The Farther Reaches of Human Nature

An Esalen Book

The Esalen Publishing Program
is edited by Stuart Miller

The Farther Reaches of Human Nature

ABRAHAM H. MASLOW

NEW YORK / THE VIKING PRESS

ACKNOWLEDGMENTS

The American Journal of Psychoanalysis: "Fusion of Facts and Values." Reprinted by permission of the Editor of *The American Journal of Psychoanalysis,* 1963, Vol. 23, No. 2, 117–31.

American Psychological Association, Inc.: "Toward a Humanistic Biology." *Journal,* August 1969, Volume 24, Number 8, pages 724–35.

George Braziller, Inc., Studio Vista Limited and Editions de la Connaissance, S.A.: From "Isomorphic Interrelationships between Knower & Known," from *Sign Image Symbol* edited by Gyorgy Kepes; Copyright © 1966 by George Braziller. Reprinted by permission.

Irwin Dorsey, Inc.: Reprinted by permission from *Eupsychian Management: A Journal* (Homewood, Ill.: Richard D. Irwin, Inc.), pp. 236–46.

Harper and Row Publishers, Inc.: From "Adolescence and Juvenile Delinquency in Two Different Cultures," from *Festschrift for Gardner Murphy,* John Peatman and E.M. Hartley, Editors.

Harvard Educational Review: "Some Educational Implications of the Humanistic Psychologies," *Harvard Educational Review,* 38, Fall 1968, 685–96. Copyright © 1968 by President and Fellows of Harvard College.

Humanitas: "Neurosis as a Failure of Personal Growth," *Humanitas,* Fall 1967, Number 2.

Journal of Humanistic Psychology: "Notes on Being-Psychology," 1962, 47–71; "Some Fundamental Questions That Face the Normative Social Psychologist," 1968, 8, 143–53; "Synanon and Eupsychia," 1967, 7, 28–35; "A Theory of Metamotivation: The Biological Rooting of the Value Life," 1967, 7, 93–127; "Abraham H. Maslow: A Bibliography," 1970, 10, 98–110.

Journal of Individual Psychology: "Emotional Blocks to Creativity," 1958, 14, 51–56; "Synergy in the Society and in the Individual," 1964, Volume 20, 153–64.

Journal of Transpersonal Psychology: "Theory Z," Volume 1, No. 2, 1969, pp. 31–47; "Various Meanings of Transcendence," 1969, Volume 1, No. 1, pp. 56–66.

McGraw-Hill Book Company: "Self-Actualization and Beyond," from *Challenges of Humanistic Psychology,* J.F.T. Bugental, editor. Copyright © 1967 by

Acknowledgments

McGraw-Hill Book Company, from *Human Relations at Work* by Keith Davis. Used with permission of McGraw-Hill Book Company.

Music Educators National Conference: "Music Education and Peak Experiences." Copyright © *Music Educators Journal*, February 1968. Reprinted with permission.

Pergamon Press, Inc.: "A Holistic Approach to Creativity" from *A Climate for Creativity:* Reports of the Seventh National Research Conference on Creativity, Calvin W. Taylor, editor. Copyright © 1971 by Pergamon Press, Inc.

Personnel Administration: "The Need for Creative People," 1965, May-June.

The Structurist: "The Creative Attitude," Number 3, 1963, published by the University of Saskatchewan, Saskatoon, Saskatchewan, Canada.

University of Nebraska Press: "Criteria for Judging Needs to Be Instinctoid," from *International Motivation Symposium*, A. M. Jones, editor, 1964.

Verlag für Psychologie: "Notes on Innocent Cognition."

The Viking Press, Inc.: "Preface" to the Compass edition of *Religion, Values and Peak-Experiences.* Copyright © 1970 by The Viking Press, Inc. (*Religion, Values and Peak-Experiences* originally published by Kappa Delta Pi, Copyright © 1964 by Kappa Delta Pi.)

Western Behavioral Sciences Institute: "Comments" and "Introduction" by Lawrence N. Solomon from a Symposium on Human Value from *Western Behavioral Science Institute Report Number 17.*

The Williams & Wilkins Company: "Some Parallels Between Sexual and Dominance Behavior of Infra-Human Primates and the Fantasies of Patients in Psychotherapy," from *The Journal of Nervous and Mental Disease.* Copyright © 1960, The Williams & Wilkins Co. Reproduced by permission.

All articles are by Abraham Maslow, unless otherwise indicated.

For Jeannie

Preface

In 1969 A. H. Maslow selected the articles which now comprise the chapters of this volume. His plan for the book included the addition of new material, an elaborate preface and epilogue, and a thorough rewriting and updating of the entire manuscript. In the early months of 1970 Miles Vich served as consulting and technical editor during the initial preparation of the manuscript.

The new material was about to be written when AHM suffered a fatal heart attack on June 8, 1970.

In the fall of 1970 I was faced with a choice between substantial editing of AHM's idiosyncratic style or the publication of the original articles as a collection of papers. I decided on the latter. At my request Miles Vich resumed work on the manuscript and has provided general editorial assistance during the preparation of the book. Editing has been limited to the necessary technical corrections, deletions of occasional repetitive statements, and the combination of two articles to form Chapter 13 (as originally planned by AHM).

Although the publishers of the original articles are acknowledged elsewhere, I want to thank especially Miles Vich (former editor of the *Journal of Humanistic Psychology*), who was much more than an editor for this volume, and Anthony Sutich (editor of the *Journal of Transpersonal Psychology*), for granting permission to use a significant number of titles.

I also appreciate the assistance of Michael Murphy and Stuart Miller of the Esalen Institute, and Richard Grossman of the Viking Press. I especially want to thank Kay Pontius, personal secretary to AHM while he was a Resident Fellow at the W. P. Laughlin Charitable Foundation. She has been extraordinarily helpful. W. P. Laughlin, Director of the Foundation and Chairman of the Board of the Saga Administrative Corporation, along with William J. Crockett of Saga, provided encouragement, friendship, and practical support.

A. H. Maslow believed that Henry Geiger was one of the few individuals who understood his work in depth and I am pleased that he could contribute the Introduction to this volume.

Bertha G. Maslow

Palo Alto, California
June 1971

Contents

Contents

Introduction: A. H. Maslow

An indisputable fact about the work of A. H. Maslow is that it gives off sparks—very nearly all his writing gives off sparks. An attempt to understand this by thinking of him as simply a psychologist would probably prove futile; he must first be thought of as a man, and then as one who worked very hard at psychology, or rather, who rendered his growth and maturity as a man into a new way of thinking about psychology. This was one of his major accomplishments—he gave psychology a new conceptual language.

He tells us that early in his professional life he found that the available language of psychology—its conceptual structure, that is— would not serve the direction of his research, and he determined to change or improve it. So he began inventing. As he put it: "I was raising legitimate questions and had to invent another approach to psychological problems in order to deal with them." The key terms of the language he developed are "self-actualization," "peak experience," and "the hierarchy of needs," ranging from "deficiency-needs" to "being-needs." There are others, but these are probably the most important.

It seems necessary to say that the core of what Maslow found out about psychology he found out from himself. It is evident from his writing that he studied himself—was able, as we say, to be "objective" about himself. "We must remember," he said in one place, "that knowledge of one's own deep nature is also simultaneously knowledge of human nature in general." As an aside, one might add here that Maslow was truly a man without vanity. He knew what he was doing and that it was important, but he maintained the sturdy humbleness he admired in others throughout his life. ("Humility" doesn't have the right ring in relation to him.) And he had that wonderful corrective humor that spiced all his relationships with other people as well as, no doubt, with himself.

One of the papers in this book tells how Maslow happened to begin his studies of self-actualization. He had two teachers he "could not be content simply to adore, but sought to understand." Why were these two "so different from the run-of-the-mill people in the world"? The resolve to seek answers to this question, it becomes clear, set the direction of his research in psychology, and disclosed, as well, his sense of the meaning of human life. Being a scientist, he sought a generalizing account of the excellences he had discovered in these two teachers. He began to collect other such subjects for study—and went on identifying and studying these people for the rest of his life. This sort of research, he often pointed out, gives you a fresh and encouraging view of mankind. It shows you what *can be*. "Healthy people" is the way he described these subjects, and later spoke of them as embodying "full humanness."

The climax of self-actualization is the peak experience. "Peak experience" is a splendidly *naturalistic* idiom, hospitable to all the similar meanings in the vocabularies of religion and mysticism, yet confined by none of them. A peak experience is what you feel and perhaps "know" when you gain authentic elevation as a human being. We don't know how the peak experience is achieved; it has no simple one-to-one relation with any deliberated procedure; we know only that it is somehow *earned*. It is like the promise of the rainbow. It comes and it goes and it cannot be forgotten. A man somehow knows better than to try to hold on to a state or condition of awareness that is not meant to last except in persistent recollection of the total acceptance that it brings. A peak experience is a coming into the realization that what "ought to be" *is*, in a way that requires no longing, suggests no straining, to make it so. It tells human beings something about themselves and about the world that is the same truth, and that becomes the pivot of value and an ordering principle for the hierarchy of meanings. It is the merging of subject and object, involving no loss of subjectivity but what seems its infinite extension. It is individuality freed of isolation. An experience of this sort gives the idea of transcendence an empirical ground. Its typical recurrence for his self-actualizers became for Maslow scientific evidence of what may be the normal psychological or inner life of persons who are fully human. The normative element in Maslow's thinking and theory was now present in principle, it remaining to check and fill out the pattern of how self-actualizers behave. He wanted to be able to say: "This is how people who are self-actualizing act and react in a wide gamut of situations, difficulties, and confrontations," and to demonstrate the psychological (educational) importance of such research. Many of his papers spell out these findings. Out of this work grew a psychology ordered by the symmetries of fully human health, intelligence, and aspiration.

There is no neglect of weakness, badness, or what used to be called "evil," in Maslow's work. It was natural for him to reach a Socratic position—the view that most if not all the evil in human life is due to ignorance. His principles of explanation—developed from the "givens" of self-actualization and the peak experience—were useful for understanding weakness, failure, and meanness, and he had no inclination to ignore these realities. He was not a sentimental man.

One may, however, encounter certain difficulties in Maslow's books, especially if the reader comes to him fresh from studies that are purely analytical and descriptive. Things that are quite clear to Maslow—or have become quite clear to him—may not seem so to the reader. He leaps along, apparently sure of his footing and where he is going, while the reader is peering for familiar landmarks of meaning. Is all that really there? he may grumble to himself. At this point it seems fair to urge that the internal connections of a lot of things about human nature and possibility were clear to Maslow because he had been thinking about them and working with them for a long, long time. And at the level of his work, the level which makes it valuable, the connections *are* internal. The unities he speaks of, one might stipulate, are there, but to see or feel as he did requires that you do the same kind of homework, pursue the same line of independent and reflective research. Yet all through his work one finds exposed nodes open to intuitive verification, good enough for any man of hungry common sense. In fact, it is those points of exposure—"insights," we call them—that make people keep on reading Maslow, that have given his books their popularity and long life. (University presses had a hard time understanding this. They would print three thousand copies of a Maslow book and regard their job as done. But Maslow's books would sell fifteen or twenty thousand in hardcover, and go a hundred thousand and more in paperback. People who read him understand why. He has a psychology that applies to *them*.)

There isn't a great deal more to say, with hundreds of pages of the man himself awaiting the reader—pages in which Maslow's later thought reaches beyond the accustomed limits of psychology, even his own psychology. But something might be added about his way of writing. What he wanted to write was not easy to express. He would stand back and send "waves" of words at the reader. He shed fresh idioms as easily as Bach wrote original tunes. He played with words, bouncing them around until they served his meaning exactly. You would not call what he did tricks of the trade of writing; they were never really tricks, but rather intense efforts to make himself understood. Intensity did not make him ponderous. So he succeeded pretty well, and the fact that he took pleasure in words and expression makes reading him a delight. That anyone so much fun to read has to be worth understanding is a legitimate conclusion about Maslow. Among psychologists, you could say this also of William James and Henry Murray, but of very few others.

One other comment seems important. There are two ways to arrive at a difficult but valuable conclusion. You can climb up a ladder of related syllogisms, tightening the rungs as you go by the use of precise language. The other is simply to *be* up there, high above distracting obstacles, seeing the final stages of the logical climb, but seeing also dozens of other passages of ascent, all reaching the same real place, the same exalted height—and, *being* there, freely able to look in all directions instead of having to cling insecurely to the ladder of reason, hoping it won't topple over. A lot of the time, you have the feeling that Maslow was already there, had been there for quite a while, until he felt at home, and was using the logical approach as a kind of "exercise," or for heuristic purposes.

Well, has a *scientist* any business getting to where he gets by such private or inexplicable means? Maybe; maybe not. But if the subject of his inquiry—*man*—moves forward in that way when he is at his best, how could you practice human science without yourself performing or at least attempting such exploits? Maybe Maslow could not help himself. He found himself up there. Maybe it is of the essence of a basic and necessary reform in psychology to declare and demonstrate that such capacities are necessary, and to be sought after, however mysterious. After all, what is culture at its best but the tone and resonance of a consensus of rarely accomplished human beings— self-actualizers—the people from whom one can learn most easily, and even joyously? And if these are the kind of people the best men are, any psychology that does not struggle to reveal the fact will be some kind of fraud.

A great orchestra is a combination of rare skills, a company of musicians who have learned to play their instruments and to know music better than most other people. If you listen to them talk music among themselves, you will not understand half of what they say, but when they *play*, then you will know that, whatever they said to each other, it wasn't just idle chatter. It is so with any distinguished human being. He speaks, in relation to his particular attainment, from a height. The meaning of what he says may not always be immediately plain, but the height, the attainment, is real. You feel it even if you cannot grasp it to your satisfaction. A fully human man is likely to have similar obscurities about him. And a psychology devoted to fully human beings—which is competent to speak of them, in some ways to measure them, appreciate them, tell something about the dynamics of their qualities—is bound to participate in some of this— depth, rather than obscurity. Now and then readers may feel a little lost. Why not? Perhaps a psychology that does not have partly this effect on the student will never get off the ground.

One aspect of Maslow's later thought deserves attention. The older he got, the more "philosophical" he became. It was impossible, he found, to isolate the pursuit of psychological truth from philosophical questions. How a man thinks cannot be separated from what he is, and the question of what he *thinks* he is, is never independent of what he is in fact, even though this, intellectually, may be an insoluble problem. At the beginning of an inquiry, Maslow held, science has no right to shut out any of the data of experience. As he said in *The Psychology of Science*, all the deliveries of human awareness must be accepted by psychology, "even contradictions and illogicalities, and mysteries, the vague, the ambiguous, the archaic, the unconscious, and all other aspects of existence that are difficult to communicate." The inchoate and by nature imprecise is nonetheless part of our knowledge about ourselves: "Knowledge of low reliability is also a part of knowledge." Man's knowledge of himself is mainly of this sort, and, for Maslow, the rules for its increase were those of an "explorer" who looks in every direction, rejects no possibilities. "The beginning stages of knowledge," he wrote, "should not be judged by the criteria derived from 'final' knowledge."

This is the statement of a philosopher of science. If, indeed, the task of the philosopher of science is to identify the appropriate means of study in a given field of research, Maslow was more than anything else a philosopher of science. He would have wholly agreed with H. H. Price, who, thirty years ago, in a discussion of the potentialities of mind, observed: "In the early stages of any inquiry it is a mistake to lay down a hard-and-fast distinction between a scientific investigation of the facts and philosophical reflection about them. . . . At the later stages the distinction is right and proper. But if it is drawn too soon and too rigorously those later stages will never be reached." Indirectly, a large part of Maslow's work involved removing the philosophical barriers that stood in the way of the advance of psychology to its own "later stages."

Of Maslow's inner life, of the themes of his thought, and of his inspiration, we know only what he has told us and what may be deduced by inference. He was not a great letter-writer. Yet it is evident that his life was filled with humanitarian concern, and in his last years with continuous reflection on what might make the foundation of a social psychology that could point the way to a better world. Ruth Benedict's conception of a synergistic society was a cornerstone of this thinking, as his later papers show. There is, however, something in one of his infrequent letters to a friend that suggests how his private hours were spent. He is speaking of a difficulty in remembering where his ideas came from, wondering, perhaps, if his delight in them, his working them over and developing their correlates, had somehow displaced recollection of their origin. Sometime between 1966 and 1968—the letter is undated—he wrote:

I'm still vulnerable to my idiotic memory. Once it frightened me—I had some of the characteristics of brain tumor, but finally I thought I'd accepted it. . . . I live so much in my private world of Platonic essences, having all sorts of conversations with Plato & Socrates and trying to convince Spinoza and Bergson of things, & getting mad at Locke and Hobbes, that I only *appear* to others to be living in the world. I've had so much trouble . . . because I seem to mimic being conscious & interpersonal, I even carry on conversations and look intellectual. But then there is absolute and complete amnesia—and then I'm in trouble with my family!

No one can say that these dialogues were "unreal." They bore too many fruits.

HENRY GEIGER

PART I

Health and
Pathology

1

Toward a Humanistic Biology[1]

My adventures in psychology have led me in all sorts of directions, some of which have transcended the field of conventional psychology—at least in the sense in which I was trained.

In the thirties I became interested in certain psychological problems, and found that they could not be answered or managed well by the classical scientific structure of the time (the behavioristic, positivistic, "scientific," value-free, mechanomorphic psychology). I was raising legitimate questions and had to invent another approach to psychological problems in order to deal with them. This approach slowly became a general philosophy of psychology, of science in general, of religion, work, management, and now biology. As a matter of fact, it became a *Weltanschauung*.

Psychology today is torn and riven, and may in fact be said to be three (or more) separate, noncommunicating sciences or groups of

[1] This is excerpted from a series of memoranda that were written during March and April 1968, at the request of the Director of the Salk Institute of Biological Studies in the hope that they might help in the move away from a value-free technologizing toward a humanized philosophy of biology. In these memoranda I leave aside all the obvious frontier questions in biology and confine myself to what I think is being neglected or overlooked or misinterpreted—all this from my special standpoint as a psychologist.

scientists. First is the behavioristic, objectivistic, mechanistic, positivistic group. Second is the whole cluster of psychologies that originated in Freud and in psychoanalysis. And third there are the humanistic psychologies, or the "Third Force" as this group has been called, a coalescence into a single philosophy of various splinter groups in psychology. It is for this third psychology that I want to speak. I interpret this third psychology to include the first and second psychologies, and have invented the words "epi-behavioristic" and "epi-Freudian" (epi = upon) to describe it. This also helps to avoid the sophomoric two-valued, dichotomized orientation, for example, of being either pro-Freudian or anti-Freudian. I am Freudian and I am behavioristic and I am humanistic, and as a matter of fact I am developing what might be called a fourth psychology of transcendence as well.

Here I speak for myself. Even among the humanistic psychologists, some tend to see themselves as *opposed* to behaviorism and psychoanalysis, rather than as including these psychologies in a larger superordinate structure. I think some of them hover on the edge of antiscience and even antirational feelings in their new enthusiasm for "experiencing." However, since I believe that experiencing is only the beginning of knowledge (necessary but not sufficient), and since I also believe that the advancement of knowledge, that is, a much broadened science, is our only ultimate hope, I had *better* speak only for myself.

It is my personally chosen task to "speculate freely," to theorize, to play hunches, intuitions, and in general to try to extrapolate into the future. This is a kind of deliberate preoccupation with pioneering, scouting, originating, rather than applying, validating, checking, verifying. Of course it is the latter that is the backbone of science. And yet I feel it is a great mistake for scientists to consider themselves *merely* and only verifiers.

The pioneer, the creator, the explorer is generally a single, lonely person rather than a group, struggling all alone with his inner conflicts, fears, defenses against arrogance and pride, even against paranoia. He has to be a courageous man, not afraid to stick his neck out, not afraid even to make mistakes, well aware that he is, as Polanyi (126)[2] has stressed, a kind of gambler who comes to tenta-

[2] Numbers in parentheses refer to the Bibliography beginning on p. 409.

tive conclusions in the absence of facts and then spends some years trying to find out if his hunch was correct. If he has any sense at all, he is of course scared of his own ideas, of his temerity, and is well aware that he is affirming what he cannot prove.

It is in this sense that I am presenting personal hunches, intuitions, and affirmations.

I think the question of a normative biology cannot be escaped or avoided, even if this calls into question the whole history and philosophy of science in the West. I am convinced that the value-free, value-neutral, value-avoiding model of science that we inherited from physics, chemistry, and astronomy, where it was necessary and desirable to keep the data clean and also to keep the church out of scientific affairs, is quite unsuitable for the scientific study of life. Even more dramatically is this value-free philosophy of science unsuitable for human questions, where personal values, purposes and goals, intentions and plans are absolutely crucial for the understanding of any person, and even for the classical goals of science, prediction, and control.

I know that in the area of evolutionary theory the arguments about direction, goals, teleology, vitalism, final causes, and the like have raged hot and heavy—my own impression, I must say, is that the debate has been muddled—but I must also submit my impression that discussing these same problems at the human psychological level sets forth the issues more clearly and in a less avoidable way.

It is still possible to argue back and forth about autogenesis in evolution, or whether pure chance collocations could account for the direction of evolution. But this luxury is no longer possible when we deal with human individuals. It is absolutely impossible to say that a man becomes a good physician by pure chance and it is time we stopped taking any such notion seriously. For my part, I have turned away from such debates over mechanical determinism without even bothering to get into the argument.

The Good Specimen and "Growing-Tip Statistics"

I propose for discussion and eventually for research the use of selected good specimens (superior specimens) as biological assays for studying the best capability that the human species has. To give several examples: For instance, I have discovered in exploratory investigations that self-actualizing people, that is, psychologically healthy, psychologically "superior" people are better cognizers and perceivers. This may be true even at the sensory level itself; for example, it would not surprise me if they turned out to be more acute about differentiating fine hue differences, etc. An uncompleted experiment that I once organized may serve as a model for this kind of "biological assay" experimentation. My plan had been to test the whole of each incoming freshman class at Brandeis University with the best techniques available at the time—psychiatric interviews, projective tests, performance tests, etc.—and select the healthiest 2 per cent of our population, a middle 2 per cent, and the least healthy 2 per cent. We planned to have these three groups take a battery of about twelve sensory, perceptive, and cognitive instruments, testing the previous clinical, personological finding that healthier people are better perceivers of reality. I predicted these findings would be supported. My plan then was to continue following these people not only through the four years of college where I could then correlate our initial test ratings with actual performance, achievement, and success in the various departments of life in a university. I also thought that it would be possible to set up a longitudinal study carried out by a longitudinally organized research team that would exist beyond our lifetimes. The idea was to seek the ultimate validations of our notions of health by pursuing the whole group through their entire lifetimes. Some of the questions were obvious, for example, longevity, resistance to psychosomatic ailments, resistance to infection, etc. We also expected that this follow-up would reveal unpredictable characteristics as well. This study was in a spirit similar to Lewis Terman's when he selected, about forty years ago, children in California with high IQs and then tested them in many ways, through the succeeding decades and up to the present time. His general finding was that children chosen because they were superior in intelligence were superior in everything else as well. The great generalization that he wound up with was that all desirable traits in a human being correlate positively.

What this kind of research design means is a change in our conception of statistics, and especially of sampling theory. What I am frankly espousing here is what I have been calling "growing-tip statistics," taking my title from the fact that it is at the growing tip of a plant that the greatest genetic action takes place. As the youngsters say, "That's where the action is."

If I ask the question, "Of what are human beings capable?" I put the question to this small and selected superior group rather than to the whole of the population. I think that the main reason that hedonistic value theories and ethical theories have failed throughout history has been that the philosophers have locked in pathologically motivated pleasures with healthily motivated pleasures and struck an average of what amounts to indiscriminately sick and healthy, indiscriminately good and bad specimens, good and bad choosers, biologically sound and biologically unsound specimens.

If we want to answer the question how tall can the human species grow, then obviously it is well to pick out the ones who are already tallest and study them. If we want to know how fast a human being can run, then it is no use to average out the speed of a "good sample" of the population; it is far better to collect Olympic gold medal winners and see how well they can do. If we want to know the possibilities for spiritual growth, value growth, or moral development in human beings, then I maintain that we can learn most by studying our most moral, ethical, or saintly people.

On the whole I think it fair to say that human history is a record of the ways in which human nature has been sold short. The highest possibilities of human nature have practically always been underrated. Even when "good specimens," the saints and sages and great leaders of history, have been available for study, the temptation too often has been to consider them not human but supernaturally endowed.

Humanistic Biology and the Good Society

It is now quite clear that the actualization of the highest human potentials is possible—on a mass basis—only under "good conditions." Or more directly, good human beings will generally need a good society in which to grow. Contrariwise, I think it should be clear that a normative philosophy of biology would involve the theory of the good society, defined in terms of "that society is good which fosters the fullest development of human potentials, of the fullest degree of humanness." I think this may at first sight be a little startling to the classical descriptive biologist who has learned to avoid such words as "good" and "bad," but a little thought will show that something of the sort is already taken for granted in some of the classical areas of biology. For instance, it is taken for granted that genes can be called "potentials" that are actualized or not actualized by their immediate surroundings in the germ plasm itself, in the cytoplasm, in the organism in general, and in the geographical environment in which the organism finds itself.

To cite a single line of experimentation (11) we can say for white rats, monkeys, and human beings that a stimulating environment in the early life of the individual has quite specific effects on the development of the cerebral cortex in what we would generally call a desirable direction. Behavioral studies at Harlow's Primate Laboratory come to the same conclusion. Isolated animals suffer the loss of various capacities, and beyond a certain point these losses frequently become irreversible. At the Jackson Labs in Bar Harbor, to take another example, it was found that dogs allowed to run loose in the fields and in packs, without human contact, lose the potentiality for becoming domesticated, that is, pets.

Finally, if children in India are suffering irreversible brain damage through lack of proteins in their dietary, as is now being reported, and if it is agreed that the political system of India, its history, its economics, and its culture are all involved in producing this scarcity, then it is clear that human specimens need good societies to permit them to actualize themselves as good specimens.

Is it conceivable that a philosophy of biology could develop in social isolation, that it could be politically entirely neutral, that it need not be Utopian or Eupsychian or reformist or revolutionary? I do not mean that the task of the biologist need go over into social action. I think this is a matter of personal taste and I know some biologists will, out of their anger at seeing their knowledge unused, go over into political effectuation of their discoveries. But quite apart from this, my immediate proposal for biologists is that they recognize that once they have swallowed the normative approach to the human species, or any other species, that is, once they have accepted as their obligation the development of the good specimen, then it becomes equally their scientific obligation to study all those conditions that conduce to the development of the good specimen, and to those conditions that inhibit such development. Obviously, this means emergence from the laboratory and into society.

The Good Specimen as the Chooser for the Whole Species

It has been my experience through a long line of exploratory investigations going back to the thirties that the healthiest people (or the most creative, or the strongest, or the wisest, or the saintliest) can be used as biological assays, or perhaps I could say, as advanced scouts, or more sensitive perceivers, to tell us less sensitive ones what it is that we value. What I mean is something like this: It is easy enough to select out, for instance, persons who are aesthetically sensitive to colors and forms and then learn to submit ourselves or to defer to their judgment about colors, forms, fabrics, furniture, and the like. My experience is that if I get out of the way and do not intrude upon the superior perceivers, I can confidently predict that what they like immediately, I will slowly get to like in perhaps a month or two. It is as if they were I, only more sensitized, or as if they were I, with less doubt, confusion, and uncertainty. I can use them, so to speak, as my experts, just as art collectors will hire art experts to help them with their buying. (This belief is supported by the work of Child (22), which shows that experienced and expert artists have similar tastes, even cross-culturally.) I hypothesize also that such sensitives are less susceptible to fads and fashions than average people are.

Now in this same way I have found that if I select psychologically healthy humans what they like is what human beings *will* come to like. Aristotle is pertinent here: "What the superior man thinks is good, that is what is *really* good."

For instance, it is empirically characteristic of self-actualizing people that they have far less doubt about right and wrong than average people do. They do not get confused just because 95 per cent of the population disagrees with them. And I may mention that at least in the group I studied they tended to agree about what was right and wrong, as if they were perceiving something real and extrahuman rather than comparing tastes that might be relative to the individual person. In a word, I have used them as value assayers or perhaps I should better say that I have learned from them what ultimate values probably are. Or to say it in another way, I have learned that what great human beings value are what I will eventually agree with, what I will come to value, and I will come to see as worthy of, as valuable in some extrapersonal sense, and what "data" will eventually support.

My theory of metamotivation (Chapter 23) ultimately rests upon this operation, namely, of taking superior people who are also superior perceivers not only of facts but of values, and then using their choices of ultimate values as possibly the ultimate values for the whole species.

I am being almost deliberately provocative here. I could phrase it, if I wished, in a far more innocent fashion simply by asking the question, "Supposing you select out psychologically healthy individuals, what will they prefer? What will motivate them? What will they struggle or strive for? What will they value?" But I do think it best to be unmistakable here. I am deliberately raising the normative and the value questions for biologists (and for psychologists and social scientists).

Perhaps it will help to say these same things from another angle. If, as I think has been demonstrated sufficiently, the human being is a choosing, deciding, seeking animal, then the question of making choices and decisions must inevitably be involved in any effort to define the human species. But making choices and decisions is a matter of degree, a matter of wisdom, effectiveness, and efficiency. The questions then come up: Who is the good chooser? Where does he come from? What kind of life history does he have? Can we teach this skill? What hurts it? What helps it?

These are, of course, simply new ways of asking the old philosophical questions, "Who is a sage? What is a sage?" And beyond that of raising the old axiological questions, "What is good? What is desirable? *What should be* desired?"

I must reassert that we have come to the point in biological history where we now are responsible for our own evolution. We have become self-evolvers. Evolution means selecting and therefore choosing and deciding, and this means valuing.

The Mind-Body Correlation

It seems to me that we are on the edge of a new leap into correlating our subjective lives with external objective indicators. I expect a tremendous leap forward in the study of the nervous system because of these new indications.

Two examples will be sufficient to justify this preparation for future research. One study by Olds (122), by now very widely known, discovered by means of implanted electrodes in the septal area of the rhinencephalon that this was in effect a "pleasure center." When the white rat was hooked up in such a fashion as to be able to stimulate his own brain via these implanted electrodes, he repeated again and again the self-stimulation as long as the electrodes were implanted in this particular pleasure center. Needless to say, displeasure or pain areas were also discovered, and then the animal, given a chance to stimulate himself, refused to do so. Stimulation of this pleasure center was apparently so "valuable" (or desirable or reinforcing or rewarding or pleasurable or whatever other word we use to describe the situation) for the animal that he would give up any other known external pleasure, food, sex—anything. We now have sufficient parallel human data to be able to guess for the human being that there are, in the subjective sense of the word, pleasure experiences that can be produced in this fashion. This kind of work is only in its beginning stages, but already some differentiation has been made between different "centers" of this sort, centers for sleep, food satiation, sexual stimulation, and sexual satiation, etc.

If we integrate this kind of experimentation with another kind, for instance that of Kamiya, then new possibilities open up. Kamiya (58), working with EEG and operant conditioning, gave the subject a visible feedback when the alpha wave frequency in his own EEG reached a certain point. In this way, by permitting human subjects to correlate an external event or signal and a subjectively felt state of affairs, it was possible for Kamiya's subjects to establish voluntary control over their own EEGs. That is, he demonstrated that it was possible for a person to bring his own alpha wave frequency to a particular desired level.

What is seminal and exciting about this research is that Kamiya discovered quite fortuitously that bringing the alpha waves to a particular level could produce in the subject a state of serenity, meditativeness, even happiness. Some follow-up studies with people who have learned the Eastern techniques of contemplation and meditation show that they spontaneously emit EEGs that are like the "serene" ones into which Kamiya was able to educate his subjects. This is to say that it is already possible to teach people how to feel happy and serene. The revolutionary consequences, not only for human betterment, but also for biological and psychological theory, are multitudinous and obvious. There are enough research projects here to keep squadrons of scientists busy for the next century. The mind-body problem, until now considered insoluble, does appear to be a workable problem after all.

Such data are crucial for the problem of a normative biology. Apparently it is now possible to say that the healthy organism itself gives clear and loud signals about what it, the organism, prefers or chooses, or considers to be desirable states of affairs. Is it too big a jump to call these "values"? Biologically intrinsic values? Instinct-like values? If we make the descriptive statement, "The laboratory rat, given a choice between pressing two auto-stimulus-producing buttons, presses the pleasure center button practically 100 per cent of the time in preference to any other stimulus-producing or self-stimulus-producing button," is this different in any important way from saying, "The rat prefers self-stimulation of his pleasure center"?

I must say that it makes little difference to me whether I use the word "values" or not. It is certainly possible to describe everything I have described without ever using this word. Perhaps as a matter of scientific strategy, or at least the strategy of communication between scientists and the general public, it might be more diplomatic if we *not* confuse the issue by speaking of values. It does not really matter, I suppose. However, what does matter is that we take quite seriously these new developments in the psychology and biology of choices, preferences, reinforcements, rewards, etc.

I should point out also that we will have to face the dilemma of a certain circularity that is built into this kind of research and theorizing. It is most clear with human beings, but my guess is that it will also be a problem with other animals. It is the circularity that is implied in saying that "the good specimen or the healthy animal chooses or prefers such and such." How shall we handle the fact that sadists, perverts, masochists, homosexuals, neurotics, psychotics, suicidals make different choices than do "healthy human beings"? Is it fair to parallel this dilemma with that of adrenalectomized animals in the laboratory making different choices from so-called "normal" animals? I should make it clear that I do not consider this an insoluble problem, merely one that has to be faced and handled, rather than avoided and overlooked. It is quite easy with the human subject to select "healthy" persons by psychiatric and psychological testing techniques and *then* to point out that people who make such and such a score, let us say in the Rorschach test, or in an intelligence test, are the same people who will be good choosers in cafeteria (food) experiments. The selection criterion then is quite different from the behavior criterion. It is also quite possible, and as a matter of fact in my own opinion quite probable, that we are within sight of the possibility of demonstrating by neurological self-stimulation that the so-called "pleasures" of perversion or murder or sadism or fetishism are not "pleasures" in the same sense that is indicated in the Olds or Kamiya experiments. Certainly this is what we already know from our subjective psychiatric techniques. Any experienced psychotherapist learns sooner or later that underlying the neurotic "pleasures" or perversions is actually a great deal of anguish, pain, and fear. Within the subjective realm itself, we know this from people who have experienced both unhealthy and healthy pleasures. They practically always report preference for the latter and learn to shudder at the former. Colin Wilson (161) has demonstrated clearly that sexual criminals have very feeble sexual reactions, not strong ones. Kirkendall (61) also shows the subjective superiority of loving sex over unloving sex.

I am now working with one set of implications that are generated by a humanistic-psychological point of view of the sort I have sketched out above. It may serve to show the radical consequences and implications for a humanistic philosophy of biology. It is certainly fair to say that these data are on the side of self-regulation, self-government, self-choice of the organism. The organism has more tendency toward choosing health, growth, biological success than we would have thought a century ago. This is in general anti-authoritarian, anti-controlling. For me it brings back into serious focus the whole *Taoistic* point of view, not only as expressed in contemporary ecological and ethological studies, where we have learned not to intrude and to control, but for the human being it also means trusting more the child's own impulses toward growth and self-actualization. This means a greater stress on spontaneity and on autonomy rather than on prediction and external control. To paraphrase a main thesis from my *Psychology of Science* (81):

> In the light of such facts, can we seriously continue to define the goals of science as prediction and control? Almost one could say the exact opposite—at any rate, for human beings. Do we ourselves want to be predicted and predictable? Controlled and controllable? I won't go so far as to say that the question of free will must necessarily be involved here in its old and classical philosophical form. But I *will* say that questions come up here and clamor for treatment which do have something to do with the subjective feeling of being free rather than determined, of choosing for oneself rather than being externally controlled, etc. In any case, I can certainly say that descriptively healthy human beings do not like to be controlled. They prefer to feel free and to be free.

Another very general "atmospheric" consequence of this whole way of thinking is that it must inevitably transform the image of the scientist, not only in his own eyes but in the eyes of the general population. There are already data (115) which indicate that, for instance, high school girls think of scientists as monsters and horrors, and are afraid of them. They do not think of them as good potential husbands, for instance. I must express my own opinion that this is not merely a consequence of Hollywood "Mad Scientist" movies; there is something real and justified in this picture, even if it is terribly exaggerated. The fact is that the classical conception of science is the man who controls, the man who is in charge, the man who does things to people, to animals, or to things. He is the master of what he surveys. This picture is even more clear in surveys of the "image of the physician." He is generally seen at the semiconscious or unconscious level as a master, a controller, a cutter, a dealer out of pain, etc. He is definitely the boss, the authority, the expert, the one who takes charge and tells people what to do. I think this "image" is now worst of all for psychologists; college students now consider them to be, very frequently, manipulators, liars, concealers, and controllers.

What if the organism is seen as having "biological wisdom"? If we learn to give it greater trust as autonomous, self-governing, and self-choosing, then clearly we as scientists, not to mention physicians, teachers, or even parents, must shift our image over to a more Taoistic one. This is the one word that I can think of that summarizes succinctly the many elements of the image of the more humanistic scientist. Taoistic means asking rather than telling. It means nonintruding, noncontrolling. It stresses noninterfering observation rather than a controlling manipulation. It is receptive and passive rather than active and forceful. It is like saying that if you want to learn about ducks, then you had better ask the ducks instead of telling them. So also for human children. In prescribing "what is best for them" it looks as if the best technique for finding out what is best for them is to develop techniques for getting *them* to tell us what is best for them.

In point of fact, we already have such a model in the good psychotherapist. This is about the way he functions. His conscious effort is not to impose his will upon the patient, but rather to help the patient—inarticulate, unconscious, semiconscious—to discover what is inside *him*, the patient. The psychotherapist helps him to discover what he himself wants or desires, what is good for him, the patient, rather than what is good for the therapist. This is the opposite of controlling, propagandizing, molding, teaching in the old sense. It definitely rests upon the implications and assumptions that I have already mentioned, although I must say that they are very rarely made, for example, such implications as trust in the health-moving direction of most individuals, of expecting them to prefer health to illness; of believing that a state of subjective well-being is a pretty good guide to what is "best for the person." This attitude implies a preference for spontaneity rather than for control, for trust in the organism rather than mistrust. It assumes that the person wants to be fully human rather than that he wants to be sick, pained, or dead. Where we do find, as psychotherapists, death wishes, masochistic wishes, self-defeating behavior, self-infliction of pain, we have learned to assume that this is "sick" in the sense that the person himself, if he ever experiences another healthier state of affairs, would far rather have that healthier state of affairs than his pain. As a matter of fact, some of us go so far as to consider masochism, suicidal impulses, self-punishment, and the like as stupid, ineffective, clumsy gropings toward health.

Something very similar is true for the new model of the Taoistic teacher, the Taoistic parent, the Taoistic friend, the Taoistic lover, and finally the more Taoistic scientist.

Taoistic Objectivity and Classical Objectivity[3]

The classical conception of objectivity came from the earliest days of scientific dealing with things and objects, with lifeless objects of study. We were objective when our own wishes and fears and hopes were excluded from the observation, and when the purported wishes and designs of a supernatural god were also excluded. This of course was a great step forward and made modern science possible. We must, however, not overlook the fact that this was true for dealing with nonhuman objects or things. Here this kind of objectivity and detachment works pretty well. It even works well with lower organisms. Here too we are detached enough, noninvolved enough so that we can be relatively noninterfering spectators. It does not *matter* to us to any great degree which way an amoeba goes or what a hydra prefers to ingest. This detachment gets more and more difficult as we go on up the phyletic scale. We know very well how easy it is to anthropomorphize, to project into the animal the observer's human wishes, fears, hopes, prejudices if we are dealing with dogs or cats, and more easily with monkeys or apes. When we get to the study of the human beings, we can now take it for granted that it is practically impossible to be the cool, calm, detached, uninvolved, noninterfering spectator. Psychological data have piled up to such a point that no one could conceivably defend this position.

Any social scientist who is at all sophisticated knows that he must

---

[3] For a fuller treatment of this topic see *The Psychology of Science: A Reconnaissance* (81).

examine his own prejudices and preconceptions *before* going in to work with any society or a subcultural group. This is one way of getting around prejudgments—to know about them in advance.

But I propose that there is another path to objectivity, that is, in the sense of greater perspicuity, of greater accuracy of perception of the reality out there outside ourselves, outside the observer. It comes originally from the observation that loving perception, whether as between sweethearts or as between parents and children, produced kinds of knowledge that were not available to nonlovers. Something of the sort seems to me to be true for the ethological literature. My work with monkeys, I am sure, is more "true," more "accurate," in a certain sense, more *objectively* true than it would have been if I had disliked monkeys. The fact was that I was fascinated with them. I became fond of my individual monkeys in a way that was not possible with my rats. I believe that the kind of work reported by Lorenz, Tinbergen, Gooddall, and Schaller is as good as it is, as instructive, illuminating, true, because these investigators "loved" the animals they were investigating. At the very least this kind of love produces interest and even fascination, and therefore great patience with long hours of observation. The mother, fascinated with her baby, who examines every square inch of it again and again with the greatest absorption, is certainly going to know more about her baby in the most literal sense than someone who is not interested in that particular baby. Something of the sort, I have found, is true between sweethearts. They are so fascinated with each other that examining, looking, listening, and exploring becomes itself a fascinating activity upon which they can spend endless hours. With a nonloved person this would hardly be the case. Boredom would set in too rapidly.

But "love knowledge," if I may call it that, has other advantages as well. Love for a person permits him to unfold, to open up, to drop his defenses, to let himself be naked not only physically but psychologically and spiritually as well. In a word, he lets himself be seen instead of hiding himself. In ordinary interpersonal relations, we are to some extent inscrutable to each other. In the love relationships, we become "scrutable."

But finally, and perhaps most important of all, if we love or are fascinated or are profoundly interested, we are less tempted to interfere, to control, to change, to improve. My finding is that, that which you love, you are prepared to leave alone. In the extreme instance of romantic love, and of grandparental love, the beloved person may even be seen as already perfect so that any kind of change, let alone improvement, is regarded as impossible or even impious.

In other words, we are content to leave it alone. We make no demands upon it. We do not wish it to be other than it is. We can be passive and receptive before it. Which is all to say that we can see it more truly as it is in its own nature rather than as we would like it to be or fear it to be or hope it will be. Approving of its existence, approving of the way it is, *as* it is, permits us to be nonintrusive, nonmanipulating, nonabstracting, noninterfering perceivers. To the extent that it is possible for us to be nonintrusive, nondemanding, nonhoping, nonimproving, to that extent do we achieve this particular kind of objectivity.

This is, I maintain, a method, a particular path to certain kinds of truth, which are better approached and achieved by this path. I do *not* maintain that it is the only path, or that all truths are obtainable in this way. We know very well from this very same kind of situation that it is also possible via love, interest, fascination, absorption, to distort certain *other* truths about the object. I would maintain only that in the full armamentarium of scientific methods, that love knowledge or "Taoistic objectivity" has its particular advantages in particular situations for particular purposes. If we are realistically aware that love for the object of study produces certain kinds of blindness as well as certain kinds of perspicuity, then we are sufficiently forewarned.

I would go as far as to say this even about "love for the problem." On the one hand it is obvious that you have to be fascinated with schizophrenia or at least interested in it to be able to stick at it and to be able to learn about it and to do research with it. On the other hand we know also that the person who becomes totally fascinated with the problem of schizophrenia tends to develop a certain imbalance with reference to other problems.

The Problem of Big Problems

I use here the title of a section in the excellent book by Alvin Weinberg (152), *Reflections on Big Science*, a book which *implies* many of the points that I would prefer to make explicit. Using his terminology I can state in a more dramatic form the purport of my memorandum. What I am suggesting is Manhattan-Project-type attacks upon what I consider to be the truly Big Problems[4] of our time, not only for psychology but for all human beings with any sense of historical urgency (a criterion of the "importance" of a research that I would now add to the classical criteria).

The first and overarching Big Problem is to make the Good Person. We must have better human beings or else it is quite possible that we may all be wiped out, and even if not wiped out, certainly live in tension and anxiety as a species. A *sine qua non* prerequisite here is of course defining the Good Person, and I have made various statements about this throughout these memoranda. I cannot stress enough that we already have some beginning data, some indicators, perhaps as many as were available for the Manhattan Project people. I myself feel confident that the great crash program would be feasible, and I am sure that I could list a hundred, or two hundred, or two thousand part problems or subsidiary problems, certainly enough to keep a huge number of people busy. This Good Person can equally be called the self-evolving person, the responsible-for-himself-and-his-own-evolution person, the fully illuminated or awakened or perspicuous man, the fully human person, the self-actualizing person, etc. In any case it is quite clear that no social reforms, no beautiful constitutions or beautiful programs or laws will be of any consequence unless people are healthy enough, evolved enough, strong enough, good enough to understand them and to want to put them into practice in the right way.

The equally Big Problem as urgent as the one I have already mentioned is to make the Good Society. There is a kind of a feedback between the Good Society and the Good Person. They need each other, they are *sine qua non* to each other. I wave aside the problem of which comes first. It is quite clear that they develop simultaneously and in tandem. It would in any case be impossible to achieve either one without the other. By Good Society I mean ultimately one species, one world. We also have beginning information (83, see also Chapter 14) on the possibility of autonomously societal, that is, nonpsychological, arrangements. To clarify, it is now clear that with the

[4] I keep Weinberg's meaningful way of capitalizing.

goodness of the person held constant, it is possible to make social arrangements that will force these people into *either* evil behavior or into good behavior. The main point is that social institutional arrangements must be taken as different from intrapsychic health, and that to some extent the goodness or badness of a person depends upon the social institutions and arrangements in which he finds himself.

The key notion of social synergy is that in some primitive cultures, and within the large, industrial cultures, there are some social trends that transcend the dichotomy between selfishness and unselfishness. That is, there are some social arrangements that set people against each other necessarily; there are other social arrangements in which a person seeking his own selfish good necessarily helps other people whether he wishes to or not. Contrariwise, the person seeking to be altruistic and to help other people must then necessarily reap selfish benefits. A single example of this would be, for instance, the economic measures like our income tax that siphons off benefits for the general population from any single person's good fortune. This is by contrast with sales taxes that take away proportionately more from poor people than they do from rich people and have, instead of a siphoning effect, what Ruth Benedict called a funneling effect.

I must stress as solemnly and seriously as I can that these are the ultimate Big Problems, coming before any other ones. Most of the technological goods and advances that Weinberg speaks about in his book, and that other people have spoken about, can be considered essentially *means* to these ends and not ends in themselves. This means that unless we put our technological and biological improvements in the hands of good men, then these improvements are either useless or dangerous. And I include here even the conquest of disease, the increase of longevity, the subduing of pain and of sorrow and of suffering in general. The point is: Who wants to make the evil man live longer? Or be more powerful? An obvious example here is the use of atomic energy and the race to achieve its military use before the Nazis did. Atomic energy in the hands of a Hitler—and there are many in charge of nations today—is certainly no blessing. It is a great danger. The same is true for *any* other technological improvements. One can always ask the criterion question: Would this be good for a Hitler or bad for a Hitler?

A by-product of our technological advance is that it is quite possible and even probable that evil men are *more* dangerous, more a threat today than they ever have been before in human history simply because of the powers given to them by advanced technology. It is quite probable that a totally ruthless man backed up by a ruthless society could not be beaten. I think that if Hitler had won, that rebellions would not have been possible, that in fact his Reich *might* have lasted a thousand years or more.

Therefore I would urge all biologists, as I would urge all other people of goodwill, to put their talents into the service of these two Big Problems.

The above considerations have strongly supported my feeling that the classical philosophy of science as morally neutral, value free, value neutral is not only wrong, but is extremely dangerous as well. It is not only amoral; it may be antimoral as well. It may put us into great jeopardy. Therefore I would stress again that science itself comes out of human beings and human passions and interests, as Polanyi (126) has so brilliantly set forth. Science itself must be a code of ethics as Bronowski (16) has so convincingly shown, since if one grants the intrinsic worth of truth, then all sorts of consequences are generated by placing ourselves in the service of this one intrinsic value. I would add as a third point that science can *seek* values, and can uncover them within human nature itself. As a matter of fact, I would claim it has already done so, at least to a level that would make this statement plausible, even though not adequately and finally proven. Techniques are now available for finding out what is good for the human species, that is, what the intrinsic values of human beings are. Several different operations have been used to indicate what these built-in values in human nature are. This is, I reiterate, both in the sense of survival value and also in the sense of growth values, that is, what makes man healthier, wiser, more virtuous, happier, more fulfilled.

This suggests what I might alternatively call strategies of future research for biologists. One is that there is a synergic feedback between the pursuit of mental health and physical health. Most psychiatrists and many psychologists and biologists now have come simply to assume that practically all diseases, and perhaps even *all* diseases without exception, can be called psychosomatic or organismic. That is, if one pursues any "physical" illness far enough and deep enough, one will find inevitably intrapsychic, intrapersonal, and social variables that are also involved as determinants. This definitely is not to etherealize tuberculosis or broken bones. It simply means that in the study of tuberculosis one finds that poverty is also a factor. As far as broken bones are concerned, once Dunbar (30) used fracture cases as a control group, assuming that *here* certainly no psychological factors could be involved, but found to her amazement that they were indeed involved. And we are now as a consequence very sophisticated about the accident-prone personality, as well as—if I may call it so—the "accident-fostering environment." Which is to say that even a broken bone is psychosomatic and "sociosomatic," if I may coin that term as well. This is all to say that even the classical biologist or physician or medical researcher, seeking to relieve human pain, suffering, illness, is well advised to be more holistic than he has been of the psychological and social determinants for the illnesses that he has been studying. For instance, there are already enough data today to indicate that a fruitful broad spectrum attack upon cancer should also include so-called "psychosomatic factors."

To say this in another way, the indications are (this is mostly extrapolation rather than hard data) that making the Good Persons, increasing psychological health, through, for example, psychiatric therapies, can probably also increase his longevity and reduce his susceptibility to disease.

Not only may lower-need deprivations produce illnesses that must be called in the classical sense "deficiency diseases," but this seems also to be true for what I have called the *metapathologies* in Chapter 23, that is, for what have been called the spiritual or philosophical or existential ailments. These too may have to be called deficiency diseases.

To summarize briefly, the loss of the basic-need satisfactions of safety and protection, belongingness, love, respect, self-esteem, identity, and self-actualization produces illnesses and deficiency diseases. Taken together, these can be called the neuroses and psychoses. However, basically need-satisfied and already self-actualizing people with such metamotives as truth, goodness, beauty, justice, order, law, unity, etc., may suffer deprivation at the metamotivational level. Lack of metamotive-gratifications, or of these values, produces what I have described as general and specific metapathologies. I would maintain these are deficiency diseases on the same continuum with scurvy, pellagra, love-hunger, etc. I should add here that the classical way of demonstrating a body need, as for vitamins, minerals, basic amino acids, etc., has been first a confrontation with a disease of unknown cause, and *then* a search for this cause. That is to say, something is considered to be a need if its deprivation produces disease. It is in exactly this same sense that I would maintain that the basic needs and metaneeds that I have described are also in the strictest sense biological needs; that is, their deprivation produces disease or illness. It is for this reason that I have used the invented term "instinctoid" to indicate my firm belief that these data have already proven sufficiently that these needs are related to the fundamental structure of the human organism itself, that there is *some* genetic basis that is involved, however weak this may be. It also leads me to be very confident of the discovery one day of biochemical, neurological, endocrinological substrates or body machinery that will explain at the biological level these needs and these illnesses (see Appendix D).

Predicting the Future

In the last few years there has been a rash of conferences, books, symposia, not to mention newspaper articles and Sunday magazine sections, about what the world will be like in the year 2000 or in the next century. I have glanced through this "literature," if one could call it that, and have generally been more alarmed than instructed by it. A good 95 per cent of it deals entirely with purely technological changes, leaving aside completely the question of good and bad, right and wrong. Sometimes the whole enterprise seems almost entirely amoral. There is much talk about new machines, prosthetic organs, new kinds of automobiles or trains or planes—in effect, bigger and better refrigerators and washing machines. Sometimes, of course, this literature frightens me as well when there is casual talk about the increased capacity for mass destruction, even to the possibility that the whole human species might be wiped out.

It is itself a sign of blindness to the real problems that are involved, that practically all of the people who get involved in these conferences are nonpersonal scientists. A huge proportion are physicists and chemists and geologists, and of the biologists a large proportion are of the molecular biology type, that is, not so much the descriptive but rather the reductive type of biological worker. The psychologists and sociologists who occasionally are chosen to speak on this problem are characteristically technologists, "experts" committed to a value-free conception of science.

In any case, it is quite clear that the questions of "improving" are very much a question of the improvement of means without regard to ends, and without regard to the clear truths that more powerful weapons in the hands of stupid or evil people simply make for more powerful stupidity or for more powerful evil. That is, these technological "improvements" may be in fact dangerous rather than helpful.

Another way of expressing my uneasiness is to point out that much of this talk about the year 2000 is at a merely material level, for example, of industrialization, modernization, increasing affluence, greater possession of more things, of increasing the capacity to produce food perhaps by farming the seas, or how to handle the population explosion by making more efficient cities, etc.

Or still another way of characterizing the sophomoric nature of much of the prediction talk is this: Large portions of it are simply helpless extrapolations from what exists today, simple projections of the curves onward from where we are. At the present rate of population growth, it is said in the year 2000 there will be so many more people; at the present rate of the growth of the cities, there will be such and such an urban situation in the year 2000, etc. It is as if we were helpless to master or to plan our own future—as if we could not reverse present trends when we disapproved of them. For instance, I would maintain that planning for the future ought to decrease present world population. There is no reason in the world, or at least no biological reason, why this could not be done if mankind wished to do it. The same would be true for the structures of the cities, the structure of automobiles, or of air travel, etc. I suspect that this kind of prediction from what is the case today is itself a by-product generated by the value-free, purely descriptive conception of science.

2

Neurosis as a Failure of Personal Growth

Rather than trying to be comprehensive, I have chosen to discuss only a few selected aspects of this topic, partly because I have been working with them, partly also because I think they are especially important, but mostly because they have been overlooked.

The frame of reference taken for granted today considers the neurosis to be, from *one* aspect, a describable, pathological state of affairs which presently exists, a kind of disease or sickness or illness, on the medical model. But we have learned to see it also in a dialectical fashion, as simultaneously a kind of moving forward, a clumsy groping forward toward health and toward fullest humanness, in a kind of timid and weak way, under the aegis of fear rather than of courage, and *now* involving the future as well as the present.

All the evidence that we have (mostly clinical evidence, but already some other kinds of research evidence) indicates that it is reasonably to assume in practically every human being, and certainly in almost every newborn baby, that there is an active will toward health, an impulse toward growth, or toward the actualization of human potentialities. But at once we are confronted with the very saddening realization that so few people make it. Only a small proportion of the human population gets to the point of identity, or of selfhood, full humanness, self-actualization, etc., even in a society like ours which is relatively one of the most fortunate on the face of the earth. This is our great paradox. We have the impulse toward full development of humanness. Then why is it that it doesn't happen more often? What blocks it?

This is our new way of approaching the problem of humanness, i.e., with an appreciation of its high possibilities and simultaneously, a deep disappointment that these possibilities are so infrequently actualized. This attitude contrasts with the "realistic" acceptance of whatever happens to be the case, and then of regarding that as the norm, as, for instance, Kinsey did, and as the television pollsters do today. We tend then to get into the situation in which normalcy from the descriptive point of view, from the value-free science point of view —that this normalcy or averageness is the best we can expect, and that therefore we should be content with it. From the point of view that I have outlined, normalcy would be rather the kind of sickness or crippling or stunting that we share with everybody else and therefore don't notice. I remember an old textbook of abnormal psychology that I used when I was an undergraduate, which was an awful book, but which had a wonderful frontispiece. The lower half was a picture of a line of babies, pink, sweet, delightful, innocent, lovable. Above that was a picture of a lot of passengers in a subway train, glum, gray, sullen, sour. The caption underneath was very simply, "What happened?" This is what I'm talking about.

I should mention also that part of what I have been doing and what I want to do here now comes under the head of the strategy and tactics of research and of preparation for research and of trying to phrase all of these clinical experiences and personal subjective experiences in such a way that we can learn more about them in a scientific way, that is, checking and testing and making more precise, and seeing if it's really so, and were the intuitions correct, etc., etc. For this purpose and also for those interested in the philosophical problems I would like to present briefly a few theoretical points which are relevant for what follows. This is the age-old problem of the relationship between facts and values, between *is* and *ought*, between the descriptive and the normative—a terrible problem for the philosophers who have dealt with it ever since there were any philosophers, and who haven't got very far with it yet. I'd like to offer some considerations which have helped me with this old philosophical difficulty, a third horn to the dilemma, you might say.

Fusion-Words

What I have in mind here is the general conclusion which comes partly from the Gestalt psychologists and partly from clinical and psychotherapeutic experience, namely, that, in a kind of a Socratic fashion, facts often point in a direction, i.e., they are vectorial. Facts just don't lie there like pancakes, just doing nothing; they are to a certain extent signposts which tell you what to do, which make suggestions to you, which nudge you in one direction rather than another. They "call for," they have demand character, they even have "requiredness," as Köhler called it (62). I get the feeling very frequently that whenever we get to know enough, that then we know what to do, or we know much better what to do; that sufficient knowledge will often solve the problem, that it will often help us at our moral and ethical choice-points, when we must decide whether to do this or to do that. For instance, it is our common experience in therapy, that as people "know" more and more consciously, their solutions, their choices become more and more easy, more and more automatic.

I am suggesting that there are facts and words which themselves are both normative and descriptive simultaneously. I am calling them for the moment "fusion-words," meaning a fusion of facts and values, and what I have to say beyond this should be understood as part of this effort to solve the "is" and "ought" problem.

I myself have advanced, as I think we all have in this kind of work, from talking in the beginning, in a frankly normative way, for example, asking the questions—what is normal, what is healthy? My former philosophy professor, who still feels fatherly toward me in a very nice way, and to whom I still feel filial, has occasionally written me a worried letter scolding me gently for the cavalier way in which I was handling these old philosophical problems, saying something like, "Don't you realize what you have done here? There are two thousand years of thought behind this problem and you just go skating over this thin ice so easily and casually." And I remember that I wrote back once trying to explain myself, saying that this sort of thing is really the way a scientist functions, and that this is part of his strategy of research, i.e., to skate past philosophical difficulties as fast as he can. I remember writing to him once that my attitude as a strategist in the advancement of knowledge had to be one, so far as philosophical problems were concerned, of "determined naïveté." And I think that's what we have here. I felt that it was heuristic, and therefore all right, to talk about normal and healthy and what was good and what was bad, and frequently getting very arbitrary about it. I did one research in which there were good paintings, and bad paintings, and with a perfectly straight face I put in the footnote, "Good paintings are defined here as paintings that I like." The thing is, if I can skip to my conclusion, that this turns out to be not so bad a strategy. In studying healthy people, self-actualizing people, etc., there has been a steady move from the openly normative and the frankly personal, step by step, toward more and more descriptive, objective words, to the point where there is today a standardized test of self-actualization (137). Self-actualization can now be defined quite operationally, as intelligence used to be defined, i.e., self-actualization is what that test tests. It correlates well with external variables of various kinds, and keeps on accumulating additional correlational meanings. As a result, I feel heuristically justified in *starting* with my "determined naïveté." Most of what I was able to see intuitively, directly, personally, is being confirmed now with numbers and tables and curves.

Full Humanness

And now I would like to suggest a further step toward the fusion-word "fully human," a concept which is still more descriptive and objective (than the concept "self-actualization") and yet retains everything that we need of normativeness. This is in the hope of moving thus from intuitive heuristic beginnings toward more and more certainty, greater and greater reliability, more and more external validation, which in turn means more and more scientific and theoretical usefulness of this concept. This phrasing and this way of thinking was suggested to me about fifteen or so years ago by the axiological writings of Robert Hartman (43), who defined "good" as the degree to which an object fulfills its definition or concept. This suggested to me that the conception of humanness might be made, for research purposes, into a kind of quantitative concept. For instance, full humanness can be defined in a cataloguing fashion, i.e., full humanness is the ability to abstract, to have a grammatical language, to be able to love, to have values of a particular kind, to transcend the self, etc., etc. The complete cataloguing definition could even be made into a kind of checklist if we wanted to. We might shudder a little at this thought, but it could be very useful if only to make the theoretical point for the researching scientist that the concept *can* be descriptive and quantitative—and yet also normative, i.e., this person is closer to full humanness than that person. Or even we could say: This person is *more* human than that one. This is a fusion-word in the sense that I have mentioned above; it is really objectively descriptive because it has nothing to do with my wishes and tastes, my personality, my neuroses; and my unconscious wishes or fears or anxieties or hopes are far more easily excluded from the conception of full humanness than they are from the conception of psychological health.

If you ever work with the concept of psychological health—or any other kind of health, or normality—you will discover what a temptation it is to project your own values and to make it into a self-description or perhaps a description of what you would like to be, or what you think people *should* be like, etc., etc. You'll have to fight against it all the time, and you'll discover that, while it's *possible* to be objective in such work, it's certainly difficult. And even then, you can't be really sure. Have you fallen into sampling error? After all, if you select persons for investigation on the basis of your personal judgment and diagnosis, such sampling errors are more likely than if you select by some more impersonal criterion (90).

Clearly, fusion-words are a scientific advance over more purely normative words, while also avoiding the worse trap of believing that science *must* be *only* value-free, and non-normative, i.e., nonhuman. Fusion concepts and words permit us to participate in the normal advance of science and knowledge from its phenomenological and experiential beginnings on toward greater reliability, greater validity, greater confidence, greater exactness, greater sharing with others and agreement with them (82).

Other obvious fusion-words are such as: *mature, evolved, developed, stunted, crippled, fully functioning, graceful, awkward, clumsy,* and the like. There are many, many more words which are less obviously fusions of the normative and the descriptive. And we may one day have to get used to thinking of fusion-words as paradigmatic, as normal, usual, and central. Then the more purely descriptive words and the more purely normative words would be thought of as peripheral and exceptional. I believe that this will come as part of the new humanistic *Weltanschauung* which is now rapidly crystallizing into a structured form.[1]

For one thing, as I have pointed out (95), these conceptions are too exclusively extrapsychic and don't account sufficiently for the quality of consciousness, for intrapsychic or subjective abilities, for instance, to enjoy music, to meditate and contemplate, to savor flavors, to be sensitive to one's *inner voices,* etc. Getting along well within one's inner world may be as important as social competence or reality competence.

But more important from the point of view of theoretical elegance and research strategy, these concepts are less objective and quantifiable than is a list of the capacities that make up the concept of humanness.

I would add that I consider none of these models to be *opposed* to the medical model. There is no need to dichotomize them from each other. Medical illnesses diminish the human being and therefore fall on the continuum of greater to lesser degree of humanness. Of course, though the medical illness model is necessary (for tumors, bacterial invasions, ulcers, etc.), it is certainly not sufficient (for neurotic, characterological, or spiritual disturbances).

Human Diminution

One consequence of this usage of "full humanness" rather than "psychological health" is the corresponding or parallel use of "human diminution," instead of "neurosis," which is anyway a totally obsolete

[1] I consider the "degree of humanness" concept to be more useful also than the concepts of "social competence," "human effectiveness," and similar notions.

word. Here the key concept is the loss or not-yet-actualization of human capacities and possibilities, and obviously this is also a matter of degree and quantity. Furthermore, it is closer to being externally observable, i.e., behavioral, which of course makes it easier to investigate than, for example, anxiety or compulsiveness or repression. Also it puts on the same continuum all the standard psychiatric categories, all the stuntings, cripplings, and inhibitions that come from poverty, exploitation, maleducation, enslavement, etc., and also the newer value pathologies, existential disorders, character disorders that come to the economically privileged. It handles very nicely the diminutions that result from drug addiction, psychopathy, authoritarianism, criminality, and other categories that cannot be called "illness" in the same medical sense as can, e.g., brain tumor.

This is a radical move away from the medical model, a move which is long overdue. Strictly speaking, neurosis means an illness of the nerves, a relic we can very well do without today. In addition, using the label "psychological illness" puts neurosis into the same universe of discourse as ulcers, lesions, bacterial invasions, broken bones, or tumors. But by now, we have learned very well that it is better to consider neurosis as rather related to spiritual disorders, to loss of meaning, to doubts about the goals of life, to grief and anger over a lost love, to seeing life in a different way, to loss of courage or of hope, to despair over the future, to dislike for oneself, to recognition that one's life is being wasted, or that there is no possibility of joy or love, etc.

These are all fallings away from full humanness, from the full blooming of human nature. They are losses of human possibility, of what might have been and could yet be perhaps. Physical and chemical hygiene and prophylaxes certainly have some little place in this realm of psychopathogenesis, but are as nothing in comparison with the far more powerful role of social, economic, political, religious, educational, philosophical, axiological, and familial determinants.

Subjective Biology

There are still other important advantages to be gained from moving over to this psychological-philosophical-educational-spiritual usage. Not least of these, it seems to me, is that it encourages the *proper* conceptual use of the biological and constitutional base which underlies any discussion of Identity or of The Real Self, of growth, of uncovering therapy, of full humanness or of diminution of humanness, of self-transcendence, or any version of these. To say it briefly, I believe that helping a person to move toward full humanness proceeds inevitably via awareness of one's identity (among other things). A very important part of this task is to become aware of what one *is*, biologically, temperamentally, constitutionally, as a member of a species, of one's capacities, desires, needs, and also of one's vocation, what one is fitted for, what one's destiny is.

To say it very bluntly and unequivocally, one absolutely necessary aspect of this self-awareness is a kind of phenomenology of one's own inner biology, of that which I call "instinctoid" (see Appendix D), of one's animality and specieshood. This is certainly what psychoanalysis tries to do, i.e., to help one to become conscious of one's animal urges, needs, tensions, depressions, tastes, anxieties. So also for Horney's distinction between a real self and a pseudo-self. Is this also not a subjective discrimination of what one truly is? And what *is* one truly if not first and foremost one's own body, one's own constitution, one's own functioning, one's own specieshood? (I have very much enjoyed, *qua theorist*, this pretty integration of Freud, Goldstein, Sheldon, Horney, Cattell, Frankl, May, Rogers, Murray, etc., etc., etc. Perhaps even Skinner could be coaxed into this diverse company, since I suspect that a listing of all his "intrinsic reinforcers" for his human subjects might very well look much like the "hierarchy of instinctoid basic needs and metaneeds" that I have proposed!)

I believe it is possible to carry through this paradigm even at the very highest levels of personal development, where one transcends one's own personality (85). I believe I make a good case for accepting the probable instinctoid character of one's highest values, i.e., of what might be called the spiritual or philosophical life. Even this personally discovered axiology I feel can be subsumed under this category of "phenomenology of one's own instinctoid nature" or of "subjective biology" or "experiential biology" or some such phrase.

Think of the great theoretical and scientific advantages of placing on one single continuum of degree or amount of humanness, not only all the kinds of sickness the psychiatrists and physicians talk about but also all the additional kinds that existentialists and philosophers and religious thinkers and social reformers have worried about. Not only this, but we can also place on the same single scale all the various degrees and kinds of health that we know about, plus even the health-beyond-health of self-transcendence, of mystical fusion, and whatever still higher possibilities of human nature the future may yet disclose.

Inner Signals

Thinking in this way has had for me at least the one special advantage of directing my attention sharply to what I called at first "the impulse voices" but which had better be called more generally something like the "inner signals" (or cues or stimuli). I had not realized sufficiently that in most neuroses, and in many other disturbances as well, the inner signals become weak or even disappear entirely (as in the severely obsessional person) and/or are not "heard" or *cannot* be heard. At the extreme we have the experientially empty person, the zombie, the one with empty insides. Recovering the self *must*, as a *sine qua non*, include the recovery of the ability to have and to cognize these inner signals, to know what and whom one likes and dislikes, what is enjoyable and what is not, when to eat and when not to, when to sleep, when to urinate, when to rest.

The experientially empty person, lacking these directives from within, these voices of the real self, must turn to outer cues for guidance, for instance eating when the clock tells him to, rather than obeying his appetite (he has none). He guides himself by clocks, rules, calendars, schedules, agenda, and by hints and cues from other people.

In any case, I think the particular sense in which I suggest interpreting the neurosis as a failure of personal growth must be clear by now. It is a falling short of what one could have been, and even, one could say, of what one *should* have been, biologically speaking, that is, if one had grown and developed in an unimpeded way. Human and personal possibilities have been lost. The world has been narrowed, and so has consciousness. Capacities have been inhibited. I think for instance of the fine pianist who couldn't play before an audience of more than a few, or the phobic who is forced to avoid heights or crowds. The person who can't study, or who can't sleep, or who can't eat many foods has been diminished as surely as the one who has been blinded. The cognitive losses, the lost pleasures, joys, and ecstasies,[2] the loss of competence, the inability to relax, the weakening of will, the fear of responsibility—all these are diminutions of humanness.

I've mentioned some of the advantages of replacing the concepts of psychological illness and health with the more pragmatic, public, and quantitative concept of full or diminished humanness, which I believe is also biologically and philosophically sounder. But before I move on, I'd like to note also that diminution can of course be either reversible or irreversible, e.g., we feel far less hopeful about the paranoid person than we do about say a nice, lovable hysterical. And of course also, diminution is dynamic, in the Freudian style. The original Freudian schema spoke of an intrinsic dialectic between the impulse and the defenses against this impulse. In this same sense, diminution leads to consequences and processes. It is only rarely a completion or a finality in a simple descriptive way. In most people these losses lead not only to all sorts of defensive processes which have been well described by Freudian and other psychoanalytic groups, for instance, to repression, denial, conflict, etc. They also lead to coping responses as I stressed long ago (110).

Conflict itself is, of course, a sign of relative health as you would know if you ever met really apathetic people, really hopeless people, people who have given up hoping, striving, and coping. Neurosis is by contrast a very hopeful kind of thing. It means that a man who is frightened, who doesn't trust himself, who has a low self-image, etc., still reaches out for the human heritage and for the basic gratifications to which every human being has a right simply by virtue of being human. You might say it's a kind of *timid* and ineffectual striving toward self-actualization, toward full humanness.

Diminution can, of course, be reversible. Very frequently, simply supplying the need gratifications can solve the problem, especially in children. For a child who hasn't been loved enough, obviously the treatment of first choice is to love him to death, to just slop it all over him. Clinical and general human experience is that it works—I don't

---

[2] What it means for one's style of life to lose peak experiences has been very well set forth in Colin Wilson's *Introduction to the New Existentialism* (159).

have any statistics, but I would suspect nine out of ten times. So is respect a wonderful medicine for counteracting a feeling of worthlessness. Which, of course, brings up the obvious conclusion that, if "health and illness" on the medical model are seen as obsolete, so also must the medical concepts of "treatment" and "cure" and the authoritative doctor be discarded and replaced.

The Jonah Complex

I would like to turn to one of the many reasons for what Angyal (4) called the evasion of growth. We have, all of us, an impulse to improve ourselves, an impulse toward actualizing more of our potentialities, toward self-actualization, or full humanness or human fulfillment, or whatever term you like. Granted this, then what holds us up? What blocks us?

One such defense against growth that I'd like to speak about specially—because it hasn't been noticed much—I shall call the Jonah complex.[3]

In my own notes I had at first labeled this defense the "fear of one's own greatness" or the "evasion of one's destiny" or the "running away from one's own best talents." I had wanted to stress as bluntly and sharply as I could the non-Freudian point that we fear our best as well as our worst, even though in different ways. It is certainly possible for most of us to be greater than we are in actuality. We all have unused potentialities or not fully developed ones. It is certainly true that many of us evade our constitutionally suggested vocations (call, destiny, task in life, mission). So often we run away from the responsibilities dictated (or rather suggested) by nature, by fate, even sometimes by accident, just as Jonah tried—in vain—to run away from *his* fate.

We fear our highest possibilities (as well as our lowest ones). We are generally afraid to become that which we can glimpse in our most perfect moments, under the most perfect conditions, under conditions of greatest courage. We enjoy and even thrill to the godlike possibilities we see in ourselves in such peak moments. And yet we

[3] This name was suggested by my friend, Professor Frank Manuel, with whom I had discussed this puzzle.

simultaneously shiver with weakness, awe, and fear before these very same possibilities.

I have found it easy enough to demonstrate this to my students simply by asking, "Which of you in this class hopes to write the great American novel, or to be a Senator, or Governor, or President? Who wants to be Secretary-General of the United Nations? Or a great composer? Who aspires to be a saint, like Schweitzer, perhaps? Who among you will be a great leader?" Generally everybody starts giggling, blushing, and squirming until I ask, "If not you, then who else?" Which of course is the truth. And in this same way, as I push my graduate students toward these higher levels of aspiration, I'll say, "What great book are you now secretly planning to write?" And then they often blush and stammer and push me off in some way. But why should I not ask that question? Who else will write the books on psychology except psychologists? So I can ask, "Do you not plan to be a psychologist?" "Well, yes." "Are you in training to be a mute or an inactive psychologist? What's the advantage of that? That's not a good path to self-actualization. No, you must want to be a first-class psychologist, meaning the best, the very best you are capable of becoming. If you deliberately plan to be less than you are capable of being, then I warn you that you'll be deeply unhappy for the rest of your life. You will be evading your own capacities, your own possibilities."

Not only are we ambivalent about our own highest possibilities, we are also in a perpetual and I think universal—perhaps even *necessary*—conflict and ambivalence over these same highest possibilities in other people, and in human nature in general. Certainly we love and admire good men, saints, honest, virtuous, clean men. But could anybody who has looked into the depths of human nature fail to be aware of our mixed and often hostile feelings toward saintly men? Or toward very beautiful women or men? Or toward great creators? Or toward our intellectual geniuses? It is not necessary to be a psychotherapist to see this phenomenon—let us call it "Counter-valuing." Any reading of history will turn up plenty of examples, or perhaps even I could say that any such historical search might fail to turn up a single exception throughout the whole history of mankind. We surely love and admire all the persons who have incarnated the true, the good, the beautiful, the just, the perfect, the ultimately successful. And yet they also make us uneasy, anxious, confused, perhaps a little jealous or envious, a little inferior, clumsy. They usually make us lose our aplomb, our self-possession, and self-regard. (Nietzsche is still our best teacher here.)

Here we have a first clue. My impression so far is that the greatest people, simply by their presence and by being what they are, make us feel aware of our lesser worth, whether or not they intend to. If this is an unconscious effect, and we are not aware of why we feel stupid or ugly or inferior whenever such a person turns up, we are apt to respond with projection, i.e., we react as if he were *trying* to make us feel inferior, as if we were the target (54). Hostility is then an understandable consequence. It looks to me so far as if conscious awareness tends to fend off this hostility. That is, if you are willing to attempt self-awareness and self-analysis of your *own* counter-valuing, i.e., of your unconscious fear and hatred of true, good, beautiful, etc., people, you will very likely be less nasty to them. And I am willing also to extrapolate to the guess that if you can learn to love more purely the highest values in others, this might make you love these qualities in yourself in a less frightened way.

Allied to this dynamic is the awe before the highest, of which Rudolf Otto (125) has given us the classical description. Putting this together with Eliade's insights (31) into sacralization and desacralization, we become more aware of the universality of the fear of direct confrontation with a god or with the godlike. In some religions death is the inevitable consequence. Most preliterate societies also have places or objects that are taboo because they are too sacred and *therefore too dangerous*. In the last chapter of my *Psychology of Science* (81) I have also given examples mostly from science and medicine of desacralizing and resacralizing and tried to explain the psychodynamics of these processes. Mostly it comes down to awe before the highest and best. (I want to stress that this awe is intrinsic, justified, *right*, suitable, rather than some sickness or failing to get "cured of.")

But here again my feeling is that this awe and fear need not be negative alone, something to make us flee or cower. These are also desirable and enjoyable feelings capable of bringing us even to the point of highest ecstasy and rapture. Conscious awareness, insight, and "working through," à la Freud, is the answer here too I think. This is the best path I know to the acceptance of our highest powers, and whatever elements of greatness or goodness or wisdom or talent we may have concealed or evaded.

A helpful sidelight for me has come from trying to understand why peak experiences are ordinarily transient and brief (88). The answer becomes clearer and clearer. *We are just not strong enough to endure more!* It is just too shaking and wearing. So often people in such ecstatic moments say, "It's too much," or "I can't stand it," or "I could die." And as I get the descriptions, I sometimes feel, Yes, they *could* die. Delirious happiness cannot be borne for long. Our organisms are just too weak for any large doses of greatness, just as they would be too weak to endure hour-long sexual orgasms, for example.

The word "peak experience" is more appropriate than I realized at first. The acute emotion must be climactic and momentary and it *must* give way to nonecstatic serenity, calmer happiness, and the intrinsic pleasures of clear, contemplative cognition of the highest goods. The climactic emotion cannot endure, but B-cognition (Being cognition) *can* (82, 85).

Doesn't this help us to understand our Jonah complex? It is partly a justified fear of being torn apart, of losing control, of being shattered and disintegrated, even of being killed by the experience. Great emotions after all can in *fact* overwhelm us. The fear of surrendering to such an experience, a fear which reminds us of all the parallel fears found in sexual frigidity, can be understood better I think through familiarity with the literature of psychodynamics and depth psychology, and of the psychophysiology and medical psychomatics of emotion.

There is still another psychological process that I have run across in my explorations of failure to actualize the self. This evasion of growth can also be set in motion by a fear of paranoia. Of course this has been said in more universal ways. Promethean and Faustian legends are found in practically any culture.[4] For instance, the Greeks called it the fear of *hubris*. It has been called "sinful pride," which is of course a permanent human problem. The person who says to himself, "Yes, I will be a great philosopher and I will rewrite Plato and do it better," must sooner or later be struck dumb by his grandiosity,

---

[4] Sheldon's excellent book on this subject (135) is not quoted often enough on this subject, possibly because it came before we were quite ready to assimilate it (1936).

his arrogance. And especially in his weaker moments, will say to himself, "Who? Me?" and think of it as a crazy fantasy or even fear it as a delusion. He compares his knowledge of his inner private self, with all its weakness, vacillation, and shortcomings, with the bright, shining, perfect, and faultless image he has of Plato. Then, of course, he'll feel presumptuous and grandiose. (What he doesn't realize is that Plato, introspecting, must have felt just the same way about himself, but went ahead anyway, overriding his doubts about himself.)

For some people this evasion of one's own growth, setting low levels of aspiration, the fear of doing what one is capable of doing, voluntary self-crippling, pseudostupidity, mock-humility are in fact defenses against grandiosity, arrogance, sinful pride, hubris. There are people who cannot manage that graceful integration between the humility and the pride which is absolutely necessary for creative work. To invent or create you must have the "arrogance of creativeness" which so many investigators have noticed. But, of course, if you have *only* the arrogance without the humility, then you are in fact paranoid. You *must* be aware not only of the godlike possibilities within, but also of the existential human limitations. You must be able simultaneously to laugh at yourself and at all human pretensions. If you can be amused by the worm trying to be a god (162), then in fact you may be able to go on trying and being arrogant without fearing paranoia or bringing down upon yourself the evil eye. This is a good technique.

May I mention one more such technique that I saw at its best in Aldous Huxley, who was certainly a great man in the sense I've been discussing, one who was able to accept his talents and use them to the full. He managed it by perpetually marveling at how interesting and fascinating everything was, by wondering like a youngster at how miraculous things are, by saying frequently, "Extraordinary! Extraordinary!" He could look out at the world with wide eyes, with unabashed innocence, awe, and fascination, which is a kind of admission of smallness, a form of humility, and then proceed calmly and unafraid to the great tasks he set for himself.

Finally, I refer you to a paper of mine (87) relevant in itself, but also as the first in a possible series. Its title, "The need to know and the fear of knowing," illustrates well what I want to say about *each* of the intrinsic or ultimate values that I've called Values of Being (B-Values). I am trying to say that these ultimate values, which

I think are also the highest needs, or metaneeds, as I call them in Chapter 23, fall, like all basic needs, into the basic Freudian schema of impulse *and* defense against that impulse. Thus it is certainly demonstrable that we need the truth and love it and seek it. And yet it is just as easy to demonstrate that we are also simultaneously *afraid* to know the truth. For instance, certain truths carry automatic responsibilities which may be anxiety-producing. One way to evade the responsibility and the anxiety is simply to evade consciousness of the truth.

I predict that we will find a similar dialectic for each of the intrinsic Values of Being, and I have vaguely thought of doing a series of papers on e.g., "The love of beauty and our uneasiness with it." "Our love of the good man and our irritation with him." "Our search for excellence and our tendency to destroy it," etc., etc. Of course, these counter-values are stronger in neurotic people, but it looks to me as if all of us must make our peace with these mean impulses within ourselves. And my impression so far is that the best way to do this is to transmute envy, jealousy, *presentiment*, and nastiness into humble admiration, gratitude, appreciation, adoration, and even worship via conscious insight and working through (see Appendix B). This is the road to feeling small and weak and unworthy and *accepting* these feelings instead of needing to protect a spuriously high self-esteem by striking out (49).

And again I think it is obvious that understanding of this basic existential problem should help us to embrace the B-Values not only in others, but also in ourselves, thereby helping to resolve the Jonah complex.

3

Self-Actualizing and Beyond

In this chapter, I plan to discuss ideas that are in midstream rather than ready for formulation into a final version. I find that with my students and with other people with whom I share these ideas, the notion of self-actualization gets to be almost like a Rorschach inkblot. It frequently tells me more about the person using it than about reality. What I would like to do now is to explore some aspects of the nature of self-actualization, not as a grand abstraction, but in terms of the operational meaning of the self-actualizing process. What does self-actualization mean in moment-to-moment terms? What does it mean on Tuesday at four o'clock?

The Beginnings of Self-Actualization Studies. My investigations on self-actualization were not planned to be research and did not start out as research. They started out as the effort of a young intellectual to try to understand two of his teachers whom he loved, adored, and admired and who were very, very wonderful people. It was a kind of high-IQ devotion. I could not be content simply to adore, but sought to understand why these two people were so different from the run-of-the-mill people in the world. These two people were

Ruth Benedict and Max Wertheimer. They were my teachers after I came with a Ph.D. from the West to New York City, and they were most remarkable human beings. My training in psychology equipped me not at all for understanding them. It was as if they were not quite people but something more than people. My own investigation began as a prescientific or nonscientific activity. I made descriptions and notes on Max Wertheimer, and I made notes on Ruth Benedict. When I tried to understand them, think about them, and write about them in my journal and my notes, I realized in one wonderful moment that their two patterns could be generalized. I was talking about a kind of person, not about two noncomparable individuals. There was wonderful excitement in that. I tried to see whether this pattern could be found elsewhere, and I did find it elsewhere, in one person after another.

By ordinary standards of laboratory research, i.e., of rigorous and controlled research, this simply was not research at all. My generalizations grew out of *my* selection of certain kinds of people. Obviously, other judges are needed. So far, one man has selected perhaps two dozen people whom he liked or admired very much and thought were wonderful people and then tried to figure them out and found that he was able to describe a syndrome—the kind of pattern that seemed to fit all of them. These were people only from Western cultures, people selected with all kinds of built-in biases. Unreliable as it is, that was the only operational definition of self-actualizing people as I described them in my first publication on the subject.

After I published the results of my investigations, there appeared perhaps six, eight, or ten other lines of evidence that supported the findings, not by replication, but by approaches from different angles. Carl Rogers' findings (128) and those of his students add up to corroboration for the whole syndrome. Bugental (20, pp. 266–275) has offered confirmatory evidence from psychotherapy. Some of the work with LSD (116), some of the studies on the effects of therapy (good therapy, that is) some test results—in fact everything I know adds up to corroborative support, though not replicated support, for that study. I personally feel very confident about its major conclusions. I cannot conceive of any research that would make major changes in the pattern, though I am sure there will be minor changes. I have made some of those myself. But my confidence in my rightness is not a scientific datum. If you question the kind of data I have from my researches with monkeys and dogs, you are bringing my competence into doubt or calling me a liar, and I have a right to object. If you question my findings on self-actualizing people (95, pp. 203–205; 89), you may reasonably do so because you don't know very much about the man who selected the people on whom all the conclusions are based. The conclusions are in the realm of prescience, but the affirmations are set forth in a form that can be put to test. In that sense, they are scientific.

The people I selected for my investigation were older people, people who had lived much of their lives out and were visibly successful. We do not yet know about the applicability of the findings to young people. We do not know what self-actualization means in other cultures, although studies of self-actualization in China and in India are now in process. We do not know what the findings of these new studies will be, but of one thing I have no doubt: When you select out for careful study very fine and healthy people, strong people, creative people, saintly people, sagacious people—in fact, exactly the kind of people I picked out—then you get a different view of mankind. You are asking how tall can people grow, what can a human being become?

There are other things that I feel very confident about—"my smell tells me," so to speak. Yet I have even fewer objective data on these points than I had on those discussed above. Self-actualization is hard enough to define. How much harder it is to answer the question: Beyond self-actualization, what? Or, if you will: Beyond authenticity, what? Just being honest is, after all, not sufficient in all this. What else can we say of self-actualizing people?

Being-Values. Self-actualizing people are, without one single exception, involved in a cause outside their own skin, in something outside of themselves. They are devoted, working at something, something which is very precious to them—some calling or vocation in the old sense, the priestly sense. They are working at something which fate has called them to somehow and which they work at and which they love, so that the work-joy dichotomy in them disappears. One devotes his life to the law, another to justice, another to beauty or truth. All, in one way or another, devote their lives to the search for what I have called (89) the "being" values ("B" for short), the ultimate values which are intrinsic, which cannot be reduced to anything more ultimate. There are about fourteen of these B-Values, including the truth and beauty and goodness of the ancients and perfection, simplicity, comprehensiveness, and several more. These B-Values are described in Chapter 9, and in the appendix to my book *Religions, Values, and Peak-Experiences* (85). They are the values of being.

Metaneeds and Metapathologies. The existence of these B-Values adds a whole set of complications to the structure of self-actualization. These B-Values behave like needs. I have called them *metaneeds*. Their deprivation breeds certain kinds of pathologies which have not yet been adequately described but which I call *metapathologies*—the sicknesses of the soul which come, for example, from living among liars all the time and not trusting anyone. Just as we need counselors to help people with the simpler problems of unmet needs, so we may need *metacounselors* to help with the soul-sicknesses that grow from the unfulfilled metaneeds. In certain definable and empirical ways, it is necessary for man to live in beauty rather than ugliness, as it is necessary for him to have food for an aching belly or rest for a weary body. In fact, I would go so far as to claim that these B-Values are the meaning of life for most people, but many people don't even recognize that they have these metaneeds. Part of the counselors' job may be to make them aware of these needs in themselves, just as the classical psychoanalyst made his patients aware of their instinctoid basic needs. Ultimately, perhaps, some professionals shall come to think of themselves as philosophical or religious counselors.

Some of us try to help our conselees move and grow toward self-actualization. These people are often all wrapped up in value problems. Many are youngsters who are, in principle, very wonderful people, though in actuality they often seem to be little more than snotty kids. Nevertheless, I assume (in the face of all behavioral evidence sometimes) that they are, in the classical sense, idealistic. I assume that they are looking for values and that they would love to have something to devote themselves to, to be patriotic about, to worship, adore, love. These youngsters are making choices from moment to moment of going forward or retrogressing, moving away from or moving toward self-actualization. What can counselors, or metacounselors, tell them about becoming more fully themselves?

Behaviors Leading to Self-Actualization

What does one do when he self-actualizes? Does he grit his teeth and squeeze? What does self-actualization mean in terms of actual behavior, actual procedure? I shall describe eight ways in which one self-actualizes.

First, self-actualization means experiencing fully, vividly, selflessly, with full concentration and total absorption. It means experiencing without the self-consciousness of the adolescent. At this moment of experiencing, the person is wholly and fully human. This is a self-actualizing moment. This is a moment when the self is actualizing itself. As individuals, we all experience such moments occasionally. As counselors, we can help clients to experience them more often. We can encourage them to become totally absorbed in something and to forget their poses and their defenses and their shyness—to go at it "whole-hog." From the outside, we can see that this can be a very sweet moment. In those youngsters who are trying to be very tough and cynical and sophisticated, we can see the recovery of some of the guilelessness of childhood; some of the innocence and sweetness of the face can come back as they devote themselves fully to a moment and throw themselves fully into the experiencing of it. The key word for this is "selflessly," and our youngsters suffer from too little selflessness and too much self-consciousness, self-awareness.

Second, let us think of life as a process of choices, one after another. At each point there is a progression choice and a regression choice. There may be a movement toward defense, toward safety, toward being afraid; but over on the other side, there is the growth choice. To make the growth choice instead of the fear choice a dozen times a day is to move a dozen times a day toward self-actualization. *Self-actualization is an ongoing process;* it means making each of the many single choices about whether to lie or be honest, whether to steal or not to steal at a particular point, and it means to make each of these choices as a growth choice. This is movement toward self-actualization.

Third, to talk of self-actualization implies that there is a self to be actualized. A human being is not a *tabula rasa*, not a lump of clay or Plasticine. He is something which is already there, at least a "cartilaginous" structure of some kind. A human being is, at minimum, his temperament, his biochemical balances, and so on. There is a self, and what I have sometimes referred to as "listening to the impulse voices" means letting the self emerge. Most of us, most of the time (and especially does this apply to children, young people), listen not to ourselves but to Mommy's introjected voice or Daddy's voice or to the voice of the Establishment, of the Elders, of authority, or of tradition.

As a simple first step toward self-actualization, I sometimes suggest to my students that when they are given a glass of wine and asked how they like it, they try a different way of responding. First, I suggest that they *not* look at the label on the bottle. Thus they will not use it to get any cue about whether or not they *should* like it. Next, I recommend that they close their eyes if possible and that they "make a hush." Now they are ready to look within themselves and try to shut out the noise of the world so that they may savor the wine on their tongues and look to the "Supreme Court" inside themselves. Then, and only then, they may come out and say, "I like it" or "I don't like it." A statement so arrived at is different from the usual kind of phoniness that we all indulge in. At a party recently, I caught myself looking at the label on a bottle and assuring my hostess that she had indeed selected a very good Scotch. But then I stopped myself: What was I saying? I know little about Scotches. All I knew was what the advertisements said. I had no idea whether this one was good or not; yet this is the kind of thing we all do. Refusing to do it is part of the ongoing process of actualizing oneself. Does *your* belly hurt? Or does it feel good? Does this taste good on *your* tongue? Do *you* like lettuce?

Fourth, when in doubt, be honest rather than not. I am covered by that phrase "when in doubt," so that we need not argue too much about diplomacy. Frequently, when we are in doubt we are not honest. Clients are not honest much of the time. They are playing games and posing. They do not take easily to the suggestion to be honest. Looking within oneself for many of the answers implies taking responsibility. That is in itself a great step toward actualization. This matter of responsibility has been little studied. It doesn't turn up in our textbooks, for who can investigate responsibility in white rats? Yet it is an almost tangible part of psychotherapy. In psychotherapy, one can see it, can feel it, can know the moment of responsibility. Then there is a clear knowing of what it feels like. This is one of the great steps. Each time one takes responsibility, this is an actualizing of the self.

Fifth, we have talked so far of experiencing without self-awareness, of making the growth choice rather than the fear choice, of listening to the impulse voices, and of being honest and taking responsibility. All these are steps toward self-actualization, and all of them guarantee better life choices. A person who does each of these little things each time the choice point comes will find that they add up to better choices about what is constitutionally right for him. He comes to know what his destiny is, who his wife or husband will be, what his mission in life will be. One cannot choose wisely for a life unless he dares to listen to himself, *his own self*, at each moment in life, and to say calmly, "No, I don't like such and such."

The art world, in my opinion, has been captured by a small group of opinion- and taste-makers about whom I feel suspicious. That is an *ad hominem* judgment, but it seems fair enough for people who set themselves up as able to say, "You like what I like or else you are a fool." We must teach people to listen to their own tastes. Most people don't do it. When standing in a gallery before a puzzling painting, one rarely hears, "That is a puzzling painting." We had a dance program at Brandeis University not too long ago—a weird thing altogether, with electronic music, tapes, and people doing surrealistic and Dada things. When the lights went up everybody looked stunned, and nobody knew what to say. In that kind of situation most people will make some smart chatter instead of saying, "I would like to think about this." Making an honest statement involves daring to be different, unpopular, nonconformist. If clients, young or old, cannot be taught about being prepared to be unpopular, counselors might just as well give up right now. To be courageous rather than afraid is another version of the same thing.

Sixth, self-actualization is not only an end state but also the process of actualizing one's potentialities at any time, in any amount. It is, for example, a matter of becoming smarter by studying if one is an intelligent person. Self-actualization means using one's intelligence. It does not mean doing some far-out thing necessarily, but it may mean going through an arduous and demanding period of preparation in order to realize one's possibilities. Self-actualization can consist of finger exercises at a piano keyboard. Self-actualization means working to do well the thing that one wants to do. To become a second-rate physician is not a good path to self-actualization. One wants to be first-rate or as good as he can be.

Seventh, peak experiences (85, 89) are transient moments of self-actualization. They are moments of ecstasy which cannot be bought, cannot be guaranteed, cannot even be sought. One must be, as C. S. Lewis wrote, "surprised by joy." But one can set up the conditions so that peak experiences are more likely, or one can perversely set up the conditions so that they are less likely. Breaking up an illusion, getting rid of a false notion, learning what one is not good at, learning what one's potentialities are *not*—these are also part of discovering what one is in fact.

Practically everyone does have peak experiences, but not everyone knows it. Some people wave these small mystical experiences aside. Helping people to recognize these little moments of ecstasy (124) when they happen is one of the jobs of the counselor or metacounselor. Yet, how does one's psyche, with nothing external in the world to point at—there is no blackboard there—look into another person's secret psyche and then try to communicate? We have to work out a new way of communication. I have tried one. It is described in another appendix in that same book, *Religions, Values, and Peak-Experiences*, under the title "Rhapsodic Communications." I think that kind of communication may be more of a model for teaching, and counseling, for helping adults to become as fully developed as they can be, than the kind we are used to when we see teachers writing on the board. If I love Beethoven and I hear something in a quartet that you don't, how do I teach you to hear? The noises are there, obviously. But I hear something very, very beautiful, and you look blank. You hear the sounds. How do I get you to hear the beauty? That is more our problem in teaching than making you learn the ABC's or demonstrating arithmetic on the board or pointing to a dissection of a frog. These latter things are external to both people; one has a pointer, and both can look at the same time. This kind of teaching is easy; the other kind is much harder, but it is part of the counselor's job. It is metacounseling.

Eighth, finding out who one is, what he is, what he likes, what he doesn't like, what is good for him and what bad, where he is going and what his mission is—opening oneself up to himself—means the exposure of psychopathology. It means identifying defenses, and after defenses have been identified, it means finding the courage to give them up. This is painful because defenses are erected against something which is unpleasant. But giving up the defenses is worthwhile. If the psychoanalytic literature has taught us nothing else, it has taught us that repression is not a good way of solving problems.

Desacralizing. Let me talk about one defense mechanism that is not mentioned in the psychology textbooks, though it is a very important defense mechanism to some youngsters of today. It is the defense mechanism of *desacralizing*. These youngsters mistrust the possibility of values and virtues. They feel themselves swindled or thwarted in their lives. Most of them have, in fact, dopey parents whom they don't respect very much, parents who are quite confused themselves about values and who, frequently, are simply terrified of their children and never punish them or stop them from doing things that are wrong. So you have a situation where the youngsters simply despise their elders—often for good and sufficient reason. Such youngsters have learned to make a big generalization: They won't listen to anybody who is grown-up, especially if the grown-up uses the same words which they've heard from the hypocritical mouth. They have heard their fathers talk about being honest or brave or bold, and they have seen their fathers being the opposite of all these things.

The youngsters have learned to reduce the person to the concrete object and to refuse to see what he might be or to refuse to see him in his symbolic values or to refuse to see him or her eternally. Our kids have desacralized sex, for example. Sex is nothing; it is a natural thing, and they have made it so natural that it has lost its poetic qualities in many instances, which means that it has lost practically everything. Self-actualization means giving up this defense mechanism and learning or being taught to resacralize.[1]

[1] I have had to make up these words because the English language is rotten for good people. It has no decent vocabulary for the virtues. Even the nice words get all smeared up—"love," for instance.

Resacralizing. Resacralizing means being willing, once again, to see a person "under the aspect of eternity," as Spinoza says, or to see him in the medieval Christian unitive perception, that is, being able to see the sacred, the eternal, the symbolic. It is to see Woman with a capital "W" and everything which that implies, even when one looks at a particular woman. Another example: One goes to medical school and dissects a brain. Certainly something is lost if the medical student isn't awed but, without the unitive perception, sees the brain only as one concrete thing. Open to resacralization, one sees a brain as a sacred object also, sees its symbolic value, sees it as a figure of speech, sees it in its poetic aspects.

Resacralization often means an awful lot of corny talk—"very square," the kids would say. Nevertheless, for the counselor, especially for the counselor of older people, where these philosophical questions about religion and the meaning of life come up, this is a most important way of helping the person to move toward self-actualization. The youngsters may say that it is square, and the logical positivists may say that it is meaningless, but for the person who seeks our help in this process, it is obviously very meaningful and very important, and we had better answer him, or we're not doing what it is our job to do.

Put all these points together, and we see that self-actualization is not a matter of one great moment. It is not true that on Thursday at four o'clock the trumpet blows and one steps into the pantheon forever and altogether. Self-actualization is a matter of degree, of little accessions accumulated one by one. Too often our clients are inclined to wait for some kind of inspiration to strike so that they can say, "At 3:23 on this Thursday I became self-actualized!" People selected as self-actualizing subjects, people who fit the criteria, go about it in these little ways: They listen to their own voices; they take responsibility; they are honest; and they work hard. They find out who they are and what they are, not only in terms of their mission in life, but also in terms of the way their feet hurt when they wear such and such a pair of shoes and whether they do or do not like eggplant or stay up all night if they drink too much beer. All this is what the real self means. They find their own biological natures, their congenital natures, which are irreversible or difficult to change.

The Therapeutic Attitude

These are the things people do as they move toward self-actualization. Who, then, is a counselor? How can he help the people who come to him to make this movement in the direction of growth?

Seeking a Model. I have used the words "therapy," "psychotherapy," and "patient." Actually, I hate all these words, and I hate the medical model that they imply because the medical model suggests that the person who comes to the counselor is a sick person, beset by disease and illness, seeking a cure. Actually, of course, we hope that the counselor will be the one who helps to foster the self-actualization of people, rather than the one who helps to cure a disease.

The helping model has to give way, too; it just doesn't fit. It makes us think of the counselor as the person or the professional who knows and reaches down from his privileged position above to the poor jerks below who don't know and have to be helped in some way. Nor is the counselor to be a teacher, in the usual sense, because what teachers have specialized in and gotten to be very good at is "extrinsic learning" (discussed in Chapter 12). The process of growing into the best human being one can be is, instead, "intrinsic learning."

The existential therapists have wrestled with this question of models, and I can recommend Bugental's book, *The Search for Authenticity* (20), for a discussion of the matter. Bugental suggests that we call counseling or therapy "ontogogy," which means trying to help people to grow to their fullest possible height. Perhaps that's a better word than the one I once suggested, a word derived from a German author, "psychogogy," which means the education of the psyche. Whatever the word we use, I think that the concept we will eventually have to come to is one that Alfred Adler suggested a long, long time ago when he spoke of the "older brother." The older brother is the loving person who takes responsibility, just as one does for his young, kid brother. Of course, the older brother knows more; he's lived longer, but he is not qualitatively different, and he is not in another realm of discourse. The wise and loving older brother tries to improve the younger, and he tries to make him better than he is, in the younger's own style. See how different this is from the "teaching-somebody-who-doesn't-know-nothin' " model!

Counseling is not concerned with training or with molding or with teaching in the ordinary sense of telling people what to do and how to do it. It is not concerned with propaganda. It is a Taoistic uncovering and *then* helping. Taoistic means the noninterfering, the "letting be." Taoism is not a laissez-faire philosophy or a philosophy of neglect or of refusal to help or care. As a kind of model of this process we might think of a therapist who, if he is a decent therapist and also a decent human being, would never dream of imposing himself upon his patients or propagandizing in any way or of trying to make a patient into an imitation of himself.

What the good clinical therapist does is to help his particular client to unfold, to break through the defenses against his own self-knowledge, to recover himself, and to get to know himself. Ideally, the therapist's rather abstract frame of reference, the textbooks he has read, the schools that he has gone to, his beliefs about the world—these should never be perceptible to the patient. Respectful of the inner nature, the being, the essence of this "younger brother," he would recognize that the best way for him to lead a good life is to be more fully himself. The people we call "sick" are the people who are not themselves, the people who have built up all sorts of neurotic defenses against being human. Just as it makes no difference to the rosebush whether the gardener is Italian or French or Swedish, so it should make no difference to the younger brother how his helper learned to be a helper. What the helper has to give is certain services that are independent of his being Swedish or Catholic or Mohammedan or Freudian or whatever he is.

These basic concepts include, imply, and are completely in accord with the basic concepts of Freudian and other systems of psychodynamics. It is a Freudian principle that unconscious aspects of the self are repressed and that the finding of the true self requires the uncovering of these unconscious aspects. Implicit is a belief that truth heals much. Learning to break through one's repressions, to know one's self, to hear the impulse voices, to uncover the triumphant nature, to reach knowledge, insight, and the truth—these are the requirements.

Lawrence Kubie (64), in "The Forgotten Man in Education,"

some time ago made the point that one, ultimate goal of education is to help the person become a human being, as fully human as he can possibly be.

Especially with adults we are not in a position in which we have nothing to work with. We already have a start; we already have capacities, talents, direction, missions, callings. The job is, if we are to take this model seriously, to help them to be more perfectly what they already are, to be more full, more actualizing, more realizing in fact what they are in potentiality.

PART II

Creativeness

4

The Creative Attitude

I

My feeling is that the concept of creativeness and the concept of the healthy, self-actualizing, fully human person seem to be coming closer and closer together, and may perhaps turn out to be the same thing.

Another conclusion I seem to be impelled toward, even though I am not quite sure of my facts, is that creative art education, or better said, Education-Through-Art, may be especially important not so much for turning out artists or art products, as for turning out better people. If we have clearly in mind the educational goals for human beings that I will be hinting at, if we hope for our children that they will become full human beings, and that they will move toward actualizing the potentialities that they have, then, as nearly as I can make out, the only kind of education in existence today that has any faint inkling of such goals is art education. So I am thinking of education through art not because it turns out pictures but because I think it may be possible that, clearly understood, it may become the paradigm for all other education. That is, instead of being regarded as the frill, the expendable kind of thing which it now is, if we take it seriously enough and work at it hard enough and if it turns out to be what some of us suspect it can be, then we may one day teach arithmetic and reading and writing on this paradigm. So far as I am concerned, I am talking about all education. This is why I am interested in education through art—simply because it seems to be good education in potential.

Another reason for my interest in art education, creativeness, psychological health, etc., is that I have a very strong feeling of a change of pace in history. It seems to me that we are at a point in history unlike anything that has ever been before. Life moves far more rapidly now than it ever did before. Think, for instance, of the huge acceleration in the rate of growth of facts, of knowledge, of techniques, of inventions, of advances in technology. It seems very obvious to me that this requires a change in our attitude toward the human being, and toward his relationships to the world. To put it bluntly, we need a different kind of human being. I feel I must take far more seriously today than I did twenty years ago, the Heraclitus, the Whitehead, the Bergson kind of emphasis on the world as a flux, a movement, a process, not a static thing. If this is so and it is obviously much more so than it was in 1900 or even in 1930—if this is so, then we need a different kind of human being to be able to live in a world which changes perpetually, which doesn't stand still. I may go so far as to say for the educational enterprise: What's the use of teaching facts? Facts become obsolete so darned fast! What's the use of teaching techniques? The techniques become obsolete so fast! Even the engineering schools are torn by this realization. M.I.T. for instance, no longer teaches engineering *only* as the acquisition of a series of skills, because practically all the skills that the professors of engineering learned when they were in school have now become obsolete. It's no use today learning to make buggy whips. What some professors have done at M.I.T., I understand, is to give up the teaching of the tried and true methods of the past, in favor of trying to create a new kind of human being who is comfortable with change, who enjoys change, who is able to improvise, who is able to face with confidence, strength, and courage a situation of which he has absolutely no forewarning.

Even today *everything* seems to be changing; international law is changing, politics are changing, the whole international scene is changing. People talk with each other in the United Nations from across different centuries. One man speaks in terms of the international law of the nineteenth century. Another one answers him in terms of something else entirely, from a different platform in a different world. Things have changed that fast.

To come back to my title, what I'm talking about is the job of trying to make ourselves over into people who don't need to staticize the world, who don't need to freeze it and to make it stable, who don't need to do what their daddies did, who are able confidently to face tomorrow not knowing what's going to come, not knowing what will happen, with confidence enough in ourselves that we will be able to improvise in that situation which has never existed before. This means a new type of human being. Heraclitian, you might call him. The society which can turn out such people will survive; the societies that *cannot* turn out such people will die.

You'll notice that I stress a great deal improvising and inspiration, rather than approaching creativeness from the vantage point of the finished work of art, of the great creative work. As a matter of fact, I won't even approach it today from the point of view of completed products at all. Why is this? Because we're pretty clearly aware now from our psychological analysis of the process of creativeness and of creative individuals, that we must make the distinction between primary creativeness and a secondary creativeness. The primary creativeness or the inspirational phase of creativeness must be separated from the working out and the development of the inspiration. This is because the latter phase stresses not only creativeness, but also relies very much on just plain hard work, on the discipline of the artist who may spend half a lifetime learning his tools, his skills, and his materials, until he becomes finally ready for a full expression of what he sees. I am very certain that many, many people have waked up in the middle of the night with a flash of inspiration about some novel they would like to write, or a play or a poem or whatever and that most of these inspirations never came to anything. Inspirations are a dime a dozen. The difference between the inspiration and the final product, for example, Tolstoy's *War and Peace*, is an awful lot of hard work, an awful lot of discipline, an awful lot of training, an awful lot of finger exercises and practices and rehearsals and throwing away first drafts and so on. Now the virtues which go with the secondary kind of creativeness, the creativeness which results in the actual products, in the great paintings, the great novels, in the bridges, the new inventions, and so on, rest as heavily upon other virtues—stubbornness and patience and hard work and so on—as they do upon the creativeness of the personality. Therefore, in order to keep the field of operation clean, you might say, it seems necessary to me to focus upon improvising on this first flash and, for the moment, not to worry about what becomes of it, recognizing that many of them do get lost. Partly for this reason, among the best subjects to study for this inspirational phase of creativeness are young children whose inventiveness and creativeness very frequently cannot be defined in terms of product. When a little boy discovers the decimal system for himself this can be a high moment of inspiration, and a high creative moment, and should not be waved aside because of some *a priori* definition which says creativeness ought to be socially useful or it ought to be novel, or nobody should have thought of it before, etc.

For this same reason I have decided for myself not to take scientific creativeness as a paradigm, but rather to use other examples. Much of the research that's going on now deals with the creative scientists, with people who have proven themselves to be creative, Nobel prize winners, great inventors, and so on. The trouble is, if you know a lot of scientists, that you soon learn that something is wrong with this criterion because scientists as a group are not nearly as creative generally as you would expect. This includes people who have discovered, who have created actually, who have published things which were advances in human knowledge. Actually, this is not too difficult to understand. This finding tells us something about the nature of science rather than about the nature of creativeness. If I wanted to be mischievous about it, I could go so far as to define science as a technique whereby noncreative people can create. This is by no means making fun of scientists. It's a wonderful thing it seems to me, for limited human beings, that they can be pressed into the service of great things even though they themselves are not great people. Science is a technique, social and institutionalized, whereby even unintelligent people can be useful in the advance of knowledge. That is as extreme and dramatic as I can make it. Since any particular scientist rests so much in the arms of history, stands on so many shoulders of so many predecessors, he is so much a part of a huge basketball team, of a big collection of people, that his own shortcomings may not appear. He becomes worthy of reverence, worthy of great respect through his participation in a great and respect-worthy enterprise. Therefore, when he discovers something, I have learned to understand this as a product of a social institution, of a collaboration. If he didn't discover it, somebody else would have pretty soon. Therefore, it seems to me that selecting our scientists, even though they have created, is not the best way to study the theory of creativeness.

I believe also that we cannot study creativeness in an ultimate sense until we realize that practically all the definitions that we have been using of creativeness, and most of the examples of creativeness that we use are essentially male or masculine definitions and male or masculine products. We've left out of consideration almost entirely the creativeness of women by the simple semantic technique of defining only male products as creative and overlooking entirely the creativeness of women. I have learned recently (through my studies of peak experiences) to look to women and to feminine creativeness as a good field of operation for research, because it gets less involved in products, less involved in achievement, more involved with the process itself, with the going-on process rather than with the climax in obvious triumph and success.

This is the background of the particular problem I am talking about.

II

The puzzle that I'm now trying to unravel is suggested by the observation that the creative person, in the inspirational phase of the creative furor, loses his past and his future and lives only in the moment. He is all there, totally immersed, fascinated and absorbed in the present, in the current situation, in the here-now, with the matter-in-hand. Or to use a perfect phrase from *The Spinster* by Sylvia Ashton-Warner, the teacher absorbed with a new method of teaching reading to her children says, "I am utterly lost in the present."

This ability to become "lost in the present" seems to be a *sine qua non* for creativeness of any kind. But also certain *prerequisites* of creativeness—in whatever realm—somehow have something to do with this ability to become timeless, selfless, outside of space, of society, of history.

It has begun to appear strongly that this phenomenon is a diluted, more secular, more frequent version of the mystical experience that has been described so often as to have become what Huxley called *The Perennial Philosophy*. In various cultures and in various eras, it takes on somewhat different coloration—and yet its essence is always recognizable—it is the same.

It is always described as a loss of self or of ego, or sometimes as a transcendence of self. There is a fusion with the reality being observed (with the matter-in-hand, I shall say more neutrally), a oneness where there was a twoness, an integration of some sort of the self with the non-self. There is universally reported a seeing of formerly hidden truth, a revelation in the strict sense, a stripping away of veils, and finally, almost always, the whole experience is experienced as bliss, ecstasy, rapture, exaltation.

Little wonder that this shaking experience has so often been considered to be superhuman, supernatural, so much greater and grander than anything conceivable as human that it could only be attributed to trans-human sources. And such "revelations" often serve as basis, sometimes the *sole* basis, for the various "revealed" religions.

And yet even this most remarkable of all experiences has now been brought into the realm of human experience and cognition. My researches on what I call peak experiences (88, 89), and Marghanita Laski's on what she calls ecstasies (66), done quite independently of each other, show that these experiences are quite naturalistic, quite easily investigated and, what is to the point right now, that they have much to teach us about creativeness as well as other aspects of the full functioning of human beings when they are most fully realizing themselves, most mature and evolved, most healthy, when, in a word, they are most fully human.

One main characteristic of the peak experience is just this total fascination with the matter-in-hand, this getting lost in the present, this detachment from time and place. And it seems to me now that much of what we have learned from the study of these peak experiences can be transferred quite directly to the enriched understanding of the here-now experience, of the creative attitude.

It is not necessary for us to confine ourselves to these uncommon and rather extreme experiences, even though it now seems clear that practically all people can report moments of rapture if they dig around long enough in their memories, and if the interview situation is just right. We can also refer to the simplest version of the peak experience, namely fascination, concentration, or absorption in *anything* which is interesting enough to hold this attention completely. And I mean not only great symphonies or tragedies; the job can be done by a gripping movie or detective story, or simply becoming absorbed with one's work. There are certain advantages in starting from such universal and familiar experiences which we all have, so that we can get a direct feeling or intuition or empathy, that is, a direct experiential knowledge of a modest, moderate version of the fancier "high" experiences. For one thing we can avoid the flossy, high-flying, extremely metaphorical vocabulary that is so common in this realm.

Well then, what are some of the things that happen in these moments?

Giving up the Past. The best way to view a present problem is to give it all you've got, to study *it* and its nature, to perceive *within* it the intrinsic interrelationships, to discover (rather than to invent) the answer to the problem within the problem itself. This is also the best way to look at a painting or to listen to a patient in therapy.

The other way is merely a matter of shuffling over past experiences, past habits, past knowledge to find out in what respects this current situation is similar to some situation in the past, i.e., to classify it, and then to use *now* the solution that once worked for the similar problem in the past. This can be likened to the work of a filing clerk. I have called it "rubricizing" (95). And it works well enough to the extent that the present *is* like the past.

But obviously it *doesn't* work in so far as the matter-in-hand is different from the past. The file-clerk approach fails then. This person confronting an unknown painting hurriedly runs back through his knowledge of art history to remember how he is supposed to react. Meanwhile of course he is hardly looking at the painting. All he needs is the name or the style or the content to enable him to do his quick calculations. He then enjoys it if he is supposed to, and doesn't if he is *not* supposed to.

In such a person, the past is an inert, undigested foreign body which the person carries about. It is not yet the person himself.

More accurately said: The past is active and alive only insofar as it has re-created the person, and has been digested into the present person. It is not or should not be something *other* than the person, something alien to it. It has now become Person (and has lost its own identity as something different and other), just as past steaks that I have eaten are now me, *not* steaks. The digested past (assimilated by intussusception) is different from the undigested past. It is Lewin's "ahistorical past."

Giving up the Future. Often we use the present not for its own sake but in order to prepare for the future. Think how often in a conversation we put on a listening face as the other person talks, secretly however preparing what we are going to say, rehearsing, planning a counterattack perhaps. Think how different your attitude would be right now if you knew you were to comment on my remarks in five minutes. Think how hard it would be then to be a good, total listener.

If we are totally listening or totally looking, we have thereby given up this kind of "preparing for the future." We don't treat the present as merely a means to some future end (thereby devaluating the present). And obviously, this kind of forgetting the future is a prerequisite to total involvement with the present. Just as obviously, a good way to "forget" the future is not to be apprehensive about it.

Of course, this is only one sense of the concept "future." The future which is within us, part of our present selves, is another story altogether (89, pp. 14–15).

Innocence. This amounts to a kind of "innocence" of perceiving and behaving. Something of the sort has often been attributed to highly creative people. They are variously described as being naked in the situation, guileless, without *a priori* expectations, without "shoulds" or "oughts," without fashions, fads, dogmas, habits, or other pictures-in-the-head of what is proper, normal, "right," as being ready to receive whatever happens to be the case without surprise, shock, indignation, or denial.

Children are more able to be receptive in this undemanding way.

So are wise old people. And it appears now that we *all* may be more innocent in this style when we become "here-now."

Narrowing of Consciousness. We have now become much less conscious of everything other than the matter-in-hand (less distractible). *Very* important here is our lessened awareness of other people, of their ties to us and ours to them, of obligations, duties, fears, hopes, etc. We become much more free of other people, which in turn, means that we become much more ourselves, our Real Selves (Horney), our authentic selves, our real identity.

This is so because *the* greatest cause of our alienation from our real selves is our neurotic involvements with other people, the historical hangovers from childhood, the irrational transferences, in which past and present are confused, and in which the adult acts like a child. (By the way, it's all right for the *child* to act like a child. His dependencies on other people can be very real. *But*, after all, he *is* supposed to outgrow them. To be afraid of what daddy will say or do is certainly out of place if daddy has been dead for twenty years.)

In a word, we become more free of the influence of other people in such moments. So, insofar as these influences have affected our behavior, they no longer do so.

This means dropping masks, dropping our efforts to influence, to impress, to please, to be lovable, to win applause. It could be said so: If we have no audience to play to, we cease to be actors. With no need to act we can devote ourselves, self-forgetfully, to the problem.

Loss of Ego: Self-Forgetfulness, Loss of Self-Consciousness. When you are totally absorbed in non-self, you tend to become less conscious of yourself, less self-aware. You are less apt to be observing yourself like a spectator or a critic. To use the language of psychodynamics, you become less dissociated than usual into a self-observing ego and an experiencing ego; i.e., you come much closer to being *all* experiencing ego. (You tend to lose the shyness and bashfulness of the adolescent, the painful awareness of being looked at, etc.) This in turn means more unifying, more oneness and integration of the person.

It also means less criticizing and editing, less evaluating, less selecting and rejecting, less judging and weighing, less splitting and analyzing of the experience.

This kind of self-forgetfulness is one of the paths to finding one's true identity, one's real self, one's authentic nature, one's deepest nature. It is almost always felt as pleasant and desirable. We needn't go so far as the Buddhists and Eastern thinkers do in talking about the "accursed ego"; and yet there *is* something in what they say.

Inhibiting Force of Consciousness (of Self). In some senses consciousness (especially of self) is inhibiting in some ways and at some times. It is sometimes the locus of doubts, conflicts, fears, etc. It is sometimes harmful to full-functioning creativeness. It is sometimes an inhibitor of spontaneity and of expressiveness (*but* the observing ego is necessary for therapy).

And yet it is also true that some kind of self-awareness, self-observation, self-criticism—i.e., the self-observing ego—*is* necessary for "secondary creativeness." To use psychotherapy as an example, the task of self-improvement is partly a consequence of criticizing the experiences that one has allowed to come into consciousness. Schizophrenic people experience many insights and yet don't make therapeutic use of them because they are too much "totally experiencing" and not enough "self-observing-and-criticizing." In creative work, likewise, the labor of disciplined construction succeeds upon the phase of "inspiration."

Fears Disappear. This means that our fears and anxieties also tend to disappear. So also our depressions, conflicts, ambivalence, our worries, our problems, even our physical pains. Even—for the moment —our psychoses and our neuroses (that is, if they are not so extreme as to prevent us from becoming deeply interested and immersed in the matter-in-hand).

For the time being, we are courageous and confident, unafraid, unanxious, unneurotic, not sick.

Lessening of Defenses and Inhibitions. Our inhibitions also tend to disappear. So also our guardedness, our (Freudian) defenses, and controls (brakes) on our impulses as well as the defenses against danger and threat.

Strength and Courage. The creative attitude requires both courage and strength and most studies of creative people have reported one or another version of courage: stubbornness, independence, self-sufficiency, a kind of arrogance, strength of character, ego-strength, etc.; popularity becomes a minor consideration. Fear and weakness cast out creativeness or at least make it less likely.

It seems to me that this aspect of creativeness becomes somewhat more understandable when it is seen as a part of the syndrome of here-now self-forgetfulness and other-forgetfulness. Such a state intrinsically implies less fear, less inhibition, less need for defense and self-protection, less guardedness, less need for artificiality, less fear of ridicule, of humiliation and of failure. All these characteristics are *part of* self-forgetfulness and audience-forgetfulness. Absorption casts out fear.

Or we can say in a more positive way, that becoming more courageous makes it easier to let oneself be attracted by mystery, by the unfamiliar, by the novel, by the ambiguous and contradictory, by the unusual and unexpected, etc., instead of becoming suspicious, fearful, guarded, or having to throw into action our anxiety-allaying mechanisms and defenses.

Acceptance: the Positive Attitude. In moments of here-now immersion and self-forgetfulness we are apt to become more "positive" and less negative in still another way, namely, in giving up criticism (editing, picking and choosing, correcting, skepticism, improving, doubting, rejecting, judging, evaluating). This is like saying that we accept. We don't reject or disapprove or selectively pick and choose.

No blocks against the matter-in-hand means that we let it flow in upon us. We let it wreak its will upon us. We let it have its way. We let it be itself. Perhaps we can even approve of its being itself.

This makes it easier to be Taoistic in the sense of humility, non-interference, receptivity.

Trust vs. Trying, Controlling, Striving. All of the foregoing happenings imply a kind of trust in the self and a trust in the world which permits the temporary giving up of straining and striving, of volition and control, of conscious coping and effort. To permit oneself to be determined by the intrinsic nature of the matter-in-hand here-now necessarily implies relaxation, waiting, receiving. The common effort to master, to dominate, and to control are antithetical to a true coming-to-terms with or a true perceiving of the materials (or the problem, or the person, etc.). Especially is this true with respect to the future. We *must* trust our ability to improvise when confronted with novelty in the future. Phrased in this way, we can see more clearly that trust involves self-confidence, courage, lack of fear of the world. It is also clear that this kind of trust in ourselves-facing-the-unknown-future is a condition of being able to turn totally, nakedly, and wholeheartedly to the present.

(Some clinical examples may help. Giving birth, urination, defecation, sleeping, floating in the water, sexual surrender are all instances in which straining, trying, controlling, have to be given up in favor of relaxed, trusting, confident letting things happen.)

Taoistic Receptivity. Both Taoism and receptivity mean many things, all of them important, but also subtle and difficult to convey except in figures of speech. All of the subtle and delicate Taoistic attributes of the creative attitude which follow have been described again and again by the many writers on creativeness, now in one way, now in another. However, everyone agrees that in the primary or inspirational phase of creativeness, some degree of receptivity or noninterference or "let-be" is descriptively characteristic and also theoretically and dynamically necessary. Our question now is how does this receptivity or "letting things happen" relate to the syndrome of here-now immersion and self-forgetfulness?

For one thing, using the artist's respect for his materials as a paradigm, we may speak of this respectful attention to the matter-in-hand as a kind of courtesy or deference (without intrusion of the controlling will) which is akin to "taking it seriously." This amounts to treating it as an end, something *per se*, with its own right to be, rather than as a means to some end other than itself; i.e., as a tool for some extrinsic purpose. This respectful treatment of its being implies that it is respectworthy.

This courtesy or respectfulness can apply equally to the problem, to the materials, to the situation, or to the person. It is what one writer (Follett) has called deference (yielding, surrender) to the authority of the facts, to the law of the situation. I can go over from a bare *permitting* "it" to be itself, to a loving, caring, approving, joyful, *eagerness* that it be itself, as with one's child or sweetheart or tree or poem or pet animal.

Some such attitude is *a priori* necessary for perceiving or understanding the full concrete richness of the matter-in-hand, in *its* own nature and in *its* own style, without our help, without our imposing ourselves upon it, in about the same way that we must hush and be still if we wish to hear the whisper from the other.

This cognition of the Being of the other (B-cognition) is fully described in Chapter 9 (and 85, 89).

Integration of the B-Cognizer (vs. Dissociation). Creating tends to be the act of a whole man (ordinarily); he is then *most* integrated, unified, all of a piece, one-pointed, totally organized in the service of the fascinating matter-in-hand. Creativeness is therefore systemic; i.e., a whole—or Gestalt—quality of the whole person; it is not added-to the organism like a coat of paint, or like an invasion of bacteria. It is the opposite of dissociation. Here-now-allness is less dissociated (split) and more one.

Permission to Dip into Primary Process. Part of the process of integration of the person is the recovery of aspects of the unconscious and preconscious, particularly of the primary process (or poetic, metaphoric, mystic, primitive, archaic, childlike).

Our conscious intellect is too exclusively analytic, rational, numerical, atomistic, conceptual and so it misses a great deal of reality, especially within ourselves.

Aesthetic Perceiving rather than Abstracting. Abstracting is more active and interfering (less Taoistic); more selecting-rejecting than the aesthetic (Northrop) attitude of savoring, enjoying, appreciating, caring, in a noninterfering, nonintruding, noncontrolling way.

The end product of abstracting is the mathematical equation, the chemical formula, the map, the diagram, the blueprint, the cartoon, the concept, the abstracting sketch, the model, the theoretical system, all of which move further and further from raw reality ("the map is *not* the territory"). The end product of aesthetic perceiving, of nonabstracting is the total inventory of the percept, in which everything in it is apt to be equally savored, and in which evaluations of more important and less important tend to be given up. Here greater richness of the percept is sought for rather than greater simplifying and skeletonizing.

For many confused scientists and philosophers, the equation, the concept, or the blueprint have become more real than the phenomenological reality itself. Fortunately now that we can understand the interplay and mutual enrichment of the concrete and the abstract, it is no longer necessary to devalue one or the other. For the moment we intellectuals in the West who have heavily and exclusively overvalued abstractness in our picture of reality, even to the point of synonymizing them, had better redress the balance by stressing concrete, aesthetic, phenomenological, nonabstracting, perceiving of *all* the aspects and details of phenomena, of the full richness of reality, including the useless portions of it.

Fullest Spontaneity. If we are fully concentrated on the matter-in-hand, fascinated with it for its own sake, having no other goals or purposes in mind, then it is easier to be fully spontaneous, fully functioning, letting our capacities flow forth easily from within, of themselves, without effort, without conscious volition or control, in an instinct-like, automatic, thoughtless way; i.e., the fullest, least obstructed, most organized action.

The one main determinant of their organization and adaptation to the matter-in-hand is then most apt to be the intrinsic nature of the matter-in-hand. Our capacities then adapt to the situation most perfectly, quickly, effortlessly, and change flexibly as the situation changes; e.g., a painter continuously adapts himself to the demands of his developing painting; as a wrestler adapts himself to his opponent; as a pair of fine dancers mutually adapt to each other; as water flows into cracks and contours.

Fullest Expressiveness (of Uniqueness). Full spontaneity is a guarantee of honest expression of the nature and the style of the freely functioning organism, and of its uniqueness. Both words, spontaneity and expressiveness, imply honesty, naturalness, truthfulness, lack of guile, nonimitativeness, etc., because they also imply a noninstrumental nature of the behavior, a lack of willful "trying," a lack of effortful striving or straining, a lack of interference with the flow of the impulses and the free "radiating" expression of the deep person.

The only determinants now are the intrinsic nature of the matter-in-hand, the intrinsic nature of the person and the intrinsic necessities of their fluctuating adaptation to each other to form a fusion, a unit; e.g., a fine basketball team, or a string quartet. Nothing outside this fusion situation is relevant. The situation is not a means to any extrinsic end; it is an end in itself.

Fusion of the Person with the World. We wind up with the fusion between the person and his world which has so often been reported as an observable fact in creativeness, and which we may now reasonably consider to be a *sine qua non*. I think that this spider web of interrelationships that I have been teasing apart and discussing can help us to understand this fusion better as a natural event, rather than as something mysterious, arcane, esoteric. I think it can even be researched if we understand it to be an isomorphism, a molding of each to each other, a better and better fitting together or complementarity, a melting into one.

It has helped me to understand what Hokusai meant when he said, "If you want to draw a bird, you must become a bird."

5

A Holistic Approach to Creativity

It has been interesting for me to compare the present-day situation in the field of creativeness with the situation about twenty or twenty-five years ago. First of all I want to say that the amount of data that has been accumulated—the sheer amount of research work —is far beyond what anybody could reasonably have expected then.

My second impression is that, in comparison with the great accumulation of methods, of ingenious testing techniques, and of sheer quantity of information, theory in this realm has not advanced very much. I want to raise the theoretical questions, that is, what disturbs me about the conceptualizations in this field of research, and the bad consequences of these disturbing conceptualizations.

I think the most important thing that I would like to communicate is my impression that the thinking and the research in the field of creativeness tends to be too atomistic and too *ad hoc*, and that it is not as holistic, organismic, or systemic as it could be and should be. Now of course I don't want to make any foolish dichotomies or polarizations here. That is, I don't want to imply any piety about holism or antagonism to dissection or atomism. The question for me is how to integrate them best, rather than choosing between them. One way of avoiding such a choosing up of sides is to use Pearson's old discrimination between a general factor ("G") and specific or special factors ("S"), both of which enter into the makeup not only of intelligence, but also of creativeness.

It seems to me terribly impressive, as I read the creativeness literature, that the relationship with psychiatric health or psychological health is so crucial, so profound, so terribly important, and so obvious, and yet it is not used as a foundation on which to build. For instance, there has been rather little relationship between the studies, let's say in the field of psychotherapy on the one hand, and of creativeness on the other. One of my graduate students, Richard Craig, has published what I consider to be a very important demonstration that there *is* such a relationship (26). We were very much impressed with the table in Torrance's book, *Guiding Creative Talent* (147), in which he pulled together and summarized the evidence on all the personality characteristics that have been demonstrated to correlate with creativeness. There are perhaps thirty or more characteristics that he considered sufficiently valid. What Craig did was to put down these characteristics in a column and then in another column beside them to list the characteristics that I had used in describing self-actualizing people (95) (which overlaps considerably with the lists many other people have used in describing psychological health, for example, Rogers' "Fully Functioning Person" or Jung's "Individuated Person" or Fromm's "Autonomous Person," and so on).

The overlap was almost perfect. There were two or three characteristics in that list of thirty or forty which had not been used to describe psychologically healthy people, but were simply neutral. There was no single characteristic which went in the other, opposite direction, which makes, let's say arbitrarily, nearly forty characteristics or perhaps thirty-seven or thirty-eight which were the same as psychological health—which added up to a syndrome of psychological health or self-actualization.

I cite this paper as a good jumping-off point for discussion because it is my very powerful conviction (as it was a long time ago) that the problem of creativeness is the problem of the creative person (rather than of creative products, creative behaviors, etc.). In other words, he is a particular or special kind of human being, rather than just an old-fashioned, ordinary human being who now has acquired new extrinsic possessions, who has now got a new skill like ice skating, or accumulated some more things that he "owns" but which are not intrinsic to him, to his basic nature.

If you think of the person, the creative person, as being the essence of the problem, then what you are confronted with is the whole problem of transformation of human nature, the transformation of the character, the full development of the whole person. This in turn necessarily involves us in the question of the *Weltanschauung*, the life philosophy, the way of living, the code of ethics, the values of society, and so on. This is in sharp and direct contrast with the *ad hoc*, causal, encapsulated, atomistic conception of theory, research, and training which I have heard implied so often, e.g., "What is *the* cause of creativity?" "What is *the* most important *single* thing we can do?" "Shall we add a three-credit course in creativity to the curriculum?" I half expect to hear someone ask soon, "Where is it localized?" or to try implanting electrodes with which to turn it on or off. In the consultations I've had with Research and Development people in industry, I also get the strong impression that they keep looking for some secret button to push, like switching a light on and off.

What I would propose in trying to achieve the creative person is that there could be hundreds and almost literally thousands of determinants of creativeness. That is, anything that would help the person to move in the direction of greater psychological health or fuller humanness would amount to changing the whole person. This more fully human, healthier person would then, epiphenomenally, generate and spark off dozens, hundreds, and millions of differences in behaving, experiencing, perceiving, communicating, teaching, working, etc., which would *all* be more "creative." He would then be simply another *kind* of person who would behave in a different way in *every* respect. And then instead of the single secret push button or trick or three-credit course which will presumably, *ad hoc*, produce more creativeness, *ad hoc*, this more holistic, organismic point of view would suggest the more likely question: "And why should not *every* course help toward creativeness?" Certainly this kind of education *of the person* should help create a better *type* of person, help a person grow bigger, taller, wiser, more perceptive—a person who, incidentally, would be more creative as a matter of course in *all* departments of life.

I give you just one example which pops into my head. One of my colleagues, Dick Jones, did a doctoral dissertation which I thought was terribly important from a philosophical point of view, but which has not been noticed enough. What he did was to run a kind of a group-therapy course with high school seniors, and then found that at the end of the year racial and ethnic prejudice had gone down, in spite of the fact that for one full year he had made it his business to avoid ever mentioning these words. Prejudice is not created by pushing a button. You don't have to train people to be prejudiced, and you can't really directly train them to be "unprejudiced." We have tried, and it doesn't work very well. But this "being unprejudiced" flies off as a spark off the wheel, as an epiphenomenon, as a byproduct, simply from becoming a better human being, whether from psychotherapy, or from any other influence that improves the person.

About twenty-five years ago my style of investigation of creativeness was very different from the classical scientific (atomistic) method. I had to invent holistic interviewing techniques. That is, I tried to get to know one single person after another as profoundly and as deeply and as fully as I could (as unique, individual persons) to the point where I felt I understood them as a whole person. It was as if I were getting very full case-histories of whole lives and whole people *without* having particular problems or questions in mind, that is, without abstracting one aspect of the person rather than another, i.e., I was doing it idiographically.

And yet it is *then* possible to be nomothetic, to *then* ask particular questions, to do simple statistics, to come to *general* conclusions. One can treat each person as an infinity, and yet infinities can be added, percentages made, just as transfinite numbers can be manipulated.

Once you get to know a sample of people profoundly and deeply, and individually in this way, then certain operations become possible that are not possible in typical classical experiments. I had a panel of about 120 people with each of whom I had spent an awful lot of time just simply getting to know them in general. Then, *after* the fact, I could then ask a question, go back to the data and answer it, and this could have been done even if all the 120 people had died. This contrasts with *ad hoc* experimentation on a single problem in which one variable would be modified and all others presumably "held constant" (although of course we know very well that there are thousands of variables which are presumably, but not actually, controlled in the classical experimental paradigm and which are very far from being held constant).

If I may be permitted to be bluntly challenging, it is my firm opinion that the cause-effect way of thinking which works pretty well in the nonliving world and which we have learned to use more or less well to solve human problems, is now dead as a general philosophy of science. It shouldn't be used any more because it just tends to lead us into *ad hoc* thinking, that is, of one cause producing one specific effect, and of one factor producing one factor, instead of keeping us sensitive to *systemic* and organismic changes of the kind that I've tried to describe, in which any single stimulus is conceived to change the whole organism, which then, as a changed organism, emits behavior changed in *all* departments of life. (This is also true for social organizations, large and small.)

For instance, if you think of physical health, and if you ask the question, "How do you get people's teeth to be better?" "How do you get their feet to be better?" or their kidneys, eyes, hair, etc., any physician will tell you that the best thing to do is to improve the general systemic health. That is, you try to improve the general (G) factor. If you can improve the diet and the mode of living and so on and so on, then these procedures, in one single blow, will improve their teeth and their kidneys and their hair and their liver and their intestines and *everything else*; that is, the whole system will be improved. In the same way general creativeness, holistically conceived, emanates from the whole system, generally improved. Furthermore, any factors that would produce a more creative person would also make a man a better father, or better teacher, or better citizen, or a better dancer, or a better anything, at least to the extent that the "G" factor is strengthened. To this is then added of course the specific (S) contributions that differentiate the good father from the good dancer or good composer.

A pretty good book on the sociology of religion is Glock and Stark (38) and I would recommend it as a rather intelligent and competent picture of this type of atomistic and *ad hoc* thinking. *Ad hoc* thinkers, S-R thinkers, cause-effect thinkers, one-cause-to-one-effect thinkers, going into a new field start the way these writers do. First of course they feel they must define religion, and of course they have to define this in such a way that it is pure and discrete, that it is not anything else. So they then proceed to isolate it, cut it away and dissect it away from everything else. So they wind up with the Aristotelian logic "A" and "Not A." "A" is all "A" and nothing but "A." It's just pure "A"; and "Not A" is pure everything else and so they have no overlap, no melting, no merging, no fusing, and so on. The old possibility (taken very seriously by all profoundly religious people) that religious attitudes can be one aspect or characteristic of practically *any* behavior—indeed of *all* behaviors—is lost on the very first page of the book. This enables them to go ahead and get into an absolute and total chaos, as beautiful a chaos as I have ever seen. They get into a blind alley—and stay there—in which religious behavior is separated off from all other behavior so that all they deal with through the whole book is the external behavior—going to church or not going to church, and saving or not saving little pieces of wood, and bowing or not bowing before this or that or the other thing, thereby leaving out of the whole book what I might call small "r" religion entirely; that is, the religious attitudes and feelings and emotions of profoundly religious people who may have nothing to do with institutions or with supernaturals or with idolatry. This is a good example of atomistic thinking, but I've got plenty of others. One can think atomistically in any department of life.

We can do the same with creativeness if we want to. We can make creativeness into a Sunday behavior also, which occurs in a particular room, in a particular building, such as a classroom, and at a particular separated-off time, e.g., on Thursdays. It's just creativeness and nothing else there in that room and at that time and at no time or place else. And only certain areas have to do with creativeness, painting, composing, writing, but not cooking or taxi driving or plumbing. But I raise the question again of creativeness being an aspect of practically any behavior at all, whether perceptual or attitudinal or emotional, conative, cognitive, or expressive. I think if you approach it in that way you get to ask all sorts of interesting questions which wouldn't occur to you if you approached it in this other dichotomized way.

It's a little like the difference in the ways you would try to learn to be a good dancer. Most people in an *ad hoc* society would go to the Arthur Murray School where you first move your left foot and then your right foot three paces and bit by bit you go through a lot of external, willed motions. But I think we would all agree, and I might even say that we *know* that it is rather characteristic of successful psychotherapy that there are *thousands* of effects among which might very well be good dancing, i.e., being more free about dancing, more graceful, less bound up, less inhibited, less self-conscious, less appeasing, and so on. In the same way I think that psychotherapy, where it is good (and we all know there is plenty of bad psychotherapy too) and is successful, then psychotherapy, in my experience, can be counted on to enhance the creativity of a person without your ever trying to or without your ever mentioning the word.

I can also mention a relevant dissertation one of our students has done, which turned up most unexpected kinds of things. This started out to be a study of peak experiences in natural childbirth, ecstacies from motherhood and so on. But it shifted considerably because what Mrs. Tanzer (145) has been finding out is that all sorts of other miraculous changes come about when childbirth is a good or great experience. When it's a good experience, many things in life change for the woman. It may have some of the flavor of the religious conversion experience, or of the great illumination effect, or the great success experience which changes radically the woman's self-image, and therefore changes all her behaviors.

I would like to say also that this general approach seems to be a much better, a more fruitful way to talk about "climate." I have tried to pin down the Nonlinear Systems organizational setup (83) and what was the cause of all the good effects there. All I can say is that the whole place was a climate of creative atmosphere. I couldn't pick one main cause as over against another. There was freedom of a *general* kind, atmospheric, holistic, global, rather than a little thing that you did on Tuesday—one particular, separable thing. The right climate, the *best* climate for enhancing creativeness would be a Utopia, or Eupsychia, as I prefer to call it, a society which was specifically designed for improving the self-fulfillment and psychological health of all people. That would be my general statement, the "G" statement. Within and against that background, we could *then* work with a particular "figure," with a particular *ad hoc*, the "S," or specific factors that make one man a good carpenter and another a good mathematician. But without that general societal background, in a bad society (which is a general systemic statement), creativeness is just less likely, less possible.

I think that the parallel from therapy can also be useful to us here. We have much to learn from the people who are interested in this realm of research and thinking. For instance, we must face their problem of what identity means, of what is the real Self, and of what therapy does and what education does, by way of helping people move toward identity. On the other hand we have a model of some kind of real Self, some kind of characteristic which is conceived biologically to some extent. It is constitutional, temperamental, "instinctoid." We are a species and we are different from other species. If this is so, if you can accept this instead of the *tabula rasa* model, the person as pure clay which is to be molded or reinforced into any predesigned shape that the arbitrary controller wants, then you must also accept the model of therapy as uncovering, unleashing, rather than the model of therapy as molding, creating and shaping. And this would be true also for education. The basic models generated by these two different conceptions of human nature would be different—teaching, learning, everything.

Is then creativeness part of the general human heritage? It does very frequently get lost, or covered up, or twisted or inhibited, or whatever, and then the job is of uncovering what all babies are, in principle, born with. Well, I think that this is a very profound and very general philosophical question that we are dealing with, a very basic philosophical stance.

Finally, I would like to make one last point which is an "S" point, not a "G" point. I would like to ask, when do we *not* want creativeness? Sometimes creativeness can be a horrible nuisance. It can be a troublesome, dangerous, messy thing, as I learned once from a "creative" research assistant who gummed up a research that I had been working at for over a year. She got "creative" and changed the whole thing in the middle of it without even telling me about it. She gummed up all the data, so that a year's work was lost, messed up. On the whole we want the trains to run on time, and generally we want dentists *not* to be creative. A friend of mine had an operation a couple of years ago, and he still remembers feeling uneasy and afraid until he met his surgeon. Fortunately, he turned out to be a nice obsessional type of man, very precise, perfectly neat with a little hairline mustache, every hair in place, a perfectly straight, controlled, and sober man. My friend then heaved a sigh of relief—this was not a "creative" man. Here was a man who would do a normal, routine, pedestrian operation, not play any tricks or try any novelties or experiments or do any new sewing techniques or anything like that. This is important, I think, not only in our society, where, with our division of labor, we ought to be able to take orders and to carry through a program and be predictable. But also it is important for each of us not only in our capacity as creative workers, but also as students of creativeness, with a tendency to deify the one side of the creative process, the enthusiastic, the great insight, the illumination, the good idea, the moment in the middle of the night when you get the great inspiration, and of underplaying the two years of hard and sweaty labor that then are necessary to make anything useful out of the bright idea.

In simple terms of time, bright ideas really take a small proportion of our time. Most of our time is spent on hard work. My impression is that our students don't know this. It may be that these dead cats have been brought to my door more because my students so frequently identify with me, because I have written about peak experiences and inspirations and so on, that they feel that this is the only way to live. Life without daily or hourly peak experiences, that's no life, so that they can't do work that is boring.

Some student tells me, "No, I don't want to do that because I don't enjoy it," and then I get purple in the face and fly up in a rage— "Damn it, you do it, or I'll fire you"—and he thinks I am betraying my own principles. I think also that in making a more measured and balanced picture of creativeness, we workers with creativity have to be responsible for the impressions we make upon other people. Apparently one impression that we are making on them is that creativeness consists of lightning striking you on the head in one great glorious moment. The fact that the people who create are good workers tends to be lost.

6
Emotional Blocks to Creativity

When I started research with this problem of creativity it was entirely an academic and professorial one. I've been amazed to be plucked at in the last couple of years by big industries of which I know nothing, or organizations like the U.S. Army Engineers whose work I don't really know at all, and I find myself a little uneasy, like many of my colleagues, on this score. I am not sure whether the work that I have done and the conclusions that I have come to, and what we "know" about creativity today is quite usable in its present form in large organizations. All I can present are essentially paradoxes, and problems, and riddles, and, at this moment, I don't know how they're going to be solved.

I think the problem of the management of creative personnel is both fantastically difficult and important. I don't quite know what we are going to do with this problem because, in essence, what I am talking about is the lone wolf. The kind of creative people that I've worked with are people who are apt to get ground up in an organization, apt to be afraid of it, and apt generally to work off in a corner or an attic by themselves. The problem of the place of the "lone wolf" in a big organization, I'm afraid, is the organization's problem and not mine.

This is also a little like trying to reconcile the revolutionary with the stable society because the people that I've studied are essentially revolutionary in the sense of turning their backs on what already exists, and in the sense of being dissatisfied with what is now the case. This is a new frontier, and I think what I'll do is just simply play the researcher and the clinician and the psychologist, toss out what I've learned and what I have to offer in the hope that one can make some use of it.

This is a new frontier in another sense that you'll all have to dig into very, very deeply—a new psychological frontier. If I can summarize in advance what I'm going to say: What we have found during the last ten years or so is that, primarily, the sources of creativeness of the kind that we're really interested in, i.e., the generation of really new ideas, are in the depths of human nature. We don't even have a vocabulary for it yet that's very good. You can talk in Freudian terms if you like, that is you can talk about the unconscious. Or in the term of another school of psychological thought, you may prefer to talk about the real self. But in any case it's a *deeper* self. It is deeper in an operational way, as seen by the psychologist, or psychotherapist, that is, it is deeper in the sense that you have to dig for it. It is deep in the sense that ore is deep. It's deep in the ground. You have to struggle to get at it through surface layers.

This is a new frontier in the sense that most people don't know about it, and also in another very peculiar sense that has never occurred before in history. *This is something that not only we don't know about, but that we're afraid to know about.* That is, there is resistance to knowing about it. This is what I'll try to make clear. I'm speaking about what I'll call primary creativeness rather than secondary creativeness, the primary creativeness which comes out of the unconscious, which is the source of new discovery—of real novelty—of ideas which depart from what exists at this point. This is something different from what I'll call secondary creativity. This is the kind of productivity demonstrated in some recent researches of a psychologist by the name of Anne Roe, who finds it in group after group of well-known people—of capable, fruitful, functional, famous people. For instance, in one research she studied all the starred biologists in the

American Men of Science. In another research she was able to study every paleontologist in the country. She was able to demonstrate a very peculiar paradox that we'll have to deal with, namely, that to a certain degree, many good scientists are what the psychopathologist or the therapist would call rather rigid people, rather constricted people, people who are afraid of their unconscious, in the sense that I have mentioned. And you may then come to a peculiar conclusion that I've come to. I am used now to thinking of two kinds of science, and two kinds of technology. Science can be defined, if you want to, as a technique whereby uncreative people can create and discover, by working along with a lot of other people, by standing upon the shoulders of people who have come before them, by being cautious and careful and so on. Now, that I'll call secondary creativeness and secondary science.

I think, however, that I can lay bare the primary creativeness which comes out of the unconscious and which I have found in the specially creative people that I have selected out to study carefully. This kind of primary creativeness is very probably a heritage of every human being. It is a common and universal kind of thing. Certainly it is found in all healthy children. It is the kind of creativeness that any healthy child had and which is then lost by most people as they grow up. It is universal in another sense, that if you dig in a psychotherapeutic way, i.e., if you dig into the unconscious layers of the person, you find it there. I shall give you only one example that you have probably all experienced yourselves. You know that in our dreams, we can be an awful lot more creative than we are in waking life. We can be more clever, and wittier, and bolder, and more original, and so on and so on. With the lid taken off, with the controls taken off, the repressions and defenses taken off, we find generally more creativeness than appears to the naked eye. I have been roaming around among my psychoanalyst friends recently trying to get from them an account of their experiences with the release of creativeness. The universal conclusion of psychoanalysts, and I am sure of all other psychotherapists as well, is that general psychotherapy may normally be expected to release creativeness which did not appear before the psychotherapy took place. It will be a very difficult thing to prove it, but that is the impression they all have. Call it expert opinion if you like. That is the impression of the people who are working at the job, for example, of helping people who would like to write but who are blocked. Psychotherapy can help them to release, to get over this block, and to get them started writing again. General experience therefore is that psychotherapy, or getting down to these deeper layers which are ordinarily repressed, will release a common heritage —something that we all have had—and that was lost.

There's a certain form of neurosis from which we can learn a great deal, in breaking into this problem, and which is an understandable kind of thing. I think I will speak about that first. This is the compulsive-obsessive neurosis.

These are rigid and tight people, people who can't play very well. These are people who try to control their emotions and so look rather cold and frozen in the extreme case. They are tense; they are constricted. And these are the people who in a normal state (of course when it's extreme it is a sickness that has to be handled by psychiatrists and psychotherapists) generally tend to be very orderly and very neat and very punctual and very systematic and very controlled and who make excellent bookkeepers, for instance, and so on. Now these people can be very briefly described in psychodynamic terms as "sharply split," possibly more sharply split than most of the rest of the population, as between what they are conscious of, what they know about themselves, and what's concealed from themselves, what is unconscious or repressed. As we learn more about these people, and learn something about the reasons for the repressions, we are also learning that these reasons obtain for all of us in a lesser degree, and so again we've learned from the extreme case something about the more average and the more normal. These people *have* to be this way. They have no alternative. They have no choice. This is the only way in which such a person can achieve safety, order, lack of threat, lack of anxiety, that is, via orderliness, predictability, control, and mastery. These desirable goals are all made possible for him by these particular techniques. The "new" is threatening for such a person, but nothing new can happen to him if he can order it to his past experience, if he can freeze the world of flux, that is, if he can make believe nothing is changing. If he can proceed into the future on the basis of "well-tried" laws and rules, habits, modes of adjustment which have worked in the past, and which he will insist on using in the future, then he feels safe and he doesn't feel anxious.

Why does he have to do this? What's he afraid of? The answer of the dynamic psychologist is—in very general terms—that he is afraid of his emotions, or of his deepest instinctual urges, or his deepest self, which he desperately represses. He's *got* to! Or else he feels he'll go crazy. This internal drama of fear and defense is within one man's skin, but it tends by this man to be generalized, projected outward on the whole world, and he is then apt to see the whole world in this fashion. What he's really fighting off are dangers within himself, but then anything that reminds him of or resembles these dangers within himself, he fights in the external world whenever he sees them. He fights against his own impulses to disorderliness by becoming extra orderly. And he will be threatened by disorderliness in the world because it reminds him, or threatens him with this revolution from the suppressed, from within. Anything that endangers this control; anything that strengthens either the dangerous hidden impulses, or else weakens the defensive walls, will frighten and threaten this kind of person.

Much is lost by this kind of process. Of course he can gain a kind of equilibrium. Such a man can live his life out without cracking up. He can hold things under control. It is a desperate effort at control. A good deal of his energy is taken up with it and so he is apt to get tired just simply controlling himself. It is a source of fatigue. But he can manage, and get along by protecting himself against the dangerous portions of his unconscious, or against his unconscious self, or his real self, which he has been taught to regard as dangerous. He must wall off everything unconscious. There is a fable of an ancient tyrant who was hunting somebody who had insulted him. He knew this someone was walled up in a certain town, so he ordered every man in that town to be killed, just to be sure that the one person wouldn't get away. The compulsive-obsessive does something like that. He kills off and walls off everything unconscious in order to be sure that the dangerous portions of it don't get out.

What I'm leading up to is that out of this unconscious, out of this deeper self, out of this portion of ourselves of which we generally are afraid and therefore try to keep under control, out of this comes the ability to play—to enjoy—to fantasy—to laugh—to loaf—to be spontaneous, and, what's most important for us here, creativity, which is a kind of intellectual play, which is a kind of permission to be ourselves, to fantasy, to let loose, and to be crazy, privately. (Every really new idea looks crazy, at first.) The compulsive-obsessive gives up his primary creativeness. He gives up the possibilities for being artistic. He gives up his poetry. He gives up his imagination. He drowns all his healthy childishness. Furthermore, this applies also to what we call a good adjustment, and what has been described very nicely as being able to fit into the right harness, that is, getting along well in the world, being realistic, common sense, being mature, taking on responsibility. I'm afraid that certain aspects of these adjustments involve a turning one's back upon what is threatening to the good adjustment. That is, these are kinds of dynamic efforts to make peace with the world and with the necessities of common sense, with the necessities of physical and biological and social realities, and this is generally at the cost of giving up a portion of our deeper selves. It is not as dramatic in us as in the case I've described, but I am afraid that it is becoming more and more apparent that what we call a normal adult adjustment involves a turning one's back on what would threaten us as well. And what does threaten us is softness, fantasy, emotion "childishness." One thing I haven't mentioned but have been interested in recently in my work with creative men (and uncreative men, too) is the horrible fear of anything that the person himself would call "femininity," "femaleness," which we immediately call "homosexual." If he's been brought up in a tough environment, "feminine" means practically everything that's creative: Imagination, fantasy, color, poetry, music, tenderness, languishing, being romantic, in general, are walled off as dangerous to one's picture of one's own masculinity. Everything that's called "weak" tends to be repressed in the normal masculine adult adjustment. And many things are called weak which we are learning are not weak at all.

Now I think I can be of service in this area by discussing these unconscious processes, what the psychoanalyst calls "primary processes," and "secondary processes." It is a tough job to try to be orderly about disorderliness, and rational about irrationality, but we've got to do it. The following notes are from what I've been writing.

These primary processes, these unconscious processes of cognizing, that is, of perceiving the world and of thinking, which interests us here, are very, very different from the laws of common sense, good logic, of what the psychoanalyst calls the "secondary processes," in which we are logical, sensible, and realistic. When "secondary processes" are walled off from the primary processes, then both the primary processes suffer and the secondary processes suffer. At the extreme, the walling off of or the complete splitting off of logic, common sense, and rationality from the deeper layers of the personality produce the compulsive-obsessive person, the compulsively rational person, the one who can't live in the world of emotion at all, who doesn't know whether he's fallen in love or not, because love is illogical, who can't even permit himself to laugh very frequently because laughing isn't logical and rational and sensible. When this is walled off, when the person is split, then you've got a diseased rationality and also diseased primary processes. These secondary processes, walled off and dichotomized, can be considered largely an organization generated by fears and by frustration, a system of defenses, repressions, and controls, of appeasement, and cunning underhanded negotiations with a frustrating and dangerous physical and social world which is the only source of gratification of needs and which makes us pay very dearly for whatever gratifications we get from it. Such a sick conscious, or ego, or conscious self becomes aware of and then lives only by what it perceives to be the laws of nature and of society. This means a kind of blindness. The compulsive-obsessive person not only loses much of the pleasures of living, but also he becomes cognitively blind to much of himself, much in other people, and even in nature. There is much he is blind to in nature even as a scientist. It is true that such people can get things done, but we must ask in the first place, as psychologists always ask, *At what cost*—to himself? (because he's not a happy person), and secondly, we also ask the question about this business of getting things done—*Which things?* And are they worthy of doing?

The best case I ever ran across of a compulsive-obsessive man was one of my old professors. He was a man who very characteristically saved things. He had all the newspapers that he had ever read, bound by weeks. I think each week was bound with a little red string, and then all the papers of the month would be put together and tied with a yellow string. His wife told me that he had a regular breakfast every day. Monday was orange juice, Tuesday was oatmeal, and Wednesday was prunes, and so on, and God help her if there were prunes on Monday. He saved his old razor blades. He had all his old razor blades saved and packaged nicely with labels on them. When he first came into his laboratory, I remember that he labeled everything, as such people will do. He had everything organized, and then put little stickers on them. I remember his spending hours trying to get a label on a little probe of the sort that didn't have any space for a label at all. And once I turned up the lid of the piano in his laboratory and there was a label on it, identifying it as "Piano." Well, this kind of man is in real trouble. He is himself extremely unhappy. Now the kinds of things that this fellow did are pertinent to the question I raised above. These people get things done, but which things do they get done! Are they worthwhile things? Sometimes they are and sometimes they are not. We know also unfortunately that many of our scientists are of this type. It happens that, in this kind of work, such a poking character can be very very useful. Such a man can spend twelve years in poking at, let's say, the microdissection of the nucleus of a one-celled animal. It takes that kind of patience and persistence and stubbornness and need-to-know that all people have. Society can most often use that sort of person.

Primary processes then in this dichotomized walled-off, feared sense —this is sick. But it *needn't* be sick. Deep down, we look at the world through the eyes of wishes and fears and gratifications. Perhaps it will help you if you think of the way in which a really young child looks at the world, looks at itself, and at other people. It is logical in the sense of having no negative, no contradictions, no separate identities, no opposites, no mutual exclusions. Aristotle doesn't exist for the primary processes. It is independent of control, taboos, discipline, inhibitions, delays, planning, calculations of possibility or impossibility. It has nothing to do with time and space or with sequence, causality, order, or with the laws of the physical world. This is a world quite other than the physical world. When it is placed under the necessity of disguising itself from conscious awareness to make things less threatening, it can condense several objects into one as in a dream. It can displace emotions from their true objects to other harmless ones. It can obscure by symbolizing. It can be omnipotent, ubiquitous, omniscient. (Remember dreams, now. Everything I've said holds for the dream.) It has nothing to do with action for it can make things come to pass without doing or without acting, simply by fantasy. For most people it is preverbal, very concrete, closer to raw experiencing, and usually visual. It is prevaluational, premoral, pre-ethical, pre-cultural. It is prior to good and evil. Now, in most civilized people just *because it has been walled off* by this dichotomizing, it tends to be childish, immature, crazy, dangerous, frightening. Remember I've given an example of the person who has completely suppressed the primary processes, completely walled off the unconscious. Such a person is a sick man in the particular way which I have described.

The person in whom the secondary processes of control, reason, order, logic, have completely crumbled, that man is a schizophrenic. He's a very, very sick man, too.

I think one can see where this leads. In the healthy person, and especially the healthy person who creates, I find that he has somehow managed a fusion and a synthesis of both primary and secondary processes; both conscious and unconscious; both of deeper self and of conscious self. And he manages to do this gracefully and fruitfully. Certainly I can report that it is *possible* to do, even though it is not very common. It is certainly possible to help this process along by psychotherapy; deeper and longer psychotherapy can be even better. What happens in this fusion is that both the primary processes and the secondary processes, partaking of each other, then change in character. The unconscious doesn't become frightening any more. This is the person who can live with his unconscious; live with, let's say, his childishness, his fantasy, his imagination, his wish fulfillment, his femininity, his poetic quality, his crazy quality. He is the person, as one psychoanalyst said in a nice phrase, "who can regress in the service of ego." This is *voluntary* regression. This person is the one who has that kind of creativeness at his disposal, readily available, that I think we're interested in.

The compulsive-obsessive kind of man that I mentioned earlier, in the extreme instance, *can't* play. He can't let go. Such a man tends to avoid parties for instance because he's so sensible and you're supposed to be a little silly at a party. Such a man is afraid to get a little tight because then his controls loosen up too much and for him this is a great danger. He has to be in control all the time. Such a person will probably make a horrible subject for hypnosis. He will probably get frightened by being anesthetized, or by any other loss of full consciousness. These are people who try to be dignified, orderly, conscious, rational at a party, where you are not supposed to be. Now this is what I mean when I say that the person who is comfortable enough with his unconscious is able to let go that much anyhow—a little crazy in this party sense; to be silly, to play along with a gag, and to enjoy it; and to enjoy being nutty for a little while anyhow—"in the service of the ego" as the psychoanalyst has said. This is like a conscious, voluntary regression—instead of trying to be dignified and controlled at all times. (I don't know why this comes to mind: It's about one person who is described as "strutting," even when he is sitting on a chair.)

Perhaps I can now say something more about this openness to the unconscious. This whole business of psychotherapy, of self-therapy, of self-knowledge is a difficult process because, as things stand now for most of us, the conscious and the unconscious are walled off from each other. How do you get these two worlds, the psychic world and the world of reality, to be comfortable with each other? In general, the process of psychotherapy, is a matter of slow confrontation, bit by bit, with the help of a technician, with the uppermost layers of the unconscious. They are exposed and tolerated and assimilated and turn out to be not so dangerous after all, not so horrible. Then comes the next layer, and then the next, in this same process of getting a person to face something which he is terribly afraid of, and then finding when he does face it, that there was nothing to be afraid of in the first place. He has been afraid of it because he has been looking at it through the eyes of the child that he used to be. This is childish misinterpretation. What the child was afraid of and therefore repressed, was pushed beyond the reach of common-sense learning and experience and growing up, and it has to stay there until it's dragged out by some special process. The conscious must become strong enough to dare friendliness with the enemy.

A fair parallel can be found in the relations between men and women throughout history. Men have been afraid of women and have therefore dominated them, unconsciously, for very much the same reasons I believe that they have been afraid of their primary processes. Remember that the dynamic psychologists are apt to think that much of the relationship of men to women is determined by the fact that women will remind men of their own unconscious, that is of their own femaleness, their own softness, their own tenderness, and so on. And therefore fighting women or trying to control them or to derogate them has been part of this effort to control these unconscious forces which are within everyone of us. Between a frightened master and a resentful slave no true love is possible. Only as men become strong enough, self-confident enough, and integrated enough can they tolerate and finally enjoy self-actualizing women, women who are full human beings. But no man fulfills himself without such a woman, in principle. Therefore strong men and strong women are the condition of each other, for neither can exist without the other. They are also the cause of the other, because women grow men and men grow women. And finally of course, they are the reward of each other. If you are a good enough man, that's the kind of woman you'll get and that's the kind of woman you'll deserve. Therefore, going back to our parallel, healthy primary processes and healthy secondary processes, that is healthy fantasy and healthy rationality, need each other's help in order to fuse into a true integration.

Chronologically, our knowledge of primary processes was derived first from studies of dreams and fantasies and neurotic processes, and later of psychotic, insane processes. Only little by little has this knowledge been freed of its taint of pathology, of irrationality, of immaturity, and primitiveness, in the bad sense. Only recently have we become aware, fully aware, from our studies of healthy people, of the creative process, of play, of aesthetic perception, of the meaning of healthy love, of healthy growing and becoming, of healthy education, that every human being is both poet and engineer, both rational and nonrational, both child and adult, both masculine and feminine, both in the psychic world and in the world of nature. Only slowly have we learned what we lose by trying daily to be *only* and *purely* rational, *only* "scientific," *only* logical, *only* sensible, *only* practical, *only* responsible. Only now are we becoming quite sure that the integrated person, the fully evolved human, the fully matured person, must be available to himself at both these levels, simultaneously. Certainly it is now obsolete to stigmatize this unconscious side of human nature as sick rather than healthy. That's the way Freud thought of it originally but we are learning different now. We are learning that complete health means being available to yourself at all levels. We can no longer call this side "evil" rather than "good," lower rather than higher, selfish rather than unselfish, beastly rather than human. Throughout human history and especially the history of Western civilization, and more especially the history of Christianity has there tended to be this dichotomy. No longer can we dichotomize ourselves into a cave man and a civilized man, into a devil and a saint. We can now see this as an illegitimate dichotomy, an illegitimate "either/or," in which by the very process of splitting and dichotomizing we create a sick "either" and a sick "or," that is to say, a sick conscious and a sick unconscious, a sick rationality, and sick impulses. (Rationality can be quite sick, as you can see on the television very quickly with all the quiz programs. I heard of one poor fellow, a specialist in ancient history, who was making an awful lot of money, who told somebody that he had gotten this way simply by memorizing the whole *Cambridge Ancient History*. He started with page one and went on right through, and now he knows every date and name in it. The poor guy! There is a story by O. Henry about a man who decided that since the encyclopedia encompassed all knowledge, he wouldn't bother going to school, but would simply memorize the encyclopedia. He started with the A's, worked his way on through the B's, C's, and so on. Now *that's* a sick rationality.)

Once we transcend and resolve this dichotomy, once we can put these together into the unity in which they are originally, for instance, in the healthy child, in the healthy adult, or in specially creative people, then we can recognize that the dichotomizing or the splitting is itself a pathological process. And then it becomes possible for one's civil war to end. This is precisely what happens in people that I call self-actualizing. The simplest way to describe them is as psychologically healthy people. It is *exactly* what we find in such people. When we pick out from the population the healthiest 1 per cent or fraction of 1 per cent, then these people have in the course of their lifetime, sometimes with the benefit of therapy, sometimes without, been able to put together these two worlds, and to live comfortably in both of them. I've described the healthy person as having a healthy child-likeness. It's hard to put it into words because the word "childlikeness" customarily means the opposite of maturity. If I say that the most mature human beings living are also childlike, it sounds like a contradiction, but actually it is not. Perhaps I could put it in terms of the party example I spoke of. The most mature people are the ones that can have the most fun. I think that's a more acceptable phrasing of it. These are also people who can regress at will, who can become childish and play with children and be close to them. I don't think it's any accident that children generally tend to like them and get along with them. They can regress to that level. Involuntary regression is of course a very dangerous thing. Voluntary regression, however, apparently is characteristic of very healthy people.

Now as for practical suggestions about achieving this fusion I don't quite know. The only really practicable one that I know in ordinary practice for making this fusion within the person is psychotherapy. And this is certainly not a practicable or even a welcome suggestion. There are possibilities, of course, of self-analysis and self-therapy. Any technique which will increase self-knowledge in depth should in principle increase one's creativity by making available to oneself these sources of fantasy, play with ideas, being able to sail right out of the world and off the earth; getting away from common sense. Common sense means living in the world as it is today, but creative people are people who don't want the world as it is today but want to make another world. And in order to be able to do that, they have to be able to sail right off the surface of the earth, to imagine, to fantasy, and even to be crazy, and nutty, and so on. The suggestion that I have to make, the practical suggestion for people who manage creative personnel, is simply to watch out for such people as they already exist and then to pluck them out and hang on to them.

I think I was able to be of service to one company by making this recommendation. I tried to describe to them what these primary-creative people are like. They are precisely the ones that make trouble in an organization, usually. I wrote down a list of some of their characteristics that would be guaranteed to make trouble. They tend to be unconventional; they tend to be a little bit queer; unrealistic; they are often called undisciplined; sometimes inexact; "unscientific," that is, by a specific definition of science. They tend to be called childish by their more compulsive colleagues, irresponsible, wild, crazy, speculative, uncritical, irregular, emotional, and so on. This sounds like a description of a bum or a Bohemian or an eccentric. And it should be stressed, I suppose, that in the early stages of creativeness, you've got to be a bum, and you've got to be a Bohemian, you've got to be crazy. The "brainstorming" technique may help us toward a recipe for being creative as this comes from people who have already successfully been creative; they let themselves be like this in the early stages of thinking. They let themselves be completely uncritical. They allow all sorts of wild ideas to come into their heads. And in great bursts of emotion and enthusiasm, they may scribble out the poem or the formula or the mathematical solution or work up the theory, or design the experiment. Then, and only then, do they become secondary, become more rational, more controlled, and more critical. If you try to be rational and controlled and orderly in this first stage of the process, you'll never get to it. Now the brainstorming technique, as I remember it, consisted in just this—in not being critical—letting yourself play with ideas—free association—letting them come out on the table, in profusion, and then only later on, tossing away those ideas which are bad, or useless, and retaining the ones which are good. If you are afraid of making this kind of crazy mistake, then you'll never get any of the bright ideas either.

Of course this kind of Bohemian business is not necessarily uniform or continued. I am talking about people who are able to be like that *when they want to be* (regression in the service of the ego; voluntary regression; voluntary craziness; voluntary going into the unconscious). These same people can afterward put on their caps and gowns and become grown-up, rational, sensible, orderly, and so on, and examine with a critical eye what they produced in a great burst of enthusiasm, and creative fervor. Then they can say sometimes, "It felt wonderful while it was being born, but it's no good," and toss it away. A truly integrated person can be both secondary and primary; both childish and mature. He can regress and then come back to reality, becoming then more controlled and critical in his responses.

I mention that this was of use to one company or at least to this one person in the company who was in charge of creative personnel, because it was precisely this sort of person he'd been firing. He had laid very great stress on taking orders well and on being well adjusted to the organization.

I don't know how an organization manager is going to work these things out. I don't know what would happen to morale. This is not my problem. I don't know how it would be possible to use such characters in the middle of an organization which has to do the orderly work that ensues upon the idea. An idea is just the beginning in a very complex process of working out. That's a problem that we'll be working out in this country more than any other place on the face of the earth, I guess, during the next decade or so. We've got to face it. Huge sums of money now are going into research and development. The management of creative personnel becomes a new problem.

However, I have no doubt that the standard of practice which has worked well in large organizations, absolutely needs modification and revision of some sort. We'll have to find some way of permitting people to be individualistic in an organization. I don't know how it will be done. I think it will have to be a practical kind of working out, just simply trying out this and trying out that and trying out the other, and finally coming to kind of an empirical conclusion. I would say that it would be a help to be able to spot these as characteristics, not only of craziness but also of creativeness. (By the way, I don't want to put in a good recommendation for everybody who behaves like this. Some of them actually *are* crazy.) Now we've got to learn to distinguish. It's a question of learning to respect or at least to look with an open eye on people of this sort and trying somehow to fit them into society. Customarily today such people are lone wolves. You will find them, I think, more in the academic situation than you will in large organizations or large corporations. They tend to be more comfortable there because they're permitted to be as crazy as they like. Everybody expects professors to be crazy, anyhow, and it doesn't make much difference to anyone. They're not beholden to anyone else except for their teaching, perhaps. But the professor has time enough ordinarily to go off into his attic or his basement and dream up all sorts of things, whether they are practical or not. In an organization you've got to give out, ordinarily. It's like a story I heard recently. Two psychoanalysts met each other at a party. One analyst walked up to the other analyst and slapped him in the face without any warning. The analyst who was slapped looked startled for a moment and then shrugged his shoulders and said, "That's *his* problem."

7

The Need for Creative People

The question is, Who is interested in creativity? And my answer is that practically everybody is. This interest is no longer confined to psychologists and psychiatrists. Now it has become a question of national and international policy as well. People in general, and especially the military, the politicians, and the thoughtful patriots, all must soon come to the following realization: there is a military stalemate and it looks as if there will continue to be. The function of the army today is essentially to prevent war rather than to make war. Therefore the continuing struggle between the large political systems, i.e., the cold war, will continue to be waged, but in a non-military fashion. That system will prevail which will appeal to other neutral people. Which turns out a better kind of person, more brotherly, more peaceable, less greedy, more lovable, more respect-worthy? Who will attract the African and Asian peoples? etc., etc.

In general, then, the more psychologically healthy (or more highly evolved) person is a political necessity. He has to be a person who is not hated, a person who can get along and be friendly, deeply friendly with anybody, including Africans and Asians, who are very quick to detect any condescension or prejudice or hatred. Certainly one of the characteristics that is necessary is that the citizen of the country which will lead and win out must not have race prejudice. He must feel brotherly, he must feel like helping, he must be a trustworthy leader rather than someone who is mistrusted. In the long run he must not be authoritarian, not sadistic, etc.

Universal Needs

But in addition to this, there is another, possibly more immediate necessity for any viable political, social, economic system, and that is to turn out more creative people. This is the same kind of consideration that weighs so heavily with our great industries, because they are all so aware of possible obsolescence. They are all aware that however rich and prosperous they may be at this moment, they may wake up tomorrow morning to find that some new product has been invented which makes them obsolete. What will happen to the automobile manufacturers if someone comes out with a cheap, personal-travel technique of some kind, one which could sell at half the price of an automobile? As a consequence, every rich corporation that can afford it pours back a very large percentage of its money into research and development of *new* products, as well as into the improvement of the old ones. The parallel on the international scene is the armament race. It is perfectly true that there is a careful balance now of deterrent weapons and bombs and bombers, etc. But supposing something happened next year of the kind that happened when the Americans invented the atom bomb?

Therefore there is also a huge amount of research and development now going on, under the head of defense or military expenditures in all the large countries. Each must try to discover first that new weapon which will make all present weapons obsolete. I think that the rulers of the powerful countries are beginning to realize that the people who are capable of discovering such things are that peculiar breed to whom they have always been reflexly antagonistic, i.e., the creative persons. Now they will have to learn about the management of creative personnel, the early selection of creative persons, the education and fostering of creative persons, and the like.

In essence, this is why I think so many more of our leaders today are interested in the theory of creativeness. The historical situation with which we are confronted helps to create an interest in creativeness among thoughtful people, among social philosophers, and many other kinds of people. Our era is more in flux, more in process, more rapidly changing than any previous one in history. The rate of acceleration of accumulation of new scientific facts, of new inventions, of new technological developments, of new psychological happenings, of increased affluence, presents every human being today with a situation different from any that has ever happened before. Among other things, this new lack of continuity and stability from past to the present into the future makes all sorts of changes necessary which many people don't realize yet. For instance the whole process of education, especially of technical and professional education, has changed entirely in the last few decades. To make it simple, there is little use in learning facts; they become obsolete too fast. There is little use in learning techniques; they become obsolete almost overnight. It is of little use, for instance, for professors of engineering to teach their students all the techniques that they themselves learned back in *their* school days; these techniques are almost useless now. In effect, we are confronted in practically every area of life with obsolescence of old facts and theories and methods. We are all a bunch of buggy-whip makers whose skills are now useless.

New Teaching Concepts

What is then the correct way of teaching people to be, e.g., engineers? It is quite clear that we must teach them to be creative persons, at least in the sense of being able to confront novelty, to improvise. They must not be afraid of change but rather must be able to be comfortable with change and novelty, and if possible (because best of all) even be able to *enjoy* novelty and change. This means that we must teach and train engineers not in the old and standard sense, but in the new sense, i.e., "creative" engineers.

This, in general, is also true of executives, leaders, and administrators in business and industry. They must be people who are capable of coping with the inevitably rapid obsolescence of any new product, or of any old way of doing things. They must be people who will not fight change but who will anticipate it, and who can be challenged enough by it to enjoy it. We must develop a race of improvisers, of "here-now" creators. We must define the skillful person or the trained person, or the educated person in a very different way than we used to (i.e., *not* as one who has a rich knowledge of the past so that he can profit from past experiences in a future emergency). Much that we have called learning has become useless. Any kind of learning which is the simple application of the past to the present, or the use of past techniques in the present situation has become obsolete in many areas of life. Education can no longer be considered essentially or only a learning process; it is now also a character training, a person-training process. Of course this is not *altogether* true, but it is very largely true, and it will become truer and truer year by year. (I think this is perhaps the most radical and blunt and unmistakable way of saying what I am trying to say.) The past has become almost useless in some areas of life. People who depend too much upon the past have become almost useless in many professions. We need a new kind of human being who can divorce himself from his past, who feels strong and courageous and trusting enough to trust himself in the present situation, to handle the problem well in an improvising way, without previous preparation, if need be.

All of this adds up to increased emphasis on psychological health and strength. It means an increased valuing of the ability to pay the fullest attention to the here-now situation, to be able to listen well, to be able to see well in the concrete, immediate moment before us. It means that we need people who are different from the average kind of person who confronts the present as if it were a repetition of the past, and who uses the present simply as a period in which he prepares for future threats and dangers, which he doesn't trust himself enough to meet unprepared when the time comes. This new kind of human being that we would need even if there were no cold war, and even if we were all united in a brotherly species, is needed simply to confront the new kind of world in which we live.

The cold war considerations that I have talked about above, as well as the new kind of world we are now confronting, force certain other necessities upon our discussion of creativeness. Since in essence we are talking about a kind of person, a kind of philosophy, a kind of character, then the stress shifts away from stress on created products, and technological innovations and aesthetic products and innovations, etc. We must become more interested in the creative process, the creative attitude, the creative person, rather than in the creative product alone.

Therefore it seems to me a better strategy to turn more attention to the inspiration phase of creativeness rather than to the working out phase of creativeness, i.e., to "primary creativeness" rather than to "secondary creativeness" (89).

We must, more often, use as our example not the finished work of art or science which is socially useful, but rather we must focus our attention on improvising, on the flexible and adaptable, efficient confronting of any here-now situation which turns up, whether it is important or unimportant. This is so because using the finished product as a criterion introduces too many confusions with good work habits, with stubbornness, discipline, patience, with good editing abilities, and other characteristics which have nothing directly to do with creativeness, or at least are not unique to it.

All of these considerations make it even *more* desirable to study creativeness in children rather than in adults. Here many of the confounding and contaminating problems are avoided. For instance here we can no longer stress social innovation or social usefulness or the created product. Also we can avoid confusing the issue by avoiding preoccupation with great inborn talent (which seems to have little connection with the universal creativeness that we are all heir to).

These are some of the reasons why I consider nonverbal education so important, e.g., through art, through music, through dancing. I am not particularly interested in the training of artists because in any case this is done in a different way. Neither am I much interested in the children having a good time, nor even in art as therapy. For that matter I am not even interested in art education, *per se*. What I am really interested in is the new kind of education which we must develop which moves toward fostering the new kind of human being that we need, the process person, the creative person, the improvising person, the self-trusting, courageous person, the autonomous person. It just happens to be a historical accident that the art educators are the ones who went off in this direction first. It could just as easily be true of mathematical education and I hope it will be one day.

Certainly mathematics or history or literature are still taught today in most places in an authoritarian, memorizing way (although already, this is not true for the very newest kind of education for improvising, for guessing, for creativeness, for pleasure that J. Bruner has been writing about, and that the mathematicians and physicists have created for the high schools). The question again is how to teach children to confront the here-now, to improvise, etc., that is, how to become creative people, able to assume the creative attitude.

The new education-through-art movement with its stress on non-objectivity is one subject in which right and wrong are much less involved, in which correctness and incorrectness can be pushed aside, and in which therefore the child can be confronted with himself, with his own courage or anxiety, with his stereotypes or his freshness, etc. A good way to say this is that where reality has been withdrawn, we have a good projective test situation, and we therefore have a good psychotherapeutic or growth situation. This is exactly what is done both in projective testing and in insight therapy; i.e., reality, correctness, adaptability to the world, physical and chemical and biological determiners are all removed, so that the psyche can reveal itself more freely. I might even go so far as to say that in this respect, education through art is a kind of therapy and growth technique, because it permits the deeper layers of the psyche to emerge, and therefore to be encouraged, fostered, trained, and educated.

PART III
Values

8
Fusions of Facts and Values

I shall begin with an explanation of what I have called peak experiences because it is in such experiences that my thesis is most easily and amply demonstrated. The term peak experiences is a generalization for the best moments of the human being, for the happiest moments of life, for experiences of ecstasy, rapture, bliss, of the greatest joy. I found that such experiences came from profound aesthetic experiences such as creative ecstasies, moments of mature love, perfect sexual experiences, parental love, experiences of natural childbirth, and many others. I use the one term—peak experiences—as a kind of generalized and abstract concept because I discovered that all of these ecstatic experiences had some characteristics in common. Indeed, I found that it was possible to make a generalized, abstract schema or model which could describe their common characteristics. The word enables me to speak of all or any of these experiences in the same moment (66, 88, 89).

When I asked my subjects, after they had described their peak experiences, how the world looked different to them during these times, I received answers which also could be schematized and generalized. Actually it is almost necessary to do this for there is no other way of encompassing the thousands of words or descriptions which have been given to me. My own boiling-down and condensation of this multitude of words, and these many descriptions of the way the world looks to them, from perhaps a hundred people, during and after peak experiences would be: truth, beauty, wholeness, dichotomy-transcendence, aliveness-process, uniqueness, perfection, necessity, completion, justice, order, simplicity, richness, effortlessness, play-fulness, and self-sufficiency.

While it is perfectly true that this is one person's condensation and boiling-down, I have little doubt but that anyone else would come up with approximately the same list of characteristics. I am confident that it would not be very different, at least not beyond differences in choice of synonyms or of particular words of description.

These words are highly abstract. How could it be otherwise? Each word has the task of including many kinds of direct experience under one rubric or one heading. This means necessarily that such a rubric would be widely encompassing, which is to say, very abstract.

These are the ways in which the world is variously characterized when seen in peak experiences. There may be differences in stress or in degree, i.e., during the peak experiences the world looks *more* honest and naked, *more* true, or is reported to look *more* beautiful than at other times.

I want to stress that these are claimed to be descriptive character-istics; the reports say these are facts about the world. They are the descriptions of what the world appears to be, what it looks like, even, they claim, of what it is. They are in the same category as the descrip-tions that a newspaper reporter or a scientific observer would use after witnessing some event. They are not "ought" or "should" statements, nor are they merely projections of the investigator's wishes. They are not hallucinations; they are not merely emotional states, lacking cog-nitive reference. They are reported as illuminations, as true and verid-ical characteristics of reality which previous blindness has hidden from them.[1]

[1] This problem of the veridicality of mystic illuminations is certainly an old problem. The very roots and origins of religion are involved, but we must be very careful not to be seduced by the absolute subjective certainty of the mystics and of the peak experiencers. To them, truth has been revealed. Most of us have experienced this same certitude in our moments of revelation.

But especially we—psychologists and psychiatrists—are at the beginning of a new age in science. In our psychotherapeutic experience, we have seen occasional illuminations, peak experiences, desolation experiences, insights and ecstasies, both in our patients and in ourselves. We are used to them; and we have learned that though not all of them are valid, some of them most certainly are.

It is the chemist, the biologist, or the engineer who will continue to have trouble with this old/new notion that truth may come in this old/new way: in a rush, in an emotional illumination, in a kind of eruption, through broken walls, through resistances, through the overcoming of fears. We are the ones who specialize in dealing with dangerous truths, with the truths which threaten self-esteem.

This scientific skepticism of the impersonal, even in the impersonal realm, is unwarranted. The history of science, or at least of the great scientists, is a story of sudden and ecstatic insights into the truth, truth which is then slowly, carefully, cautiously validated by more pedestrian workers who function more like coral insects than like eagles. I think, for instance, of visions like Kekule's dream of the benzene ring.

Too many people of limited vision define the essence of science as cautious checking, validating of hypotheses, finding out if other people's ideas are correct or not. But, insofar as science is also a technique of discovery, it will have to learn how to foster peak-experience insights and visions and then how to handle them as data. Other examples of Being-knowledge—veridical perception of hitherto unperceived truth in peak experiences—come from the perspicuity gained through Being-love, from certain religious experiences, from certain group-therapy experiences of intimacy, from intellectual illuminations, or from profound aesthetic experiences.

In the last few months, a brand-new possibility for the validation

However, one thing that mankind has learned during three thousand years of recorded history is that this subjective certainty is not enough; there must also be external validation. There must be some way of checking the truth of the claim, some measure of the fruits, some pragmatic test; we must approach these claims with some reserve, some caution, some soberness. Too many visionaries, seers, and prophets have turned out to be incorrect after *feeling* absolutely certain.

This kind of disillusioning experience is one of the historical roots of science: the mistrust of claims of personal revelation. Official, classical science has long since rejected private revelations and illuminations as not being worthy data in themselves.

of B-knowledge (illumination-knowledge) has opened up. In three different universities, LSD was able to cure alcoholism in about 50 per cent of the cases (1). Once we have recovered from our happiness at learning about this great blessing, this unexpected miracle and, since we are insatiable human beings, we inevitably ask: "How about the ones who don't recover?" I quote from a letter from Dr. A. Hoffer, dated February 8, 1963:

> We have deliberately used P.E. (peak experience) as a therapeutic weapon. Our alcoholics who receive LSD or mescaline are given P.E. using music, visual stimuli, words, suggestion, anything which will give them what they say is a P.E. We have treated over five hundred alcoholics and certain general rules can be enunciated. One is that in general the majority of alcoholics who respond by sobriety after treatment have had P.E. Conversely, hardly any who have not had P.E. respond.
>
> We also have strong data which suggest that affect is the chief component of P.E. When LSD subjects are first given penicillamine for two days they have an experience which is identical with the one normally gained from LSD, but where there is a marked dampening of affect. They observe all the visual changes, have all the changes in thinking, but they are emotionally flat and are more nonparticipant observers than participants. These subjects do not have P.E. In addition, only 10 per cent do well after treatment compared to our expected 60 per cent recovery on several large follow-up studies.

Now we make our big jump: This same list of described characteristics of reality, of the world, seen at certain times, is just about the same as what have been called the eternal values, the eternal verities. We see here the old familiar trinity of truth, beauty, and goodness. That is to say, this list of described characteristics is also simultaneously a list of values. These characteristics are what the great religionists and philosophers have valued, and this is practically the same list that most serious thinkers of mankind have agreed upon as the ultimate or highest value of life.

To repeat, my first statement is in the realm of science, defined as public. Anyone can do the same thing; anyone can check for himself; anyone can use the same procedure that I have used and can, objectively if he wishes, record on tape the things that are said in answer to the questions I posed and then make them public. That is, what I am reporting is public, repeatable, confirmable or not; it is even quantifiable if you wish. It is stable and reliable in the sense that when I repeat the operation I get approximately the same results. Even by the most orthodox, positivistic definitions of nineteenth-century science, this is a scientific statement. It is a cognitive statement, a description of the characteristics of reality, of the cosmos, of the world out there, outside the person who is reporting and describing, *of the world as perceived*. These data can be worked with in the traditional fashion of science, and their degree of truth or untruth can be determined.[2]

And yet, exactly the same statement about the way the world looks, is also a value statement. These are the most inspiring values of life; these are the ones that people are willing to die for; these are the ones they are willing to pay for with effort, pain, and torture. These are also the "highest" values in the sense that they come most often to the best people, in their best moments, under the best conditions. These are the definitions of the higher life, of the good life, of the spiritual life, and, I may also add, these are the far goals of psychotherapy, and the far goals of education in the broadest sense. These are qualities for which we admire the great men of human history, that characterize our heroes, our saints, even our Gods.

Therefore, this cognitive statement is the same as this valuing statement. *Is* becomes the same as *ought*. *Fact* becomes the same as *value*. The world which is the case, which is described and perceived, becomes the same as the world which is valued and wished for. The world which *is* becomes the world which *ought* to be. That which ought to be has come to pass, in other words, facts have here fused with values.[3]

---

[2] Further researches are possible for anyone who is interested in doing them. My students and I have done some. For instance, in one very simple experiment, done only in order to show what it was possible to do, we found that college girls had such peak experiences significantly more often from the experience of being loved. College men, on the other hand, significantly more often got their peaks from victory, success, from overcoming, and from achievement. This coincides with our common-sense knowledge, and also with our clinical experience. Many other researches of this sort can be done; the field is wide open for research especially now that we know peak experiences can often be deliberately brought about by drugs.

[3] At the very beginning, I wish to avoid confusion over the word "ought" as I am using it here, with the "neurotic shoulds" of Horney as set forth, for instance, in Chapter 3 of *Neurosis and Human Growth* (49). What man is

Difficulty with the Word "Values." It is clear that what I have discussed has something to do with values (21, 93), no matter how the word is defined. However, "values" are defined in many ways, and mean different things to different people. As a matter of fact, it is so confusing semantically that I am convinced we will soon give up this catchall word in favor of more precise and more operational definitions for each of the many submeanings that have been attached to it.

To use another image, we can think of the concept "values" as a big container holding all sorts of miscellaneous and vague things. Most of the philosophical writers about values have tried to find a simple formula or definition which would tie together everything in the container, even though many of the things inside were there by accident. They ask—"What does the word *really* mean?"—forgetting that it doesn't really mean anything, that it's just a label. Only pluralistic description can serve, that is, a catalogue of all the different ways in which the word "value" is actually used by different people.

What follows is a series of brief observations, hypotheses, and questions about various facets of this problem; various ways in which facts and values may be said to fuse or to approach fusion, in various senses of the word "values" and in various senses of the word "facts." This is like a shift from a debate among lexicographers to a focus on operations and actual happenings in the realm of psychology and psychotherapy: from the world of semantics to the world of nature. Actually, this would be a first step toward bringing these problems into the realm of science (broadly defined to include experiential data as well as objective data).

Psychotherapy as an "Ought-Is-Quest." I want now to apply this kind of thinking to the phenomenon of psychotherapy and self-therapy. The questions that people ask in the search for identity, real self, etc., are very largely "ought" questions: What ought I to do? What ought I to be? How should I solve this conflict situation? Should I pursue this career or that one? Should I get divorced or not? Should I live or die?

---

supposed to be is often extrinsic, arbitrary, *a priori*, perfectionistic—in a word, unrealistic. I am using the word "ought" here as intrinsic to the organism, as actual potentiality which can actually be fulfilled and which had better be fulfilled under pain of illness.

Most untutored people are quite willing to answer these questions directly. "If I were you . . ." they say, and then proceed with suggestions and advice. But technically trained people have learned that this doesn't work or is even harmful. We don't say what we think another ought to do.

What we have learned is that ultimately, the best way for a person to discover what he ought to do is to find out who and what he is, because the path to ethical and value decisions, to wiser choices, to oughtness, is via "isness," via the discovery of facts, truth, reality, the nature of the particular person. The more he knows about his own nature, his deep wishes, his temperament, his constitution, what he seeks and yearns for and what really satisfies him, the more effortless, automatic, and epiphenomenal become his value choices. (This is one of the great Freudian discoveries, and one which is often overlooked.) Many problems simply disappear; many others are easily solved by knowing what is in conformity with one's nature, what is suitable and right.[4] (And we must also remember that knowledge of one's own deep nature is also simultaneously knowledge of human nature in general.)

That is to say, we help him to search for "oughtness" via "facticity." Discovering one's real nature is simultaneously an *ought* quest and an *is* quest. This kind of value quest, since it is a quest for knowledge, facts, and information, that is, for the truth, is squarely within the jurisdiction of a sensibly defined science. As for the psychoanalytic method as well as all other noninterfering, uncovering, Taoistic therapeutic methods, I can say with equal accuracy that they are scientific

[4] The achievement of identity, authenticity, self-realization, etc., definitely does *not* automatically solve *all* ethical problems. Even after the pseudoproblems fade away, there are many real problems left. But, of course, even these real problems are likely to be handled better by a man with clear eyes. Honesty with oneself and clear knowledge of one's nature is an inevitable prerequisite to authentic moral decisions. But I do not wish to imply that it is enough to be authentic and self-knowing. Authentic self-knowledge is definitely not enough for many decisions; it is absolutely necessary, but it is not sufficient. And also, I leave aside here the undoubted educational characteristics of psychotherapy, i.e., the unwitting indoctrination with the therapist's value, if only by being a model. The questions are: What is central? What is peripheral? What is to be maximized? What minimized? Do we aim for pure self-discovery by uncovering, and what is pragmatically correct to aim for? I wish also to point out that refusing to impose oneself upon the patient or to indoctrinate him can be achieved via either the Freudian mirror detachment or the B-loving "encounter" of the existential psychotherapists.

methods on the one hand, and value-discovering on the other; this kind of therapy is an ethical quest, even a religious quest in the naturalistic sense.

Observe here that the *process* of therapy and the *goals* of therapy (another contrast between *is* and *ought*) *are* indistinguishable. To separate the two becomes merely ludicrous or tragic. The immediate *goal* of therapy is to find out what the person is; the *process* of therapy is also finding out what the person is. Do you want to find out what you ought to be? Then find out who you are! "Become what thou art!" The description of what one ought to be is almost the same as the description of what one deeply is.[5]

Here "value," in the sense of *telos*, of the end toward which you are striving, the terminus, the Heaven, exists right now. The self, toward which one is struggling, exists right now in a very real sense, just as real education, rather than being the diploma that one gets at the end of a four-year road, is the moment to moment to moment process of learning, perceiving, thinking. Religion's Heaven, which one is supposed to enter after life is over—life itself being meaningless —is actually available in principle all through life. It is available to us now, and is all around us.

Being and Becoming are, so to speak, side by side, simultaneously existing, now. Traveling can give end-pleasure; it need not be only a means to an end. Many people discover too late that the retirement made possible by the years of work doesn't taste as sweet as the years of work did.

Acceptance. Another kind of fusion of fact and value comes from what we call acceptance. Here the fusion comes not so much from an improvement of actuality, the *is*, but from a scaling down of the *ought*, from a redefining of expectations so that they come closer and closer to actuality and therefore to attainability.

What I mean by this can be exemplified in the course of therapy, when our overperfect demands upon ourselves, our idealized image of ourselves, break down under insight. The self-image of the perfectly brave man, the perfectly maternal woman, or the perfectly logical and rational person, collapses as we permit ourselves to discover our bits of cowardliness, envy, hostility, or selfishness.

Very often, this is a depressing and even a crushing realization.

[5] The real self is also partly constructed and invented.

We may feel totally sinful, or depraved or unworthy. We see our *is* as extremely far away from our *ought*.

But, it is also quite characteristic that in successful therapy we go through the process of acceptance. From being horrified with ourselves, we move toward resignation. But from resignation we sometimes move on toward thinking: "After all that's not so bad. It's really quite human and quite understandable that a loving mother might sometimes resent her baby." And sometimes we see ourselves going even beyond this stage to a fully loving acceptance of humanness, and out of full understanding of the failing, finally see it as desirable, beautiful, as a glory. The woman, fearful and resentful of maleness, can finally come to be pleased with it, to be even religiously awed by it to the point of ecstasy. What was seen first as an evil can become a glory. By redefining her notion of masculinity, her husband can change before her eyes into being what he ought to be.

We can all experience this with children if we give up our censoriousness, our definitions of what they ought to be, our demands for them. To the extent that we can occasionally do this, we can then see them transiently as perfect, as *now* actually being acutely and poignantly beautiful, remarkable, totally lovable. Our subjective experience of willing and wishing—i.e., of not being content—can then fuse with the subjective experience of satisfaction, of agreement, and of the finality that we feel when the ought has come to pass. I quote an interesting passage from Alan Watts who says this very well: ". . . in the moment of death many people undergo the curious sensation not only of accepting but of having willed everything that has happened to them. This is not willing in the imperious sense; it is the unexpected discovery of an identity between the willed and the inevitable." (151)

Here we are also reminded of various experiments by Carl Rogers' (128) group which showed that in the course of successful therapy the ego ideal and the actual self slowly come closer and closer toward fusion. In Horney's phrasing, the real self and the idealized image are slowly modified and move toward fusion, that is, toward becoming the same thing rather than widely different things. (49) Similar is the more orthodox Freudian notion of the harsh and punishing superego, which, in the course of psychotherapy, is scaled down, becomes more benevolent, more accepting, more loving, more self-approving;

this·is another way of saying that one's ideal for one's self, and one's actual perception of one's self come closer together so as to permit self-respect and hence, self-love.

The example which I prefer is that of the dissociated or multiple personality, in which the presenting personality always is an over-conventionalized, prissy, goody-goody type, so rejecting the underlying impulses as to repress them altogether, so that he can get satisfaction only by total breakthrough of the psychopathic, childlike, impulsive, pleasure-seeking, uncontrolled aspect of the self. Dichotomizing them distorts both "personalities"; fusing them involves real change in both "personalities." Getting rid of arbitrary "oughts" and "shoulds" makes possible an embracing and enjoying of what is.

A few rare psychotherapists, like scoptophiliacs, use uncovering as a kind of debunking or lowering of the patient, as if a mask is torn away, and the patient is revealed to be "not so much." This is a kind of dominance maneuver, a kind of one-upmanship. It becomes a form of social climbing, a way of feeling powerful, strong, dominant, above, even godlike. For some who don't think very much of themselves this is a method of becoming intimate.

This partly implies that what is revealed—the fears, the anxieties, the conflicts—are defined as low, bad, evil. For instance, Freud, even toward the end of his life, did not really like the unconscious and still defined it mostly as something dangerous and evil that had to be brought under control.

Fortunately, most therapists I know are quite different in this respect. In general, the more they know the depths of human beings, the more they like them and respect them. They *like* humanness, and do not condemn it on the basis of some pre-existing definition or Platonic essence to which it fails to measure up. They find it possible to think men heroic, saintly, wise, talented, or great, even when these men are patients and reveal themselves and their "weaknesses" and "evils."

Or, to say it in another way, if one becomes disillusioned with humanness as one gets to see it more deeply, then this is the same as saying that one had illusions or expectations which could not be realized or could not stand the light of day, i.e., which were false and unreal. I remember a subject in one of my sexological researches about twenty-five years ago (I am not sure this would happen today in the same way) who lost her religion because she simply could not believe in a God who had invented such a nasty, dirty, and disgusting way of making babies. Here I am reminded of the writings of various monks in medieval times who were tortured by the incompatibility of their animal nature (e.g., defecation) and their religious aspirations. Our professional experience permits us to smile at such unnecessary, self-created foolishness.

In a word, basic human nature has been called dirty, evil, or barbaric because some of its characteristics were *a priori* defined to be so. If you define urination or menstruation as dirty, then the human body becomes dirty by this semantic trick. A man I once knew tortured himself with agonies of guilt and shame every time he was sexually attracted by his wife; he was "semantically" evil, evil by arbitrary definition. Redefining then, in a more reality-accepting way, is a way of reducing the distance between what is and what ought to be.

Unitive Consciousness. Under the best conditions what is, is valued. (What ought to be has been achieved.) I have already pointed out that this fusion can take place in either of two directions, one by improving the actuality so that it comes closer to the ideal, the other by scaling down the ideal, so that ideality may come closer to what actually exists.

Perhaps now, I can add a third way, namely, the unitive consciousness. This is the ability to simultaneously perceive in the fact—the *is*— its particularity, *and* its universality; to see it simultaneously as here and now, and yet also as eternal, or rather to be able to see the universal in and through the particular and the eternal in and through the temporal and momentary. In my own phrasing, this is a fusion of the Being-realm and the Deficiency-realm: to be aware of the B-realm while immersed in the D-realm.

This is nothing new. Any reader of Zen, Taoistic, or mystical literatures knows what I am talking about. Every mystic has tried to describe this vividness and particularity of the concrete object and, at the same time, its eternal, sacred, symbolic quality (like a Platonic essence). And now, in addition, we have many such descriptions from the experimenters (Huxley, for instance) with the psychedelic drugs.

I can use our perception of the child as a common example of this kind of perception. In principle, any baby may become anything. It has vast potentials and, therefore, in a certain sense, *is* anything. If we have any sensitivity, we should be able to sense these potentials when looking at the baby, and therefore be awed. This particular baby may be seen as possibly the future president, the future genius, the future scientist, or hero. He actually in fact, at this moment, in a realistic sense, has and is these potentials. Part of his facticity is the various kinds of possibilities that he embodies. Any rich and full perception of the baby perceives these potentials and these possibilities.

In the same way, any full perception of any woman or man includes their God and Goddess, priest and priestess possibilities, and mysteries embodied in and shining through the actual and limited human individuals before one's eyes: what they stand for, what they could be, what they remind us of, what we can be poetic about. (How is it possible for a sensitive person always to remain unawed by the sight of a woman suckling her infant or baking bread, or of a man interposing himself between his family and the danger that confronts them?)

Every good therapist must have this kind of unitive perception of his patient or he can never become a decent therapist. He must be able to give the patient simultaneously "unconditional positive regard" (Rogers)—regard him as a unique and sacred person—at the same time that he is also implying that the patient is lacking something, that he is imperfect, that he needs to be improved.[6] Some such sacredness of the patient as a human individual is required; we owe it to any patient no matter how horrible the deeds he has committed. This is the kind of philosophy implied by the movement to abolish capital punishment, or to forbid the degradation of the individual beyond a particular point, or forbid cruel and unusual punishment.

To perceive unitively we must be able to perceive both the sacred and profane aspects of a person: Not perceiving these universal, eternal, infinite, essential symbolic qualities is certainly a kind of reduction to the concrete and to the *sachlich*, the thinglike. It is

[6] This simultaneous acceptance and fusing of seemingly contradictory perceptions is often paralleled in religious, God-language. For instance, the following is from a letter from a religious woman: "I see a parallel in the growth-safety idea and the dichotomy idea (selfish-unselfish) with the actual-potential idea. God sees and loves us in our present condition and yet sees our potential and requires of us growth toward the potential. As we become more Godlike, can we not too, be accepting of a person in his present state while beckoning to him to take the next step?"

therefore a kind of partial blindness. (See below for "ought-blindness.")

The relevance of this for our topic lies in the fact that this is a technique for perceiving simultaneously the *is* and the *ought*, the immediate, concrete actuality and also what might be, what could be, the end-value that not only could come to pass but is there now, existing before our eyes. Also, this is a technique that I have been able to teach to some; therefore, in principle, it sets before us the possibility of deliberately, voluntarily fusing facts and values. It is hard to read Jung, Eliade or Campbell or Huxley without being permanently affected in our perceptions, without bringing facts and values closer together. We need not wait for peak experiences to bring about fusion!

"*Ontification.*" Another relevant way of saying this involves turning to another facet of the same problem. Practically any means-activity (a means-value) can be transformed into an end-activity (an end-value) if one is wise enough to want to do this. A job entered into for the sake of earning a living, can be loved for its own sake. Even the dullest, dreariest job, as long as it is worthwhile in principle, can be sanctified, sacralized (ontified, changed from a mere means into an end, a value in itself). The Japanese movie *Ikuri* makes this point very well. The dreariest kind of bureaucratic job is ontified when death by cancer approaches, and life must become meaningful and worthwhile, what it ought to be. This is still another way of fusing fact and value; one can transform the fact into an end-value simply by seeing it as such and, therefore, making it be so. (I have the feeling that sacralizing or seeing unitively is in some way different from ontifying, even though they overlap.)

The Vectorial Nature of Facts. I begin this approach with a quotation from Wertheimer (155):

> What is the structure? The situation, seven plus seven equals . . . is a system with a lacuna, a gap (*eine Leerstelle*). It is possible to fill the gap in various ways. The one completion—fourteen—corresponds to the situation, fits in the gap, is what is structurally demanded in this system, in this place, with its function in the whole. It does justice to the situation. Other completions, such as fifteen, do not fit. They are not the right ones. They are determined by caprice, in blindness or in violation of the function this gap has in the structure.

We have here the concepts of "systems," of the "gap," of different kinds of "completion," of the demands of the situation; the "requiredness."

The case is similar if a good mathematical curve has a gap, a place in which something is lacking. For the filling in of the gap, there are often, from the structure of the curve, determinations which indicate that the one completion is appropriate to the structure, is sensible, the right one; other completions are not. This is connected with the old concept of inner necessity. And not only logical operations, conclusions, etc., but also happenings, doings, being, can be, in this sense, sensible or senseless, logical or illogical.

We may formulate: Given a situation, a system with a *Leerstelle*, whether a given completion (*Lueckenfüllung*) does justice to the structure, is the "right" one, is often determined by the structure of the system, of the situation. There are requirements, structurally determined; there are possible in pure cases unambiguous decisions as to which completion does justice to the situation, which does not, which violates the requirements of the situation. . . . Here sits a hungry child; yonder a man, who is building a small house, and lacks a single brick. I have in one hand a piece of bread and in the other a brick. I give the hungry child the brick and take the soft bread to the man. Here we have two situations, two systems. The allotment is blind to the functions of the gap filling.

And then in a footnote, Wertheimer adds:

I cannot deal with this [a clarification of the terms "requiredness," etc.] here. I may only mention that the usual simple dichotomy of to be and ought to be has to be revised. "Determinations," "requirements" of such an order are objective qualities.

Similar statements were made by most of the other writers in *Documents of Gestalt Psychology* (45). As a matter of fact, the whole literature of Gestalt psychology is testimony to the fact that facts are dynamic and not just static; that they are not scalar (magnitude only) but rather vectorial (having both magnitude and direction) as Köhler (62) especially has pointed out. Even stronger examples can be found in the writings of Goldstein, Heider, Lewin, and Asch (39, 44, 75, 76, 7).

Facts don't just lie there, like oatmeal in a bowl; they do all sorts of things. They group themselves, and they complete themselves; an incompleted series "calls for" a good completion. The crooked picture on the wall begs to be straightened; the incompleted problem perseverates and annoys us until we finish it. Poor gestalten make themselves into better gestalten and unnecessarily complex percepts or memories simplify themselves. The musical progression demands the right chord which it needs for completion; the imperfect tends toward perfection. An unfinished problem points inexorably to its proper solution. "The logic of the situation demands . . ." we say. Facts have authority and demand-character. They may require of us; they may say "No" or "Yes." They lead us on, suggest to us, imply the next thing to do and guide us in one direction rather than another. Architects speak about the requirements of the site. Painters will say that the canvas "calls for" some more yellow. A dress designer will say that her dress needs a particular kind of hat to go with it. Beer goes with Limburger better than it goes with Roquefort or, as some people say, beer "likes" the one cheese more than it does the other.

Goldstein's work (39) especially demonstrates organismic "oughtiness." A damaged organism isn't satisfied just to be what it is, merely damaged. It strives, presses, and pushes; it fights and struggles with itself in order to make itself into a unity again. From being a Unity, minus a lost capacity, it presses toward becoming a new kind of Unity in which the lost capacity no longer destroys its Unity. It governs itself, makes itself, recreates itself. It is certainly active and not passive. That is, the Gestalt and Organismic psychologies are not only is-perceptive but they are also vector-perceptive (ought-perceptive?) instead of being ought-blind as the behaviorisms are, in which organisms only get passively "done-to," instead of also "doing," "calling for." From this point of view Fromm, Horney, and Adler may also be seen as *Is* and *Ought* perceptive. Sometimes I find it useful to think of the so-called neo-Freudians as synthesizing Freud (who wasn't holistic enough) with Goldstein and the Gestalt psychologists, rather than simply as deviants from Freud.

What I should like to maintain is that many of these dynamic characteristics of facts, these vectorial qualities, fall well within the semantic jurisdiction of the word "value." At the very least, they bridge the dichotomy between fact and value which is conventionally and unthinkingly held by most scientists and philosophers to be a defining characteristic of science itself. Many people define science as morally and ethically neutral, as having nothing to say about ends or oughts. They thus open the door to the inevitable consequence that if ends have to come from somewhere, and that if they cannot come from knowledge, then they must come from outside of knowledge.

The Creation of "Oughtiness" by "Facticity." This leads by easy stages into a more inclusive generalization, namely that increase in the "factiness" of facts, of their "facty" quality, leads simultaneously to increase in the "oughty" quality of these facts. Factiness generates oughtiness, we might say.

Facts create oughts! The more clearly something is seen or known, and the more true and unmistakable something becomes, the more ought-quality it acquires. The more "is" something becomes, the more "ought" it becomes—the more requiredness it acquires, the louder it "calls for" particular action. The more clearly perceived something is, the more "oughty" it becomes and the better a guide to action it becomes.

In essence, what this means is that when anything is clear enough or certain enough, true enough, real enough, beyond the point of doubt, then that something raises within itself its own requiredness, its own demand-character, its own suitabilities. It "calls for" certain kinds of action rather than others. If we define ethics, morals, and values as guides to action, then the easiest and best guides to the most decisive actions are very facty facts; the more facty they are, the better guides to action they are.

We can use an uncertain diagnosis as an example of this point. We know the unsureness, the wobbling and the wavering, the tolerance, the suggestibility, and the indecisiveness of the young psychiatrist who is interviewing someone and is not quite sure of what is what. When he gets many other clinical opinions and a whole battery of tests which support each other; and if these coincide with his own perceptions and he checks them repeatedly, he becomes absolutely certain, for instance, that the patient is a psychopath; then his behavior changes in a very important way toward certainty, toward decisiveness and sureness, toward knowing exactly what to do and when and how to do it. This feeling of certainty arms him against disagreement and contradiction by relatives, or by anyone else who thinks differently. He can drive right on through opposition simply because he is certain; this is another way of saying that he perceives the truth of the matter without any doubts. This knowledge enables him to plow ahead in spite of the pain he may have to inflict upon the patient, in spite of tears, protest, or hostility. You don't mind exerting strength if you are sure of yourself. Sure knowledge means sure ethical decision. Certainty in the diagnosis, then, means certainty in the treatment.

I have an example in my own experience of how moral sureness can come from factual certainty. As a graduate student I did researches in hypnosis. There was a university rule that hypnosis was forbidden, on the grounds, I gather, that it did not exist. But I was so certain that it did exist (because I was doing it), and I was so convinced that it was a royal road to knowledge and a necessary kind of research, that I was able to be absolutely psychopathic about my researches. I startled myself by my lack of scruples; I did not mind lying or stealing or hiding. I just did what had to be done because I was absolutely certain that it was the right thing to do. (Notice that the phrase "right thing to do" is *simultaneously a cognitive word and an ethical word*.)[7] I just knew better than they did. I was not necessarily angry at these people; I just simply regarded them as ignorant in the matter and paid no attention to them. (Here I pass by the very difficult problems of unjustified feelings of certainty; that is another problem.)

Another example: Parents are weak only when they are uncertain; they are definite and strong and clear when they are certain. If you know exactly what you are doing you do not fumble even if your child cries, has pains, or protests. If you know that you have to pull out a thorn or an arrow, or if you know that you have to cut in order to save the child's life, you can go ahead surely, definitely.

This is where knowledge brings certainty of decision, action, choice and what to do, and, therefore, strength of arm. This is very much like the situation with a surgeon or dentist. The surgeon opening up the abdomen and finding an inflamed appendix knows that it had better be cut out because if it bursts it will kill the person. This is an example of truth dictating what must be done, of the *is* dictating the *ought*.

All of this relates to the Socratic belief that no man will willingly choose falsehood over truth, or evil over good. The assumption here is that ignorance makes the bad choice possible. Not only this, but also

---

[7] "Wrong," "bad," "correct" are also such cognitive-evaluative words. A further illustration is the story of the English professor who told his students of two inelegant words that he did not want them to use in their writing. One was "lousy" and one was "swell." After an expectant hush, one student asked, "Well, what are they?"

the whole of Jeffersonian democratic theory is based on the conviction that full knowledge leads to right action, and that right action is impossible without full knowledge.

Perception of Facts and Values in Self-Actualizing People. Some years ago, I reported that self-actualizing people were 1) very good perceivers of reality and truth, and also 2) that they were generally unconfused about right and wrong, and made ethical decisions more quickly and more surely than average people (95). The first finding has been supported often enough since then; also I think we can understand it better today than was possible twenty years ago.

However, the second finding has remained something of a puzzle. Of course, we know more today of the psychodynamics of psychological health, and so we can feel more comfortable with this finding, and more inclined to expect that it will be confirmed as a fact by research in the future.

The context of our present discussion permits me to offer my strong impression (which must, of course, be confirmed by other observers) that these two findings may be intrinsically connected. That is, I think that the clear perception of values is in part a consequence of the clear perception of facts or, perhaps, they may even be the same thing.

What I have called B-cognition, the perception of the Being, the otherness, or the intrinsic nature of the person or thing, occurs more often in healthier people and seems to be not only a perception of the deeper *facticity* but also, at the same time, of the *oughtiness* of the object. That is to say, oughtiness is an *intrinsic* aspect of deeply perceived facticity; it is itself a fact to be perceived.

This oughtiness, demand character, or requiredness or built-in request-for-action, seems to affect only those people who can see clearly the intrinsic nature of the percept. Therefore, B-cognition can lead to moral sureness and decisiveness, in just about the same sense that the high IQ can lead to a clear perception of a complicated set of facts, or in about the same sense that a constitutionally sensitive aesthetic perceiver tends to see very clearly what color-blind people cannot see or what other people do not see. It makes no difference that one million color-blind people cannot see that the rug is colored green. They may think it is colored gray, but this will make no difference to the person who clearly, vividly, and unmistakably perceives the truth of the matter.

Because healthier, more perceptive people are less ought-blind—because they can let themselves perceive what the facts wish, what they call for, what they suggest, demand or beg for—because they can therefore permit themselves to be Taoistically guided by the facts —they will therefore have less trouble with all value decisions that rest in the nature of reality, or that are part of the nature of reality.

Insofar as the facty aspect of a percept is separable from the oughty aspect of that same percept, then it may help to speak separately of is-perceptiveness and is-blindness, and ought-perceptiveness and ought-blindness. I believe that the average person can then be described as is-perceptive but ought-blind. The healthy person is more ought-perceptive. Psychotherapy conduces to greater ought-perceptiveness. The greater moral decisiveness of my self-actualizing subjects may come directly from greater is-perceptiveness, greater ought-perceptiveness, or both.

Even if it complicates this issue, I cannot resist adding here that ought-blindness may be understood partly as a blindness to potentialities, to ideal possibilities. As an instance, let me cite Aristotle's ought-blindness about slavery. When he examined slaves he found that they were, in fact, slavish in character. This descriptive fact was then assumed by Aristotle to be the true, innermost, instinctual nature of slaves. Therefore, slaves are slaves by nature and they ought to be slaves. Kinsey made a similar mistake by confusing simple, surface, description with "normality." He couldn't see what "might" be. This was also true for Freud and his weak psychology of the female. Females in his time did not ordinarily amount to much in fact; but to fail to see their potentialities for further development was like failing to see that a child can grow into adulthood given a chance. Blindness to future possibilities, change, development, or potentialities leads inevitably to a kind of status quo philosophy in which "what is" (being all there is or can be) must then be taken as the norm. Pure description merely is, as Seeley has said about descriptive social scientists, an invitation to join the conservative party.[8] "Pure" value-free

---

[8] Thus far I have placed under the rubric "ought-perception" several separate kinds of perception. One is the perception of the Gestalt-vectorial (dynamic or directional) aspects of the perceptual field. Second is the perception of the future as now existing, i.e., of potentialities and possibilities for future growth and development. Third is the unitive type of perception in which the eternal and symbolic aspects of the percept are perceived simultaneously with its con-

description is, among other things, simply *sloppy* description.

Taoistic Listening. One finds what is right for oneself by listening carefully and Taoistically to one's inner voices, by listening in order to let oneself be molded, guided, directed. The good psychotherapist helps his patient in the same way—by helping the patient hear his drowned-out inner voices, the weak commands of his own nature on the Spinozistic principle that true freedom consists of accepting and loving the inevitable, the nature of reality.

Similarly, one finds out what is right to do with the world by the same kind of listening to *its* nature and voices, by being sensitive to *its* requiredness and suggestions, by hushing so that *its* voices may be heard; by being receptive, noninterfering, nondemanding, and letting-be.

We do this all the time in our daily lives. Carving a turkey is made easier by the knowledge of where the joints are, how to handle the knife and fork—that is, by possessing full knowledge of the facts of the situation. If the facts are fully known, they will guide us and tell us what to do. But what is also implied here is that the facts are very soft-spoken and that it is difficult to perceive them. In order to be able to hear the fact-voices it is necessary to be very quiet, to listen very receptively—in a Taoistic fashion. That is, if we wish to permit the facts to tell us their oughtiness, we must learn to listen to them in a very specific way which can be called Taoistic—silently, hushed, quietly, fully listening, noninterfering, receptive, patient, respectful of the matter-in-hand, courteous to the matter-in-hand.

This also is a modern phrasing of the old Socratic doctrine that no man with full knowledge could ever do evil. While we cannot go that far since we now know of sources of evil behavior other than ignorance, still we can agree with Socrates that ignorance of the facts is a major source of evil behavior. This is the same as saying that the facts themselves carry, within their own nature, suggestions about what *ought* to be done with them.

Fitting a key into a sticky lock is another kind of activity which had best be done Taoistically, gently, delicately, by feeling one's way. I

---

crete, immediate, and limited aspects. I am not sure how similar or how different from this is what I have called "ontification," the deliberate perception of an activity as an end and not only a means. Since they are different operations, I will keep them apart for the time being.

think we can all understand that this is also a very good way, and sometimes the best way, to solve geometry problems (156), therapeutic problems, marital problems, vocational choice, and others, as well as problems of conscience, of right and wrong.

This is an inevitable consequence of accepting the oughty quality of facts. If this quality is there, then it has to be perceived. We know that this is not an easy thing to do, and we shall have to study the conditions which maximize ought-perceptiveness.

9

Notes on Being-Psychology[1]

I. Definition of Being-Psychology
by Its Subject Matter, Problems, Jurisdictions

(Could also be called Onto-Psychology, Transcendental Psychology, Psychology of Perfection, Psychology of Ends)

1. Deals with ends (rather than with means or instruments); with end-states, end-experiences (intrinsic satisfactions and enjoyments); with persons insofar as they are ends-in-themselves (sacred, unique, noncomparable, equally valuable with every other person rather than as instruments or means-to-ends); with techniques of making means into ends, of transforming means-activities into end-activities. Deals with objects *per se*, as they are in their own nature, not insofar as they are self-validating, intrinsically valid, inherently valuable, *per se* valuable, needing no justification. Here-now states

[1] These pieces are not yet in final form, nor do they form a complete structure. They build upon the ideas presented in (89) and (95), and carry these ideas further toward their ideal limit. They were written during my tenure as Andrew Kay Visiting Fellow at the Western Behavioral Sciences Institute, La Jolla, California in 1961. Additional notes on Being-psychology are available in (84) and (86).

in which the present is experienced fully, *per se* (as end-in-itself), and not as repetition of past or prelude to future.

2. Deals with states of *finis* and of *telos;* i.e., of completion, climax, finality, ending, totality, consummation, finishing (states in which nothing is lacking, nothing more is needed or wanted, no improvement is possible). States of pure happiness, joy, bliss, rapture, ecstasy, fulfillment, realization, states of hopes fulfilled, of problems solved, of wishes granted, of needs gratified, of goals attained, of dreams realized. Already being there; having arrived rather than striving to get there. Peak experiences. States of pure success (transient disappearance of all negation).

2a. Unhappy, tragic states of completion and finality, insofar as they yield B-cognition. States of failure, of hopelessness, of despair, of collapse of defenses, acute failure of value system, acute confrontation with real guilt, can *force* perception of truth and reality (as an end and no longer as a means) in some instances where there is enough strength and courage.

3. States felt to be, perceived to be perfect. Concepts of perfection. Ideals, models, limits, examplars, abstract definitions. The human being insofar as he potentially is, or can be conceived to be perfect, ideal, model, authentic, fully human, paradigmatic, godlike, exemplary, or insofar as he has potentialities and vectors in these directions (i.e., man as he *might* be, *could* be, or potentially *is* under best conditions; the ideal limits of human development, to which he approaches, but never attains permanently). His Destiny, Fate. These ideal human potentialities extrapolated out from the ideal far goals of psychotherapy, education, family training, end product of growth, self-development, etc. (See "Operations Which Define B-Values.") Deals with Definition of Core and with defining characteristics of the human being; his nature; his "intrinsic core" or "inner core"; his essence, his presently existing potentialities; his *sine qua nons* (instincts, constitution, biological nature, inherent, intrinsic human nature). This makes possible definition (quantitatively) of "full humanness" or "degree of humanness" or "degree of human diminution." Philosophical Anthropology in European sense. Differentiate *"sine qua non,"* defining characteristics (which define the concept "humanness"), *from* the exemplar (model, Platonic idea, ideal possibility, perfect idea, hero, template, die). Former is the

minimum; latter is the maximum. Latter is pure, static Being which the former tries to Become. Former has very low entrance requirements to the class, e.g., human is featherless biped. Also membership is all-or-none, in or out.

4. States of desirelessness, purposelessness, of lack of D-need (deficiency-need), of being unmotivated, noncoping, nonstriving, of enjoying rewards, of having been satisfied. Profit taking. (Able, therefore, "to leave one's interests, wishes, and aims entirely out of sight; thus of entirely renouncing one's own personality for a time, so as to remain pure knowing subject . . . with clear vision of the world"—Schopenhauer.)

4a. States of fearlessness; anxiety-free states. Courage. Unhampered, freely flowing, uninhibited, unchecked human nature.

5. Metamotivation (dynamics of action when all the D-needs, lacks, wants, have been satisfied). Growth motivation. "Unmotivated" behavior. Expression. Spontaneity.

5a. States and processes of pure (primary and/or integrated) creativeness. Pure here-now activity ("freedom" from past or future insofar as this is possible). Improvisation. Pure fitting of person and situation (problem) to each other, moving toward person-situation fusion as an ideal limit.

6. Descriptive, empirical, clinically or personologically or psychometrically described states of fulfillment of the promise (or destiny, vocation, fate, call), of the self; (self-actualization, maturity, the fully evolved person, psychological health, authenticity, attainment of "real self," individuation, the creative personality, identity, realizing or actual-izing of potentiality).

7. Cognition of Being (B-cognition). Transactions with extrapsychic reality which are centered upon the nature of that reality rather than upon the nature of, or interests of, the cognizing self. Penetration to the essence of things or persons. Perspicuity.

7a. Conditions under which B-cognition occurs. Peak experiences. Nadir-or-desolation experiences. B-cognition before death. B-cognition under acute psychotic regression. Therapeutic insights as B-cognition. Fear and evasion of B-cognition; dangers of B-cognition.

(1.) Nature of the percept in B-cognition. Nature of reality as *described* and as *ideally extrapolated* under B-cognition, i.e.

under "best" conditions. Reality conceived to be independent of the perceiver. Reality unabstracted. (See note on B-cognition and D-cognition.)

(2.) Nature of the perceiver in B-cognition. Veridical because detached, desireless, unselfish, "disinterested," Taoistic, fearless, here-now (See note on Innocent Perceiving), receptive, humble (not arrogant), without thought of selfish profit, etc. Ourselves as most efficient perceivers of reality.

8. Transcending time and space. States in which they are forgotten (absorption, focal attention, fascination, peak experiences, Nadir experiences), irrelevant or hampering or harmful. Cosmos, people, objects, experiences seen insofar as they are timeless, eternal, spaceless, universal, absolute, ideal.

9. The sacred; sublime, ontic, spiritual, transcendent, eternal, infinite, holy, absolute; states of awe; of worship, oblation, etc. "Religious" states insofar as they are naturalistic. Everyday world, objects, people seen under the aspect of eternity. Unitive Life. Unitive consciousness. States of fusion of temporal and eternal, of local and universal, of relative and absolute, of fact and value.

10. States of innocence (using child or animal as paradigm). (See B-cognition), (using mature, wise, self-actualizing person as paradigm). Innocent perceiving (ideally no discrimination of important and unimportant; everything equally probable; everything equally interesting; less differentiation of figure and ground; only rudimentary structuring and differentiation of environment; less means-ends differentiation, as everything tends to be equally valuable in itself; no future, no prognosis, no foreboding, therefore no surprises, apprehensions, disappointments, expectations, predictions, anxieties, rehearsals, preparations, or worries; one thing is as likely to happen as another; noninterfering-receptiveness; acceptance of whatever happens; little choosing, preferring, selecting, discriminating; little discrimination of relevance from irrelevance; little abstraction; wonder.) Innocent behaving (spontaneity, expressiveness, impulsiveness; no fear, controls, or inhibitions; no guile, no ulterior motives; honesty; fearlessness; purposeless; unplanned, unpremeditated, unrehearsed; humble (not arrogant); no impatience (when future unknown); no impulse to improve world, or reconstruct it

(Innocence overlaps with B-cognition very much; perhaps they will turn out to be identical in the future).

11. States tending toward ultimate holism, i.e., the whole cosmos, all of reality, seen in a unitary way; insofar as everything is everything else as well, insofar as anything is related to everything; insofar as all of reality is a single thing which we perceive from various angles. Bucke's cosmic consciousness (18). Fascinated perception of a portion of the world as if it were the whole world. Techniques of seeing something as if it were all there was, e.g., in art and photography, cropping, magnification, blowing up, etc. (which cut off object from all its relations, context, imbeddedness, etc., and permit it to be seen in itself, absolutely, freshly). Seeing *all* its characteristics rather than abstracting in terms of usefulness, danger, convenience, etc. The Being of an object is the whole object; abstracting necessarily sees it from the point of view of means and takes it out of the realm of the *per se*.

Transcending of separateness, discreteness, mutual exclusiveness, and of law of excluded middle.

12. The observed or extrapolated characteristics (or Values) of Being. (See List of B-Values). The B-realm. The Unitive Consciousness. See attached memo for the operations that give definition to the B-Values [section IV below].

13. All states in which dichotomies (polarities, opposites, contradictories) are resolved (transcended, combined, fused, integrated), e.g., selfishness and unselfishness, reason and emotion, impulse and control, trust and will, conscious and unconscious, opposed or antagonistic interests, happiness and sadness, tears and laughter, tragic and comic, Apollonian and Dionysian, romantic and classical, etc. All integrating processes which transform oppositions into synergies, e.g., love, art, reason, humor, etc.

14. All synergic states (in world, society, person, nature, self, etc.). States in which selfishness becomes the same as unselfishness (when by pursuing "selfish ends" I *must* benefit everyone else; and when by being altruistic, I benefit myself, i.e., when the dichotomy is resolved and transcended). States of society when virtue pays, i.e., when it is rewarded extrinsically as well as intrinsically; when it doesn't cost too much to be virtuous, or intelligent, or perspicuous, or beautiful or honest, etc. All states which foster and encourage the

B-Values to be actualized. States in which it is easy to be good. States which discourage resentment, counter-values and counter-morality (hatred and fear of excellence, truth, goodness, beauty, etc.). All states which increase the correlation between the true, the good, the beautiful, etc., and move them toward their ideal unity with each other.

15. States in which the Human Predicament (Existential Dilemma) is transiently solved, integrated, transcended, or forgotten, e.g., peak experience, B-humor and laughter, the "happy ending," triumph of B-justice, the "good death," B-love, B-art, B-tragedy or comedy, all integrative moments, acts, and perceptions, etc.

II. Collation of the Various Ways in Which the Word "Being" Has Been Used in Toward a Psychology of Being (89)

1. It has been used to refer to the whole cosmos, to everything that exists, to all of reality. In peak experiences, in states of fascination, of focal attention, attention can narrow down to a single object or person which is then reacted to "as if" it were the whole of Being, i.e., the whole of reality. This implies that it is all holistically interrelated. The only complete and whole thing there is is the whole Cosmos. Anything short of that is partial, incomplete, shorn away from intrinsic ties and relations for the sake of momentary, practical convenience. It refers also to Cosmic Consciousness. Also implies hierarchical integration rather than dichotomizing.

2. It refers to the "inner core," the biological nature of the individual—his basic needs, capacities, preferences; his irreducible nature; the "real self" (Horney); his inherent, essential, intrinsic nature. Identity. Since "inner core" is both species-wide (every baby has the need to be loved) and individual (only Mozart was perfectly Mozartian), the phrase can mean either "being fully human" and/or "being perfectly idiosyncratic."

3. Being can mean "expressing one's nature," rather than coping, striving, straining, willing, controlling, interfering, commanding (in the sense that a cat is being a cat, as contrasted with the sense in which a female impersonator is being a female, or a stingy person "tries" to be generous). It refers to effortless spontaneity (as an intel-

ligent person expresses intelligence, as a baby is babyish) which permits the deepest, innermost nature to be seen in behavior. Since spontaneity is difficult, most people can be called the "human impersonators," i.e., they are "trying" to be what they think is human, rather than just being what they are. It therefore also implies honesty, nakedness, self-disclosure. Most of the psychologists who have used it include (covertly) the hidden, not-yet-sufficiently-examined assumption that a neurosis is *not* part of the deepest nature, the inner core, or the real Being of the person, but is rather a more superficial layer of the personality which conceals or distorts the *real self*, i.e., neurosis is a defense against real Being, against one's deep, biological nature. "Trying" to be may not be as good as "being" (expressing), but it is also better than *not* trying, i.e., hopelessness, not coping, giving up.

4. Being can refer to the *concept* "human being," "horse," etc. Such a concept has defining characteristics, includes and excludes from membership within it by specific operations. For human psychology this has limitations because any person can be seen *either* as a member, or example, of the concept or class "human being," *or* as the sole member of the unique class "Addison J. Sims."

Also, we can use the class concept in two extremely different ways, minimum or maximum. The class can be defined minimally so that practically no one is excluded. This gives us no basis for grading quality or for discriminating among human beings in any way. One is either a member of the class or not a member of the class, either in or out. No other status is possible.

Or else the class can be defined by its perfect exemplars (models, heroes, ideal possibilities, Platonic ideas, extrapolations out to ideal limits and possibilities). This usage has many advantages, but its abstract and static quality must be kept in mind. There is a profound difference between describing carefully the best actual human beings I can get (self-actualizing people), none of whom are perfect, and on the other hand, describing the ideal, the perfect, the conceptually pure concept of the exemplar, constructed by extrapolating out ahead from the descriptive data on actual, imperfect people. The *concept* "self-actualizing people" describes not only the people but also the ideal limit which they approach. This should make no difficulty. We are used to blueprints and diagrams of "the" steam engine, or automobile, which are certainly never confused with, e.g., a photograph of my automobile or your steam engine.

Such a conceptual definition gives the possibility also of distinguishing the essential from the peripheral (accidental, superficial, nonessential). It gives criteria for discriminating the real from the not-real, the true from the false, the necessary from the dispensable or expendable, the eternal and permanent from the passing, the unchanging from the changeable.

5. Being can mean the "end" of developing, growing, and becoming. It refers to the end product or limit, or goal, or *telos* of becoming rather than to its process, as in the following sentence: "In this way, the psychologies of being and of becoming can be reconciled, and the child, simply being himself, can yet move forward and grow." This sounds very much like Aristotle's "final cause," or the telos, the final product, the sense in which the acorn now has within its nature the oak tree which it will become. (This is tricky because it is our tendency to anthropomorphize and say that the acorn is "trying" to grow up. It is not. It is simply "being" an infant. In the same way that Darwin could not use the word "trying" to explain evolution, so also must we avoid this usage. We must explain its growth forward toward its limit as an epiphenomenon of its being, as "blind" byproducts of contemporary mechanisms, and processes.)

III. The Being-Values (as Descriptions of the World Perceived in Peak Experiences)

The characteristics of being are also the values of being. (Paralleled by the characteristics of fully human people, the preferences of full human people; the characteristics of selfhood [identity] in peak experiences; the characteristics of ideal art; the characteristics of ideal children; the characteristics of ideal mathematical demonstrations, of ideal experiments and theories, of ideal science and knowledge; the far goals of all ideal [Taoistic noninterfering] psychotherapies; the far goals of ideal humanistic education; the far goals and the expression of some kinds of religion; the characteristics of the ideally good environment and of the ideally good society.)

1. *Truth:* honesty; reality; (nakedness; simplicity; richness;

essentiality; oughtness; beauty; pure; clean and unadulterated completeness).

2. *Goodness:* (rightness; desirability; oughtness; justice; benevolence; honesty); (we love it, are attracted to it, approve of it).

3. *Beauty:* (rightness; form; aliveness; simplicity; richness; wholeness, perfection; completion; uniqueness; honesty).

4. *Wholeness:* (unity; integration; tendency to oneness; interconnectedness; simplicity; organization; structure; order, not dissociated; synergy; homonomous and integrative tendencies).

4a. *Dichotomy-transcendence:* (acceptance, resolution, integration, or transcendence of dichotomies, polarities, opposites, contradictions); synergy (i.e., transformation of oppositions into unities, of antagonists into collaborating or mutually enhancing partners).

5. *Aliveness:* (process; not-deadness; spontaneity; self-regulation; full-functioning; changing and yet remaining the same; expressing itself).

6. *Uniqueness:* (idiosyncrasy; individuality; noncomparability; novelty; quale; suchness; nothing else like it).

7. *Perfection:* (nothing superfluous; nothing lacking; everything in its right place, unimprovable; just-rightness; just-so-ness; suitability; justice, completeness; nothing beyond; oughtness).

7a. *Necessity:* (inevitability; it must be *just* that way; not changed in any slightest way; and it is good that it *is* that way).

8. *Completion:* (ending; finality; justice; it's finished; no more changing of the Gestalt; fulfillment; *finis* and *telos;* nothing missing or lacking; totality; fulfillment of destiny; cessation; climax; consummation closure; death before rebirth; cessation and completion of growth and development).

9. *Justice:* (fairness; oughtness; suitability; architectonic quality; necessity; inevitability; disinterestedness; nonpartiality).

9a. *Order:* (lawfulness; rightness; nothing superfluous; perfectly arranged).

10. *Simplicity:* (honesty; nakedness; essentiality; abstract, unmistakability; essential skeletal structure; the heart of the matter; bluntness; only that which is necessary; without ornament, nothing extra or superfluous).

11. *Richness:* (differentiation; complexity; intricacy; totality; nothing missing or hidden; all there; "nonimportance"; i.e., every-

thing is equally important; nothing is unimportant; everything left the way it is, without improving, simplifying, abstracting, rearranging).

12. *Effortlessness:* (ease; lack of strain, striving, or difficulty; grace; perfect and beautiful functioning).

13. *Playfulness:* (fun; joy; amusement; gaiety; humor; exuberance; effortlessness).

14. *Self-sufficiency:* (autonomy; independence; not-needing-anything-other-than-itself-in-order-to-be-itself; self-determining; environment-transcendence; separateness; living by its own laws; identity).

IV. Operations Which Define the Meanings of the Being-Values in Testable Form

1. First seen as described characteristics of self-actualizing (psychologically healthy) people, as reported by themselves and as perceived by investigator and by people close to them (Values 1, 2, 3, 4, 4a, 5, 6, 7, (?), 8, 9, 9a, 10, 11, 12, 13, 14, and also perspicuity, acceptance, ego-transcendence, freshness of cognition, more peak experiences, *Gemeinschaftsgefühl*, B-love, nonstriving, B-respect, creativeness$_{sa}$[2]).

2. Seen as preferences, choices, desiderata, values of self-actualizing people, in themselves, in other people, in the world (granted fairly good environmental conditions and fairly good chooser). Some likelihood that many more than self-actualizing people have same, though weaker preferences, needing, however, *very* good environmental conditions and *very* good condition of the chooser. The probability of preference for any and all of the B-Values increases with increase in a) psychological health of the chooser. The probability of preference for any and all of the B-Values increases with increase in a) psychological health of the chooser, b) synergy of the environment, and c) strength, courage, vigor, self-confidence, etc. of chooser.

Hypothesis: The B-Values are what many (most? all?) people deeply *yearn for* (discoverable in deep therapy).

Hypothesis: The B-Values are ultimate satisfiers, whether or not

---

[2] The author suggests the use of qualifying subscripts for many subjective terms, in this case "sa," indicating self-actualizing. (See 95, p. 362.)—ED.

consciously sought, preferred, or yearned for; i.e., bring feelings of perfection, completion, fulfillment, serenity, destiny fulfilled, etc. Also in terms of producing good effects (therapeutic and growth).[3]

3. Reported to the investigator as characteristics of the world (or as trends toward such characteristics) perceived in the peak experiences by the peak experiencers (i.e., the way the world looks in the various peak experiences). These data supported in general by the common reports in the literatures on mystic experience, love experience, aesthetic experience, creative experiences, parental and reproductive experiences, intellectual insight, therapeutic insights (not always), athletic sports, bodily experiences (sometimes), and by some aspects of religious writings.

4. Reported to the investigator as characteristics of the self by peak experiencers ("acute identity-experiences"); (all values with possible exception of 9, plus creativeness$_{sa}$; here-now quality; non-striving which may be taken as exemplifying 5, 7, 12; poetic communication).

5. Observed by the investigator as characteristics of the behavior of the peak experiencers (same as #4 preceding).

6. Same for other B-cognitions when there is sufficient strength and courage; e.g., some foothill experiences; some Nadir and desolation experiences (psychotic regression, confrontation with death, destruction of defenses, illusions or value-systems, tragedy and tragic experiences, failures, confrontation with human predicament or existential dilemma); some intellectual and philosophical insights, constructions and workings-through; B-cognition of the past ("embracing the past"). This "operation" or source of data not sufficient in itself; i.e., needs other validations. Sometimes supports findings by other operations, sometimes contradicts them.

7. Observed as characteristics of "good" art ("good" so far means "preferred by this investigator"); e.g., painting, sculpture, music, dancing, poetry, and other literary arts; (all values except 9, and with some exceptions to 7 and 8).

A pilot experiment: Children's nonrepresentational paintings rated by artistic judges on ten-point scale from "most generally aesthetic quality" to "least generally aesthetic quality," another set of judges rating all these paintings on ten-point scale for "wholeness," another

[3] See Chapter 3 in *Toward a Psychology of Being* (89).

set of judges rating for "aliveness," another set of judges rating for "uniqueness." All four variables correlate positively. *A pilot investigation:* leaves impression that it is possible by examination of paintings or short stories to make a better-than-chance judgment about the health of the artist.

Testable Hypothesis: That the correlation between beauty, wisdom, and goodness and psychological health increases with age. People in increasing age decades to be rated for health, beauty, goodness, and wisdom, each rating by different sets of judges. Correlation should be positive throughout and should be higher for people in the thirties, still higher in the forties, etc. So far hypothesis supported by casual observation.

Hypothesis: Rating novels in all fifteen B-Values will show that "poor" novels (so rated by judges) are less close to the B-Values than "good" novels. Same for "good" music and "poor" music. Non-normative statements are possible also; e.g., which painters, which words, what kind of dancing help to heighten or to strengthen or exemplify individuality, honesty, self-sufficiency, or other B-Values. Also, which books, poems are preferred by more matured people. How possible is it to use healthy people as "biological assays" (more sensitive and efficient perceivers and choosers of B-Values, like canaries in a coal mine)?

8. What little we know about the characteristics of and the determinants of increasing and decreasing psychological health in children of all ages in our culture indicates on the whole that increasing health means movement toward various and perhaps all of the B-Values. "Good" external conditions in school, family, etc., may then be defined as conducive to psychological health or toward the B-Values. Phrasing this in terms of testable hypotheses would yield, e.g., psychologically healthier children are more honest (beautiful, virtuous, integrated, etc. . . .) than less healthy children, health to be measured by projective tests or behavior samples or psychiatric interview, or absence of classical neurotic symptoms, etc.

Hypothesis: Psychologically healthier teachers should produce movement toward the B-Values in their students, etc.

Question in non-normative style: Which conditions increase and which decrease integration in children? Honesty, beauty, playfulness, self-sufficiency, etc.?

9. "Good" (Value 2) or "elegant" mathematical demonstrations are the ultimate in "simplicity" (10), in abstract truth (1), in perfection and completion and "order" (7, 8, 9). They can be and often are seen as very beautiful (3). Once done, they look easy and *are easy* (12). This move toward, yearning for, love for, admiration for, even in some people need for perfection, etc., is roughly paralleled by all machine makers, engineers, production engineers, toolmakers, carpenters, specialists in administration and organization in business, army, etc. They too show *Drang nach* the above B-Values. This should be measurable in terms of choices between: e.g., an elegantly simple machine, and an unnecessarily complex one, a well balanced hammer and a clumsily balanced hammer, a "fully" functioning engine and a partially functioning one (5), etc. Healthier engineers, carpenters, etc., should spontaneously demonstrate greater preference for and closeness to the B-Values in all their products, which should be more preferred, command a higher price, etc., than the less "B-ward" products of less developed and evolved engineers, carpenters, etc. Something similar is probably also true of the "good" experiment, the "good" theory and for "good" science in general. It is probable that a strong determinant of the use of the word "good" in these contexts is "closer to the B-Values" in about the same sense as is true for mathematics.

10. Most (insight, uncovering, nonauthoritarian, Taoistic) psychotherapists, of whatever school, when they can be induced to speak of the ultimate goals of psychotherapy, will even today, speak of the fully human, authentic, self-actualizing, individuated person, or some approximation thereof both in the descriptive sense and in the sense of the ideal, abstract concept. When teased out into subdetails, this usually means some or all of the B-Values; e.g., honesty (1), good behavior (2), integration (4), spontaneity (5), movement toward fullest development and maturing and harmonizing of potentialities (7, 8, 9), being what one fully is in essence (10), being all that one can be and accepting one's deeper self in all its aspects (11), effortless, easy functioning (12), ability to play and to enjoy (13), independence, autonomy, and self-determination (14). I doubt that any therapist would seriously object to any of these, although some might want to add.

Massive evidence on the actual effects of successful and unsuccessful psychotherapy comes from the Rogers group, and all of it, without exception so far as I am aware, supports or is compatible with the hypothesis that the B-Values are the far goal of psychotherapy. This operation—i.e., before and after psychotherapy—is available for putting to the test the as yet untested hypothesis that therapy also increases the beauty of the patient and also his sensitiveness to, yearning for, and enjoyment of beauty. A parallel set of hypotheses for humor$_{sa}$ is also testable.

Pilot experiment: Unquantified observation from two-year-long experiments with group therapy; both the college boys and the college girls in general looked more beautiful or handsome both to me and to the participants themselves (and actually became more beautiful, attractive as measured by the judgment of strangers) because of increased self-love and self-respect and increased pleasure in pleasing the group members (out of increased love for them). In general, if we stress the uncovering aspect of therapy, then whatever it reveals was there already in some sense. Therefore, whatever emerges or is revealed by uncovering therapy is very likely to be constitutionally or temperamentally or genetically intrinsic to the organism; i.e., its essence, its deepest reality, is biologically given. That which is dissipated by uncovering therapy is thereby proven to be, or at least indicated to be, *not* intrinsic, or inherent, but rather accidental, superficial, acquired by or imposed upon the organism. The relevant evidence which indicates that the B-Values are strengthened or actualized by uncovering therapy therefore supports the belief that these B-Values are attributes or defining characteristics of the deepest, most essential, most intrinsic human nature. This general proposition is quite testable in principle. Rogers' technique of "moving toward and away from" in therapy (129) offers a wide range of possibilities of research on what helps movement toward and away from B-Values.

11. The far goals of "creative," "humanistic," or "whole person" education, especially nonverbal (art, dance, etc.) education, overlap very considerably with the B-Values, and may turn out to be identical with them, plus all sorts of psychotherapeutic additions which are probably means rather than ends. That is, this kind of education half-consciously wants the same kind of end product as ideal psychotherapy. All the kinds of research that have been done and will be done on the effects of therapy can, therefore, in principle be paralleled

with "creative" education. As with therapy, so also with education, can be seen the possibility of winding up with a usable, normative concept—i.e., that education is "good" which best "be-ifies" the student; i.e., helps him to become more honest, good, beautiful, integrated, etc. This probably holds true also for higher education, if the acquisition of skills and tools is excluded, or seen only as a means to ultimate Being-ends.

12. About the same is true for certain versions of the large theistic and nontheistic religions, and for both the legalistic and mystical versions of each of these. On the whole they propagate: a) a God who is the embodiment of most of the B-Values; b) the ideal, religious, and Godly man is one who best exemplifies or at least yearns for these same "Godlike" B-Values; c) all techniques, ceremonials, rituals, dogmas can be seen as means toward achieving these ends; d) heaven is the place or state, or time of achievement of these values. Salvation, redemption, conversion, are all acceptances of the truth of the above, etc. Since these propositions are supported by selected evidence, they need a principle of selection outside themselves; i.e., they are compatible with B-psychology, but do not prove it to be true. The literature of religion is a useful storehouse if one knows what to pick and use. As with other propositions above, we may turn things about and offer as theoretical proposition to try out, e.g., B-Values are definers of "true" or functional, usable, helpful religion. This criterion is probably best satisfied now by a combination of Zen and Tao and Humanism.

13. It is my impression that *most* people move away from B-Values under hard or bad environmental conditions that threaten the D-need gratifications, e.g., concentration camps, prison camps, starvation, plague, terror, hostility from the environment, abandonment, rootlessness, widespread breakdown of value systems, absence of value systems, hopelessness, etc. It is not known why a *few* people under these very same "bad" conditions, move toward the B-Values. However, both kinds of movement are testable.

Hypothesis: That one useful meaning of "good conditions" is "synergy," defined by Ruth Benedict as "social-institutional conditions which fuse selfishness and unselfishness, by arranging it so that when I pursue 'selfish' gratifications, I automatically help others, and when I try to be altruistic, I automatically reward and gratify myself also; i.e., when the dichotomy or polar opposition between selfishness and altruism is resolved and transcended." Thus the hypotheses: a good society is one in which virtue pays; the more the synergy in a society or subgroup or pair or within a self, the closer we come to the B-Values; poor social or environmental conditions are those which set us against each other by making our personal interests antagonistic to each other, or mutually exclusive, or in which the personal gratifications (D-needs) are in short supply so that not all can satisfy their needs, except at the expense of others. Under good conditions, we have to pay little or nothing for being virtuous, for pursuing the B-Values, etc.; under good conditions, the virtuous businessman is more successful financially; under good conditions, the successful person is loved rather than hated or feared or resented; under good conditions, admiration is more possible (unmixed with erotization or dominatization, etc.).

14. There is some evidence to indicate that what we call "good" jobs and "good" working conditions on the whole help to move people toward the B-Values; e.g., people in less desirable jobs value safety and security most, while people in the most desirable jobs most often value highest the possibilities for self-actualization. This is a special case of "good" environmental conditions. Again the possibility is implied here of moving toward non-normative statements, e.g. which work conditions produce greater wholeness, honesty, idiosyncrasy, etc., thereby replacing the word "good" with the phrase "conducing to the B-Values."

15. The hierarchy of basic needs and their order of prepotency was discovered by the operation of a "reconstructive biology," i.e., the frustration of which needs produce neurosis. Perhaps one day not too far off we shall have sensitive enough psychological instruments to put to the test the hypothesis that threat to or frustration of any of the B-Values produces a kind of pathology or existential illness, or a feeling of human diminution, i.e., that they are also "needs" in the above sense (that we yearn for them in order to complete ourselves or become fully human). At any rate, it is possible now to ask the researchable questions which have not yet been researched, "What are the effects of living in a dishonest world, an evil world, an ugly world, a split, disintegrated world, a dead, static world, a world of clichés and stereotypes, an incomplete, unfinished world, a world

without order or justice, an unnecessarily complicated world, an over-simplified, overabstract world, an effortful world, a humorless world, a world without privacy or independence?"

16. I have already pointed out that one usable operational meaning of the "good society" is the degree to which it offers all its members the basic need satisfactions and the possibilities of self-actualization and human fulfillment. To this phrasing can be added the proposition "the good society" (by contrast with the poor society) exemplifies, values, strives for, makes possible the achievement of the B-Values. This can also be phrased non-normatively, as we have done above. The abstractly ideal Eupsychia would perfectly achieve the B-Values. To what extent is the good society (Eupsychia) the same as the synergic society?

V. How Can Being-Love Bring Disinterest, Neutrality, Detachment, Greater Perspicuity?

When does Love sometimes bring blindness? When does it mean *greater* and when lesser perspicuity?

The point at which a corner is turned is when the love becomes so great and so pure (unambivalent) for the object itself that *its* good is what we want, not what it can do for us, i.e., when it passes beyond being means and becomes an end (with our permission). As with the apple tree for instance: We can love *it* so much that we don't want it to be anything else; we are happy it is as it is. Anything that interferes with it ("butts in") can do *only* harm and make it *less* an apple tree, or less perfectly living by its own intrinsic, inherent rules. It can look so perfect that we're afraid to touch it for fear of lessening it. Certainly, if it is seen as perfect, there is no possibility of improving it. As a matter of fact, the effort to improve (or decorate, etc.) is itself a proof that the object is seen as less than perfect, that the picture of "perfect development" in the improver's head is conceived by him to be better than the final end of the apple tree itself; i.e., he can do better than the apple tree, he knows better; he can shape it better than it can itself. So we feel half-consciously that the dog-improver is not really a dog-lover. The real dog-lover will be enraged by the tail cropping, the ear cropping or shaping, the selective breeding that makes this dog fit a pattern from some magazine, at the cost of making it nervous, sick, sterile, unable to give birth normally, epileptic, etc. (And yet such people do call themselves dog-lovers.) Same for people who train dwarf-trees, or teach bears to ride a bicycle, or chimpanzees to smoke cigarettes.

Real love then is (sometimes at least) noninterfering and nondemanding and can delight in the thing itself; therefore, it can gaze at the object without guile, design, or calculation of any selfish kind. This makes for less abstracting (or selecting of parts or attributes or single characteristics of the object), less viewing of less-than-the-whole, less atomizing or dissecting. This is the same as saying that there is less active or Procrustean structuring, organizing, shaping, molding, or fitting-to-theory, or to a preconception; i.e., the object remains more whole, more unified, which amounts to saying, more itself. The object is less measured against criteria of relevance or irrelevance, importance or unimportance, figure or ground, useful or useless, dangerous or not-dangerous, valuable or valueless, profit or no-profit, good or bad, or other criteria of selfish human perceiving. Also the object is less apt to be rubricized, classified, or placed in a historical sequence, or seen as simply a member of a class, as a sample, or instance of a type.

This means that all the (unimportant as well as important) aspects or characteristics of (holistic) parts of the object (peripheral as well as central) are more apt to be given equal care or attention, and that *every* part is apt to be delightful and wonderful; B-love, whether of a lover, or a baby or a painting or a flower, almost always guarantees this kind of distributed looking-with-care-intense-and-fascinated.

Seen in this holistic context, little flaws are apt to be seen as "cute," charming, endearing, *because* idiosyncratic, because they give character and individuality to the object, because they make it what-it-is-rather-than-something-else, perhaps also *just* because they are unimportant, peripheral, nonessential.

Therefore, the B-lover (B-cognizer) will see details that will evade the D-lover or nonlover. Also he will more easily see the *per se* nature of the object itself, in its own right and in its own style of being. Its own delicate and cartilaginous structure is more likely to be yielded to by receptive looking, which is nonactive, noninterfering, less arrogant. That is, its perceived shape is more determined by its own shape when B-cognized than when a structure is imperiously imposed upon it by the perceiver, who will therefore be more likely to be too brusque, too impatient, too much the butcher hacking a carcass apart, for his own appetite, too much the conqueror demanding unconditional surrender, too much the sculptor modeling clay which has no structure of its own.

VI. Under What Condition and by Which People Are Being-Values Chosen or Not Chosen?

The evidence available shows that B-Values are more often chosen by "healthy" people (self-actualizing, mature, productive characters, etc.). Also by a preponderance of the "greatest," most admired, most loved people throughout history. (Is this why they are admired, loved, considered great?)

Animal experimentation on choice shows that strong habits, previous learning, etc., lowers the biological efficiency, flexibility, adaptability of self-healing choice, e.g., in adrenalectomized rats. Experiments with familiarization demonstrate that people will continue to choose and to prefer even the inefficient, the annoying, and the initially nonpreferred if previously forced to choose them over a ten-day period. General experience with human beings supports these findings, e.g., in the area of good habits. Clinical experience indicates that this preference for the habitual and familiar is greater and more rigid, compulsive, and neurotic in people who are more anxious, timid, rigid, constricted, etc. Clinical evidence and some experimental evidence indicate that ego-strength, courage, health, and creativeness make more likely in adults and children the choice of the new, the unfamiliar, the unhabitual.

Familiarization in the sense of adaptation also can cut the tendency to choose the B-Values. Bad smells cease to smell bad. The shocking tends to cease shocking. Bad conditions are adapted to and not noticed any more, i.e., cease to be conscious, even though their bad *effects* may continue without conscious awareness, e.g., effects of continued noise or of continued ugliness, or of chronically poor food.

Real choice implies equal and simultaneous presentation with the alternatives. For instance, people used to a poorly reproducing phonograph preferred it to a hi-fi phonograph. People used to the hi-fi preferred *that*. But when both groups were exposed to *both* poor and good music reproduction, both groups finally chose the better reproduction of the hi-fi (Eisenberg).

The preponderance of the experimental literature on discrimination shows that it is more efficient when the alternatives are simultaneously present and close together rather than far apart. We may expect that the selection of the more beautiful of two paintings, or the more honest of two wines, or the more alive of two human beings, will be more likely the closer together they are in space and time.

Proposed experiment: If the gamut of qualities is from 1 (poor cigars, wine, fabric, cheese, coffee, etc.) to 10 ("good" cigars, wine, etc.), the persons used to level 1 may very well choose 1, if the only alternative choice is at the other extreme, e.g., 10. But it is probable that the person will choose 2 rather than 1, 3 rather than 2, etc., and in this way be brought to choose level 10 finally. The alternative choices ought to be within the same realm of discourse, i.e., not too far apart. Using this same technique for those who initially prefer the very good wine, i.e., giving them a choice between 10 and 9, 9 and 8, 5 and 4, etc., they will probably continue to choose the higher value.

In the various senses above, uncovering insight therapy can be seen as leading up to a "real choice" process. The ability to make real choice is much greater after successful therapy than it was before, i.e., it is constitutionally rather than culturally determined, it is determined by the self rather than by the external or internal "others." The alternatives are conscious rather than unconscious, fear is minimized, etc. Successful therapy increases the tendency to prefer B-Values as well as to exemplify them.

This implies that characterological determinants of choosers must also be held constant or taken into account; e.g., learning that the "better" choice (higher in the hierarchy of values, going toward B-Values) tastes better by actually tasting it is more difficult for traumatized, negatively conditioned, or generally neurotic people, for shy, timid people, for narrowed, impoverished, coarcted people, for rigid, stereotyped, conventionalized people, etc. (because they may be afraid to try the experience, or to experience the taste, or may deny the experience, suppress it, repress it, etc.). This characterological control holds true in principle both for constitutional determinants and for acquired determinants.

Many experiments show that social suggestion, irrational advertising, social pressure, propaganda, have considerable effect against freedom of choice and even freedom of perception; i.e., the choices may be misperceived and then mis-chosen. This deleterious effect is greater in conforming rather than in independent, stronger people. There are clinical and social-psychological reasons for predicting that this effect is greater in younger than in older people. However, all of these effects, and similar ones, from e.g., subliminal conditioning, propaganda, prestige suggestion, or false advertising, subliminal stimuli, covert positive reinforcement, etc., rest upon blindness, ignorance, lack of insight, concealment, lying, and unawareness of the situation. Most of these effects can be eliminated by making the ignorant chooser consciously aware of the way in which he has been manipulated.

Really free choice—in which the inner, intrinsic nature of the chooser is the main determinant—is therefore enhanced by freedom from social pressure, by an independent rather than dependent personality, by chronological maturity, by strength and courage rather than by weakness and fear, and by truth, knowledge, and awareness. Satisfying each of these conditions should increase the percentage of B-choices.

The hierarchy of values, in which the B-Values are the "highest" is in part determined by the hierarchy of basic needs, by the prepotency of deficit-needs over growth-needs, by the prepotency of homeostasis over growth, etc. In general, where there are two lacks to be gratified, the more prepotent, i.e., the "lower," is chosen to be gratified. Therefore, an expectable, highly probable preference for B-Values rests in principle upon prior gratification of lower, more prepotent values. This generalization generates many predictions; for example, the safety-need-frustrated person will prefer the true to the false, the beautiful to the ugly, the virtuous to the evil, etc., less often than will the safety-need-gratified person.

This implies a restatement of the age-old problem: In what senses are "higher" pleasures (e.g., Beethoven) superior to "lower" pleasures (e.g., Elvis Presley)? How can this be *proven* to one "stuck" in the lower pleasures? Can it be taught? Especially can it be taught to one who doesn't want to be taught?

What are the "resistances" to the higher pleasures? The general answer (in addition to all the above considerations) is: The higher pleasures taste (feel) better than the lower ones, for instance, to anyone who can be induced to experience them both. But all the special, experimental conditions above are necessary in order for the person to be able to make a real choice, i.e., to be able fully and freely to compare the two tastes. Growth is theoretically possible *only* because the "higher" tastes are better than the "lower" and because the "lower" satisfaction becomes boring. (See Chapter 4 in *Toward a Psychology of Being* for discussion of "growth-through-delight-and-eventual-boredom-with consequent-seeking-for-new-higher-experience.")

Constitutional factors of another type also determine choices and therefore values. Chickens, laboratory rats, farm animals have all been found to vary from birth in efficiency of choice, especially of a good diet; i.e., some animals are efficient choosers and some are poor choosers, in a biological sense. That is, these latter poor choosers, will sicken or die if left to choose for themselves. The same is reported in an unofficial way for human infants by child psychologists, pediatricians, etc. All these organisms also vary in the energy with which they will struggle for satisfaction and the overcoming of frustration. In addition, constitution work with human adults shows that the different body types show some difference in choices of satisfactions. Neurosis is a powerful destroyer of choice-efficiency, preference for B-Values, preference for real need-satisfactions, etc. It is even possible to define psychological ill health by the degree to which that is chosen which is "bad" for the health of the organism, e.g., drugs, alcohol, bad diet, bad friends, bad jobs, etc.

Cultural conditions, in addition to all the obvious effects, are a main determinant of the range of choices possible, e.g., of careers, of diet, etc. Specifically, economic-industrial conditions are also important; e.g., large scale, profit-seeking, mass-distribution industry is very good at supplying us with, for example, inexpensive and well made clothes, and very bad at supplying us with good, unpoisoned foods such as chemical-free bread, insecticide-free beef, hormone-free fowl, etc.

Therefore, we may expect B-Values to be more strongly preferred by: 1. people who are more healthy, matured, 2. older, 3. stronger, more independent, 4. more courageous, 5. more educated, etc. One of the conditions which will increase the percentage of choice of B-Values is absence of great social pressure.

All the above can easily be cast in a non-normative form for those who get uneasy over the use of the terms "good" and "bad," "higher" and "lower," etc., even though these can be defined operationally. For instance, the nonhuman Martian could ask, "When and by whom and under what conditions is truth chosen rather than falsehood, integrated rather than disintegrated, complete rather than incomplete, orderly rather than disorderly, etc.?"

Another old question can also be rephrased in this more manageable way; i.e., Is man basically good or evil? No matter how we choose to define these words, man turns out to have both good and evil impulses, and to behave in both good and evil ways. (Of course, this observation doesn't answer the question of which is deeper, more basic, or more instinctlike.) For purposes of scientific investigation we had better rephrase this question to read: Under what conditions and when will who choose the B-Values, i.e., be "good"? What minimizes or maximizes this choice? What kind of society maximizes this choice? What kind of education? Of therapy? Of family? These questions in turn open up the possibility of asking, How can we make men "better"? How can we improve society?

10

Comments from a
Symposium on Human Values

These four papers[1] seem to be utterly dissimilar and yet in one way they are not really so. They assume and share certain basic

[1] Presented by Charlotte Buhler, Herbert Fingarette, Wolfgang Lederer, and Alan Watts on December 15, 1961, at the California State Psychological Association Meeting, San Francisco. Symposium Chairman Dr. Lawrence N. Solomon summarized each author's position:

In the lead paper, Dr. Buhler takes off from a psychoanalytic orientation to explore life's basic tendencies as a possible basis for a value system consonant with nature. She presents some of the empirical operations utilized to approach this area and suggests what appears to her, at this time, to be a most promising technique.

Dr. Fingarette tackles the philosophical problem of moral guilt and raises the profoundly meaningful question of whether or not behavior must always reflect an inner acceptance (on some level of consciousness) of the wish behind the deed. His affirmative answer to this question leads to some interesting conclusions regarding the distinction between moral and neurotic guilt.

Dr. Lederer, in his paper, shares with the reader his experiences as an analyst and, specifically, those significant events which led to his belief that psychotherapy must, in this day and age, be value-oriented. A therapist can no longer "listen long and silently, with free-floating attention, without criticism, without giving advice—uninvolved." Values enter psychotherapy when the therapist becomes sufficiently liberated to follow his own understanding and conscience in his therapeutic encounters with today's patient: the young man without identity.

(149

changes in belief about values, revolutionary changes that have come about only recently and that we should be conscious of.

There is no appeal in any of these papers to an extrahuman source or locus of values. No supernatural is involved, no sacred book, no hallowed tradition. All the speakers agree that the values which are to guide human action must be found within the nature of human and natural reality itself.

Not only is the locus of values implied to be natural but so also is the procedure for discovering these values. They are to be uncovered (or discovered) by human effort and by human cognition, by appealing to the experimental, clinical, and philosophical experiences of human beings. No powers are involved here that are not human powers.

The further implication is that they are to be *found*, that is, discovered or uncovered, rather than (or as well as) invented, constructed, or created. This implies further that they exist *in some sense* and *in some degree* and that they are, so to speak, waiting for us to see them. In this sense, values are being treated like other secrets of nature which we may not know much about at the moment but which will undoubtedly yield to our probing and searching.

All four papers by implication discard that simplistic conception of science which conceives it to be "objective" in the conventional sense, *only* public, *only* "out there," and which expects all scientific statements to be thrown into physicalistic form, if not now then in the future.

Such an acceptance of the psyche must of course destroy an exclusively objectivistic theory of science. Some people will feel that such "mentalism" will destroy *all* science, but I disagree with such a foolish notion. On the contrary, I claim that science with the psyche left in is far *more* powerful, rather than *less* powerful. For instance, I think that this larger and more inclusive conception of science can certainly handle problems of value with ease. As we know, the nar-

---

Dr. Watts' paper presents, for the Western reader, what may appear to be a novel, but at the same time fundamentally important, conceptualization of the nature of man. Drawing upon the Taoistic traditions, he portrays the human being inside the skin and the world outside the skin as having the skin as a common boundary between them which *belongs to both*. Such thinking lends itself easily to conceptualizations about the behavior of a unified field, and has meaningful implications for any theory of values and morality.

rower science which tried to be purely objectivistic and impersonal could then find no place *at all* for values, goals, or ends and so had to define them out of existence. Either their factuality had to be denied, or else put forever beyond the reach of scientific cognition (which made them "unimportant" and not worthy of serious examination). To talk about values became "unscientific" or even antiscientific, and so they were turned over to poets, philosophers, artists, religionists, and other softheaded though warmhearted people.

In other words these papers are essentially "scientific" even though in an older and more original sense of the word "science." These papers are not essentially different in spirit or approach, I would guess, from a discussion of vitamins around the year 1920 or 1925. They, too, were then in the clinical, pre-experimental stage as we are today.

If this is so, then of course we should keep discussion and hypothesizing open and diverse. We should not close off possibilities prematurely. The diversity of approaches in this symposium seems to be fitting and proper and could have been even greater if there had been time. This is no time for orthodoxies and I am glad to notice that the fierce and bitter arguments among the schools of twenty years ago have been replaced by a more humble recognition of collaboration and division of labor.

I believe it will also be humbling for us if we admit freely that we are impelled to our interest in values not only by the intrinsic logic of science and philosophy but also by the current historical position of our culture, or rather of our whole species. Throughout history values have been discussed only when they became moot and questionable. Our situation is that the traditional value systems have all failed, at least for thoughtful people. Since it seems to be impossible for us to live without values to believe in and approve of, we are now in the process of casting about in a new direction, namely, the scientific one. We are trying the new experiment of differentiating value-as-fact from value-as-wish, hoping thereby to discover values that we can believe in because they are true rather than because they are gratifying illusions.

PART IV

Education

11

Knower and Known

My general thesis is that many of the communication difficulties between persons are the byproduct of communication barriers *within* the person; and that communication between the person and the world, to and fro, depends largely on their isomorphism (i.e., similarity of structure or form); that the world can communicate to a person only that of which he is worthy, that which he deserves or is "up to"; that to a large extent, he can receive from the world, and give to the world, only that which he himself is. As Georg Lichtenberg said of a certain book, "Such works are like mirrors; if an ape peeps in, no apostle will look out."

For this reason, the study of the "innards" of the personality is one necessary base for the understanding of what a person can communicate to the world, and what the world is able to communicate to him. This truth is intuitively known to every therapist, every artist, every teacher, but it should be made more explicit.

Of course I take communication here in the very broadest sense. I include all the processes of perception and of learning, and all the forms of art and of creation. And I include primary-process cognition (archaic, mythological, metaphorical, poetic cognition) as well as verbal, rational, secondary-process communication. I want to speak of what we are blind and deaf to as well as what gets through to us; of what we express dumbly and unconsciously as well as what we can verbalize or structure clearly.

A main consequence of this general thesis—that difficulties with the outer parallel difficulties within the inner—is that we should expect communication with the outer world to improve along with improvement in the development of the personality, along with its integration and wholeness, and along with freedom from civil war among the various portions of the personality, i.e., perception of reality should improve. One then becomes more perceptive in the sense implied by Nietzsche when he says that one must have earned for oneself the distinction necessary to understand him.

Splits within the Personality

First of all, what do I mean by failure of internal communication? Ultimately the simplest example is that of dissociation of the personality, of which the most dramatic and most usually known form is the multiple personality. I have examined as many of these cases as I could find in the literature, and a few I had access to myself, along with the less dramatic fugues and amnesias. They seem to me to fall into a general pattern which I can express as a tentative general theory, which will be of use to us in our present task because it tells something about the splits in *all* of us.

In every case I know, the "normal" or presenting personality has been a shy or quiet or reserved person, most often a female, rather conventional and controlled, rather submissive and even self-abnegating, unaggressive and "good," tending to be mousy, and easily exploited. In every case I know of, the "personality" that broke through into consciousness and into control of the person was the very opposite, impulsive rather than controlled, self-indulgent rather than self-abnegating, bold and brassy rather than shy, flouting the conventions, eager for a good time, aggressive and demanding, immature.

This is, of course, a split that we can see in *all* of us in a less extreme form. This is the inward battle between impulse and control, between individual demands and the demands of society, between immaturity and maturity, between irresponsible pleasure and responsibility. To the extent that we succeed in being *simultaneously* the mischievous, childish rascal *and* the sober, responsible, impulse-controlling citizen, to that extent are we less split and more integrated. This, by the way, is the ideal therapeutic goal for multiple personalities: to retain both or all three personalities, but in a graceful fusion or integration under conscious or preconscious control.

Each of these multiple personalities communicates with the world, to and fro, in a different way. They talk differently, write differently, indulge themselves differently, make love differently, select different friends. In one case I had contact with, "the willful child" personality had a big, sprawling, child's handwriting, vocabulary, and misspelling; the "self-abnegating, exploitable" personality had a mousy, conventional, good-schoolgirl handwriting. One "personality" read and studied books. The other could not, being too impatient and uninterested. How different would have been their art productions, had we thought to get them.

In the rest of us, too, those portions of ourselves which are rejected and relegated to unconscious existence can and inevitably *do* break through into open effects upon our communication, both intake and output, affecting our perceptions as well as our actions. This is easily enough demonstrated by projective tests on one side and art expression on the other.

The projective test shows how the world looks to us, or better said, it shows how we organize the world, what we can take out of it, what we can let it tell us, what we choose to see, and what we choose *not* to listen to or see.

Something similar is true on our expressive side. We express what we are (95). To the extent that we are split, our expressions and communications are split, partial, onesided. To the extent that we are integrated, whole, unified, spontaneous, and fully functioning, to that extent are our expressions and communications complete, unique and idiosyncratic, alive and creative rather than inhibited, conventionalized, and artificial, honest rather than phony. Clinical experience shows this for pictorial and verbal art expressions, and for expressive movements in general, and probably also for dance, athletic, and other total bodily expressions. This is true not only for the communicative effects that we *mean* to have upon other people; it seems also to be true for the effects we do not mean to have.

Those portions of ourselves that we reject and repress (out of fear or shame) do not go out of existence. They do not die, but rather go underground. Whatever effects these underground portions of our human nature may thereafter have upon our communications tend either to be unnoticed by ourselves or else to be felt as if they were not part of us, e.g., "I don't know what made me say such a thing." "I don't know what came over me."

To me this phenomenon means that expression is not alone a cultural thing; it is also a biological phenomenon. We *must* talk about the instinctoid elements in human nature, those intrinsic aspects of human nature which culture cannot kill but only repress, and which continue to affect our expression—even though in a sneaky way—in spite of all that culture can do. Culture is only a necessary cause of human nature, not a sufficient cause. But so also is our biology only a necessary cause and not a sufficient cause of human nature. It is true that only in a culture can we learn a spoken language. But it is just as true that in that same cultural environment a chimpanzee will *not* learn to speak. I say this because it is my vague impression that communication is studied too exclusively at the sociological level and not enough at the biological level.

Pursuing this same theme, of the ways in which splits within the personality contaminate our communications to the world and from the world, I turn to several well-known pathological examples. I cite them also because they seem to be exceptions to the general rule that the healthy and integrated person tends to be a superior perceiver and expresser. There is both clinical and experimental evidence in large quantity for this generalization; for instance, the work of H. J. Eysenck and his colleagues. And yet, there are exceptions that force us to be cautious.

The schizophrenic is one in whom the controls and defenses are collapsing or have collapsed. The person then tends to slip into his private inner world, and his contact with other people and with the natural world tends to be destroyed. But this involves also some destruction of the communications to and from the world. Fear of the world cuts communication with it. So also can inner impulses and voices become so loud as to confuse reality-testing. But it is also true that the schizophrenic patient sometimes shows a selective superiority.

Because he is so involved with forbidden impulses and with primary-process cognition, he is reported occasionally to be extraordinarily acute in interpreting the dreams of others or in ferreting out the buried impulses of others, for instance, concealed homosexual impulses.

It can also work the other way about. Some of the best therapists with schizophrenics were schizophrenics themselves. And here and there we see a report that former patients can make exceptionally good and understanding ward attendants. This works on about the same principle as Alcoholics Anonymous. Some of my psychiatrist friends are now seeking this participant-understanding by having an experience of being transiently psychotic with LSD or mescaline. One way of improving communication with a Y is to *be* a Y.

In this area we can learn much also from the psychopathic personality, especially the "charming" type. They can be described briefly as having no conscience, no guilt, no shame, no love for other people, no inhibitions, and few controls, so that they pretty well do what they want to do. They tend to become forgers, swindlers, prostitutes, polygamists, and to make their living by their wits rather than by hard work. These people, because of their own lacks, are generally unable to understand in others the pangs of conscience, regret, unselfish love, compassion, pity, guilt, shame, or embarrassment. What you are not, you cannot perceive or understand. It cannot communicate itself to you. And since what you are does sooner or later communicate itself, eventually the psychopath is seen as cold, horrible, and frightening, even though at first he seems so delightfully carefree, gay, and unneurotic.

Again we have an instance in which sickness, though it involves a *general* cutting of communications, also involves, in specialized areas, a greater acuteness and skill. The psychopath is extraordinarily acute at discovering the psychopathic element in *us*, however carefully we conceal it. He can spot and play upon the swindler in us, the forger, the thief, the liar, the faker, the phony, and can ordinarily make a living out of this skill. He says "You can't con an honest man," and seems very confident of his ability to detect any "larceny in the soul." (Of course, this implies that he can detect the *absence* of larceny, which means in turn that the character becomes visible in mien and demeanor, at least to the intensely interested observer, i.e., it communicates itself to those who can understand it and identify with it.)

Masculinity and Femininity

The close relationship between intra- and interpersonal communication is seen with especial clarity in the relations between masculinity and femininity. Notice that I do not say "between the sexes," because my point is that the relations *between* the sexes are very largely determined by the relation between masculinity and femininity *within* each person, male or female.

The most extreme example I can think of is the male paranoid who very frequently has passive homosexual yearnings, in a word, a wish to be raped and injured by the strong man. This impulse is totally horrifying and unacceptable to him, and he struggles to repress it. A main technique that he uses (projection) helps him to deny his yearning and to split it off from himself, and at the same time permits him to think about and talk about and be preoccupied with the fascinating subject. It is the *other* man who wants to rape him, not he who wishes to be raped. And so there is a suspiciousness in these patients which can express itself in the most pathetically obvious ways, e.g., they will not let anyone get behind them, they will keep their backs to the wall, etc.

This is not so crazy as it sounds. Men throughout history have regarded women as temptresses, because they—the men—were tempted by them. Men tend to become soft and tender, unselfish and gentle when they love a woman. If they happen to live in a culture in which these are nonmasculine traits, then they get angry at women for weakening them (castrating them), and they invent Samson and Delilah myths to show how horrible women are. They project malevolent intentions. They blame the mirror for what it reflects.

Women, especially "advanced" and educated women in the United States of America, are frequently fighting against their own very deep tendencies to dependency, passivity, and submissiveness (because this unconsciously means to them a giving up of selfhood or personhood). It is then easy for such a woman to see men as would-be dominators and rapists and to treat them as such, frequently by dominating *them*.

For such reasons and others, too, men and women in most cultures and in most eras have misunderstood each other, have not been truly friendly with each other. It can be said in our present context that their intercommunications have been and are still bad. Usually one sex has dominated the other. Sometimes they manage to get along by cutting off the women's world from the men's, and making a complete division of labor, with concepts of masculine and feminine character that are very wide apart, with no overlapping. This makes for peace of a certain sort but certainly not for friendship and mutual understanding. What do the psychologists have to suggest about the improvement of understanding between the sexes? The psychological solution stated with especial clarity by the Jungians but also generally agreed upon is as follows: The antagonism between the sexes is largely a projection of the unconscious struggle *within* the person, between his or her masculine and feminine components. To make peace between the sexes, make peace within the person.

The man who is fighting within himself all the qualities he and his culture define as feminine will fight these same qualities in the external world, especially if his culture values maleness more than femaleness, as is so often the case. If it be emotionality, or illogic, or dependency, or love for colors, or tenderness with babies, he will be afraid of these in himself and fight them and try to be the opposite. And he will tend to fight them in the external world too by rejecting them, by relegating them to women entirely, etc. Homosexual men who solicit or accost are very frequently brutally beaten up by the men they approach, most likely because of the fears they arouse by being tempting. And this conclusion is certainly fortified by the fact that the beating up often comes *after* the homosexual act.

What we see here is an extreme dichotomizing, either/or, Aristotelian thinking of the sort that Goldstein, Adler, Korzybski, *et al.*, considered so dangerous. My psychologist's way of saying the same thing is "dichotomizing means pathologizing; and pathologizing means dichotomizing." The man who thinks you can be *either* a man, *all* man, *or* a woman, and *nothing but* a woman, is doomed to struggle with himself, and to eternal estrangement from women. To the extent that he learns the facts of psychological "bisexuality," and becomes aware of the arbitrariness of either/or definitions and the pathogenic nature of the process of dichotomizing, to the degree that he discovers that differences can fuse and be structured with each other, and need not be exclusive and mutually antagonistic, to that extent will he be a more integrated person, able to accept and enjoy the "feminine" within himself (the "Anima," as Jung calls it). If he can make peace with his female inside, he can make peace with the females outside, understand them better, be less ambivalent about them, and even admire them more as he realizes how superior their femaleness is to his own much weaker version. You can certainly communicate better with a friend who is appreciated and understood than you can with a feared, resented, and mysterious enemy. To make friends with some portion of the outside world, it is well to make friends with that part of it which is within yourself.

I do not wish to imply here that one process necessarily comes before the other. They are parallel and it can start the other way about, i.e., accepting X in the outside world can help achieve acceptance of that same X in the inside world.

Primary- and Secondary-Process Cognition

The repudiation of the inner psychic world in favor of the external world of common-sense "reality" is stronger in those who *must* deal successfully with the outer world primarily. Also, the tougher the environment is, the stronger the repudiation of the inner world must be, and the more dangerous it is to a "successful" adjustment. Thus the fear of poetic feeling, of fantasy, of dreaminess, of emotional thinking, is stronger in men than in women, in adults than in children, in engineers than in artists.

Observe also that we have here another example of the profound Western tendency, or perhaps general human tendency to dichotomize, to think that between alternatives or differences, one must choose *either* one *or* the other, and that this involves repudiation of the not-chosen, as if one couldn't have both.

And again we have an instance of the generalization that what we are blind and deaf to within ourselves, we are also blind and deaf to in the outer world, whether it be playfulness, poetic feeling, aesthetic sensitivity, primary creativity, or the like.

This example is especially important for another reason, namely that it seems to me that reconciling this dichotomy may be *the* best place for educators to begin in the task of resolving *all* dichotomies.

That is, it may be a good and practicable starting point for teaching humanity to stop thinking in a dichotomous way in favor of thinking in an integrative way.

This is one aspect of the great frontal attack upon an overconfident and isolated rationalism, verbalism, and scientism that is gathering force. The general semanticists, the existentialists, the phenomenologists, the Freudians, the Zen Buddhists, the mystics, the Gestalt therapists, the Humanistic psychologists, the Jungians, the self-actualization psychologists, the Rogerians, the Bergsonians, the "creative" educationists, and many others, are all helping to point out the limits of language, of abstract thought, of orthodox science. These have been conceived as controllers of the dark, dangerous, and evil human depths. But now as we learn steadily that these depths are not only the wellsprings of neuroses, but also of health, joy, and creativeness, we begin to speak of the *healthy* unconscious, of healthy regression, healthy instincts, healthy nonrationality, and healthy intuition. We begin also to desire the salvaging of these capacities for ourselves.

The general theoretical answer seems to lie in the direction of integration and away from splitting and repressing. Of course all these movements which I have mentioned can too easily themselves become splitting forces. Antirationalism, antiabstractionism, antiscience, antiintellectualism are also splits. Properly defined and conceived, intellect is one of our greatest, most powerful integrating forces.

Autonomy and Homonomy

Another paradox that faces us as we try to understand the relations between inner and outer, between self and world is the very complex interrelation between autonomy and homonomy. We can easily agree with Angyal (5) that there are within us these two general directions or needs, one toward selfishness and one toward unselfishness. The trend toward autonomy, taken by itself, leads us toward self-sufficiency, toward strength over against the world, toward fuller and fuller development of our own inner unique Self out of its own laws, its own inner dynamics, autochthonous laws of the psyche rather than of the environment. These psychic laws are different from, separate from, and even opposed to the laws of the nonpsychic worlds of the external reality. This quest for identity, or search for self (individuation, self-actualization) has certainly been made familiar to us by the growth and self-actualization psychologists, not to mention the existentialists, and the theologians of many schools.

But we are also aware of the equally strong tendency, seemingly contradictory, toward giving up the self, toward submerging ourselves in the not-self, toward giving up will, freedom, self-sufficiency, self-control, autonomy. In its sick forms this results in the wild romanticism of blood, earth, and instinct, in masochism, in contempt for the human being, in the search for values either *outside* the human being altogether or else in his lowest animal nature, both of which rest on contempt for the human being.

Elsewhere I have made the differentiation between the high homonomy and the low homonomy (89). Here I should like to differentiate the high autonomy from the low autonomy. I wish then to show how these differentiations can help us to understand the isomorphism between inner and outer, and thereby lay a theoretical base for improvement of communication between the personality and the world.

The autonomy and strength which is found in emotionally secure people is different from the autonomy and strength of insecure people (95). Very broadly, and without too much inaccuracy, we can say that insecure autonomy and strength is a strengthening of the personality as *over against* the world, in an either/or dichotomy in which they are not only quite separate but also mutually exclusive, as if they were *enemies*. We might call this selfish autonomy and strength. In a world in which one is either hammer or anvil, these are the hammers. In the monkeys in which I first studied the different qualities of strength, this was called autocratic or fascistic dominance. In the college students who were later studied it was called insecure high-dominance (95).

Secure high-dominance was another matter altogether. Here there was affection for the world and for others, big-brotherly responsibility and a feeling of trust in and identification with the world rather than of antagonism and fear toward it. The superior strength of these individuals was therefore used for enjoyment, for love, and for helping others.

On various grounds we can now find it possible to speak of these differentiations as between psychologically healthy and unhealthy autonomy, and between psychologically healthy and unhealthy homonomy. We find also that this differentiation enables us to see that they are interrelated rather than opposed to each other; for as the person grows healthier and more authentic, the high autonomy and the high homonomy grow together, appear together and tend finally to fuse and to become structured into a higher unity which includes them both. The dichotomy between autonomy and homonomy, between selfishness and unselfishness, between the self and non-self, between the pure psyche and outer reality, now tends to disappear, and can be seen as a byproduct of immaturity and of incomplete development.

While this transcendence of dichotomy can be seen as a usual thing in self-actualizing persons, it can *also* be seen in most of the rest of us in our most acute moments of integration within the self, and between self and the world. In the highest love between man and woman, or parent and child, as the person reaches the ultimates of strength, of self-esteem, of individuality, so also does he simultaneously merge with the other, lose self-consciousness and more or less transcend the self and selfishness. The same can happen in the creative moment, in the profound aesthetic experience, in the insight experience, in giving birth to a child, in dancing, in athletic experiences, and others which I have generalized as peak experiences (89). In all of these peak experiences it becomes impossible to differentiate sharply between the self and the not-self. As the person becomes integrated so does his world. As he feels good, so does the world look good. And so on.

Observe first of all that this is an empirical statement and not a philosophical or theological one. Anyone can repeat these findings. I am definitely speaking of human experiences and not of supernatural ones.

Secondly, observe that this implies a disagreement with various theological statements which imply that transcending the limits of self means spurning or repudiating, or *losing* the self or the individuality. In the peak experiences of ordinary people and in self-actualizing people as well, these are end products of the development of greater and greater autonomy, of the achievement of identity; and they are the products of self-transcendence, not of self-obliteration.

Thirdly, observe that they are transient experiences, and not permanent ones. If this is a going into another world, then there is always a coming back to the ordinary world.

Full Functioning, Spontaneity, B-Cognition

We begin to know something in a scientific way about the more integrated personality as it affects receiving and emitting communications. For instance, the many studies by Carl Rogers (128) and his collaborators indicate that as the person improves in psychotherapy, he becomes more integrated in various ways, more "open to experience" (more efficiently perceiving), and more "fully functioning" (more honestly expressive). This is our main body of experimental research, but there are also many clinical and theoretical writers who parallel and support these general conclusions at every point.

My own pilot explorations (not exact enough to be called researches in the contemporary sense) come to the same conclusions from another angle, i.e., the direct exploration of the relatively healthy personality. First of all, these explorations support the finding that integration is one defining aspect of psychological health. Secondly, they support the conclusion that healthy people are more spontaneous and more expressive, that they emit behavior more easily, more totally, more honestly. Thirdly, they support the conclusion that healthy people perceive better (themselves, other people, all of reality) although, as I have indicated, this is not a *uniform* superiority. A current story has the psychotic saying, "2 plus 2 equals 5," while the neurotic says, "2 plus 2 equals 4, but I can't *stand* it!" I might add that the valueless person—a new kind of illness—says, "2 plus 2 equals 4. So what!" And the healthier person says in effect, "2 plus 2 equals 4. How interesting!"

Or to put it another way, Joseph Bossom and I have recently published an experiment (13) in which we found that secure people tended to see photographed faces as more warm than did insecure perceivers. The question remains for future research, however, as to whether this is a projection of kindness, or of naïveté, or more efficient perception. What is called for is an experiment in which the faces perceived have *known* levels of warmth or coolness. Then, we may ask, are the secure perceivers who perceive or attribute more warmth right or wrong? Or are they right for warm faces and wrong for cool faces? Do they see what they want to see? Do they want to like what they see?

A last word about B-cognition. This seems to me to be the purest and most efficient kind of perception of reality (although this remains to be tested experimentally). It is the truer and more veridical perception of the percept because most detached, most objective, least contaminated by the wishes, fears, and needs of the perceiver. It is noninterfering, nondemanding, most accepting. In B-cognition dichotomies tend to fuse, categorizing tends to disappear, and the percept is seen as unique.

Self-actualizing people tend more to this kind of perceiving. But I have been able to get reports of this kind of perception in practically *all* the people I have questioned, in the highest, happiest, most perfect moments of their lives (peak experiences). Now, my point is this: Careful questioning shows that as the percept gets more individual, more unified and integrated, more enjoyable, more rich, so also does the perceiving individual get more alive, more integrated, more unified, more rich, more healthy for the moment. They happen simultaneously and can be set off on either side, i.e., the more whole the percept (the world) becomes, the more whole the person becomes. And also, the more whole the person becomes, the more whole becomes the world. It is a dynamic interrelation, a mutual causation. The meaning of a message clearly depends not alone on its content, but also on the extent to which the personality is able to respond to it. The "higher" meaning is perceptible only to the "higher" person. The taller he is, the more he can see.

As Emerson said, "What we are, that only can we see." But we must now add that what we see tends in turn to make us what it is and what we are. The communication relationship between the person and the world is a dynamic one of mutual forming and lifting-lowering of each other, a process that we may call "reciprocal isomorphism." A higher order of persons can understand a higher order of knowledge; but also a higher order of environment tends to lift the level of the person, just as a lower order of environment tends to lower it. They make each other more like each other. These notions are also applicable to the interrelations between persons, and should help us to understand how persons help to form each other.

12

Education and Peak Experiences

If one took a course or picked up a book on the psychology of learning, most of it, in my opinion, would be beside the point—that is, beside the "humanistic" point. Most of it would present learning as the acquisition of associations, of skills and capacities that are *external* and not *intrinsic* to the human character, to the human personality, to the person himself. Picking up coins or keys or possessions or something of the sort is like picking up reinforcements and conditioned reflexes that are, in a certain, very profound sense, expendable. It does not really matter if one has a conditioned reflex; if I salivate to the sound of a buzzer and then this extinguishes, nothing has happened to me; I have lost nothing of any consequence whatever. We might almost say that these extensive books on the psychology of learning are of no consequence, at least to the human center, to the human soul, to the human essence.

Generated by this new humanistic philosophy is also a new conception of learning, of teaching, and of education. Stated simply, such a concept holds that the function of education, the goal of education—the human goal, the humanistic goal, the goal so far as human beings are concerned—is ultimately the "self-actualization" of a person, the becoming fully human, the development of the fullest height that the human species can stand up to or that the particular individual can come to. In a less technical way, it is helping the person to become the best that he is able to become.

Such a goal involves very serious shifts in what we would teach in a course in the psychology of learning. It is not going to be a matter of associative learning. Associative learning in general is certainly useful, extremely useful for learning things that are of no real consequence, or for learning means—techniques which are after all interchangeable. And many of the things we must learn are like that. If one needs to memorize the vocabulary of some other language, he would learn it by sheer rote memory. Here, the laws of association can be a help. Or if one wants to learn all sorts of automatic habits in driving, responding to a red signal light or something of the sort, then conditioning is of consequence. It is important and useful, especially in a technological society. But in terms of becoming a better person, in terms of self-development and self-fulfillment, or in terms of "becoming fully human," the greatest learning experiences are very different.

In my life, such experiences have been far more important than classes, listening to lectures, memorizing the branches of the twelve cranial nerves and dissecting a human brain, or memorizing the insertions of the muscles, or the kinds of thing that one does in medical schools, in biology courses, or other such courses.

Far more important for me have been such experiences as having a child. Our first baby changed me as a psychologist. It made the behaviorism I had been so enthusiastic about look so foolish that I could not stomach it any more. It was impossible. Having a second baby, and learning how profoundly different people are even before birth, made it impossible for me to think in terms of the kind of learning psychology in which one can teach anybody anything. Or the John B. Watson theory of "Give me two babies and I will make one into this and one into the other." It is as if he never had any children. We know only too well that a parent cannot make his children into anything. Children make themselves into something. The best we can do and frequently the most effect we can have is by serving as something to react against if the child presses too hard.

Another profound learning experience that I value far more highly than any particular course or any degree that I have ever had was my personal psychoanalysis: discovering my own identity, my own self. Another basic experience—far more important—was getting married. This was certainly far more important than my Ph.D. by way of instructiveness. If one thinks in terms of the developing of the kinds of wisdom, the kinds of understanding, the kinds of life skills that we would want, then he must think in terms of what I would like to call *intrinsic* education—*intrinsic* learning; that is, learning to be a human being in general, and second, learning to be *this* particular human being. I am now very busily occupied in trying to catch up with all the epiphenomena of this notion of intrinsic education. Certainly one thing I can tell you. Our conventional education looks mighty sick. Once you start thinking in this framework, that is, in terms of becoming a good human being, and if then you ask the question about the courses that you took in high school, "How did my trigonometry course help me to become a better human being?" an echo answers, "By gosh, it didn't!" In a certain sense, trigonometry was for me a waste of time. My early music education was also not very successful, because it taught a child who had a very profound feeling for music and a great love for the piano *not* to learn it. I had a piano teacher who taught me in effect that music is something to stay away from. And I had to relearn music as an adult, all by myself.

Observe that I have been talking about ends. This is a revolutionary repudiation of nineteenth-century science and of contemporary professional philosophy, which is essentially a technology and not a philosophy of ends. I have rejected thereby, as theories of human nature, positivism, behaviorism, and objectivism. I have rejected thereby the whole model of science and all its works that have been derived from the historical accident that science began with the study of nonpersonal, nonhuman things, which in fact had no ends. The development of physics, astronomy, mechanics, and chemistry was in fact impossible until they had become value-free, value-neutral, so that pure descriptiveness was possible. The great mistake that we are now learning about is that this model, which developed from the study of objects and of things, has been illegitimately used for the study of human beings. It is a terrible technique. It has not worked.

Most of the psychology on this positivistic model, on this objectivistic, associationistic, value-free, value-neutral model of science, as it piles up like a coral reef or like mountains and mountains of small facts about this and that, is certainly not false, but merely trivial. I would like to point out here that, in order not to sell my own science short, I think we do know a great deal about things that *do* matter to the human being, but I would maintain that what has mattered to the human being that we have learned has been learned mostly by non-physicalistic techniques, by the humanistic science techniques of which we have become more conscious.

In speaking of the world situation at the opening ceremonies of a recent Lincoln Center Festival, Archibald MacLeish said in part:

> What is wrong is not the great discoveries of science—information is always better than ignorance, no matter what information or what ignorance. What is wrong is the belief behind the information, the belief that information will change the world. It won't. Information without human understanding is like an answer without its question—meaningless. And human understanding is only possible through the arts. It is the work of art that creates the human perspective in which information turns to truth. . . .

In a certain sense I disagree with MacLeish, although I can understand why he said this. What he is talking about is information *short of this new revolution*, short of the humanistic psychologies, short of the conceptions of the sciences that not only repudiate the notion of being value-free and value-neutral, but actually assume as an obligation, as a duty, the necessity for discovery of values—the empirical discovery, demonstration, and verification of the values that are inherent in human nature itself. This work is now busily going on.

What Mr. MacLeish said was appropriate for the era from 1920 to 1930. It is appropriate today if one doesn't know about the new psychologies. "And human understanding is only possible through the arts." That *was* true. Fortunately, it is no longer true. It now is possible to gather *information* that can contribute to human understanding, that carries imbedded within it value hints, vectorial and directional information, information that goes someplace.

"It is the work of art that creates the human perspective in which information turns to truth." I deny that, and we had better argue about that. We must have some criteria for distinguishing good art from bad art. They do not yet exist in the realms of art criticism so far as I know. They are *beginning* to exist, and I would like to leave one hint, an empirical hint. A possibility is beginning to emerge that we would have some objective criteria for discriminating good art from bad art.

If your situation is like mine, you know that we are in a complete and total confusion of values in the arts. In music, just try to prove something about the virtues of John Cage as against Beethoven—or Elvis Presley. In painting and architecture similar confusion is present. We have no shared values anymore. I don't bother to read music criticism. It is useless to me. So is art criticism, which I have also given up reading. Book reviews I find useless frequently. There is a complete chaos and anarchy of standards. For instance, the *Saturday Review* recently carried a favorable review of one of Jean Genet's crummy books. Written by a professor of theology, it was total confusion. It was the approach that Evil now has become Good because there is some kind of paradox while playing with words: If evil becomes totally evil, then it somehow becomes good, and there were rhapsodies to the beauties of sodomy and drug addiction, which, for a poor psychologist who spends much of his time trying to rescue people from the anguish of these kinds of things, were incomprehensible. How can a grown man recommend this book as a chapter in ethics and a guide to the young?

If Archibald MacLeish says that works of art lead to the truth, Archibald MacLeish is thinking about particular works of art that Archibald MacLeish has picked out, but ones his son might not agree with. And *then*, MacLeish really has nothing much to say. There is no way of convincing anybody about this point. I think this could be some symbol of the way in which I feel that we are at a turning point. We are moving around the corner. Something new is happening. There are discernible differences—and these are not differences in taste or arbitrary values. These are empirical discoveries. They are new things that are being found out, and from these are generated all sorts of propositions about values and education.

One is the discovery that the human being *has higher needs*, that he has instinctlike needs, which are a part of his biological equipment—the need to be dignified, for instance, and to be respected, and the need to be free for self-development. The discovery of higher needs carries with it all sorts of revolutionary implications.

Secondly, the point I have already made about the social sciences: Many people are beginning to discover that the physicalistic, mechanistic model was a mistake and that it has led us . . . where? To atom bombs. To a beautiful technology of killing, as in the concentration camps. To Eichmann. An Eichmann cannot be refuted with a positivistic philosophy or science. He just cannot; and he never got it until the moment he died. He didn't know what was wrong. As far as he was concerned, nothing was wrong; he had done a good job. He *did* do a good job, if you forget about the ends and the values. I point out that professional science and professional philosophy are dedicated to the proposition of forgetting about the values, excluding them. This, therefore must lead to Eichmanns, to atom bombs, and to who knows what!

I'm afraid that the tendency to separate good style or talent from content and ends can lead to this kind of danger.

The great discoveries Freud made, we can now add to. His one big mistake, which we are correcting now, is that he thought of the unconscious merely as undesirable evil. But unconsciousness carries in it also the roots of creativeness, of joy, of happiness, of goodness, of its own human ethics and values. We know that there is such a thing as a healthy unconscious as well as an unhealthy one. And the new psychologies are studying this at full tilt. The existential psychiatrists and psychotherapists are actually putting it into practice. New kinds of therapies are being practiced.

So we have a good conscious and a bad conscious—and a good unconscious and a bad unconscious. Furthermore, the good is real, in a non-Freudian sense. Freud was committed by his own positivism. Remember, Freud came out of a physicalistic, chemicalistic science. He was a neurologist. And a sworn oath that is in print called for a project to develop a psychology that could be entirely reduced to physical and chemical statements. This is what he dedicated himself to. He himself disproved his point, of course.

And about this higher nature that I claim we have discovered, the question is, how do we explain it? The Freudian explanation has been reductive. Explain it away. If I am a kind man, this is a reaction formation against my rage to kill. Somehow, here the killing is more basic than the kindness. And the kindness is a way of trying to cover up, repress, and defend myself against realizing the fact that I am truly a murderer. If I am generous, this is a reaction formation against stinginess. I am really stingy inside. This is a very peculiar thing. Somehow there is the begging of the question that is so obvious now. Why did he not say, for instance, that maybe killing people was a reaction formation against loving them? It is just as legitimate a conclusion and, as a matter of fact, more true for many people.

But to return to the principal idea, this exciting new development in science, this new moment in history. I have a very strong sense of being in the middle of a historical wave. One hundred and fifty years from now, what will the historians say about this age? What was really important? What was going? What was finished? My belief is that much of what makes the headlines is finished, and the "growing tip" of mankind is what is now growing and will flourish in a hundred or two hundred years, if we manage to endure. Historians will be talking about this movement as the sweep of history, that here, as Whitehead pointed out, when you get a new model, a new paradigm, a new way of perceiving, new definitions of the old words, words which now mean something else, suddenly, you have an illumination, an insight. You can see things in a different way.

For instance, one of the consequences generated by what I have been talking about, is a flat denial, an *empirical* denial (not pious, or arbitrary, or *a priori*, or wishful) of the Freudian contention of a necessary, intrinsic, built-in opposition between the needs of the individual and the needs of society and civilization. It just is not so. We now know something about how to set up the conditions in which the needs of the individual become synergic with, not opposed to, the needs of society, and in which they both work to the same ends. This is an empirical statement, I claim.

Another empirical statement is about the peak experiences. We have made studies of peak experiences by asking groups of people and individuals such questions as, What was the most ecstatic moment of your life? Or as one investigator asked, Have you experienced transcendent ecstasy? One might think that in a general population, such questions might get only blank stares, but there were many answers.

Apparently, the transcendent ecstasies had all been kept private, because there is no way of speaking about them in public. They are sort of embarrassing, shameful, not "scientific"—which, for many people, is the ultimate sin.

In our investigations of peak experiences, we found many, many triggers, many kinds of experiences that would set them off. Apparently most people, or almost all people, have peak experiences, or ecstasies. The question might be asked in terms of the single most joyous, happiest, most blissful moment of your whole life. You might ask questions of the kind I asked. How did you feel different about yourself at that time? How did the world look different? What did you feel like? What were your impulses? How did you change if you did? I want to report that the two easiest ways of getting peak experiences (in terms of simple statistics in empirical reports) are through music and through sex. I will push aside sex education, as such discussions are premature—although I am certain that one day we will not giggle over it, but will take it quite seriously and teach children that like music, like love, like insight, like a beautiful meadow, like a cute baby, or whatever, that there are many paths to heaven, and sex is one of them, and music is one of them. These happen to be the easiest ones, the most widespread, and the ones that are easiest to understand.

For our purposes in identifying and studying peak experiences, we can say it is justified to make a list of kinds of triggers. The list gets so long that it becomes necessary to make generalizations. It looks as if any experience of real excellence, of real perfection, of any moving toward the perfect justice or toward perfect values tends to produce a peak experience. Not always. But this is the generalization I would make for the many kinds of things that we have concentrated on. Remember, I am talking here as a scientist. This doesn't sound like scientific talk, but this is a new kind of science. A dissertation will soon be published which will show that out of this humanistic science has come, I would say, one of the real childbearing improvements since Adam and Eve. It is a dissertation (145) on peak experiences in natural childbirth. And this can be a potent source of peak experiences. We know just how to encourage peak experiences; we know the best way for women to have children in such a fashion that the childbearing mother is apt to have a great and mystical experience, a religious experience if you wish—an illumination, a revelation, an insight. That is what they call it, by the way, in the interviews—to simply become a different kind of person because, in a fair number of peak experiences, there ensues what I have called "the cognition of being."

We must make a new vocabulary for all these untilled, these unworked problems. This "cognition of being" means really the cognition that Plato and Socrates were talking about; almost, you could say, a technology of happiness, of pure excellence, pure truth, pure goodness, and so on. Well, why *not* a technology of joy, of happiness? I must add that this is the only known technique for inducing peak experiences in fathers. It had occurred to us, as my wife and I had first gotten to these surveys in college students, that many triggers were discovered. One of them was that while women talked about peak experiences from having children, men didn't. Now we have a way to teach men also to have peak experiences from childbirth. This means, in a certain condensed sense, being changed, seeing things differently, living in a different world, having different cognitions, in a certain sense some move toward living happily ever after. Now these are data, various paths to mystical experiences. I think that I had better pass them by as they are so numerous.

So far, I have found that these peak experiences are reported from what we might call "classical music." I have not found a peak experience from John Cage or from an Andy Warhol movie, from abstract-expressionistic kind of painting, or the like. I just haven't. The peak experience that has reported the great joy, the ecstasy, the visions of another world, or another level of living, has come from classical music—the great classics. Also I must report that this melts over, fuses over, into dancing or rhythm. So far as this realm of research is concerned, there really isn't much difference between them; they melt into each other. I may add, even, that when I was talking about music as a path to peak experiences, I included dancing. For me they have already melted together. The rhythmic experience, even the very simple rhythmic experience—the good dancing of a rumba, or the kinds of things that the kids can do with drums: I don't know whether you want to call that music, dancing, rhythm, athletics, or something else. The love for the body, awareness of the body, and a reverence of the body—these are clearly good paths to peak experiences. These in turn are good paths (not guaranteed, but statistically likely to be good paths) to the "cognition of being," to the perceiving of the Platonic essences, the intrinsic values, the ultimate values of being, which in turn is a therapeutic-like help toward both the curing-of-sicknesses kind of therapy and also the growth toward self-actualization, the growth toward full humanness.

In other words, peak experiences often have consequences. They can have very, very important consequences. Music and art in a certain sense can do the same; there is a certain overlap. They can do the same there as psychotherapy, if one keeps his goals right, and if one knows just what he is about, and if one is conscious of what he is going toward. We can certainly talk, on the one hand, of the breaking up of symptoms, like the breaking up of clichés, of anxieties, or the like; or on the other hand, we can talk about the development of spontaneity, and of courage, and of Olympian or Godlike humor and suchness, sensory awareness, body awareness, and the like.

Far from least, it happens that music and rhythm and dancing are excellent ways of moving toward the discovering of identity. We are built in such a fashion that this kind of trigger, this kind of stimulation, tends to do all kinds of things to our autonomic nervous systems, endocrine glands, to our feelings, and to our emotions. It just does. We just do not know enough about physiology to understand why it does. But it does, and these are unmistakable experiences. It is a little like pain, which is also an unmistakable experience. In experientially empty people, which includes a tragically large proportion of the population, people who do not know what is going on inside themselves and who live by clocks, schedules, rules, laws, hints from the neighbors—other-directed people—this is a way of discovering what the self is like. There are signals from inside, there are voices that yell out, "By gosh this is good, don't ever doubt it!" This is a path, one of the ways that we try to teach self-actualization and the discovery of self. The discovery of identity comes via the impulse voices, via the ability to listen to your own guts, and to their reactions and to what is going on inside of you. This is also an experimental kind of education that, if we had the time to talk about it, would lead us into another parallel educational establishment, another *kind* of school.

Mathematics can be just as beautiful, just as peak-producing as music; of course, there are mathematics teachers who have devoted themselves to preventing this. I had no glimpse of mathematics as a study in aesthetics until I was thirty years old, until I read some books on the subject. So can history, or anthropology (in the sense of learning another culture), social anthropology, or paleontology, or the study of science. Here again I want to talk data. If one works with great creators, great scientists, the creative scientists, *that* is the way they talk. The picture of the scientist must change, and is giving way to an understanding of the creative scientist, and the creative scientist lives by peak experiences. He lives for the moments of glory when a problem solves itself, when suddenly through a microscope he sees things in a very different way, the moments of revelation, of illumination, insight, understanding, ecstasy. These are vital for him. Scientists are very, very shy and embarrassed about this. They refuse to talk about this in public. It takes a very, very delicate kind of a midwifery to get these things out, but I have gotten them out. They are there, and if one can manage to convince a creative scientist that he is not going to be laughed at for these things, then he will blushingly admit the fact of having a high emotional experience from, for example, the moment in which the crucial correlation turns out right. They just don't talk about it, and as for the usual textbook on how you do science, it is total nonsense.

My point here is that it is possible; that if we are conscious enough of what we are doing, that is, if we are philosophical enough in the insightful sense too, we may be able to use those experiences that most easily produce ecstasies, that most easily produce revelations, experiences, illumination, bliss, and rapture experiences. We may be able to use them as a model by which to re-evaluate history teaching or any other kind of teaching.

Finally, the impression that I want to try to work out—and I would certainly suggest that this is a problem for everyone involved in arts education—is that effective education in music, education in art, education in dancing and rhythm, is intrinsically far closer than the usual "core curriculum" to intrinsic education of the kind that I am talking about, of learning one's identity as an essential part of education. If education doesn't do that, it is useless. Education is learning to grow, learning what to grow toward, learning what is good and bad, learning what is desirable and undesirable, learning what to choose and what not to choose. In this realm of intrinsic learning, intrinsic teaching, and intrinsic education, I think that the arts, and especially the ones that I have mentioned, are so close to our psychological and biological core, so close to this identity, this biological identity, that rather than think of these courses as a sort of whipped cream or luxury, they must become basic experiences in education. I mean that this kind of education can be a glimpse into the infinite, into ultimate values. This intrinsic education may very well have art education, music education, and dancing education as its core. (I think dancing is the one I would choose first for children. It is the easiest for the two-, three-, or four-year-old children—just plain rhythm.) Such experiences could very well serve as the model, the means by which perhaps we could rescue the rest of the school curriculum from the value-free, value-neutral, goal-less meaninglessness into which it has fallen.

13

Goals and Implications
of Humanistic Education

J ust before he died, Aldous Huxley was on the brink of an enormous breakthrough, on the verge of creating a great synthesis between science, religion, and art. Many of his ideas are illustrated in his last novel, *Island* (52). Although *Island* is not very significant as a work of art, it is very exciting as an essay on what man is capable of becoming. The most revolutionary ideas in it are those pertaining to education, for the educational system in Huxley's Utopia is aimed at radically different goals than the educational system of our own society.

If we look at education in our own society, we see two sharply different factors. First of all, there is the overwhelming majority of teachers, principals, curriculum planners, school superintendents, who are devoted to passing on the knowledge that children need in order to live in our industrialized society. They are not especially imaginative or creative, nor do they often question *why* they are teaching the things they teach. Their chief concern is with efficiency, that is, with implanting the greatest number of facts into the greatest possible number of children, with a minimum of time, expense, and effort. On the other hand, there is the minority of humanistically oriented educators who have as their goal the creation of better human beings, or in psychological terms, self-actualization and self-transcendence.

Classroom learning often has as its unspoken goal the reward of pleasing the teacher. Children in the usual classroom learn very quickly that creativity is punished, while repeating a memorized response is rewarded, and concentrate on what the teacher wants them to say, rather than understanding the problem. Since classroom learning focuses on behavior rather than on thought, the child learns exactly how to behave while keeping his thoughts his own.

Thought, in fact, is often inimical to extrinsic learning. The effects of propaganda, indoctrination, and operant conditioning all disappear with insight. Take advertising, for example. The simplest medicine for it is the truth. You may worry about subliminal advertising and motivational research, but all you need are the data which prove that a particular brand of toothpaste stinks, and you'll be impervious to all the advertising in the world. As another example of destructive effect of truth upon extrinsic learning, a psychology class played a joke on their professor by secretly conditioning him while he was delivering a lecture on conditioning. The professor, without realizing it, began nodding more and more, and by the end of the lecture he was nodding continually. As soon as the class told the professor what he was doing, however, he stopped nodding, and of course after that no amount of smiling on the part of the class could make him nod again. Truth made the learning disappear. Extending this point, we ought to ask ourselves how much classroom learning is actually supported by ignorance, would be destroyed by insight.

Students, of course, have been steeped in attitudes of extrinsic learning and respond to grades and examinations as the chimps responded to the poker chips. In one of the best universities in the country a boy sat on the campus reading a book, and a friend passing by asked him why he was reading that particular book as it hadn't been assigned. The only reason for reading a book could be the extrinsic rewards that it would bring. In the poker-chip milieu of the university, the question was logical.

The difference between the intrinsic and the extrinsic aspects of a college education is illustrated by the following story about Upton

Sinclair. When Sinclair was a young man, he found that he was unable to raise the tuition money needed to attend college. Upon careful reading of the college catalogue, however, he found that if a student failed a course, he received no credit for the course, but was obliged to take another course in its place. The college did not charge the student for the second course, reasoning that he had already paid once for his credit. Sinclair took advantage of this policy and got a free education by deliberately failing all his courses.

The phrase "earning a degree" summarizes the evils of extrinsically oriented education. The student automatically gets his degree after investing a certain number of hours at the university, referred to as credits. All the knowledge taught in the university has its "cash value" in credits, with little or no distinction made between various subjects taught at the university. A semester of basketball coaching, for example, earns the student as many credits as a semester in French philology. Since only the final degree is considered to have any real value, leaving college before the completion of one's senior year is considered to be a waste of time by the society and a minor tragedy by parents. You have all heard of the mother bemoaning her daughter's foolishness in leaving school to get married during her senior year since the girl's education had been "wasted." The learning value of spending three years at the university has been completely forgotten.

In the ideal college, there would be no credits, no degrees, and no required courses. A person would learn what he wanted to learn. A friend and I attempted to put this ideal into action by starting a series of seminars at Brandeis called "Freshman Seminars—Introduction to the Intellectual Life." We announced that the course would have no required reading or writing and give no credits, and that whatever was discussed would be of the student's own choosing. We also stated who we were—a professor of psychology and a practicing psychiatrist, expecting that the description of the seminar and of our own interests would indicate to the student who should come and who should not. The students who came to this seminar came of their own volition and were at least partially responsible for its successes and failures. The exact opposite holds true for the classical schoolroom—it is compulsory, people have been forced into it one way or another.

In the ideal college, intrinsic education would be available to anyone who wanted it—since anyone can improve and learn. The student body might include creative, intelligent children as well as adults; morons as well as geniuses (for even morons can learn emotionally and spiritually). The college would be ubiquitous—that is, not restricted to particular buildings at particular times, and the teachers would be any human beings who had something that they wanted to share with others. The college would be lifelong, for learning can take place all through life. Even dying can be a philosophically illuminating, highly educative experience.

The ideal college would be a kind of educational retreat in which you could try to find yourself; find out what you like and want; what you are and are not good at. People would take various subjects, attend various seminars, not quite sure of where they were going, but moving toward the discovery of vocation, and *once they found it*, they could then make good use of technological education. The chief goals of the ideal college, in other words, would be the *discovery of identity*, and with it, the *discovery of vocation*.

What do we mean by the discovery of identity? We mean finding out what your real desires and characteristics are, and being able to live in a way that expresses them. You learn to be authentic, to be honest in the sense of allowing your behavior and your speech to be the true and spontaneous expression of your inner feelings. Most of us have learned to avoid authenticity. You may be in the middle of a fight, and your guts are writhing with anger, but if the phone rings, you pick it up and sweetly say hello. Authenticity is the reduction of phoniness toward the zero point.

There are many techniques for teaching authenticity. The T-group is an effort to make you aware of who you really are, of how you really react to other people, by giving you a chance to be honest, to tell what is really going on inside of you instead of presenting façades or giving polite evasions.

People whom we describe as healthy, strong, and definite seem to be able to hear their inner-feeling-voices more clearly than most people. They know what they want, and they know equally clearly what they don't want. Their inner preferences tell them that one color doesn't go with another, and that they don't want wool clothing because it makes them itch, or that they dislike superficial sexual relations. Other people, in contrast, seem to be empty, out of touch with their own inner signals. They eat, defecate, and go to sleep by the clock's cues, rather than by the cues of their own bodies. They use external criteria for everything from choosing their food ("it's good for you") and clothing ("it's in style") to questions of values and ethics ("my daddy told me to").

We do a very good job of confusing our young children about their own inner voices. A child may say, "I don't want any milk," and his mother replies, "Why, you know you want some milk." Or he may say, "I don't like spinach," and she tells him, "We love spinach." An important part of self-knowledge is being able to hear clearly these signals from the inside, and the mother is not helping her child when she confuses their clarity for him. It would be just as easy for her to say, "I know you don't like spinach, but you have to eat it anyway for such-and-such reasons."

Aesthetic people seem to have clearer impulse voices than most people about matters of colors, relationships of appearances, suitability of patterns, etc. People with high IQs seem to have similarly strong impulse voices about perceiving truth, seeing that this relationship is true and that one is not, in the same way that aesthetically gifted people seem to be able to see that this tie goes well with this jacket but not that one. Presently a lot of research is being done on the relationship between creativity and high IQ in children. Creative children seem to be those who have strong impulse voices that tell them what is right and what is wrong. Noncreative high IQ children seem to have lost their impulse voices and become domesticated, so that they look to the parent or the teacher for guidance or inspiration.

Healthy people seem to have clear impulse voices about matters of ethics and values, as well. Self-actualizing people have to a large extent transcended the values of their culture. They are not so much merely Americans as they are world citizens, members of the human species first and foremost. They are able to regard their own society objectively, liking some aspects of it, disliking others. If an ultimate goal of education is self-actualization, then education ought to help people transcend the conditioning imposed upon them by their own culture and become world citizens. Here the technical question of how to enable people to overcome their enculturation arises. How do you awaken the sense of brotherhood to all mankind in a young child that is going to enable him to hate war as an adult and do all that he can to avoid it? The churches and Sunday schools have carefully avoided this task, and instead teach the children colorful Bible tales.

Another goal which our schools and teachers should be pursuing is the discovery of vocation, of one's fate and destiny. Part of learning who you are, part of being able to hear your inner voices, is discovering what it is that you want to do with your life. Finding one's identity is almost synonymous with finding one's career, revealing the altar on which one will sacrifice oneself. Finding one's lifework is a little like finding one's mate. One custom is for young people to "play the field," to have a lot of contacts with people, a love affair or two, and perhaps a serious trial marriage before getting married. In this way they discover what they like and don't like in members of the opposite sex. As they become more and more conscious of their own needs and desires, those people who know themselves well enough eventually just find and recognize one another. Sometimes very similar things happen when you find your career, your lifework. It feels right and suddenly you find that twenty-four hours aren't a long-enough time span for the day, and you begin bemoaning the shortness of human life. In our schools, however, many vocational counselors have no sense of the possible goals of human existence, or even of what is necessary for basic happiness. All this type of counselor considers is the need of the society for aeronautical engineers or dentists. No one ever mentions that if you are unhappy with your work, you have lost one of the most important means of self-fulfillment.

Summarizing what we have said, the schools should be helping the children to look within themselves, and from this self-knowledge derive a set of values. Yet values are not taught in our schools today. This may be a holdover from the religious wars in which the church and the state were made separate and the rulers decided that the discussion of values would be the church's concern, whereas the secular schools would concern themselves with other problems. Perhaps it is fortunate that our schools, with their grievous lack of a real philosophy and of suitably trained teachers, do *not* teach values, just as it is fortunate they have not taught sex education for the same reasons.

Among the many educational consequences generated by the humanistic philosophy of education is a different conception of the self.

This is a very complex conception, difficult to describe briefly, because it talks for the first time in centuries of an *essence*, of an *intrinsic* nature, of specieshood, of a kind of animal nature. This is in sharp contrast with the European existentialist, most especially with Sartre, for whom man is *entirely* his own project, *entirely* and merely a product of his own arbitrary, unaided will. For Sartre and all those whom he has influenced, one's self becomes an arbitrary choice, a willing by fiat to be something or do something without any guidelines about which is better, which is worse, what's good and what's bad. In essentially denying the existence of biology, Sartre has given up altogether any absolute or at least any species-wide conception of values. This comes very close to making a life-philosophy of the obsessive-compulsive neurosis in which one finds what I have called "experiential emptiness," the absence of impulse voices from within.

The American humanistic psychologists and existential psychiatrists are mostly closer to the psychodynamicists than they are to Sartre. Their clinical experiences have led them to conceive of the human being as having an essence, a biological nature, membership in a species. It is very easy to interpret the "uncovering" therapies as helping the person to *discover* his Identity, his Real Self, in a word, his own subjective biology, which he can *then* proceed to actualize, to "make himself," to "choose."

The trouble is that the human species is the only species which finds it hard to be a species. For a cat there seems to be no problem about being a cat. It's easy; cats seem to have no complexes or ambivalences or conflicts, and show no signs of yearning to be dogs instead. Their instincts are very clear. But *we* have no such unequivocal animal instincts. Our biological essence, our instinct remnants, are weak and subtle, and they are hard to get at. Learnings of the extrinsic sort *are more powerful than our deepest impulses*. These deepest impulses in the human species, at the points where the instincts have been lost almost entirely, where they are extremely weak, extremely subtle and delicate, where you have to dig to find them, *this* is where I speak of introspective biology, of biological phenomenology, implying that one of the necessary methods in the search for identity, the search for self, the search for spontaneity and for naturalness is a matter of closing your eyes, cutting down the noise, turning off the thoughts, putting away all busyness, just relaxing in a kind of Taoistic and receptive fashion (in much the same way that you do on the psychoanalyst's couch). The technique here is to just wait to see what happens, what comes to mind. This is what Freud called free association, free-floating attention rather than task orientation, and if you are successful in this effort and learn how to do it, you can forget about the outside world and its noises and begin to hear these small, delicate impulse voices from within, the hints from your animal nature, not only from your common species-nature, but also from your own uniqueness.

There's a very interesting paradox here, however. On the one hand I've talked about uncovering or discovering your idiosyncrasy, the way in which you are different from everybody else in the whole world. Then on the other hand I've spoken about discovering your specieshood, your humanness. As Carl Rogers has phrased it: "How does it happen that the deeper we go into ourselves as particular and unique, seeking for our own individual identity, the more we find the whole human species?" Doesn't that remind you of Ralph Waldo Emerson and the New England Transcendentalists? Discovering your specieshood, at a deep enough level, merges with discovering your selfhood. Becoming (learning how to be) fully human means *both* enterprises carried on simultaneously. You are learning (subjectively experiencing) what you peculiarly are, how you are you, what your potentialities are, what your style is, what your pace is, what your tastes are, what your values are, what direction your body is going, where your personal biology is taking you, i.e., how you are *different* from others. And at the same time it means learning what it means to be a human animal like other human animals, i.e., how you are *similar* to others.

One of the goals of education should be to teach that life is precious. If there were no joy in life, it would not be worth living. Unfortunately many people never experience joy, those all-too-few moments of total life-affirmation which we call peak experiences. Fromm (35) spoke about the life-wishers who often experienced joy, and the death-wishers who never seemed to experience moments of joy and whose hold on life was very weak. The latter group would take all sorts of idiotic chances with their lives, as though they were hoping that an accident would save them from the trouble of committing suicide. Under adverse conditions, such as in concentration camps, those to whom every moment of life was precious struggled to keep alive, while the others let themselves die without resistance. We are beginning to find out through such agencies as Synanon that drug addicts, who are killing a part of themselves, will give up drugs easily of you offer them instead some meaning to their lives. Psychologists have described alcoholics as being fundamentally depressed, basically bored with life. They describe their existence as an endless flat plain with no ups or downs. Colin Wilson (159), in his book, *Introduction to the New Existentialism*, pointed out that life has to have meaning, has to be filled with moments of high intensity that validate life and make it worthwhile. Otherwise the desire to die makes sense, for who would want to endure endless pain or endless boredom?

We know that children are capable of peak experiences and that they happen frequently during childhood. We also know that the present school system is an extremely effective instrument for crushing peak experiences and forbidding their possibility. The natural child-respecting teacher who is not frightened by the sight of children enjoying themselves is a rare sight in classrooms. Of course, with the traditional model of thirty-five children in one classroom and a curriculum of subject matter which has to be gotten through in a given period of time, the teacher is forced to pay more attention to orderliness and lack of noise than she is making learning a joyful experience. But then our official philosophies of education and teachers' colleges seem to have as an implicit assumption that it is dangerous for a child to have a good time. Even the difficult tasks of learning to read and subtract and multiply, which are necessary in an industrialized society, can be enhanced and made joyful.

What can the schools do to counteract the death wish in kindergarten, to strengthen the wish for life in the first grade? Perhaps the most important thing they can do is to give the child a sense of accomplishment. Children get a great deal of satisfaction in helping someone younger or weaker than themselves accomplish something. The child's creativity can be encouraged by avoiding regimentation. Since the children imitate the attitudes of the teacher, the teacher can be encouraged to become a joyful and self-actualizing person.

The parents convey their own distorted patterns of behavior to the child, but if the teacher's are healthier and stronger, the children will imitate these instead.

In the first place, unlike the current model of teacher as lecturer, conditioner, reinforcer, and boss, the Taoist helper or teacher is receptive rather than intrusive. I was told once that in the world of boxers, a youngster who feels himself to be good and who wants to be a boxer will go to a gym, look up one of the managers, and say, "I'd like to be a pro, and I'd like to be in your stable. I'd like you to manage me." In this world, what is then done characteristically is to try him out. The good manager will select one of his professionals and say, "Take him on in the ring. Stretch him. Strain him. Let's see what he can do. Just let him show his very best. Draw him out." If it turns out that the boxer has promise, if he's a "natural," then what the good manager does is to take that boy and train him to be, if this is Joe Dokes, a *better Joe Dokes*. That is, he takes his style as given and builds upon that. He does not start all over again, and say, "Forget all you've learned, and do it this new way," which is like saying, "Forget what kind of body you have," or "Forget what you are good for." He takes him and builds upon his *own* talents and builds him up into the very best Joe Dokes-type boxer that he possibly can.

It is my strong impression that this is the way in which much of the world of education could function. If we want to be helpers, counselors, teachers, guiders, or psychotherapists, what we must do is to accept the person and help him learn what kind of person he is already. What is his style, what are his aptitudes, what is he good for, not good for, what can we build upon, what are his good raw materials, his good potentialities? We would be nonthreatening and would supply an atmosphere of acceptance of the child's nature which reduces fear, anxiety, and defense to the minimum possible. Above all, we would care for the child, that is, enjoy him and his growth and self-actualization (117). So far this sounds much like the Rogerian therapist, his "unconditional positive regard," his congruence, his openness and his caring. And indeed there is evidence by now that this "brings the child out," permits him to express and to act, to experiment, and even to make mistakes; to let himself be seen. Suitable feedback at this point, as in T-groups or basic encounter groups, or nondirective counseling, then helps the child to discover what and who he is. We must learn to treasure the "jags" of the child in school, his fascination, absorptions, his persistent wide-eyed wonderings, his Dionysian enthusiasms. At the very least, we can value his more diluted raptures, his "interests," and hobbies, etc. They can lead to much. Especially can they lead to hard work, persistent, absorbed, fruitful, educative.

And conversely I think it is possible to think of the peak experience, the experience of awe, mystery, wonder, or of perfect completion, as the goal and reward of learning as well, its end as well as its beginning (67). If this is true for the *great* historians, mathematicians, scientists, musicians, philosophers, and all the rest, why should we not try to maximize these studies as sources of peak experiences for the child as well?

I must say that whatever little knowledge and experience I have to support these suggestions comes from intelligent and creative children rather than from retarded or underprivileged or sick ones. However, I must also say that my experience with such unpromising adults in Synanon, in T-groups (141), in Theory-Y industry (83), in Esalen-type educative centers (32), in Grof-type work with psychedelic chemicals (40), not to mention Laing-type work with psychotics (65), and other such experiences, has taught me never to write *anybody* off in advance.

Another important goal of intrinsic education is to see that the child's basic psychological needs are satisfied. A child cannot reach self-actualization until his needs for security, belongingness, dignity, love, respect, and esteem are all satisfied. In psychological terms, the child is free from anxiety because he feels himself to be loveworthy, and knows that he belongs in the world, that someone respects and wants him. Most of the drug addicts who come to Synanon have had a life devoid of almost all need-gratification. Synanon creates an atmosphere in which they are treated as if they were four-year-olds, and then slowly lets them grow up in an atmosphere which will allow their fundamental needs to be satisfied one by one.

Another goal of education is to refreshen consciousness so that we are continually aware of the beauty and wonder of life. Too often in this culture we become desensitized so that we never really see things we look at or hear the things we listen to. Laura Huxley had a little cube of magnifying glasses into which you could insert a tiny flower and look at the flower while it was illuminated from lights at the sides of the cubes. After a while the watcher would become lost in the experience of total attention, and from that would arise the psychedelic experience, which is seeing the absolute concreteness of a thing and the wonder of its existence. A very good trick for refreshening the quality of daily experience is imagining that you are going to die—or that the other person you are with is going to die. If you are actually threatened by death, you perceive in a different way with closer attention than you do ordinarily. If you know that a particular person is going to die, you see him more intensely, more personally, without the casual categorizing that marks so much of our experience. You must fight stereotyping, never allowing yourself to get used to anything. Ultimately the best way of teaching, whether the subject is mathematics, history, or philosophy, is to make the students aware of the beauties involved. We need to teach our children unitive perception, the Zen experience of being able to see the temporal and the eternal simultaneously, the sacred and the profane in the same object.

We must once again learn to control our impulses. The days in which Freud treated overinhibited people are now long past, and today we are confronted with the opposite problem—that of expressing every impulse immediately. It is possible to teach people that controls are not necessarily repressive. Self-actualized people have a system of Apollonian controls in which the control and the gratification work together to make the gratification more pleasurable. They know, for example, that eating is more fun if you sit down at a well-set table with well-cooked food even though it takes more control to prepare the table and the food. Something similar is true for sex.

One of the tasks of real education is to transcend pseudoproblems and to grapple with the serious existential problems of life. All neurotic problems are pseudoproblems. The problems of evil and suffering, however, are real and must be faced by everybody sooner or later. Is it possible to reach a peak experience through suffering? We have found that the peak experience contains two components— an emotional one of ecstasy and an intellectual one of illumination. Both need not be present simultaneously. For example, the sexual orgasm can be extremely satisfying emotionally but not illuminate the person in any way. In confrontation with pain and death, a non-ecstatic illumination can occur, as pointed out in Marghanita Laski's book, *Ecstasy* (66). We now have a fairly extensive literature on the psychology of death in which it is evident that some people do experience illumination and gain philosophical insight as they approach death. Huxley, in his book, *Island* (52), illustrates how a person can die with reconciliation and acceptance rather than being dragged out of life in an undignified way.

Another aspect of intrinsic education is learning how to be a good chooser. You can teach yourself to choose. Place yourself before two glasses of sherry, a cheap one and an expensive one, and see which one you like the best. Try seeing if you can tell the difference between two brands of cigarettes with your eyes closed. If you can't tell the difference, there is none. I found myself that I can tell the difference between good and cheap sherry, so I now buy expensive sherry. On the other hand, I can't tell the difference between good gin and cheap gin, so I buy the cheapest gin I can. If I can't tell the difference, why bother?

What do we really mean by self-actualization? What are the psychological characteristics that we are hoping to produce in our ideal educational system? The self-actualized person is in a state of good psychological health; his basic needs are satisfied so what is it that motivates him to become such a busy and capable person? For one thing, all self-actualized people have a cause they believe in, a vocation they are devoted to. When they say, "my work," they mean their mission in life. If you ask a self-actualized lawyer why he entered the field of law, what compensates for all the routine and trivia, he will eventually say something like, "Well, I just get mad when I see somebody taking advantage of somebody else. It isn't fair." Fairness to him is an ultimate value; he can't tell you *why* he values fairness any more than an artist can tell you why he values beauty. Self-actualizing people, in other words, seem to do what they do for the sake of ultimate, final values, which is for the sake of principles which seem *intrinsically worthwhile*. They protect and love these values, and if the values are threatened, they will be aroused to indignation, action, and often self-sacrifice. These values are not abstract to the self-actualizing person; they are as much a part of them as their bones and arteries. Self-actualizing people are motivated by the eternal verities, the B-Values, by pure truth and beauty in perfection. They go beyond polarities and try to see the underlying oneness; they try to integrate everything and make it more comprehensive.

The next question is, are these values instinctoid, inherent in the organism, just as the need for love or vitamin D are inherent in the organism? If you eliminate all vitamin D from your diet, you will become sick. We can call love a need for the same reason. If you take away all love from your children, it can kill them. Hospital staffs have learned that unloved babies die early from colds. Do we need truth in the same way? I find that if I am deprived of truth, I come down with a peculiar kind of sickness—I become paranoid, mistrusting everybody and trying to look behind everything, searching for hidden meanings to every event. This sort of chronic mistrustfulness is certainly a psychological disease. So I would say that being deprived of truth results in a pathology—a metapathology. A metapathology is the illness which results in being deprived of a B-Value.

The deprivation of beauty can cause illness. People who are aesthetically very sensitive become depressed and uncomfortable in ugly surroundings. It probably affects their menstruation, gives them headaches, etc.

I performed a series of experiments on beautiful and ugly surroundings to prove this point. When subjects saw pictures of faces to be judged in an ugly room, they viewed the people as being psychotic, paranoid, or dangerous, indicating that faces and presumably human beings look bad in ugly surroundings. How much the ugliness affects you depends on your sensitivity and the ease with which you can turn your attention away from the obnoxious stimuli. To carry the point further, living in an unpleasant environment with nasty people is a pathological force. If you choose beautiful and decent people to spend your time with, you will find that you feel better and more uplifted.

Justice is another B-Value, and history has given us plenty of examples of what happens to people when they are deprived of it over a long period of time. In Haiti, for example, people learn distrust of everything, cynicism about all other human beings, believing that underneath everything there must be rot and corruption.

The metapathological state of uselessness is of great interest to me. I have met many youngsters who fulfill all the criteria of self-actualization; their basic needs are gratified, they are using their capacities well and show no obvious psychological symptoms.

Yet they are disrupted and disturbed. They mistrust all the B-Values, all the values that people over thirty espouse, and regard such words as truth, goodness, and love as empty clichés. They have even lost faith in their ability to make a better world, and so all they can do is protest in a meaningless and destructive way. If you don't have a value-life, you may not be neurotic, but you suffer from a cognitive and spiritual sickness, for to a certain extent your relationship with reality is distorted and disturbed.

If B-Values are as necessary as vitamins and love, and if their absence can make you sick, then what people have talked about for thousands of years as the religious or platonic or rational life seems to be a very basic part of human nature. Man is a hierarchy of needs, with the biological needs at the base of the hierarchy and the spiritual needs at the top. Unlike the biological needs, however, the B-Values are not hierarchical in and of themselves. One is as important as the next, and each one can be defined in terms of all the others. Truth, for example, must be complete, aesthetic, comprehensive, and strangely enough, it must be funny in an Olympian godlike sense. Beauty must be true, good, comprehensive, etc. Now if the B-Values are all definable in terms of each other, we know from factor-analysis that some general factor underlies them all—a G-factor, to use the statistical term. The B-Values are not separate piles of sticks, but rather the different facets of one jewel. Both the scientist who is devoted to truth and the lawyer who is devoted to justice are devoted to the same thing. Each has found out that the aspect of the general value which suits him best is the one he is using in his life's work.

An interesting aspect of the B-Values is that they transcend many of the traditional dichotomies, such as selfishness and unselfishness, flesh and spirit, religious and secular. If you are doing the work that you love and are devoted to the value that you hold highest, you are being as selfish as possible, and yet are also being unselfish and altruistic. If you have introjected truth as a value so that it is as much a part of you as your blood, then if a lie is told anywhere in the world, it hurts you to find out about it. The boundaries of yourself in that sense now extend far beyond your personal sphere of interests to include the entire world. If an injustice is being committed against a person in Bulgaria or China, it is also being committed against you. Though you may never meet the person involved, you can feel his betrayal as your own.

Take the dichotomy of "religious" and "secular." The form of religion that was offered to me as a child seemed so ludicrous that I abandoned all interest in religion and experienced no desire to "find God." Yet my religious friends, at least those who had gotten beyond the peasants' view of God as having a skin and beard, talk about God the way I talk about B-Values. The questions that theologians consider of prime importance nowadays are questions such as the meaning of the universe, and whether or not the universe has a direction. The search for perfection, the discovery of adherence to values is the essence of the religious tradition. And many religious groups are beginning to declare openly that the external trappings of religion, such as not eating meat on Friday, are unimportant, even detrimental, because they confuse people as to what religion really is, and are beginning once again to commit themselves in practice as well as in theory to the B-Values.

People who enjoy and are committed to the B-Values also enjoy their basic need-gratifications more because they make them sacred. To lovers who view each other in terms of the B-Values as well as in terms of need fulfillment, sexual intercourse becomes a sacred ritual. To live the spiriutal life, you don't have to sit on top of a pillar for ten years. Being able to live in the B-Values somehow makes the body and all its appetites holy.

If we were to accept as a major educational goal the awakening and fulfillment of the B-Values, which is simply another aspect of self-actualization, we would have a great flowering of a new kind of civilization. People would be stronger, healthier, and would take their own lives into their hands to a greater extent. With increased personal responsibility for one's personal life, and with a rational set of values to guide one's choosing, people would begin to actively change the society in which they lived. The movement toward psychological health is also the movement toward spiritual peace and social harmony.

PART V
Society

14

Synergy in the
Society and in the Individual

I would like to dedicate this chapter to the memory of Ruth Benedict,[1] who invented and developed the concept of synergy in a series of lectures she gave at Bryn Mawr College in 1941. This concept is not familiar only because her manuscript was lost. When I first read these lectures I was horrified to find that the copy she had given me was the only one in existence. I was afraid that she would not publish it—she seemed not to care much whether it was published or not. I was also afraid that it might be lost. This fear turned out to be well founded. Margaret Mead, her executrix, has hunted through all her files and papers, but has never been able to find the manuscript. But I had someone type out as many parts as possible. These excerpts are to be published soon (9, 41), so I will use only a few of them in this chapter.

[1] Ruth Benedict (1887–1948) was professor of anthropology, Columbia University, and a poet, under the name of Ann Singleton. Her main field of interest was the American Indian. During World War II, she studied Japanese culture, furnishing basic information for Allied propaganda. Among her books are *Patterns of Culture; Race, Science and Politics;* and *The Chrysanthemum and the Sword.*—Ed. note, Heinz L. Ansbacher.

Development and Definition of Synergy

Ruth Benedict tried in her last years to overcome and to transcend the doctrine of cultural relativity with which her name has been associated incorrectly. My recollection is that she was extremely irritated by this identification. Her *Patterns of Culture* (10) she felt was essentially an essay in holism. It was a holistic rather than an atomistic effort to describe societies as unitary organisms of wholes, with a feel, a flavor, a tone that she tried to describe in her own poetic way.

As things stood while I was studying anthropology in 1933–1937, cultures were unique, idiosyncratic. There was no scientific way of handling them, no generalization you could make. Each one seemed to be different from every other. There was nothing you could say about any culture except from within. Benedict kept struggling with the effort to achieve a comparative sociology. It came as it would to a poetess, in an intuitive way. She kept struggling with words which she did not dare to say in public in her capacity as a scientist, because they were normative, involved rather than cool, words that could be said over a martini but not in print.

Development. As she described it, she had huge sheets of newsprint upon which she wrote all that was known about four pairs of cultures that she selected because she felt that they were different. She had an intuition, a feeling, and she phrased it in different ways which I have written down in old notes.

One culture in each pair was anxious and the other was not. One was surly (obviously an unscientific word); they were surly people and she didn't like surly people. The four cultures on the one side were all surly and nasty people, and the four on the other side were nice people. She spoke at other times, as the war threatened us, of low morale and high morale cultures. She spoke on the one hand of hatred and aggression, and on the other hand of affection. What was there general to all the four cultures that she disliked and opposite to what was general to the four that she liked? She spoke tentatively of these as insecure and secure cultures.

The good ones, the secure ones, those she liked, felt drawn to, were the Zuni, the Arapesh, the Dakota, and one of the Eskimo groups (I forget which one). My own field work (unpublished) added the

Northern Blackfoot as a secure culture. The nasty, surly ones, that she would shiver a little about and shudder over were the Chuckchee, the Ojibwa, the Dobu, and the Kwakiutl.

She tried one after another all the generalizations that she might be able to make of these cultures, all the standard can-openers, you might call them, that were available at that time. She compared them on the basis of race, geography, climate, size, wealth, complexity. But these criteria failed to work, that is, to be common to the four secure ones and absent in the four insecure ones. No integration was possible on these bases, no logic, no taxonomy. She asked, which cultures commit suicide and which don't. Which have polygamy and which don't. Which are matrilineal and which are patrilineal? Which have big houses and which have small houses? None of these principles of classification worked.

Finally what *did* work was what I can only call the *function* of behavior rather than the overt behavior itself. She realized that behavior was not the answer, that she had to look for the function of the behavior, the meaning that it purported, what it tried to say, what character structure it expressed. It is this jump which I think was a revolution in the theory of anthropology and of society, laying the basis for a comparative sociology, a technique for comparing societies and placing them on a continuum instead of regarding each as unique and *per se*. The following is from her manuscript:

Take, for example, suicide. Suicide has repeatedly been shown to be related to the sociological environment; it goes up under certain conditions and goes down under others. In America it is one index of psychological catastrophe because it is an act which cuts the Gordian knot of a situation with which a man is no longer able or willing to deal. But suicide, listed as a common trait of culture, may be an act with very different significance in some other culture where it is common. In old Japan, it was the honorable act of any warrior who had lost his battle; it was an act which reinstated honor more than life—the whole duty of man in the Samurai code. In primitive society suicide is sometimes the final loving duty of a wife or sister or mother in the extravagance of mourning; it is the reaffirmation that love of a close relative is more than anything else in life and that when that relative is dead, life is no longer worthwhile. Where this is the highest moral code of such a society, suicide is a final affirmation of ideals. On the other hand, suicide in some tribes is more like the Chinese idea of suicide, as they say, "on the doorstep" of another man; meaning that suicide is an accepted way of revenging himself against one who has wronged him or against whom he holds a grudge. Such suicide in primitive tribes where it exists is the most effective, and sometimes the only, action one can take against another, and it stacks up with action at law in other cultures, not with any of the kinds of suicide we have already spoken of.

Definition. Instead of secure and insecure Benedict finally chose the concepts "high synergy" and "low synergy" which are less normative, more objective, and less open to suspicion of projection of one's own ideals and tastes. She defined these terms as follows:

> Is there any sociological condition which correlates with strong aggression and any that correlates with low aggression? All our ground plans achieve the one or the other in proportion as their social forms provide areas of mutual advantage and eliminate acts and goals that are at the expense of others in the group. . . . From all comparative material, the conclusion that emerges is that *societies where non-aggression is conspicuous have social orders in which the individual by the same act and at the same time serves his own advantage and that of the group.* . . . Non-aggression occurs (in these societies) not because people are unselfish and put social obligations above personal desires, but when social arrangements make these two identical. Considered just logically, production—whether raising yams or catching fish—is a general benefit and if no man-made institution distorts the fact that every harvest, every catch adds to the village food supply, a man can be a good gardener and also be a social benefactor. He is advantaged and his fellows are advantaged. . . .
>
> I shall speak of cultures with low synergy where the social structure provides for acts which are mutually opposed and counteractive, and cultures with high synergy where it provides for acts which are mutually reinforcing. . . . *I spoke of societies with high social synergy where their institutions insure mutual advantage from their undertakings, and societies with low social synergy where the advantage of one individual becomes a victory over another, and the majority who are not victorious must shift as they can* [my italics].

These societies have high synergy in which the social institutions are set up so as to transcend the polarity between selfishness and unselfishness, between self-interest and altruism, in which the person who is simply being selfish necessarily reaps rewards for himself. The society with high synergy is one in which virtue pays.

I would like to deal with some of the manifestations and aspects of high and low synergy. I am using my notes, which are twenty-five years old; and I must apologize for not knowing which is Benedict and which is my own thinking. I have made use of this concept through the years in various ways, and there has been a kind of fusion.

High and Low Synergy in Primitive Societies

Siphoning vs. Funneling of Wealth. With regard to the economic institutions, Benedict found that the overt, superficial, face-value kind of things—whether the society was rich or poor, etc.—did not matter. What did matter was that the secure, high-synergy societies had what she called a siphon system of wealth distribution, whereas the insecure, low synergy cultures had what she called funnel mechanisms of wealth distribution. I can summarize funnel mechanisms very briefly, metaphorically; they are any social arrangement that guarantees that wealth attracts wealth, that to him that hath is given and from him that hath not is taken away, that poverty makes more poverty and wealth makes more wealth. In the secure, high-synergy societies, on the contrary, wealth tends to get spread around, it gets siphoned off from the high places down to the low places. It tends, one way or another, to go from rich to poor, rather than from poor to rich.

An example of a siphon mechanism is the "giveaway" during the Sun Dance ceremony of the Northern Blackfoot Indians as I saw it. In this ceremony all the tepees of the society gathered in one huge circle. The rich men of the tribe (rich meaning those who have worked hard and accumulated a great deal) would have accumulated mounds of blankets, food, bundles of various sorts, and sometimes very pathetic things—cases of Pepsi-Cola as I remember. As many possessions as a man could have accumulated during the previous year were piled up.

I am thinking of one man I saw. At one point in the ceremony, in the Plains' Indian tradition, he strutted, and, we would say, boasted, that is, told of his achievements. "You all know that I have done so and so, you all know that I have done this and that, and you all know how smart I am, how good a stock man I am, how good a farmer, and how I have therefore accumulated great wealth." And then, with a very lordly gesture, a gesture of great pride but without being humiliating, he gave this pile of wealth to the widows, to the orphaned children, and to the blind and diseased. At the end of the Sun Dance ceremony he was stripped of all his possessions, owning nothing but the clothes he stood in. He had, in this synergic way (I won't say either selfishly or unselfishly because clearly the polarity has been transcended) given away everything he had, but in that process had demonstrated what a wonderful man he was, how capable, how intelligent, how strong, how hard-working, how generous, and therefore how wealthy.

I remember my confusion as I came into the society and tried to find out who was the richest man, and found that the rich man had nothing. When I asked the white secretary of the reserve who was the richest man, he mentioned a man none of the Indians had mentioned, that is, the man who had on the books the most stock, the most cattle and horses. When I came back to my Indian informants and asked them about Jimmy McHugh, about all his horses, they shrugged with contempt. "He keeps it," they said, and, as a consequence, they hadn't even thought to regard him as wealthy. White-Headed Chief was "wealthy" even though he owned nothing. In what way then did virtue pay? The men who were formally generous in this way were the most admired, most respected, and the most loved men in the tribe. These were the men who benefited the tribe, the men they could be proud of, the men who warmed their hearts.

To say it another way, if White-Headed Chief, this generous man, had discovered a gold mine or stumbled across some pile of wealth, everyone in the tribe would have been happy because of his generosity. If he had been an ungenerous man, as happens so frequently in our society, then the tendency would have been as it is for our friends who have suddenly acquired great wealth; it is apt to set them over against us. Our institutions encourage the development of jealousy, envy, resentment, distance, and finally a real likelihood of enmity, in a situation like this.

Among the siphon systems of wealth distribution that Benedict listed, the giveaway of this type was one. Another was ritual hospitality as in many tribes where the rich man will immediately have all his relatives come to visit and he will take care of them. There were also generosity, mutual-reciprocity relationships, cooperative techniques of food sharing and so on. In our own society, I think our graded income and property taxes would be an instance of a siphon mechanism. In theory, if a wealthy person gets twice as wealthy, this is good for me and you because so much of that goes into the common treasury. Let us assume it is used for the common good.

As for funnel mechanisms, examples are exorbitant rent, usurious interest (by comparison we know nothing of usurious interest even on the waterfront; as I recall it, the Kwakiutl rate of interest was 1200 per cent a year), slave labor and forced labor, exploitation of labor, excessive profits, relatively greater taxation of the poor than of the rich, and so on.

I think you can see Benedict's point about the purport, the effect, or the flavor of the institution. Giving away money is in itself, as sheer behavior, meaningless. I consider this to be true at the psychological level also. So many psychologists do not realize that behavior is a defense against the psyche as often as it is a direct expression of it. It's a way of hiding motivations and emotions, intent, and purport, as well as of revealing them, and therefore must never be taken at face value.

Use vs. Ownership. We can also look at the relation of ownership to actual use of possessions. My interpreter, who spoke English quite well, had been to the Canadian schools, had got some college education, and was therefore wealthy, for in this kind of tribe intelligence correlated very closely with wealth, even in our sense. He was the only man in the society who owned an automobile. We were together most of the time, so I could see that he hardly ever used his car. People would come and say, "Teddy, how about the key to your car?" And he would pass over the key. As near as I could make out, owning the car for him meant paying for the gas, fixing the tires, coming out and rescuing people in the middle of the reservation who didn't know how to handle it, and so on. This car belonged to anybody who needed it and could ask for it. Obviously the fact that he possessed the only car in the whole society was a point of pride, of pleasure and gratification rather than attracting to him envy, malice, and hostility. The others were glad he had the car and would have been glad if five people had cars instead of just one.

Comforting vs. Frightening Religion. The distinction in terms of synergy also holds for the religious institutions. You will find that the god or gods or the ghosts or the supernaturals in the secure or high-synergy societies tend uniformly to be rather benevolent, helpful, friendly, sometimes even in a way that some in our society call sacrilegious. Among the Blackfoot, for instance, the personal ghost that any man would have for himself privately, the one he had seen in a vision perhaps on a mountain, could actually be invoked at a poker game. There was so much comfort with these personal gods that it was perfectly all right for a man with an inside straight to call a halt to the game and go off in a corner and commune with his ghost to decide whether to draw or not. In the insecure or low-synergy societies on the other hand, the gods, the supernaturals, and the ghosts were uniformly ruthless, terrifying, and so on.

I checked this relationship with some students at Brooklyn College in a very informal way (around 1940). There were a couple of dozen youngsters whom I had tested as secure or insecure in a questionnaire that I had constructed. I asked those who were religious in a formal way one question: Suppose you woke up out of your sleep and felt somehow that God was either in the room or looking in at you, how would you feel? The tendency was for the secure people to feel comforted, and protected; and for the insecure to feel terrified.

Now on a much larger scale, it is approximately this kind of thing that you can find in the secure and insecure societies. Western notions of the god of vengeance and wrath as over against the god of love indicate that our own religious documents are composed of a kind of a mixture of what you might call secure and insecure religion. In the insecure societies the persons who have religious power generally use this for personal profit of some sort, for what we would call selfish purposes, whereas religious power in a secure society is intended to be used, as in the Zuni for instance, for bringing rain, for making the crops better, for bringing benefit to the whole society.

This kind of contrasting psychological purport or upshot can be distinguished in the style of prayer, the style of leadership, the family relationship, the relationships between men and women, the phrasing of sexuality, the style of emotional ties, of kinship, of friendship, and so on. If you have the feel for this differentiation, you should be able to predict right on down the line what you could expect in these two kinds of societies. I will add just one more thing, a little unexpected I think to our Western minds. The societies with high synergy all have techniques for working off humiliation, and the societies with low synergy uniformly do not. In the latter, life is humiliating, embarrassing, and hurting. It *must* be. In Benedict's four insecure societies the humiliation rankled, lasted, somehow never ended; whereas in the secure societies there was a way of bringing it to a close, of paying your debt and being done with it.

High and Low Synergy in Our Society

It must have occurred to you by now that our own society is one of mixed synergy. We have high-synergy and low-synergy institutions.

We have a wide pervasiveness of high synergy in philanthropy, for instance, which does not occur in many other cultures at all. Our society is a very generous culture and frequently in a very nice, very secure way.

On the other hand, there are obviously institutions in our society which set us against each other, making us into rivals necessarily, which put us into a situation where we must scrap for a limited amount of goods. This is like the zero-sum game where one can win and the other must therefore lose.

Perhaps I can illustrate by a simple familiar example, the grading system as it is used in most colleges, especially grading on a curve. I have been in situations like that, and could see very well how it felt to be placed against my brothers, to have their good become my hurt. Supposing my name begins with Z and the grades are called off alphabetically, and we know there are only six A's. Of course, I must sit there and hope that the people before me will get poor grades. Every time someone gets a bad grade, this is good for me. Every time someone gets an A, this is bad for me, since it lowers my chances of getting an A. And it is easy enough to say, "I hope he drops dead."

This synergy principle is so important, not only for a general objectively comparative sociology, not only for the tantalizing possibility that this comparative sociology also opens up the way for a supracultural system of values by which to evaluate a culture and everything within it, not only because it furnishes a scientific basis for Utopian theory, but also for more technical social phenomena in other areas.

For one thing, it seems to me that not enough psychologists, particularly social psychologists, are aware of the great and important things that are happening in an area which does not even have a very good name yet, which we may call organization theory, or the social psychology of industry perhaps, or the theory of enterprise or business. The book read as a primer by most people interested in this field is McGregor's *The Human Side of Enterprise* (114). I suggest that you look at what he calls the Theory-Y level of social organization as an example of high synergy. It illustrates the possibility of arranging social institutions, whether in business, in an army, or in a university, in such a fashion that the people within the organization are coordinated with each other and are perforce made into colleagues and teammates rather than into rivals. I have studied such a business during the last few years, and I assure you it is possible to describe it, to some extent at least, in terms of high synergy, or secure social organization. I hope that these new social psychologists will try using Benedict's concepts to contrast carefully such an organization with one which is based on the doctrine that there is a limited amount of good and "if I get some you must get less."

I would refer you also to Likert's recent book, *New Patterns of Management* (78), which is a collection of extensive, careful researches on various aspects of what we can call synergy in industrial organizations. There is even one place in which Likert actually discusses what he calls the "influence pie" (p. 57), trying to work with a paradox which he found difficult, namely that the good foremen, the good leaders, the ones who would rate high in terms of actual results gave power *away* more than the others. What could you say about the fact that the more power you give away the more you have? Likert's treatment of this paradox is interesting because you see a Western mind struggling with a not very Western concept.

I would say no Utopia can be constructed henceforth by the knowledgeable person without making peace with the concept of synergy. It looks to me at this time as if any Utopia, or Eupsychia (which I think is a better name), must have as one of its foundations a set of high-synergy institutions.

Synergy in the Individual

Identification. The synergy concept can also be applied on the individual level, to the nature of interpersonal relationships between two persons. It makes a fairly decent definition of the high love relationship, what I have written about as Being-love (89, pp. 39–41). Love has been defined variously as if your interests were my interests, or as if two hierarchies of basic needs pooled into one, or as if my feet hurt when you have a corn, or as if my happiness rested upon your happiness. Most of the definitions of love that have been offered imply identification of this sort. But this is also a good parallel with the notion of high synergy, that somehow two people have arranged their relationship in such a fashion that one person's advantage is the other person's advantage rather than one person's advantage being the other's disadvantage.

Some recent studies of sex life and family life in the lower economic classes in this country (e.g., 61) and in England (142) describe what they call the exploitative relationship, which is clearly a relationship with low synergy. Here there is always the question of who wears the pants in the family, or who is the boss, or who loves whom more, with the conclusion that whoever loves more is a sucker or must get hurt, and so on. All of these are low-synergy statements and imply a limited amount of good, rather than an unlimited amount.

I think that the concept of identification, which has come not only from Freud and Adler but from other sources as well, can stand broadening on this new basis. Perhaps we could say that love can be defined as the expansion of the self, the person, the identity. I think we have all experienced this, with children, with wives or husbands, with people who are very close to us. There is a feeling, especially with helpless children I would say, that you would rather have the cough than have your child cough during the night. It just hurts more when the child coughs than when you do. You are stronger; therefore, if you could only take the cough it would be better all around. Clearly this is a melting of the psychological skin between two entities. This is, I would suggest, another direction for the notion of identification.

Fusing the Selfish-Unselfish Dichotomy. Here I would like to take a jump beyond Benedict. She seems too often to have been talking in terms of a straight-line continuum, a polarity, a dichotomizing of selfish and unselfish. But it seems obvious to me that she clearly *implied* a transcendence of this dichotomy in the strict, Gestalt sense of the creation of a superordinate unity which would demonstrate that what had seemed a duality was so only because it had not yet developed far enough into unity. In highly developed, psychiatrically healthy people, self-actualizing people, whichever you choose to call them, you will find if you try to rate them that they are extraordinarily unselfish in some ways, and yet also that they are extraordinarily selfish in other ways. Those who know Fromm's work on healthy and unhealthy selfishness, or Adler's on *Gemeinschaftsgefühl*, will know what I mean here. Somehow the polarity, the dichotomy, the assumption that more of one means less of the other, all this fades. They melt into each other and you have now a single concept for which we have no word yet. High synergy from this point of view can represent a transcending of the dichotomizing, a fusion of the opposites into a single concept.

Integrating the Cognitive and the Conative. Finally, I have found the concept of synergy useful for the understanding of intrapersonal psychodynamics. Sometimes this usefulness is very obvious, as in seeing integration within the person as high synergy, and intrapsychic dissociations of the ordinary pathological sort as low synergy, i.e., as a person torn and set against himself.

In the various studies on free choice in various animal species and in human infants, I think a further improvement in theoretical phrasing can be made with the aid of synergy theory. We can say that these experiments demonstrate a synergic working or fusing of cognition and conation. These are situations in which, so to speak, head and heart, rational and nonrational speak the same language, in which our impulses lead us in a wise direction. This applies as well to Cannon's concept of homeostasis, which he called the "wisdom" of the body.

There are situations in which especially anxious, insecure people tend to assume that what they want must necessarily be bad for them. What tastes good is probably fattening. What is wise or right to do, or what you ought to do, is very likely something that you have to spur yourself on to do. You have to force yourself to do it, because of this deep assumption in so many of us that what we wish for, what we yearn for, what we like, what tastes good, is probably not wise, not good, not correct. But the appetite and other free-choice experiments indicate, on the contrary, that it is more likely that we enjoy what is good for us, at least with fairly good choosers and under fairly good conditions.

I will conclude with a statement by Erich Fromm that has always impressed me very much. "Sickness consists essentially in wanting what is not good for us."

15

Questions for the
Normative Social Psychologist[1]

Note that the description of the seminar implies practicality, actual attainability, rather than dreams, fantasies, or wish fulfillments. In order to stress this point, not only must your paper describe your good society, but it must also have some specification about the methods of achieving it, i.e., politics. Next year the title of the course will be changed to "Normative Social Psychology." This is to stress that the empirical attitude will prevail in this class. This means that we will talk in terms of degree, of percentages, of the reliability of evidence, of missing information that needs to be obtained, of needed investigations and researches, of the possible. We will not waste our

[1] This chapter is based on notes given out at the beginning of the Spring 1967 semester-long seminar for seniors and graduate students at Brandeis University. In addition to furnishing a common background of assumptions, rules, and problems for the assigned reading and papers, I hoped also that these notes would help keep the group in the realm of empirical and scientific endeavor.

The catalogue description of the proposed seminar read: "Utopian Social Psychology: Seminar for graduate students in Psychology, Sociology, Philosophy or any of the social sciences. Discussion of selected Utopian and Eupsychian writings. The seminar will concern itself with the empirical and realistic questions: How good a society does human nature permit? How good a human nature does society permit? What is possible and feasible? What is not?"

time on dichotomizing, on black or white, either/or, on the perfect, on the unattainable, or on the inevitable. (There is no inevitable.) It will be assumed that reform is possible, as are also progress, improvement. But *inevitable* progress toward the attainment, in some future moment, of a perfect ideal, is not likely, and we will not bother talking about it. (Deterioration or catastrophe are also possible.) In general, merely being against something will not be sufficient. Better alternatives should be presented at the same time. We will assume a holistic approach to the problem of reforming or revolutionizing or improving an individual man or the whole society. Futhermore, we will assume that it is not necessary to change one first before the other can be changed, i.e., the man or the society. We will assume that they can both be worked at simultaneously.

Make the general assumption that no normative social thinking is possible until we have some idea of *the individual goal*, i.e., the kind of person to aim to be and by which to judge the adequacy of any society. I proceed on the assumption that the good society, and therefore the immediate goal of any society which is trying to improve itself, is the self-actualization of all individuals, or some norm or goal approximating this. (Transcendence of self—living at the level of Being —is assumed to be most possible for the person with a strong and free identity, i.e., for the self-actualizing person. This will necessarily involve consideration of societal arrangements, education, etc., that make transcendence more possible.) The question here is: Do we have a trustworthy, reliable conception of the healthy or desirable or transcending or ideal person? Also this normative idea is itself moot and debatable. Is it possible to improve a society without having some idea of what one considers to be an improved human being?

We must also have some notion, I assume, of the *autonomous social requirements* (which are independent of the intrapsychic or of individual psychological health or maturity). I assume that the idea of personal improvement, one person by one person, is not a practicable solution of the problem of improving the society. Even the best individuals placed under poor social and institutional circumstances behave badly. One can set up social institutions which will guarantee that individuals will be at each other's throats; or one can set up social institutions which will encourage individuals to be synergic with each other. That is, one can set up social conditions so that one person's advantage would be to another person's advantage rather than the other person's disadvantage. This is a basic assumption and is debatable, and ought to be demonstrable (83, pp. 88–107).

1. *Is the norm to be universal (for the whole human species), or national (with political and military sovereignty), or subcultural (with a smaller group within a nation or state) or familial and individual?* I assume that universal peace is not possible so long as there are separate and sovereign nations. Because of the kind of wars which are possible today (and which I think are unavoidable so long as we have national sovereignty) any normative social philosopher must assume in the long run limited sovereignty of nations, e.g., like that proposed by the United World Federalists, etc. I assume that the normative social thinker will be automatically working toward such a goal at all times. But once this is assumed, then the questions come up of improving the nation-states as they now exist, of local subdivisions like the states within the U.S., or subcultural groupings in the United States, like the Jews or the Chinese, or, finally, the question of making an oasis out of the individual family. This does not exclude even the question of how a single person can make his own life and his own environment more Eupsychian. I assume that all of these are simultaneously possible; they do not in theory or in practice mutually exclude each other. (I suggest as a basis for discussion "The Theory of Social Improvement; The Theory of the Slow Revolution," in my *Eupsychian Management* [83, pp. 247–260]).

2. *Selected or unselected societies.* For my conception of Eupsychia, see page 350 in *Motivation and Personality* (95). Also "Eupsychia, the Good Society," *Journal of Humanistic Psychology* (91). Also scattered sections in my *Eupsychian Management* (83). My definition of Eupsychia is clearly a selected subculture, i.e., it is made up only of psychologically healthy or mature or self-actualizing people and their families. Through the history of Utopias, this question has sometimes been faced and sometimes not. I assume it *always* has to be consciously decided upon. In your papers you must specify whether you are speaking about the whole human species, unselected, or about a selected-out smaller group, with specified entrance requirements. Also you must address yourself to the question of exiling or assimilating disruptive individuals if you do have a selected Utopian group.

Must individuals be kept in the society once they have been selected or born into it? Or do you think you need provisions for exile or imprisonment, etc.? For criminals, evildoers, etc.? (I assume on the basis of your knowledge of psychopathology and psychotherapy, and of social pathology, and of the history of Utopian attempts, that any unselective group may be destroyed by sick or immature individuals. But since our techniques of selection are still very poor, my opinion is that any group trying to be Utopian or Eupsychian must also be able to expel dystopian individuals who slip by the selection techniques.)

3. *Pluralism. The acceptance and use of individual differences in constitution and in character.* Many Utopias proceeded as if all human beings were interchangeable and were equal to each other. We must accept the fact that there are very wide ranges of variation in intelligence, character, constitution, etc. Permission for individuality or for idiosyncrasy or individual freedom must specify the range of individual differences to be taken into consideration. In the fantasy Utopias there have been no feeble-minded people, no insane, no seniles, etc. Furthermore, there is frequently built in, in a covert fashion, some norm for the desirable human person which seems to me far too narrow in view of our actual knowledge of range of variations in human beings. How fit all kinds of people into *one* set of rules or laws? Do you want to allow for a wide pluralism, e.g., of styles and fashions in clothes, shoes, etc.? In the United States we now permit a very wide, though not complete, range of choice among foods, but a very narrow range of choice among fashions in clothes. Fourier, for instance, founded his whole Utopian scheme on the full acceptance and use of a very wide range of constitutional differences. Plato on the other hand had only three kinds of human beings. How many kinds do you want? Can there be a society without deviants? Does the concept of self-actualization make this question obsolete? If you accept the widest range of individual differences and the pluralism of characters and talents, then this is a society that in effect accepts much (or all) of human nature. Does self-actualization mean in effect the acceptance of idiosyncrasy or of deviants? To what extent?

4. *Pro-industrial or anti-industrial? Pro-science or anti-science? Pro-intellectual or anti-intellectual?* Many Utopias have been Thoreauvian. rural, essentially agricultural (e.g., Borsodi's School of Living). Many

of them have been a move away from and against the cities, machines, the money economy, division of labor, etc. Do you agree? How possible is decentralized, ruralized industry? How possible Taoistic harmony with the surroundings? Garden cities? Garden factories? i.e., with housing always attached so no commuting? Must modern technology necessarily enslave human beings? There certainly are small groups of people in various places in the world who are moving back to agriculture, and certainly this is feasible for small groups. Is it feasible for the whole human species? But also some intentional communities were and are built around manufacturing rather than agriculture or handicrafts.

There is sometimes seen in antitechnology, anticity philosophies a sort of covert anti-intellectualism, antiscience, anti-abstract thought. These are seen by some people as desacralizing, divorced from basic concrete reality, bloodless, opposed to beauty and emotion, unnatural, etc. (82, 126).

5. *Centralized-central, planning-socialistic, or decentralized-anarchic societies.* How much planning is possible? Must it be centralized? Must it be coercive? Most intellectuals know little or nothing about philosophical anarchism. (I recommend *Manas* [79].) One basic aspect of the *Manas* philosophy is a philosophical anarchism. It stresses decentralization rather than centralization, local autonomy, personal responsibility, a mistrust of large organizations of any kind or of large accumulations of power of any kind. It mistrusts force as a social technique. It is ecological and Taoistic in its relationship to nature and to reality, etc. How much hierarchy is necessary within a community, e.g., a kibbutz or a Fromm-type factory, or a partnership-owned farm or factory, etc.? Is command necessary? Power over other people? Power to enforce majority will? Power to punish? The scientific community can be taken as an example of a leaderless Eupsychian "subculture," decentralized, voluntary yet coordinated, productive, and with a powerful and effective code of ethics (which works). With this may be contrasted the Synanon subculture (highly organized, hierarchically structured).

6. *The question of evil behavior.* In many Utopias this question is simply missing. It is either wished away or overlooked. There are no jails, nobody is punished. Nobody hurts anybody else. There is no crime, etc. I accept as a basic assumption that the problem of bad be-

havior, or psychopathological behavior, of evil behavior, of violence, jealousy, greed, exploitation, laziness, sinfulness, malice, etc., must be consciously confronted and managed. ("The short and sure path to despair and surrender is this, to believe that there is somewhere a scheme of things that will eliminate conflict, struggle, stupidity, cupidity, personal jealousy"—David Lilienthal.) The question of evil must be discussed both intrapersonally and in terms of the societal arrangements, i.e., psychologically *and* sociologically (which means also historically).

7. *The dangers of unrealistic perfectionism.* I assume that perfectionism, i.e., thinking that ideal or perfect solutions may be demanded, is a danger. The history of Utopias shows many such unrealistic, unattainable, nonhuman fantasies (e.g., let us all love each other. Let us all share equally. All people must be treated as equals in all ways. Nobody must have any power over anybody else. Application of force is always evil. "There are no bad people; there are only unloved people"). A common sequence here is perfectionism or unrealistic expectations *leading to* inevitable failure *leading to* disillusionment, *leading to* apathy, discouragement, or active hostility to all ideals and all normative hopes and efforts. That is, perfectionism very often (always?) tends ultimately to lead to active hostility against normative hopes. Improvability has often been thought impossible when perfectibility turned out to be impossible.

8. *How to handle aggression, hostility, fighting, conflict?* Can these be abolished? Is aggression or hostility in some sense instinctive? Which social institutions foster conflict? Which minimize it? Granted that wars are unavoidable in a human species divided up into sovereign nations, could force be conceivably unneeded in a united world? Would such a world government need a police force or an army? (As a basis for discussion, I suggest Chapter 10 "Is Destructiveness Instinctoid?" in my *Motivation and Personality* [95], and Appendix B.) My general conclusions are: that aggression, hostility, strife, conflict, cruelty, sadism certainly all exist commonly and perhaps universally on the psychoanalytic couch, i.e., in fantasy, in dream, etc. I assume that aggressive behavior can be found in everyone as an actuality or a possibility. Where I see no aggressiveness at all, I suspect repression or suppression or self-control. I assume that the *quality* of aggression changes very markedly as one moves from psychological immaturity

or neurosis up toward self-actualization or maturity in that sadistic or cruel or mean behavior is a quality of aggression found in undeveloped or neurotic or immature people, but that as one moves toward personal maturity and freedom, the quality of this aggression changes into reactive or righteous indignation and into self-affirmation, resistance to exploitation and domination, passion for justice, etc. I also assume that successful psychotherapy changes the *quality* of aggression in this second direction, i.e., changing it from cruelty into healthy self-affirmation. I assume also that verbal airing of aggression makes actual aggressive behavior less likely. I assume that social institutions can be set up in such a way as to make aggression of any quality more likely or less likely. I assume that some outlet for violence is more necessary for young males than for young females. Are there techniques for teaching young people how to handle and express their aggressions wisely, in a satisfying fashion, and yet not in a fashion harmful to others?

9. *How simple should life be?* What are the desirable limits to the complexity of life?

10. *How much privacy for the individual person, the child, the family must a society allow?* How much togetherness, community activity, fellowship, sociability, community life? How much privacy, "let-be," nonintrusiveness?

11. *How tolerant can a society be? Can everything be forgiven? What cannot be tolerated? What must be punished?* How tolerant can a society be of stupidity, falsehood, cruelty, psychopathy, criminality, etc.? How much protection must be built into the social arrangements for, e.g., aments, seniles, ignorant, crippled, etc.? This question is also important because it raises the question of overprotection, and of hampering the ones who don't need protection, which may lead to hampering the freedom of thought, discussion, experimentation, idiosyncrasy, etc. It also raises the question of the dangers of the germ-free atmosphere, of the tendency in Utopian writers to somehow remove all danger as well as all evil.

12. *How wide can the range of public tastes be that must be accepted? How much tolerance for what you disapprove of? How much tolerance for degrading, value-destroying, "low tastes." How about drug addiction, alcohol, LSD, cigarettes? How about the tastes on TV, movies, newspapers?* It is claimed that this is what the public

wants, and probably this is not too far off the statistical truth. How much will you interfere with what the statistical public wants? Do you plan equal votes for superiors, for geniuses, for the talented, the creative, the capable on the one hand, and feebleminded on the other hand? What would you do with the British Broadcasting Corporation? Should it always teach? How much should it reflect the Neilsen ratings? Ought there to be three channels for different kinds of people, five channels? Do the makers of movies, TV shows, etc., have any responsibility for educating and improving public taste? Whose business is this? Or is it nobody's business? What should be done, for instance, about homosexuals, pederasts, exhibitionists, sadists, and masochists? Should homosexuals be allowed to solicit children? Supposing a pair of homosexuals carry on their sexual life in complete privacy—should the society interfere? If a sadist and a masochist please each other privately, is this public business? Should they be allowed to advertise publicly for each other? Should transvestites be allowed public exposure? Should exhibitionists be punished or limited or confined?

13. *The problem of the leader (and the follower), the capable, the excellent, the strong, the boss, the entrepreneur.* Is it possible wholly to admire and love our (factual) superiors? Is it possible to be post-ambivalent? How protect them from envy, *ressentiment*, "the evil eye"? If all newborn infants were given complete equality of opportunity, all sorts of individual differences in capacity, talent, intelligence, strength, etc., would appear during the life span. What to do about these? Should greater rewards, greater pay, more privileges be given to the more talented, the more useful, the ones who produce more? Where would the "gray eminence" idea work, i.e., paying the powerful people *less* (in money) than other people, while perhaps paying them off in nonmonetary terms, i.e., in terms of higher need and metaneed gratifications, e.g., being permitted freedom, autonomy, self-actualization? How possible is the vow of poverty (or at least simplicity) for leaders, bosses, etc.? How much freedom should be given to the entrepreneur, to the person with the high need for achievement, to the organizer, to the initiator, to the person who enjoys running things, being boss, wielding power? How get voluntary self-subordination? Who will collect the garbage? How will the strong and the weak relate to each other? The more capable and the less

capable? How achieve love, respect, and gratitude for authority (policeman, judge, lawmaker, father, captain)?

14. *Is permanent contentment possible? Is immediate contentment possible?* As a basis for discussion I suggest the chapter "On Low Grumbles, High Grumbles, and Metagrumbles" (Chapter 18). Also various writings of Colin Wilson on what he calls the "St. Neot margin" (159). Also, *Work and the Nature of Man* (46). It can be assumed that contentment is for practically all people a transient state, no matter what the social conditions may be, and that it is useless to seek for permanent contentment. Compare with concepts of Heaven, Nirvana, the benefits expected from great wealth, from leisure, retirement, etc. Parallel to this the finding that solving "lower" problems brings not so much contentment as more but "higher" problems, and "higher" grumbles.

15. *How shall males and females adapt to each other,* *enjoy each other, respect each other?* Most Utopias have been written by males. Would females have different conceptions of a good society? Most Utopians also have been either obviously patriarchal or covertly so. In any case throughout most of history females were regarded as inferior to males in intellect, in executive capacity, in creativeness, etc. Now that females, at least in the advanced countries, have been emancipated and self-actualization is possible for them also, how will this change the relationships between the sexes? What kind of change is necessary in the male in order to accommodate to this new female? Is it possible to transcend the simple dominance-subordination hierarchy? What would a Eupsychian marriage be like, i.e., between the self-actualizing male and the self-actualizing female? What kinds of functions, duties, what kinds of work would the females do in Eupsychia? How would the sex life change? How would femininity and masculinity be defined?

16. *The question of institutionalized religions, personal religions, the "spiritual life," the life of values, the metamotivated life.* All known cultures have a religion of one sort or another, and presumably always have had. For the first time nonreligion or humanism or noninstitutionalized personal religion is possible. What kind of religious or spiritual or value-life would exist in Eupsychia, or in a small Eupsychian community? If group religions, religious institutions, the historical religions continued, how would they be changed?

How would they differ from what they were in the past? How shall children be reared and educated toward self-actualization and beyond to the value-life (spiritual, religious, etc.)? Toward being good members of a Eupsychia? Can we learn from other cultures, from the ethnological literature, from the high-synergy cultures?

17. *The question of intimacy groups, of families, brotherhoods, fraternities, fellowships.* There seems to be an instinctoid need for belongingness, for roots, for a face-to-face group in which affection and intimacy are given freely. It is pretty clear that these would have to be smallish groups, certainly not over fifty or one hundred. In any case it is unlikely that intimacy and affection is possible between millions of people, and therefore any society must organize itself from below upward starting with intimacy groups of some sort. In our society it is the blood family, at least in the cities. There are religious fellowships, sororities, fraternities. The T-groups and encounter groups practice candor, feedback, honesty with each other, efforts toward friendship, expressiveness, and intimacy. Is it possible to institutionalize something of this sort? An industrial society tends to be highly mobile, i.e., people tend to move around a lot. Must this cut the roots and the ties to other people? Also—must these groups be cross-generational? Or can they be peer groups? It looks as if children and adolescents are not capable of complete self-rule (unless perhaps if specifically brought up toward this end). Is it possible to have some nonadult peer groups living by their own values, that is, without fathers, mothers, without elders?

Problem: is intimacy possible without sex?

18. *The effective helper; the hurtful helper. Effective nonhelping (Taoistic noninterference). The Bodhisattva.* Assuming that in any society the stronger would want to help the weaker, or in any case, would have to, what is the best way to help others (who are weaker, poorer, less capable, less intelligent)? What is the best way to help them become stronger? How much of their autonomy and responsibility for themselves is it wise to take upon yourself if you are the stronger or older person? How can you help other people if they are poor and you are rich? How can a rich nation help poor nations? For discussion purposes, I will define arbitrarily the Bodhisattva as a person a) who would like to help others, b) who agrees he will be a better helper as he himself becomes more mature, healthy, more fully

human, c) who knows when to be Taoistic and noninterfering, i.e., nonhelping, d) who *offers* his help or makes it available to be chosen or not chosen as the other person wishes, and, e) who assumes that a good way to self-growth is via helping others. This is to say that if one wishes to help other people, then a very desirable way to do this is to become a better person oneself. Problem: How many nonhelping persons can a society assimilate, i.e., people looking for their own personal salvation, hermits, pious beggars, people who meditate alone in a cave, people who remove themselves from society and go into privacy, etc?

19. *Institutionalizing sex and love.* My guess is that the advanced societies are now moving toward beginning the sex life approximately at the age of puberty without marriage or without other ties. There are "primitive" societies that do something of the sort, i.e., pretty complete premarital promiscuity plus a postmarital monogamy or near-monogamy. In these societies the marriage partner is chosen hardly at all for sexual reasons since sex is freely available, but rather as a matter of personal taste and also as a partner in the culture, e.g., for having children, for economic division of labor, etc. Is this a reasonable guess? What does it imply? There has already appeared a tremendous range of variation in sexual drive or sexual need, especially in women (in our culture). It is unwise to assume that everybody is equally strongly sexed. How is it possible to accept in a good society a wide range of difference in sexual appetite?

Sexuality, love, and family folkways are now in very rapid transition in many parts of the world, including many Utopian communities, e.g., promiscuity groups, group marriage, "swap clubs," nonlegal marriages, etc. (See for instance the novels of Robert Rimmer.) Many kinds of arrangements are being suggested and actually tried out. The data from these "experiments" are not yet available, but will be one day and will then have to be considered.

20. *The problem of choosing the best leaders.* In our society there are many groups, e.g., adolescents, that seem often to prefer bad leaders to good ones. That is, they choose people who will lead them to destruction and to defeat—losers rather than winners—paranoid characters, psychopathic personalities, blusterers. Any good society that hopes to grow must be able to choose as leaders those individuals

who are best suited for the job in fact, in actual talents, and capacity. How can such good choices be enhanced? What kinds of political structure make it more possible for, e.g., a paranoid person to have great power? What kinds of political structures make this less possible or impossible?

21. *What are the best social conditions for bringing human nature to full humanness?* This is a normative way of phrasing the study of personality-culture. The new literature of social psychiatry is pertinent here, and also the new literature of the mental-hygiene and the social-hygiene movement, the various forms of group therapy that are now being experimented with, the Eupsychian educational communities like Esalen Institute. This is the point at which to bring up the question of how to make the classroom more Eupsychian—the schools, universities, and education in general—and then on to each of the other social institutions. Eupsychian management (or Theory-Y management) is an example of this kind of normative social psychology. In it society and each of the institutions within the society are defined as "good" to the extent that they help people toward fuller humanness, and they are defined as bad or psychopathogenic to the extent that they diminish humanness. At this point as well as at other points the questions of social pathology and of individual pathology must undoubtedly be discussed.

22. *Can a health-fostering group itself be a path toward self-actualization?* (See the materials on the Eupsychian factory, on Synanon, the intentional community, etc.) Some people are convinced that the interests of the individual *must* be opposed to the interests of a group, an institution, an organization, a society—civilization itself. The history of religions shows frequently a split between the individual mystics whose private illuminations set them *against* the church. Can a church foster individual development? Can the schools? Factories?

23. *How is "idealism" related to practicality, "materialism," realism?* I assume that lower basic needs are prepotent to higher needs, which in turn are prepotent to metaneeds (intrinsic values). This means that materialism is prepotent to "idealism" but also that they both exist and are psychological realities which must be taken into account in any Eupsychian or Utopian thinking.

24. *Many Utopias have visualized a world composed exclusively of sane, healthy, and effective citizens. Even if a society selects only such individuals originally, yet some will become sick, aged, weak, or incapable. Who will take care of them?*

25. *I assume that the abolition of social injustices will permit the unmistakable appearance of "biological injustices,"* of genetic, pre-natal and natal inequalities, e.g., one child is born with a healthy heart while another is born with a bad heart—which of course is not fair. Neither would it be fair that one is more talented or intelligent or strong or beautiful than another. Biological injustices may be harder to bear than social injustices, where alibis are more possible. What can a good society do about this?

26. *Is ignorance, misinformation, concealment of truth, censoring, blindness necessary in the society or any portion of it?* Are certain truths reserved for the governing group? Dictatorships, benevolent or not, seem to require some concealing of truth. What truths are considered dangerous, e.g., to the young, etc.? Jeffersonian democracy *needs* full access to truth.

27. *Many actual and fantasied Utopias have relied on a wise, benevolent, shrewd, strong, effective leader, a philosopher-king. But can this be counted on?* (See Frazier in Skinner's *Walden Two* [140] for a modern version.) Who will pick this ideal leader? How guarantee that this leadership will not fall into the hands of tyrants? Are such guarantees possible at all? What happens when the good leader dies? How possible are leaderlessness, decentralization of power, retention of power by each individual and leaderless groups?

28. *At least some of the successful Utopian communities, past and present, e.g., Bruderhof, have built into the culture candor mechanisms for private or public confession, discussion of each other, mutual honesty, truthfulness, and feedback.* Currently this is true of the T-groups (encounter groups) of Synanon and Synanon-like groups of Eupsychian (Theory Y) factories and industries, various types of therapy groups, etc. See *Esalen* brochures (32); *The Tunnel Back: Synanon* (164); pages 154–187 in my *Eupsychian Management* (83); *The Lemon Eaters* (141); the back files of the *Journal of Applied Behavioral Sciences* (56), of the *Journal of Humanistic Psychology* (57), etc.

29. *How integrate enthusiasm with skeptical realism?* Mysticism with practical shrewdness and good reality-testing? Idealistic and perfect and therefore unattainable goals (needed as compass directions) with good-natured acceptance of the unavoidable imperfections of means?

16

Synanon and Eupsychia[1]

First of all, so that there will not be any misunderstanding, I must admit that I have led a very sheltered life. I did not know anything at all about much of what is going on here, and the reason that I came down was to get another angle on the lives of people who weren't so sheltered as I was. I wanted to see what I could learn. The use that I can be to you is as a naïve person, from your point of view, someone who is taking a look at things that you are used to and perhaps noticing things that you would overlook simply because they are so familiar. Perhaps I can help in this way simply by telling you the kinds of reactions I have had and the kinds of questions I am coming away with.

My background is as a theoretical and research psychologist. I have done clinical psychotherapy in the past, but in a situation that is very, very different from the one here, using different approaches and with different kinds of people—such as college students and privileged characters generally. I have spent a whole lifetime learning

[1] This paper (editor, Arthur Warmoth) is based on an impromptu talk given at Daytop Village, an offshoot from Synanon, Staten Island, N. Y., on August 14, 1965. Synanon is a community run by former drug addicts to which addicts come to be cured.

to be pretty careful with people, to be sort of delicate and gentle, and to treat them as if they were like brittle china that would break easily. The first thing that interested me in what is going on here is the evidence that indicates that maybe the whole attitude is wrong. What I have read about Synanon, as well as what I saw last night and this afternoon, suggests that the whole idea of the fragile teacup which might crack or break, the idea that you mustn't say a loud word to anybody because it might traumatize him or hurt him, the idea that people cry easily or crack or commit suicide or go crazy if you shout at them—that maybe these ideas are outdated.

The assumption in your groups seems to be, on the contrary, that people are very tough, and not brittle. They can take an awful lot. The best thing to do is get right at them, and not to sneak up on them, or be delicate with them, or try to surround them from the rear. Get right smack into the middle of things right away. I've suggested that a name for this might be "no-crap therapy." It serves to clean out the defenses, the rationalizations, the veils, the evasions, and politenesses of the world. The world is half-blind, you might say, and what I've seen here is the restoring of sight. In these groups people refuse to accept the normal veils. They rip them aside and refuse to take any crap or excuses or evasions of any sort.

Well, I have been asking questions, and I have been told that this assumption works fine. Did anybody ever commit suicide or crack in any way? No. Has anyone gone crazy from this rough treatment? No. I watched it last night. There was extremely direct talking, and it worked fine. Now this contradicts a whole lifetime of training, and that makes it terribly important to me as a theoretical psychologist who has been trying to figure out what human nature is like in general. It raises a real question about the nature of the whole human species. How strong are people? How much can they take? The big question is how much honesty can people take. How is it good for them, how bad for them? I'm reminded of a line from T. S. Eliot, "Mankind cannot bear very much reality." He is suggesting that people cannot take it straight. On the other hand, the kind of experience that you are having here indicates that not only can people take honesty, but also that it may be very helpful, very therapeutic. It may move things faster. This is true even when the honesty hurts.

I heard from a friend of mine, who is very much interested in

Synanon, about a drug addict who had been through this kind of thing and who, for the first time in his life, had experienced real intimacy, real friendship, real respect. This was his first experience of honesty and directness, and he felt for the first time in his life that he could be himself and that people wouldn't kill him for it. It was delightful: The more himself he was, the better they liked him for it. And he said something that affected me very much. He was thinking about a friend of his whom he liked and who he felt would benefit from this kind of thing. And he said what seemed a really crazy thing: "Isn't it a pity that he is not an addict, because if he were an addict he could come to this wonderful place." In a way, this is a little Utopia, a place out of the world where you can get real straightforwardness, real honesty and the respect that is implied by honesty, and the experience of a real group working together as a team.

Another thought that came to me here: Could it be that this has some of the elements of the good society, and that the insanity is outside? Years ago I worked with the Northern Blackfoot Indians. They are wonderful people. I was interested in that kind of person, and I spent some time with them and got to know them. And yet I had a funny experience. I came into the reservation with the notion that the Indians are over there on a shelf, like a butterfly collection or something like that. And then slowly I shifted and changed my mind. Those Indians on the reservation were decent people; and the more I got to know the whites in the village, who were the worst bunch of creeps and bastards I've ever run across in my life, the more it got paradoxical. Which was the asylum? Who were the keepers and who the inmates? Everything got all mixed up, as it does for the small, good society. It is not like creating crutches, but rather like creating an oasis in a desert.

Another thought came out of our conversation at lunch. The process here basically poses the question of what people need universally. It seems to me that there is a fair amount of evidence that the things that people need as basic human beings are few in number. It is not very complicated. They need a feeling of protection and safety, to be taken care of when they are young so that they feel safe. Second, they need a feeling of belongingness, some kind of a family, clan, or group, or something that they feel that they are in and belong to by right. Third, they have to have a feeling that people have affection for them, that they are worth being loved. And fourth, they must experience respect and esteem. And that's about it. You can talk about psychological health, about being mature and strong, adult and creative, mostly as a consequence of this psychological medicine—like vitamins. Now, if this is true, then most of the American population suffers from lack of these vitamins. There are all sorts of games cooked up to cover the truth, but the truth is that the average American citizen does not have a real friend in the world. Very few people have what a psychologist would call real friendships. The marriages are mostly no good in that ideal sense as well. You could say that the kinds of problems we have, the open troubles—not being able to resist alcohol, not being able to resist drugs, not being able to resist crime, not being able to resist anything—that these are due to the lack of these basic psychological gratifications. The question is, does Daytop supply these psychological vitamins? My impression as I wandered around this place this morning is that it does. Remember what they are: first of all, safety, being anxiety-free, free of fear; next, belongingness, you have to belong to a group; next, affection, you have to have people who like you; and finally, respect, you have to have some respect from people. Could it be that Daytop is effective because it provides an environment where these feelings are possible?

I have a lot of impressions and thoughts rushing in on me. I've been asking a thousand questions and trying out a thousand ideas, but this all seems to be part of it. Let me say it this way: Do you think that this straight honesty, this bluntness that even sounds cruel at times, provides a basis for safety, affection, and respect? It hurts, it must hurt. Each of you has gone through it. Do you think that it is a good idea? There was a prospect here just interviewed, and I sat in on it. The swords were out, and there was no gentleness about it. It was very straight, very direct, very blunt. So, do you think that this works for you? This is one question that I am very much interested in hearing answered. Another is, does this particular kind of group functioning, with everybody clicking together and everything being taken care of by the group, does this supply this feeling of belongingness? And had this feeling been missing before? It seems possible that this brutal honesty, rather than being an insult, implies a kind of respect. You can take it as you find it, as it really is. And this can be a basis for respect and friendship.

I remember hearing an analyst talking a long time ago, long before group therapy. He was talking about this honesty too. What he was saying sounded foolish at the time, as if he was being cruel or something. What he said was that "I place upon my patients the fullest load of anxiety that they can bear." Do you realize what that implies? As much as they can take, that is what he is going to dish out, because the more he can dish out, the faster the whole thing will move. It doesn't seem so foolish in the light of experience here.

And this brings out the idea of education, and of Daytop as an educational institution. It is an oasis, a little good society which supplies the things all societies should supply but don't. In the long run, Daytop brings up the whole question of education and the use which cultures make of it. Education does not mean just books and words. The lessons of Daytop are for education in the larger sense of learning how to become a good adult human being.

[*Note: At this point a discussion began that involved a lively inter- action between Dr. Maslow and the residents of Daytop. Unfortu- nately, the many interesting comments by the residents were not caught on the tape, so that the remainder of this transcription contains only those remarks by Dr. Maslow that were sufficiently extensive and self-contained to be understandable out of the context of the inter- action.*]

Concerning Daytop and the theory of self-actualization. In prin- ciple, everyone can become self-actualized. If everyone does not, it is because something has happened to gum up the process. What is added to the data here is that, more than I had realized, the search for maturity, for responsibility, for a good life is so powerful that it can take all this rough stuff that you dish out. At least this is true for some people. People sort of have to fight their way in here past the pain, the embarrassment, and so forth; and this impressed me as a stronger need for actualizing one's self than even I had realized. Of course, the people here are the ones that *could* take it. Who *couldn't* take it? How many people has this honesty turned away because it was too painful?

On the development of responsibility. It looks as if one way to breed grown-up people is to give them responsibility, to assume that they can take it, and to let them struggle and sweat with it. Let them work it out themselves, rather than overprotecting them, indulging them, or doing things for them. Of course, on the other hand, there is complete neglect, but that is another story. I gather that what is happening here is just this sort of development of a sense of responsibility. You don't take any crap from anybody, and if you have to do something you have to do it. There don't seem to be any excuses.

I can give an example of what I mean from the Blackfoot Indians. These are strong characters, self-respecting men, and they were the bravest of warriors. They were tough characters, they could take it. If you watched to see how they developed this, I think it was through greater respect for their children. I can give you a couple of examples. I can remember a little baby, a toddler, trying to open a door to a cabin. He could not make it. This was a big, heavy door and he was shoving and shoving. Well, Americans would get up and open the door for him. The Blackfoot Indians sat down there for half an hour while that baby struggled with that door, until he was able to get it done for himself. He had to grunt and sweat, and then everyone praised him because he was able to get it done himself. I would say that the Blackfoot Indian respected the child more than the American observer.

Another example was a little boy that I was very fond of. He was about seven or eight years old, and I found by looking very close that he was a kind of rich kid, in a Blackfoot way. He had several horses and cattle in his name, and he owned a medicine bundle of particular value. Someone, a grown-up, turned up who wanted to buy the medicine bundle, which was the most valuable thing that he had. I learned from his father that what little Teddy did when he was made this offer —remember he was only seven years old—was to go into the wilderness by himself to meditate. He went away for about two or three days and nights, camping out, thinking for himself. He did not ask his father or his mother for advice, and they didn't tell him anything. He came back and announced his decision. I can just see us doing that with a seven-year-old kid.

On the new social therapy. This is a thought which may turn out to be of professional interest to you. There is a new kind of job opening up that is an activist's job, and it is one that demands experience rather than book training. It is a sort of a combination of an old-fashioned minister and a teacher. You have to be concerned with people. You have to like working with them directly, rather than at a distance; and you have to have as much knowledge of human nature as possible. I have suggested calling it "social therapy." Well, this seems to be developing very gradually over the last year or two. The people who are doing best are not the people with Ph.D.s and so on; they are the people who have been on the streets and who know what it is all about themselves. They know what they're talking about. They know, for example, when to push hard and when to take it easy.

With one-third of the American population and with about 98 per cent of the rest of the world what you might call "not privileged"; and with the sudden effort to try to teach the illiterate how to read; and of psychiatry to help people to maturity and responsibility; and so on, there is already a great shortage of people to do these jobs. My impression is that it has turned out that ordinary academic training might help some but is not enough. At the present time, much of this is being pushed into the hands of social workers; and the average social worker, if I know anything about his training, generally won't know what is going on. In terms of actual experience, that is. So it might be better to man all these new agencies at least partly with people who are wise by experience rather than by lectures. Well, one of the interesting things about Daytop is that it is being run by people who have been through the mill of experience. You people know how to talk to others in the same boat. And this is a job; it may be a new type of profession.

On the current social revolution. I could give you a half hour of examples of the way it takes place in different spots. The churches are all changing, religion is changing. There is a revolution going on. There are some spots which are more growing points than others; but they are all growing in the same Eupsychian direction, that is, in the direction of more fully human people. This is the direction of people as strong and creative and joyful as people are capable of being, people enjoying life, psychologically and physically healthy people. You can speak about Eupsychian religion and it's happening. I have a book, *Eupsychian Management* (83), that is about the work situation, jobs, factories, and so on. There is a revolution going on there, too. In some places the whole job situation is being set up in such a fashion that it is good for human nature, not bad for it. Human nature is developed rather than diminished by these procedures.

There are books and articles and investigations about marriage and love and sex in the same way. All of them pointing toward an ideal of a sort that tells us the direction in which we are going, in the direction of a man being as tall as he can be, as fully human, as fully developed as you can get.

Now, it is perfectly true that the mass of society is still like a dead weight. But there are so many growing points, so many different spots, that you begin to call it the wave of the future. This isn't the only spot in the world where these things are being talked about, you know. There are dozens of others. We don't hear about most of them because they develop independently. If you get a bright idea, if I make a discovery, some beautiful idea that I work up, I've learned that if I can cook it up, several other people are cooking it up at the same time. It is always a response to what is going on, and the more sensitive people will respond.

This is going on in education as well. I think that it would be possible, if we got together and pooled all the experiences, bad and good, that we could all pool together, to take the skin off the whole damn educational system. But we could also rebuild it. We could make good suggestions—and we should have an educational system. Well, this is explosive because it demands a human reality, human needs, and human development, rather than a sort of traditional heritage from a thousand years ago which is outdated.

It is difficult to speak about Eupsychian education. I think that you can contribute some with the thought that I suggested to you that you consider this as a sort of pilot experiment. Act as if the whole world were looking over your shoulder to see what will happen out of your efforts—what works, what doesn't work, what's good and what's bad, what succeeds and what fails.

Partly, we can do this because the United States is the richest country in the world. We can afford to sit around here instead of grubbing in the fields for a little rice or something of the sort just to keep alive. It's not exactly luxury, but we can sit and talk, whereas there are not many other societies on the face of the earth where you could spend this much time talking and not starve to death. In that sense, we are a sort of pilot experiment where things can be tried out. You can take your experience as an object lesson, or as a biologist would talk of the growing tip of a plant. Instead of another world altogether, this is the growing tip, as you might say when you feel optimistic. When you feel pessimistic, of course, it looks as if most of society is dead weight. It is traditional, conventional, outdated. There are all sorts of moral lessons that we are being given that were good for 1850. It depends on your mood to some extent. But I think that it is a fair way to look at it, to say that this is not just a little backwater. Maybe it's the growing tip of mankind.

On encounters. May I tell you something. I've been in only one encounter group—last night—and I don't know how I would react if I'd been in that thing for a long time. Nobody has ever been that blunt with me in my whole life. It is certainly a striking contrast to the conventional world, the world of university professors. Faculty meetings are certainly not like these encounters. They don't mean a damn thing and I try to avoid them if I can—all the politeness, nobody will say "boo!" If I may say it, I remember thinking of one professor that he would not say "shit" if he were in it up to his neck. Well, this is different; it shook me up a little last night. In the world I come from everyone is so polite because they are avoiding confrontation. There are a lot of prissy old maids around—I mean masculine "old maids." I think it would be a wonderful thing if it were possible for you to get in on one of our faculty meetings and have a real encounter. It would turn the whole thing upside down. And I have a suspicion that it would be for the best.

A major research question. That raises a question that I am asking around here. It is a very important question, and you don't really have the answer, I guess. The question is why do some people stay and others not? That also means, if you take this as a kind of educational institution, how good will it be for how much of the population? How many customers do you expect? How many people won't it work for? You know, the people who never show up do not get counted as failures.

You people here overcame a hurdle, you overcame a fear. What is your theory about the people who don't jump over the fear? What is the difference between them and you? This is a practical question, since you people will be the graduates who will be running places like this somewhere else in the future. Then you must face the problem of how to make a larger percentage stay.

On psychotherapy. You see, the problem is the same for psychoanalysis, for individual psychotherapy. The theory that they have developed out of their experience is that it is just this directness that will drive people away from therapy. What they do is to work people in very gently and allow them months before they really start digging at the problem. They try to establish a relationship first and then put a little pressure on. This is contradicted here where nobody waits for six months; the intensive therapy starts right away. It is a question of what works best, and for whom, for how many. Compared with regular psychoanalytic procedure, it seems that things move very fast here.

That reminds me of something else. The theory that I was brought up with, and that I have used in therapy, is that it does not do much good to *give* people the truth. The thing to do is to help them to discover the truth about themselves for themselves. And the figuring is that it is going to take a long time because the truth is not such a nice thing to see. You have to face it gradually. I report to you that by comparison with that picture—that procedure—what happens here is that the truth is being dished out and shoved right in your face. Nobody sits and waits for eight months until you discover it for yourself. At least the people who stay can accept it, and it appears to be good for them. That is in contradiction to a whole psychiatric theory.

On self-knowledge and groups. Somehow the group is a help. Nobody quite knows why, by the way. All they know is that somehow it works. I have a mass of impressions that I have not really sorted out yet. I am not sure what to make of it since it takes time thinking about it. From the kind of talking that we did last night, I very definitely have the feeling that the group would feed back things that you could not get in a hundred years of psychoanalysis from one person. Talking about what somebody looks like and what you look like to somebody else, and then having six other people agreeing about the impression you give, is revealing. Maybe it is not possible to form your own identity or a real picture of yourself unless you also get the picture of what you look like to the world. Well, that is a new assumption. In psycho-analysis that assumption isn't made. What you look like to other people isn't taken into account. It is just simply what you can discover in yourself from your own guts, from your own insides, from your own dreams and fantasies.

I have the feeling that if I stayed with that group, I would hear things I had never heard before. It would be the kind of stuff I would get if there were a candid motion picture camera that could show me myself as other people see me. Then I could weigh it and think about it, ask are they right or are they wrong? How much truth is there in it? I have a feeling that this would make for more knowledge of myself. This self-knowledge would be useful in the search for identity.

After you get over the pain, eventually self-knowledge is a very nice thing. It feels good to know about something rather than to wonder about it, to speculate about it. "Maybe he didn't speak to me because I'm bad, maybe they behaved that way because I'm bad." For the average man, life is just a succession of maybes. He doesn't know why people smile at him or why they don't. It is a very comfortable feeling not to have to guess. It is good to be able to know.

17

On Eupsychian Management

One basic question is, what conditions of work, what kinds of work, what kinds of management, and what kinds of reward or pay will help human nature to grow healthily, to its fuller and fullest stature. That is, what conditions of work are best for personal fulfillment. But we can also turn this about to ask, granted a fairly prosperous society and fairly healthy or normal people, whose most basic needs—gratifications in food, shelter, clothes, etc.—can be taken for granted, then how can such people be used best to foster the aims and values of an organization? How had they best be treated? Under what conditions will they work best? What rewards, nonmonetary as well as monetary, will they work for best?

Eupsychian (pronounced yew-sigh-key-an) conditions of work are often good not only for personal fulfillment, but also for the health and prosperity of the organization, as well as for the quantity and quality of the products or services turned out by the organization.

The problem of management (in any organization or society) can then be approached in a new way: how to set up social conditions in any organization so that the goals of the individual merge with the goals of the organization. When is this possible? When is it impossible? Or harmful? Which are the forces that foster social and individual synergy? Which forces, on the other hand, increase the antagonism between society and the individual?

Such questions obviously touch upon the profoundest issues of personal and social life, of social, political, and economic theory, and even of philosophy in general. For instance, my *Psychology of Science* (81) demonstrates the need for and the possibility of a humanistic science to transcend the self-imposed limits of value-free, mechano-morphic science.

And it can also be assumed that classical economic theory, based as it is on an inadequate theory of human motivation, could also be revolutionized by accepting the reality of higher human needs, including the impulse to self-actualization and the love for the highest values. I am sure that something similar is also true for political science, for sociology, and for all human and social sciences and professions.

This is all to emphasize that this is not about some new tricks of management, or some "gimmicks" or superficial techniques that can be used to manipulate human beings more efficiently for ends not their own. This is not a guide to exploitation.

No, it is rather a clear confrontation of one basic set of orthodox values by another newer system of values which claims to be not only more efficient but also more true. It draws some of the truly revolutionary consequences of the discovery that human nature has been sold short, that man has a higher nature which is just as "instinctoid" as his lower nature, and that this higher nature includes the needs for meaningful work, for responsibility, for creativeness, for being fair and just, for doing what is worthwhile and for preferring to do it well.

To think of "pay" in terms of money alone is clearly obsolete in such a framework. It is true that the lower need-gratifications can be bought with money—but when these are already fulfilled, then people are motivated only by higher kinds of "pay," e.g., belongingness, affection, dignity, respect, appreciation, honor, as well as the opportunity for self-actualization and the fostering of the highest values— truth, beauty, efficiency, excellence, justice, perfection, order, lawfulness, etc.

There is obviously much to think about here, not only for the Marxian or the Freudian, but also for the political or military authoritarian or the "bossy" boss or for the liberal.

18

On Low Grumbles, High
Grumbles, and Metagrumbles

The general principle from which the whole thing proceeds is something like this: People can live at various levels in the motivation hierarchy, that is, they can live a high life or a low life, they can live barely at the level of survival in the jungle, or they can live in an Eupsychian society with good fortune and with all the basic needs taken care of so that they can live at a higher level and think about the nature of poetry or mathematics or that kind of thing.

There are various ways of judging the motivational level of life. For instance, one can judge the level at which people live by the kind of humor that they laugh at. The person living at the lowest-need levels is apt to find hostile and cruel humor very amusing, e.g., the old lady who is getting bitten by a dog or the town moron who is being plagued by the other children, etc. The Abraham Lincoln type of humor—the philosophical, educational type of humor—brings a smile rather than a belly laugh; it has little to do with hostility or conquest. This higher type of humor cannot be understood at all by the person living at the lower-need levels.

The projective tests also can serve as an example of the way in which the motivational level at which we are living expresses itself in all kinds of symptoms and expressive acts. The Rorschach test can be used to indicate what the person is actively striving for, what he wishes, needs, and craves. All the basic needs which have been fully gratified tend to be forgotten by the individual and to disappear from consciousness. Gratified basic needs just simply cease to exist in a certain sense, at least in consciousness. Therefore, what the person is craving and wanting and wishing for tends to be that which is just out ahead of him in the motivational hierarchy. Focusing on this particular need indicates that all the lower needs have been satisfied, and it indicates that the needs which are still higher and beyond what the person is craving for have not yet come into the realm of possibility for him, so he doesn't even think about that. This can be judged from Rorschach tests. Also, this can be judged from dreams and dream analysis.

In the same way it was my thought that the level of complaints—which is to say, the level of what one needs and craves and wishes for—can be an indicator of the motivational level at which the person is living; and if the level of complaints is studied in the industrial situation, it can be used also as a measure of the level of health of the whole organization, especially if one has a large enough sampling.

For instance, take the workers living in the authoritarian jungle industrial situation in which fear and want and even simple starvation are a real possibility, and determine the choice of job and the way in which bosses will behave and the submissiveness with which workers will accept cruelty, etc., etc. Such workers who have complaints or grumbles are apt to be falling short of basic needs which are low in the hierarchy. At this lowest level this means complaints about cold and wet and danger to life and fatigue and poor shelter and all of these basic biological necessities.

Certainly, in the modern industrial situation, if one runs across complaints of this sort, then this is an indication of extremely poor management and an extremely low level of living in the organization. In even average industrial situations, this kind of complaint, this sort of low grumble hardly ever comes up. On the positive side, that is, those complaints which represent a wish or craving out ahead of what is now available—these are at this same low level approximately. That is, the worker in Mexico might be making positive grumbles at the security and safety level, at such things as being fired arbitrarily, of not being able to plan his family budget because he does not know how long the job will last. He may complain about a total lack of job security, about the arbitrariness of the foreman, about the kinds of indignities that he has to take in order to keep his job, etc. I think we can call low grumbles those grumbles which come at the biological and at the safety level, perhaps, also, at the level of gregariousness and belonging to the informal, sociable group.

The higher-need levels would be mostly at the level of esteem and self-esteem, where questions would be involved of dignity, of autonomy, of self-respect, of respect from the other; feelings of worth, of getting praise and rewards and credit for one's accomplishments and the like. Grumbles at this level would probably be mostly about something that involved loss of dignity or the threat to self-esteem or to prestige. Now, so far as the metagrumbles are concerned, what I have in mind here are the metamotivations which hold in the self-actualizing life. More specifically, these can be summed up as the B-Values. These metaneeds for perfection, for justice, for beauty, for truth, and the like also show themselves in the industrial situation, where there might very well be complaints about inefficiency (even when this does not affect the pocket of the complainer). In effect, then, he is making a statement about the imperfection of the world in which he lives (again not a selfish complaint but an impersonal and altruistic philosopher's complaint, one might almost call it). Or he might complain about not being given the full truth, all the facts, or about other blocks in the free flow of communications.

This preference for truth and honesty and all the facts again is one of the metaneeds rather than one of the "basic" needs, and people who have the luxury of complaining at this level are strictly living a very high-level life. In the society which is cynical, which is run by thieves or by tyrants or by nasty people, one would get no such complaints as this—the complaints would be at a lower level. Complaints about justice are also metagrumbles, and I see plenty of them in the protocols from the workers in a well-managed place. They are apt to complain about an injustice even where it is to their personal financial advantage. Another kind of metagrumble is the complaint about a virtue not being rewarded, and about villainy getting these rewards, i.e., a failure of justice.

In other words, everything above implies very strongly that human beings will always complain. There is no Garden of Eden, there is no paradise, there is no heaven except for a passing moment or two. Whatever satisfactions are given to human beings, it is inconceivable that they should be perfectly content with these. This in itself would be a negation of the highest reaches of human nature because it would imply that no improvements could be made after this point—and this, of course, is nonsense. We cannot conceive of a million years of further development bringing such a perfection to pass. Human beings will always be able to tuck in under their belts whatever gratifications, whatever blessings, whatever good fortune are available. They'll be absolutely delighted with these blessings for a little while. And then, as soon as they get used to them, they'll forget about them and start reaching out into the future for still higher blessings, as they restlessly perceive how things could be even more perfect than they are at this moment. This looks to me like an eternal process going on into the future forever (160).

Therefore, I am concerned to stress this point very heavily because I see in the management literature a considerable amount of disappointment and disillusionment, and an occasional giving up of the whole philosophy of enlightened management and going back to authoritarian management, because the management has been sharply disappointed by the lack of gratitude, by the continuation of complaints when the better conditions came to pass. But we should, according to motivation theory, never expect a cessation of complaints; we should expect only that these complaints will get to be higher and higher complaints, i.e., that they will move from the lower-grumble level to higher-grumble levels and finally to metagrumble levels. This is in accordance in principle with what I have written about human motivation being never-ending and simply proceeding to higher and higher levels all the time as conditions improve. And it also conforms with my concept of frustration levels. That is, I repudiated the simple acceptance of frustration as being always necessarily bad; I assumed that there were hierarchies of frustration and that moving from a low-frustration to a high-frustration level is a sign of blessedness, of good fortune, of good social conditions, and of good personal maturity, etc. To complain about the garden programs in the city where I live, to have committees of women heatedly coming in and complaining that the rose gardens in the parks are not sufficiently cared for, is in itself a wonderful thing because it indicates the height of life at which the complainers are living. To complain about rose gardens means that your belly is full, that you have a good roof over your head, that your furnace is working, that you're not afraid of bubonic plague, that you're not afraid of assassination, that the police and fire departments work well, that the government is good, that the school system is good, that local politics are good, and many other preconditions are already satisfied. *This is the point: The high-level complaint is not to be taken as simply like any other complaint; it must be used to indicate all the preconditions which have been satisfied in order to make the height of this complaint theoretically possible.*

If an enlightened and intelligent management understands all the above deeply, then such a management will expect that improvement in conditions would raise the complaint level and raise the frustration level as outlined above, *rather than expecting that improved conditions will make all complaints disappear.* There will then be little danger that they will become disillusioned and angry when much trouble and money and effort goes into making some improvements in work conditions and then the complaints continue. What we must learn to look for is, Have these complaints gone up in motivational level? This is the real test and this is, of course, all that can be expected. But furthermore, I suppose this means that we must learn to be very happy about such a thing, not merely to be contented with it.

Some special problems do emerge here. One such problem is the question of what to call justice and injustice. There are certainly going to be many petty complaints about comparisons between others and one's self—maybe that someone has a better light, or a better chair or somewhat better rate of pay or something of this sort. Such things can become extremely petty, with people comparing the size of the desks that they'll have in their offices or whether they'll have two flowers or one flower in the vase and that sort of thing. Frequently, we will have to make an *ad hoc* judgment in the particular sense as to whether this is at the level of justice in the metaneeds or whether it is simply a surface indication of dominance hierarchy and of elbowing forward in this hierarchy, and trying to go up the ladder in terms of prestige. Or even it could be, as in Dalton's book where there are several examples of this sort of thing, that one could tell from the context that this was clearly referring to safety need. One example I remember is that it was noticed that if the boss's secretary behaved in a friendly fashion with one person and in a neglectful fashion with another person, that this meant that the latter person was about to be fired. In other words, one must make a guess in the particular instance about the motivation level.

Another one perhaps more difficult is to try to make some analysis of the meaning of money in a motivational way. Money can mean practically anything in the motivational hierarchy. It can mean low or middle or high values or metavalues as well. When I've tried to specify the particular need level, there were certainly some instances in which I simply failed—in such cases I just let them slide altogther and considered the instances unratable, and pushed them aside without attempting to rate them in the motivational hierarchy.

There will certainly be other instances that will be difficult to rate. Probably the most cautious thing to do is simply not to try to rate them, to put them aside as unusable data. Certainly, if one were making a huge and careful and personal study, then one could go back and reinterview the persons to see just exactly what they did mean in a motivational sense by a particular complaint, e.g., about money. But in the present study this is not feasible or possible or even necessary. This is especially true if we use the same criterion of rating for the two outfits which are being used for experimental purposes, that is, the well-managed plant and the poorly managed plant.

The meaning of really bad conditions. Let us keep in mind what bad conditions really are at the extreme. In the management literature we don't have any instances of really bad conditions of the kind that any casual or nonprofessional laborer is used to, where conditions come close to the verge of civil war. Perhaps we could take as an example for the end of the scale something like a prisoner-of-war camp or a jail or a concentration camp. Or else within this country we could take the small one- or two-man business in a highly competitive and cutthroat activity where nickels and dimes are important; where the boss can survive only by bleeding his employees to the last drop, to the point of desperation where they simply have to quit; where he tries to make a living by hanging on to them as long as possible, squeezing out as much profit as he can before they quit. Let us not fall into the delusion of thinking of a relatively less well-managed large corporation as having "bad conditions"—these are not bad at all. Let us remember that 99 per cent of the human species would give several years of their lives to get a job in the worst-managed large corporation we have in the whole country. We must have a wider scale for comparison. I think it would probably be desirable for research such as this to start making a collection of really bad instances in our own experience.

Another complication. One characteristic of good conditions that is emerging to view these days for the first time, and certainly surprised me when I first ran across it, is that good conditions, though they have a growth effect on most of the population, nevertheless also have a bad, even catastrophic, effect on a certain small proportion of the population. Freedom and trust given to authoritarians, for instance, will simply bring out bad behavior in these people. Freedom and permissiveness and responsibility will make really dependent and passive people collapse in anxiety and fear. I don't know much about this because I started noticing it only a few years ago. But it's a good thing to keep in mind in this kind of work. We should accumulate more naturalistic instances of this before we try making any theories about it and certainly before we try making any experiments. Put it this way: A fair proportion of the population at the psychopathological end are, for example, very easily tempted to steal but perhaps never realize this because they work in a situation where they are watched all the time, so that the temptation hardly ever comes up to consciousness. Suppose, for example, that a bank suddenly goes "liberal," takes off all the controls, fires the detectives, and so on, and trusts the employees; then, certainly one employee in ten or in twenty—I really don't know what proportion—will be assailed for the first time in his conscious life with temptations to steal. Some of them may give in if they think they can get away with it.

The big point here is not to think that good conditions inevitably make all human beings into growing, self-actualizing, people. Certain forms of neurosis don't respond in this way. Certain kinds of constitution or temperament are much less apt to respond in this way. And finally, the little bit of larceny and sadism and all the other sins which you can find in practically any human being on the face of the earth may be called forth by these "good conditions," when the person is trusted and put completely on his own honor and the like. I am reminded of the way the honor system worked when I was an undergraduate student at Cornell University in 1926 and 1927. It was really amazing that about 95 per cent (or more) of the student population, I would estimate, were very honored, very pleased by this system, and it worked perfectly for them. But there was always that 1 or 2 or 3 per cent for whom it didn't work, who took advantage of the whole business to copy, to lie, to cheat on examinations, and so on. The honor system still cannot be used generally in situations where the temptations are too great, where the stakes are too great.

All of the above ideas and techniques could in principle be applied to many other social-psychological situations. For instance, in the college situation, we could judge the level of enlightenment in which the whole community was living by the grumbles, by the height of the grumbles of the faculty, of the administration, and of the students. There can be in such a situation a whole hierarchy of complaints, of gratifications being sought for. The same thing is true for a marriage and might even turn out to be a way of judging the goodness of the marriage, or its health, one might say, i.e., by the level of the complaints and grumbles in the marriage. A wife who complained about her husband forgetting to bring her flowers once, or taking too much sugar in his coffee, or something of the sort is certainly at a different level from the wife who complains that her husband broke her nose or knocked her teeth out or scarred her or the like. In general the same thing could be true for children's complaints about their parents. Or for children's complaints about their school or their teachers.

I think I could make a generalization of this, that the health or the level of development of any human interpersonal organization can in theory be judged by this same technique of rating the height in the hierarchy of the complaints and grumbles. The one thing to remember is that no matter how good the marriage or the college or the school or the parents, there will be perceived ways of improving the situation, i.e., there will be complaints and grumbles. It should also be taken for granted that it is necessary to divide these into the negative and positive, that is, that there will be very quick and sharp complaints about any more basic gratifications which are taken away or threatened or jeopardized, even though the person doesn't notice these gratifications or takes them for granted entirely when they are easily available. That is, if you ask a person what's good about his place, he won't think to tell you that his feet don't get wet because the floors aren't flooded, or that he is protected against lice and cockroaches in his office, or the like. He will simply take all of these for granted and won't put them down as pluses. But if any of these taken-for-granted conditions disappears, then of course you'll hear a big howl. To say it another way, these gratifications do not bring appreciation or gratitude, even though they do bring violent complaints when they are taken away. Then, on the other hand, in contrast, we must talk about the positive grumbles or complaints or suggestions about improvement. These are generally comments about what is just higher in the hierarchy of motivation, what is just out ahead, what is the next wish wished for.

I suppose that, in principle, an easily possible extension of this research on grumbles, would be, first of all, to collect real instances of bad bosses in the extreme sense and of bad conditions in the extreme sense. For instance, one upholsterer that I know—who feels murderous about his boss but who simply cannot get a better job because in that industry no better jobs are available—is made perpetually angry by the fact that his boss whistles for him instead of calling him by name. This insult is chronic and deliberate and makes him angrier and angrier over the months. Another instance occurred in my own experience in working in hotel dining rooms and restaurants when I was in college. I signed up for a summer job at a resort hotel as a waiter (around 1925), and then paid my way up to the hotel and was made a busboy instead at much lower wages, and as it turned out, without any tips at all. I was simply swindled in this situation—I didn't have the money to go back with, and anyway it was too late to get another job for the summer; the boss promised he would make me a waiter very soon, and I took his word for it. As a busboy without tips I was working at the rate of about ten or twenty dollars a month. This was a seven-day-a-week job, about fourteen hours a day, with no days off. Also, this man asked the staff to take on the additional task of preparing all of the salads because he said the salad man, whose job this was, was delayed for a day or two. After a few days of the staff doing this additional work, we asked him where the salad man was, and he said he was coming the following day. This kind of thing kept up for about two weeks, but it became very clear that the man was simply swindling us all and trying to snatch an extra dollar or two out of the situation.

Finally, for the July Fourth holiday, there were three or four hundred guests in the hotel, and we were asked to stay up most of the night before preparing some very fancy dessert which looked pretty but which took a huge amount of time. The staff all got together and agreed to do this without complaint; but then after we had set the first course of dinner on the Fourth, the whole staff walked out and quit the job. This was, of course, a great sacrifice financially to the workers because it was already late to get good jobs and possibly too late to get any job, and yet the hatred and the desire to retaliate was so great that the satisfaction of doing so remains with me to his day, thirty-five years later. This is what I mean by really bad conditions and what I mean by civil war.

Well, anyway, collecting this sort of treatment, this sort of instance, might be the basis for making up a checklist in order to make well-managed workers more aware of their blessings (which normally they won't even notice, which they will take for granted, as normal). That is, instead of asking them to volunteer complaints, it might be desirable to have a checklist of really bad conditions and ask them if any of these things happen; for instance, if there are any bugs or if it's too cold, or too hot or too noisy or too dangerous or if corrosive chemicals spatter on them or if they are physically hurt or attacked by anybody or if there are no safety precautions on dangerous machines, etc., etc. Any man presented with a check list of two hundred such items could then realize that the absence of all these two hundred bad conditions was itself a positive good.

PART VI

Being-Cognition

19

Notes on Innocent Cognition

"Suchness" is a synonym for the Japanese word *sono-mama*. (Descriptions are found in the book by Suzuki, *Mysticism: Christian and Buddhist* [144], especially pages 99 and 102.) Literally it means the "as-it-isness" of things. It is also expressed by the English suffix "-ish," as in tigerish, meaning just like a tiger, or nine-year-oldish, or Beethovenish, or the German word *amerikanisch*. These all refer to the peculiar and characteristic defining whole-quality, or Gestalt, of the object which makes it exactly what it is, gives it its particular idiographic nature, which differentiates it from everything in the whole world.

The old psychological word "quale" means what suchness means, with reference to sensation. Quale is that quality that is impossible to describe or define, which makes red color different from blue color. It is the reddishness or the suchness of the red that is different from the suchness of the blue.

We also in the English language imply something of the sort when we say of a particular person, "He would!" This means for us that this was expectable, that it fits with his nature, it conforms to his nature, it is characteristic of him, etc.

Suzuki, on page 99, where he defines *sono-mama* for the first time as suchness, goes on to imply that this is the same as the unitive consciousness, the same as "living in the light of eternity." He quotes William Blake, implying that he is speaking of *sono-mama* when he says, "To hold infinity in the palm of your hand and eternity in an hour." Here Suzuki is very clearly implying that this suchness, or *sono-mama*, is the same as Being-cognition (89) and yet, also, he implies that "seeing things *sono-mama*," in their suchness, is the same as concrete perception.

Goldstein's description (39) of brain-injured people who are reduced to the concrete (for instance, when he describes the ways in which their color vision has been reduced to the concrete and the ability to abstract has been lost) is very much like Suzuki's description of suchness. That is, brain-injured people do not see a general category green, or blue, but they see each particular color in its own suchness, not related to anything else, not on a continuum of any kind, not more or less anything else, not better than or worse than, not greener than or less green than, but simply as if it were the only color in the whole world and there was nothing to compare it with. This is what I understand as one element of suchness (noncomparability). If I am right in this reading, then we have to be extremely careful to avoid a possible confusion between Goldsteinian reduction to the concrete and secondly, the ability to perceive freshly and concretely of the healthy man who is not reduced to the concrete. And furthermore we must differentiate this all from Being-cognition, in general, because Being-cognition can be not only of the concrete suchness, but it can also be abstraction in various senses of the word abstract, not to mention the fact that it can be cognition of the whole cosmos.

It is also desirable to discriminate all of the foregoing from the peak experience itself (89), or the *satori* experience that Suzuki describes. For instance, B-cognition (B for Being) always comes when one has a peak experience, but it may come without a peak experience, and it may come even from a tragic experience. Then, also, we have to make a differentiation between the two kinds of peak experience and the two kinds of B-cognition. In the first place, there is the cosmic consciousness of Bucke (18), or of various mystics, in which the whole of the cosmos is perceived and everything in it is seen in relationship with everything else, including the perceiver. This has been described by my subjects in such words as "I could see that I belonged in the universe and I could see where I belonged in it; I could see how important I was and yet, also how unimportant and small I was, so at the same time that it made me humble, it made me feel important." "I was very definitely a necessary part of the world, I was in the family, so to speak, and not outside looking in, not separate from the world, not on a cliff looking across at another cliff, but rather I was in the heart of things, I was in the family, in this very big family and belonged in it instead of being like an orphan, or an adopted child, or like somebody looking in from the outside through the window, from the outside looking into the house." This is one kind of peak experience, one kind of B-cognition, and must be sharply differentiated from the other kind in which fascination occurs, and in which there is an extreme narrowing of consciousness down to the particular percept, for example, the face or the painting, the child or the tree, etc., and in which the rest of the world is totally forgotten and in which the ego itself is also totally forgotten. This is when there is so much absorption and fascination with the percept, and everything else in the world is so much forgotten that there is a felt transcendence, or at least self-consciousness is lost, or the self is gone, and the world is gone, which means that the percept becomes the whole of the cosmos. This percept is seen as if it were the whole world. For the time being, it's the only thing there is. Therefore, all the laws of perception that apply to seeing the whole world now apply to seeing this cut-off percept with which we are fascinated and which has become the whole world. These are two different kinds of peak experiences and two different kinds of B-cognition. Suzuki goes on to refer, without discriminating, to both of these kinds of experience. That is, sometimes he talks about seeing the whole world in a little wild flower. Then at other times, he talks in a religious and mystical way of satori as identification with God, or with heaven, or with the whole of the universe.

This cut-down and narrowed fascination is very much like the Japanese concept of *muga*. This is the state in which you are doing whatever you are doing with a total wholeheartedness, without thinking of anything else, without any hesitation, without any criticism or doubt or inhibition of any kind whatsoever. It is a pure and perfect and total spontaneous acting without any blocks of any kind. This is possible only when the self is transcended or forgotten.

This *muga* state is frequently spoken of as if it were the same as the satori state. Much of the Zen literature speaks of *muga* as if it were total absorption with whatever one was doing at the time, for example, chopping wood with all one's heart and might. And yet the Zen people also talk about this as if it were the same as the mystic unification with the cosmos. These are clearly very different in certain respects.

So also ought we to be critical of the Zen attack on abstract thought, as if only concrete suchness was worth anything and as if abstraction could be only a danger. This, of course, we can't agree with. This would be a voluntary self-reduction to the concrete, with the bad consequences which are clearly set forth by Goldstein.

From such considerations, it is clear that we psychologists cannot accept the concrete perception as the only truth, or the only good, and that we cannot accept abstraction as only a danger. We must remember the description of the self-actualizing person as able to concrete and also as able to abstract, as the situation calls for; and also we must remember that he is able to enjoy both.

There is an excellent example, starting on page 100 in Suzuki, to make exactly this point. There the little flower is seen in its suchness and it is also seen as the same as God, as full of heavenly splendor, standing in the midst of the light of eternity, etc., etc. Here the flower clearly is seen not only in a purely concrete suchness, but is seen either as the whole of world with everything else being excluded, or else is being seen in a B-cognizing way as symbolic of the whole world, i.e., as a B-flower, rather than a D-flower (D for deficiency). When the flower is seen as a B-flower, certainly all of these things are true about eternity and the mystery of being, of heavenly splendor and so on, and everything is seen in the B-realm; that is, seeing the flower is like glimpsing through the flower the whole of the B-realm.

Then Suzuki goes on to criticize Tennyson for the way in which, in his poem, he plucked the flower and then reflected on and abstracted about it, or maybe even dissected it. Suzuki makes this out to be a bad thing. He contrasts it with the way in which the Japanese poet handled this same experience. He didn't pluck the flower, he didn't mutilate it. He left it where he found it. To quote from Suzuki, page 102, "He does not detach it from the totality of its surroundings, he contemplates it in its *sono-mama* state, not only in itself, but in the situation as it finds itself—the situation in its broadest and deepest possible sense."

On page 104, Suzuki quotes from Thomas Traherne. The first quote is a very good one to illustrate the unitive consciousness, that is, the fusion of the B-realm and the D-realm, and so also is the second quote on the same page. But on page 105, trouble begins, where Suzuki talks about the state of innocence as if the unitive consciousness, the fusing of the temporal and the eternal, is somehow akin to the state of the child whom Traherne describes at the foot of page 105 as having primal innocence. Suzuki says this is to revisit the Garden of Eden, to regain paradise, where the tree of knowledge has not yet begun to bear fruit. "It is our eating the forbidden fruit of knowledge which has resulted in our constant habit of intellectualizing. But we have never forgotten, methodically speaking, the original abode of innocence." Suzuki makes this biblical innocence, this Christian notion of innocence correspond with "being *sono-mama*," that is of seeing suchness. This I think is a very bad mistake. The Christian fear of knowledge, as in the Garden of Eden fable in which knowledge was the cause of the downfall of Adam and Eve, has remained in Christianity ever since as a kind of anti-intellectualism, a fear of the knower, the scientist, etc., along with the feeling that faith, or piety, or simplicity, of the St. Francis of Assisi kind of innocence is somehow better than the intellectual kind of knowledge. And in some aspects of the Christian tradition there is even a feeling that these two are mutually exclusive, that is, if you know too much, you can't have a simple, innocent faith and certainly since faith is better than knowledge, it is better not to study too much or to go to school too much, or be a scientist, or the like. And it is certainly true in all the "primitive" sects I know, that they are uniformly anti-intellectual and mistrust learning and knowledge as if this was something "belonging only to God and not to man."[1]

But ignorant innocence is not the same as wise or sophisticated

---

[1] I have speculated on the possibility that "knowledge" in this legend could also mean "knowledge" in the old sexual sense, i.e., eating the apple may have meant discovering the forbidden sexuality, losing innocence in that way rather than by the traditional interpretation. Hence, perhaps also, the traditional Christian antisexuality.

innocence. Furthermore, the concrete perception of the child and his ability to perceive suchness is definitely not the same as the concrete perception and the suchness perception of the self-actualizing adult. These are quite different in at least this sense. The child has not been reduced to the concrete; he hasn't even grown up to the abstract yet. He is innocent because he is ignorant. This is very, very different from the "second innocence" or the "second naïveté," as I have called it, of the wise, self-actualizing, old adult who knows the whole of the D-realm, the whole of the world, all its vices, its contentions, poverties, quarrels, and tears, and yet is able to rise above them, and to have the unitive consciousness in which he is able to see the B-realm, to see the beauty of the whole cosmos, in the midst of all the vices, contentions, tears, and quarrels. Through defects, or in defects, he is able to see perfection. This is a very different kind of thing from the childish innocence of the ignorant child that Traherne describes. This state of innocence is definitely not the same as that which is achieved by saintly men, or by sages, by men who have gone through the D-realm and who have worked with it and fought with it, have been made unhappy by it and yet who are fully able to transcend it.

This adult innocence or "self-actualizing innocence" probably overlaps with, or maybe even is synonymous with, the unitive consciousness in which "B" (the realm of Being) is fused and integrated with "D" (the realm of deficiencies). This is a way then of differentiating out the healthy, realistic, knowledgeable and human perfection that can be, in fact, more or less attained by strong, powerful, and self-actualizing people, and which rests squarely on the fullest knowledge of the "D" realm. This is quite different from the B-cognition of the child who yet knows nothing of the world and had better be said to have ignorant-innocence. This is also different from the fantasy world of some religious people, including Traherne, in which the whole of the D-realm is somehow denied (in the Freudian sense). They stare at it and don't see it. They won't admit its existence. This kind of unhealthy fantasy is like perceiving only "B" without any "D." This is unhealthy because it is only a fantasy, or else it is based on denial or childish ignorance, on lack of knowledge, or on lack of experience.

What this amounts to is differentiating and discriminating the high nirvana from the low nirvana, union upward from union downward (93), the high regression from the low regression, the healthy regression from the unhealthy regression. The temptation for some religious people is to make the perception of heaven, or the perception of the B-world a regression to childhood or to this ignorant-innocence, or else a return to the Garden of Eden before the fruit of knowledge was eaten, which is practically the same thing. It is like saying that it is only knowledge that makes you miseráble. Which then implies— "Then be stupid and ignorant and you will never be miserable." "Then you will be in heaven, then you will be in the Garden of Eden, then you won't know anything about the world of tears and quarrels."

But it is a general principle that "you can't go home again," you can't really regress, the adult cannot become a child in the strict sense. You can't "undo" knowledge, you can't really become innocent again; once you have seen something, you can't undo the seeing. Knowledge is irreversible, perceiving is irreversible, knowing is ir- reversible; in this sense you can't go home again. You can't really regress, not even by giving up your sanity or strength altogether. You can't long for some mythological Garden of Eden, and if you are an adult you can't long for childhood because you just can't get it. The only possible alternative for the human being is to understand the possibility of going on ahead, growing older, going on ahead to the second naïveté, to the sophisticated innocence, to the unitive con- sciousness, to an understanding of B-cognition so that it is possible in the midst of the D-world. Only in this way can the D-world be tran- scended, only by real knowledge and only by growth, only by the fullest adulthood.

It is therefore necessary to stress the distinction between the such- ness of a) persons reduced to the concrete, including brain-injured people, b) the concrete perception of the child who has not yet grown up to abstractness, c) the concrete perception of the healthy adult, which is quite compatible with the ability to abstract as well.

This phrasing applies as well to the Wordsworth kind of nature mysticism. The child is really not a good model for self-actualization; it is not a good model for B-cognition; it is not a good model for con- crete perception, or for *sono-mama*, or for the perception of suchness. This is because he does not transcend the abstract; he hasn't even got to it yet.

It is also desirable to say for Meister Eckhart and for Suzuki and for many other religious people that the way in which they define the unitive consciousness, i.e., the fusion of the eternal with the temporal, is by denying the temporal altogether. (For instance, see the quote from Eckhart, at the top of page 111, where he speaks about the now-moment.) These people hover on the edge of denying the reality of the world in favor of treating as reality only the sacred or the eternal or the Godlike. But these must be seen in the temporal; the sacred must be seen in and through the profane. The B-realm must be seen through the D-realm. I would add that it can be seen in no other way since there isn't any B-realm in the geographical sense of being on the other shore someplace, or being quite different from the world, being something other than it, something not-world in the Aristotelian sense. There is only the world, only one world, and the business of fusing "B" and "D" is really a matter of being able to retain both the "D" and "B" attitudes toward the one world. If we say anything else, then we fall into the trap of the otherworldliness which finally winds up in fables of a heaven above the clouds, some place which is like another house, or another room, which we can see and feel and touch, and in which religion becomes otherworldly and supernatural rather than this-worldly and humanistic and naturalistic.

Since talking about "B" realm and "D" realm might be misunderstood as referring to two separate realms in actual physical space or actual physical time, which are separate and discrete from each other, I had better stress that talk of "B" realm and "D" realm is actually talk about two kinds of perception, two kinds of cognition, two attitudes toward the one world. It might also be better to talk about the unitive attitude, rather than about unitive consciousness. An example of the kind of confusion that could be eliminated by thinking of "B" and "D" cognition as simply two attitudes or styles of perceiving can be seen later in Suzuki's book where he finds it necessary to talk about transmigration, incarnation, reincarnation, souls, and the like. This is the result of hypostatizing these attitudes into real objective things. If I speak of these two kinds of cognition as attitudes, then these transmigrations, etc., simply do not apply, any more than they would to the new kind of perception that a person would have of a Beethoven symphony after he had taken a course in the structure of music. This also implies that the meaning, or the structure in the Beethoven symphony was there before the lessons took place; it was only that a certain blindness was lifted from the perceiver. He could now perceive, now that he had the right attitude, knew what to look for and how to look for it, and could see the structure of the music and the meaning of the music and what Beethoven was trying to say, what he was trying to communicate, etc.

20

Further Notes on Cognition

Characteristics of Being-Cognition and Deficiency-Cognition of the World[1]

B-COGNITION

1. Seen as whole, as complete, self-sufficient, as unitary. Either Cosmic Consciousness (Bucke), in which whole cosmos is perceived as single thing with oneself belonging in it; or else the person, object, or portion of the world seen is seen as if it were the whole world, i.e., rest of world is forgotten. Integrative perceiving of unities.

D-COGNITION

Seen as part, as incomplete, not self-sufficient, as dependent upon other things.

---

[1] Improved from A. H. Maslow, Chapter 6, of *Toward a Psychology of Being* (89). See Chapter 7 for characteristics of the B-cognizer (of the self) in the peak experiences.

B-COGNITION

Unity of the world or object perceived.

2. Exclusively, fully, narrowly attended to; absorption, fascination, focal attention; total attention. Tends to de-differentiate figure and ground. Richness of detail; seen from many sides. Seen with "care," totally, intensely, with complete investment. Totally cathected. Relative importance becomes unimportant; all aspects equally important.

3. No comparing (in Dorothy Lee's sense). Seen *per se*, in itself, by itself. Not in competition with anything else. Sole member of the class (in Hartman's sense).

4. Human-irrelevant.

5. Made richer by repeated experiencing. More and more perceived. "Intra-object richness."

6. Seen as unneeded, as purposeless, as not desired, as unmotivated perceiving. Perceived as if it had no reference to the needs of the perceiver. Can therefore be seen

D-COGNITION

Attended to with simultaneous attention to all cause that is relevant. Sharp figure-ground differentiation. Seen imbedded in relationships to all else in world, as part of the world. Rubricized; seen from some aspects only; selective attention and selective inattention to some aspects; seen casually, seen only from some point of view.

Placing on a continuum or within a series; comparing, judging, evaluating. Seen as a member of a class, as an instance, a sample.

Relevant to human concerns; e.g., what good is it, what can it be used for, is it good for or dangerous to people, etc.

Repeated experiencing impoverishes, reduces richness, makes it less interesting and attractive, takes away its demand-character. Familiarization leads to boredom.

Motivated perceiving. Object seen as need-gratifier, as useful or not useful.

B-COGNITION

D-COGNITION

as independent, in its own right.

7. Object-centering. Self-forgetful, ego-transcending, unselfish, disinterested. Therefore, it-centered. Identification and fusion of perceiver and perceived. So absorbed and poured into the experience that self disappears, so that whole experience can be organized around the object itself as a centering point or organizing point. Object uncontaminated and unconfused with self. Abnegation of the perceiver.

Organized around ego as a centering point, which means projection of the ego into the percept. Perception not of the object alone but of the object-mixed-with-self-of-the-perceiver.

8. The object is permitted to be itself. Humble, receptive, passive, choiceless, undemanding. Taoistic, noninterference with the object or percept. Let-be acceptance.

Active shaping, organizing, and selecting by the perceiver. He shifts it, rearranges it. He works at it. This must be more fatiguing than B-cognizing, which probably is fatigue-curing. Trying, striving, effort. Will, control.

9. Seen as end in itself, self-validating. Self-justifying. Intrinsically interesting for its own sake. Has intrinsic value.

A means, an instrument, not having self-contained worth but having only exchange-value, or standing for something else, or a ticket to some other place.

10. Outside of time and space. Seen as eternal, universal. "A minute is a day; a day is a minute." Disorientation of perceiver in time and space, not conscious of surround-

In time and space. Temporal. Local. Seen *in* history, and in the physical world.

B-COGNITION

ings. Percept not related to surroundings. Ahistorical.

11. The characteristics of Being are perceived as Values of Being.

12. Absolute (because timeless and spaceless, because detached from the ground, because taken *per se*, because rest of world and history all forgotten). This is compatible with the perception of process and shifting, alive organizations *within* the perception—but it is strictly *within* the perception.

13. Resolution of dichotomies, polarities, conflicts. Inconsistences seen to exist simultaneously and to be sensible and necessary, i.e., to be seen as a higher unity or integration, or under a superordinate whole.

14. Concretely (*and* abstractly) perceived. All aspects at once. Therefore ineffable (to ordinary language); describable, if at all, by poetry, art, etc., but even this will make sense only to one who has already had same experience.

D-COGNITION

D-Values are means-values, i.e., usefulness, desirability-undesirability, suitability for a purpose. Evaluations, comparisons, condemnations, approvals, or disapprovals, judgments upon.

Relative to history, to culture, to characterology, to local values, to the interests and needs of man. It is felt to be *passing*. Depends on man for its reality; if man were to disappear, *it* would disappear. Shifting from one syndrome to another as a whole, i.e., it is now a bit in this syndrome, now a bit in *that* syndrome.

Aristotelean logic, i.e., separate things seen as dissected and cut off and quite different from each other, mutually exclusive, often with antagonistic interests.

Only abstract, categorized, diagrammatic, rubricized, schematized. Classifying. "Reduction to the abstract."

Essentially aesthetic experience (in Northrop's sense). Nonchoosing preferring or selecting. Seen in its suchness (different from the concrete perception of young children, of primitive adults, or of brain-injured people because it coexists with abstract ability).

15. The idiographic object; the concrete, unique instance. Classification impossible (except for abstracted aspects) because sole member of its class.

Nomothetic, general, statistical lawfulness.

16. Increase of dynamic isomorphism between inner and outer worlds. As the essential Being of the world is perceived by the person, so also does he concurrently come closer to his own Being; and vice versa.

Decreased isomorphism.

17. Object often perceived as sacred, holy, "very special." It "demands" or "calls for" awe, reverence, piety, wonder.

Object "normal," everyday, ordinary, familiar, nothing special, "familiarized away."

18. World and self often (not always) seen as amusing, playful, comic, funny, absurd, laughable; but also as poignant. Laughter (which is close to tears). Philosophical humor, humor$_{sa}$. World, per-

Lesser forms of humor, if seen at all. Serious things quite different from amusing things. Hostile humor, humorlessness. Solemnity.

B-COGNITION	D-COGNITION
son, child, etc., seen as cute, absurd, charming, lovable. May produce mixed laughing-crying. Fusion of comic-tragic dichotomy.	
19. Noninterchangeable. Not replaceable. No one else will do.	Interchangeable. Replaceable.

Innocent Cognition (as an Aspect of B-Cognition)

In innocence; i.e., to the innocent, everything moves toward becoming equally probable; everything is equally important; everything is equally interesting. The best way to try to understand this is to see it through the eyes of the child. For instance, to the child the word importance doesn't mean anything at first. That which catches the eye, anything that glitters or happens to strike the eye by accident is as important as anything else. There seems to be only rudimentary structuring and differentiation of the environment (what comes forward as figure and what recedes into the background as ground).

If one expects nothing, if one has no anticipations or apprehensions, if in a certain sense there is no future, because the child is moving totally "here-now," there can be no surprise, no disappointment. One thing is as likely as another to happen. This is "perfect waiting," and spectatorship without any demands that one thing happen rather than another. There is no prognosis. And no prediction means no worry, no anxiety, no apprehension or foreboding. Any child's reaction to pain, for instance, is total, without inhibition, without control of any kind. The whole organism goes into a yell of pain and rage. Partly this can be understood as a concrete reaction to the concrete here-now moment. This is possible because there is no expectation of the future, hence no preparation for the future, no rehearsal or anticipation. Neither is there any eagerness when the future is unknown ("I can't wait"). There is certainly no impatience.

In the child there is a total unquestioning acceptance of whatever happens. Since there is also very little memory, very little leaning on the past, there is little tendency in the child to bring the past into the present or into the future. The consequence is that the child is totally here-now, or totally innocent one could say, or totally without past and future. These are all ways of defining further concrete perception, B-cognition (of the child), and also the occasional B-cognition of the sophisticated adult who has managed to achieve the "second naïveté."

This is all related to my conception of the creative personality as one who is totally here-now, one who lives without the future or past. Another way of saying this is: "The creative person is an innocent." An innocent could be defined as a grown person who can still perceive, or think, or react like a child. It is this innocence that is recovered in the "second naïveté," or perhaps I will call it the "second innocence" of the wise old man who has managed to recover the ability to be childlike.

Innocence may also be seen as the direct perception of the B-Values, as in the H. C. Andersen fable of the child who was able to see the King had no clothes on, when all the adults had been fooled into thinking the King was clothed (just as in Asch's experiment [7]).

Innocence on the behavioral side, is unself-conscious spontaneity when absorbed or fascinated; i.e., lack of self-awareness, which means loss of self or transcendence of it. Then behavior is totally organized by fascination with the interesting world outside the self, which then means "not trying to have an effect on the onlooker," without guile or design, without even being aware that one is an object of scrutiny. The behavior is purely experience and not a means to some interpersonal end.

PART VII

Transcendence and the Psychology of Being

21

Various Meanings of Transcendence

1. Transcendence in the sense of loss of self-consciousness, of self-awareness, and of self-observing of the adolescent depersonalization type. It is the same kind of self-forgetfulness which comes from getting absorbed, fascinated, concentrated. In this sense, meditation or concentration on something outside one's own psyche can produce self-forgetfulness and therefore loss of self-consciousness, and in this particular sense of transcendence of the ego or of the conscious self.

2. Transcendence in the metapsychological sense of transcending one's own skin and body and bloodstream, as in identification with the B-Values so that they become intrinsic to the Self itself.

3. Transcendence of time. For example, my experience of being bored in an academic procession and feeling slightly ridiculous in cap and gown, and suddenly slipping over into being a symbol under the aspect of eternity rather than just a bored and irritated individual in the moment and in the specific place. My vision or imagining was that the academic procession stretched way, way out into the future, far, far away, further than I could see, and it had Socrates at its head, and the implication was, I suppose, that many of the people far ahead

had been there and in previous generations, and that I was a successor and a follower of all the great academics and professors and intellectuals. Then the vision was also of the procession stretching out behind me into a dim, hazy infinity where there were people not yet born who would join the academic procession, the procession of scholars, of intellectuals, of scientists and philosophers. And I thrilled at being in such a procession and felt the great dignity of it, of my robes, and even of myself as a person who belonged in this procession. That is, I became a symbol; I stood for something outside my own skin. I was not exactly an individual. I was also a "role" of the eternal teacher. I was the Platonic essence of the teacher.

This kind of transcendence of time is also true in another sense, namely that I can feel friendly, in a very personal and affectionate way, with Spinoza, Abraham Lincoln, Jefferson, William James, Whitehead, etc., as if they still lived. Which is to say that in specific ways they *do* still live.

In still another sense, one can transcend time, namely in the sense of working hard for not yet born great-grandchildren or other successors. But this is in the sense in which Allen Wheelis (157) in his novel, *The Seeker*, had his hero on the point of death thinking that the best thing he could do would be to plant trees for future generations.

4. Transcendence of culture. In a very specific sense, the self-actualizing man, or the transcendent self-actualizing man, is the universal man. He is a member of the human species. He is rooted in a particular culture but he rises above that culture and can be said to be independent of it in various ways and to look down upon it from a height, perhaps like a tree which has its roots in the soil but whose branches are spread out very high above and are unable to look down upon the soil in which the roots are rooted. I have written about the resistance to enculturation of the self-actualizing person. One can examine one's own culture in which one is rooted in a detached and objective way of a certain kind. This parallels the process in psychotherapy of simultaneously experiencing and of self-observing one's own experience in a kind of critical or editorial or detached and removed way so that one can criticize it, approve or disapprove of it and assume control, and, therefore, the possibility of changing it

exists. One's attitude toward one's culture, the parts of it which one has consciously accepted, is quite different from the unthinking and blind, unaware, unconscious total identification with one's culture in a nondiscriminating way.

5. Transcendence of one's past. Two attitudes toward one's past are possible. One attitude may be said to be a transcendent attitude. One can have a B-cognition of one's own past. That is, one's own past can be embraced and accepted into one's present self. This means full acceptance. It means forgiving one's self because of understanding one's self. It means the transcendence of remorse, regret, guilt, shame, embarrassment, and the like.

This is different from viewing the past as something before which one was helpless, something that happened to one, situations in which one was only passive and completely determined by outside determinants. In a certain sense this is like taking responsibility for one's past. It means "having become an agent as well as now being an agent."

6. Transcendence of ego, self, selfishness, ego-centering, etc., when we respond to the demand-character of external tasks, causes, duties, responsibilities to others and to the world of reality. When one is doing one's duty, this also can be seen to be under the aspect of eternity and can represent a transcendence of the ego, of the lower needs of the self. Actually, of course, it is ultimately a form of meta-motivation, and identification with what "calls for" doing. This is a sensitivity to extrapsychic requiredness. This in turn means a kind of Taoistic attitude. The phrase "being in harmony with nature" implies this ability to yield, to be receptive to, or respond to, to live with extrapsychic reality as if one belonged with it, or were in harmony with it.

7. Transcendence as mystical experience. Mystic fusion, either with another person or with the whole cosmos or with anything in between. I mean here the mystical experience as classically described by the religious mystics in the various religious literatures.

8. Transcendence of death, pain, sickness, evil, etc., when one is at a level high enough to be reconciled with the necessity of death, pain, etc. From a godlike, or Olympian point of view, all these are necessary, and can be understood as necessary. If this attitude is

achieved, as for instance it can be in the B-cognition, then bitterness, rebelliousness, anger, resentment may all disappear or at least be much lessened.

9. (Overlaps with above.) Transcendence is to accept the natural world, is to let *it* be *itself* in the Taoistic fashion, is the transcendence of the lower needs of the self—that is, of one's selfish within-the-skin demands, of one's egocentric judgments upon extrapsychic things as being dangerous or not dangerous, edible or not edible, useful or not useful, etc. This is the ultimate meaning of the phrase "to perceive the world objectively." This is one necessary aspect of B-cognition. B-cognition implies a transcendence of one's ego, lower needs, selfishness, etc.

10. Transcendence of the We-They polarity. Transcendence of the Zero-Sum game as between persons. This means to ascend up to the level of synergy (interpersonal synergy, synergy of social institutions or of cultures).

11. Transcendence of the basic needs (either by gratifying them so that they disappear normally from consciousness, or by being able to give up the gratifications and to conquer the needs). This is another way of saying "to become primarily metamotivated." It implies identification with the B-Values.

12. Identification-love is a kind of transcendence, e.g., for one's child, or for one's beloved friend. This means "unselfish." This means transcendence of the selfish Self. It implies also a wider circle of identifications, i.e., with more and more and more people approaching the limit of identification with all human beings. This can also be phrased as the more and more inclusive Self. The limit here is identification with the human species. This can also be expressed intrapsychically, phenomenologically, as experiencing one's self to be one of the band of brothers, to belong to the human species.

13. All examples of Angyal-type homonomy, either high or low (5).

14. Getting off the merry-go-round. Walking through the abattoir without getting bloody. To be clean even in the midst of filth. To transcend advertising means to be above it, to be unaffected by it, to be untouched. In this sense one can transcend all kinds of bondage, slavery, etc., in the same way that Frankl, Bettelheim, *et al.* could transcend even the concentration camp situation. Use the example of

The New York Times front-page picture in 1933 of an old Jewish man with a beard being paraded before the jeering crowd in Berlin in a garbage truck. It was my impression that he had compassion for the crowd and that he looked upon them with pity and perhaps forgiveness, thinking of them as unfortunate and sick and subhuman. Being independent of other people's evil or ignorance or stupidity or immaturity even when this is directed toward oneself is possible, though very difficult. And yet one *can*, in such a situation, gaze upon the whole situation—including oneself in the midst of the situation—as if one were looking upon it objectively, detachedly from a great and impersonal or suprapersonal height.

15. Transcending the opinions of others, i.e., of reflected appraisals. This means a self-determining Self. It means to be able to be unpopular when this is the right thing to be, to become an autonomous, self-deciding Self; to write one's own lines, to be one's own man, to be not manipulatable or seduceable. These are the resisters (rather than the conformers) in the Asch-type experiment. Resistance to being rubricized, to be able to be role-free, i.e., to transcend one's role and to be a person rather than being the role. This includes resisting suggestion, propaganda, social pressures, being outvoted, etc.

16. Transcending the Freudian superego and coming up to the level of intrinsic conscience, and intrinsic guilt, deserved and suitable remorse, regret, shame.

17. Transcendence of one's own weakness and dependency, to transcend being a child, to become one's own mother and father to one's self, to become parental and not only filial, to be able to be strong and responsible in addition to being dependent, to transcend one's own weakness, and to rise to being strong. Since we always have both of these within us simultaneously, this is really a matter of degree in large part. But after all, it can be said meaningfully, of some individuals, that they are primarily weak, and that they primarily relate to all other human beings as the weak relate to the strong, and that all mechanisms of adaptation, coping mechanisms, defense mechanisms, are the defenses of weakness against strength. It's the same for dependency and independence. It's the same for irresponsibility and responsibility. It's the same for being the captain of the ship, or the driver of the car on the one hand, and of being merely the passenger on the other hand.

18. Transcending the present situation in the sense of Kurt Goldstein (39), "to relate to existence also in terms of the possible as well as the actual." This is, to rise above being stimulus-bound and here-now situation-bound, and actuality-bound. Goldstein's reduction to the concrete can be transcended. Perhaps the best phrase here is to rise to the realm of the possible as well as of the actual.

19. Transcendence of dichotomies (polarities, black and white oppositions, either-or, etc.). To rise from dichotomies to superordinate wholes. To transcend atomism in favor of hierarchical-integration. To bind separates together into an integration. The ultimate limit here is the holistic perceiving of the cosmos as a unity. This is the ultimate transcendence, but any step along the way to this ultimate limit is itself a transcendence. Any dichotomy may be used as an example; for instance, selfish versus unselfish, or masculine versus feminine, or parent versus child, teacher versus student, etc. All these can be transcended so that the mutual exclusiveness and oppositeness and Zero-Sum game quality is transcended, in the sense of rising above to a higher viewpoint where one can see that these mutually exclusive differences in opposites can be coordinated into a unity which would be more realistic, more true, more in accord with actual reality.

20. Transcendence of the D-realm in the B-realm. (Of course this overlaps with every other kind of transcendence. As a matter of fact, they each overlap with each other.)

21. Transcendence of one's own will (in favor of the spirit of "not my will be done but Thine"). To yield to one's destiny or fate and to fuse with it, to love it in the Spinoza sense or in the Taoistic sense. To embrace, lovingly, one's own destiny. This is a rising above one's own personal will, being in charge, taking control, *needing* control, etc.

22. The word transcend also means "surpass" in the sense simply of being able to do more than one thought one could do, or more than one had done in the past, e.g., simply to be able to run faster than one used to, or to be a better dancer or pianist, or a better carpenter, or whatever.

23. Transcendence also means to become divine or godlike, to go beyond the merely human. But one must be careful here not to make anything extrahuman or supernatural out of this kind of statement. I am thinking of using the word "metahuman" or "B-human" in order

to stress that this becoming very high or divine or godlike is part of human nature even though it is not often seen in fact. It is still a potentiality of human nature.

To rise above dichotomized nationalism, patriotism, or enthnocentrism, in the sense of "them" against "us," or of we-they, or Ardrey's (6) enmity-amity complex. For example, Piaget's little Genevan boy who couldn't imagine being both Genevan and Swiss. He could think of being only either Genevan or Swiss. It takes more development in order to able to be more inclusive and superordinate, more integrative. My identification with nationalism, patriotism, or with my culture does not necessarily mitigate against my identification and more inclusive and higher patriotism with the human species or with the United Nations. As a matter of fact, such a superordinate patriotism is, of course, not only more inclusive, but therefore more healthy, more fully-human, than the strict localism which is regarded as antagonistic or as excluding others. That is, I can be a good American, and of course *must* be an American (that's the culture I grew up in, which I can never shake off and I don't want to shake off in favor of being a world citizen). Stress that the world citizen who has no roots, who doesn't belong any place, who is utterly and merely cosmopolitan, is not as good a world citizen as one who grew up in the family, in a place, in a home with a particular language, in a particular culture, and therefore has a sense of belongingness on which to build toward higher need and metaneed levels. To be a full member of the human species does not mean repudiating the lower levels; it means rather including them in the hierarchical integration, e.g., cultural pluralism, enjoying the differences, enjoying different kinds of restaurants with different kinds of food, enjoying travel to other countries, enjoying the ethnological study of other cultures, etc.

24. Transcendence can mean to live in the realm of Being, speaking the language of Being, B-cognizing, plateau-living. It can mean the serene B-cognition as well as the climactic peak-experience kind of B-cognition. After the insight or the great conversion, or the great mystic experience, or the great illumination, or the great full awakening, one can calm down as the novelty disappears, and as one gets used to good things or even great things, live casually in heaven and be on easy terms with the eternal and the infinite. To have got over being surprised and startled and to live calmly and serenely among

the Platonic essences, or among the B-Values. The phrase to use here for contrast with the climactic or emotionally poignant great insight and B-cognition would be plateau-cognition. Peak experiences must be transient, and in fact are transient so far as I can make out. And yet an illumination or an insight remains with the person. He can't really become naïve or innocent again or ignorant again in the same way that he was. He cannot "un-see." He can't become blind again. And yet there must be a language to describe getting used to the conversion or the illumination or to living in the Garden of Eden. Such an awakened person normally proceeds in a unitive way or in a B-cognizing way as an everyday kind of thing—certainly, whenever he wishes to. This serene B-cognition or plateau-cognition can come under one's own control. One can turn it off or on as one pleases.

The (transient) attainment of full-humanness or of finality or being an end is an example of transcendence.

25. The attainment of Taoistic (B-level) objectivity in the transcendence of noninvolved, neutral, noncaring, spectator-type objectivity (which itself transcends the purely egocentric and immature lack of objectivity).

26. Transcending—the split between facts and values. Fusion of facts and values in which they become one (see Chapter 8).

27. A transcendence of negatives (which include evil, pain, death, etc., but also include more than that) is seen in the report from the peak experiences in which the world is accepted as good and one is reconciled to the evils that one perceives. But this is also a transcendence of inhibitions, of blocks, of denials, of refusals.

28. Transcendence of space. This can be in the very simplest sense of getting so absorbed in something that one forgets where one is. But it can also rise to the very highest sense in which one is identified with the whole human species and therefore in which one's brothers on the other side of the earth are part of oneself, so that in a certain sense one is on the other side of the earth as well as being here in space. The same is true for the introjection of the B-Values since they are everywhere, and since they are defining characteristics of the self, and one's self is everywhere too.

29. Overlapping with several of the above is the transcendence of effort and of striving, of wishing and hoping, of any vectorial or intentional characteristics. In the simplest sense this is, of course, the sheer

enjoyment of the state of gratification, of hope fulfilled and attained, of being there rather than of striving to get there, of having arrived rather than of traveling toward. This is also in the sense of "being fortuitous" or of Mrs. Garrett's use of the phrase, "high carelessness." It is the Taoistic feeling of letting things happen rather than of making them happen, and of being perfectly happy and accepting of this state of nonstriving, nonwishing, noninterfering, noncontrolling, nonwilling. This is the transcendence of ambition, of efficiencies. This is the state of having rather than of not having. Then of course one lacks nothing. This means it is possible to go over to the state of happiness, of contentment, of being satisfied with what is. Pure appreciation. Pure gratitude. The state and the feeling of good fortune, good luck, the feeling of grace, of gratuitous grace.

Being in an end-state means the transcendence of means in various senses. But this has to be very carefully spelled out.

30. Specially noteworthy for research purposes as well as therapy purposes is to pick out of the special kinds of transcendence, the transcendence of fear into the state of not-fearing or of courage (these are not quite the same thing).

31. Also useful would be Bucke's (18) use of cosmic consciousness. This is a special phenomenological state in which the person somehow perceives the whole cosmos or at least the unity and integration of it and of everything in it, including his Self. He then feels as if he belongs by right in the cosmos. He becomes one of the family rather than an orphan. He comes inside rather than being outside looking in. He feels simultaneously small because of the vastness of the universe, but also an important being because he is there in it by absolute right. He is part of the universe rather than a stranger to it or an intruder in it. The sense of belongingness can be very strongly reported here, as contrasting with the sense of ostracism, isolation, aloneness, of rejection, of not having any roots, of belonging no place in particular. After such a perception, apparently one can feel permanently this sense of belonging, of having a place, of being there by right, etc. (I have used this cosmic consciousness type of B-cognition in the peak experience to contrast with another type, namely, that which comes from narrowing down consciousness and zeroing in in an intense and total absorption and fascination with one person or one thing or one happening which somehow then stands for the

whole world, the whole cosmos. I have called this the narrowing-down kind of peak experience and B-cognition.)

32. Perhaps a special and separate statement ought to be made of transcendence in the particular meaning of introjection of and identification with B-Values, with the state of being primarily motivated by them thereafter.

33. One can even transcend individual differences in a very specific sense. The highest attitude toward individual differences is to be aware of them, to accept them, but also to enjoy them and finally to be profoundly grateful for them as a beautiful instance of the ingenuity of the cosmos—the recognition of their value, and wonder at individual differences. This is certainly a higher attitude and I suppose therefore a kind of transcendence. But also, and quite different from this ultimate gratitude for individual differences, is the other attitude of rising above them in the recognition of the essential commonness and mutual belongingness and identification with all kinds of people in ultimate humanness or species-hood, in the sense that everyone is one's brother or sister, then individual differences and even the differences between the sexes have been transcended in a very particular way. That is, at different times one can be very aware of the differences between individuals; but at another time one can wave aside these individual differences as relatively unimportant for the moment by contrast with the universal humanness and *similarities* between human beings.

34. A particular kind of transcendence useful for certain theoretical purposes is the transcendence of human limits, imperfections, shortcomings, and finiteness. This comes either in the acute end experiences of perfection or in the plateau experiences of perfection, in which one can *be* an end, a god, a perfection, an essence, a Being (rather than a Becoming), sacred, divine. This can be phrased as a transcendence of ordinary, everyday humanness in favor of extraordinary humanness or metahumanness or some such phrasing. This can be an actual phenomenological state; it can be a kind of cognizing; it can also be a conceived limit of philosophy or ideal—for instance, the platonic essences or ideas. In such acute moments, or to some extent in plateau cognition, one becomes perfect, or can see oneself as perfect, e.g., in that moment I can love all and accept all, forgive all, be reconciled even to the evil that hurts me. I can understand and

enjoy the way things are. And I can then even feel some subjective equivalent of what has been attributed to the gods only, i.e., omniscience, omnipotence, ubiquity (i.e., in a certain sense one can *become* in such moments a god, a sage, a saint, a mystic). Perhaps the best word in order to stress that this is part of human nature, even though at its best, is the word metahumanness.

35. Transcendence of one's own credo, or system of values, or system of beliefs. This is worth discussing separately because of the special situation in psychology in which the first force, the second force, and the third force have been seen as mutually exclusive by many. Of course this is erroneous. Humanistic psychology is more inclusive rather than exclusive. It is epi-Freudian and epipositivistic science. These two points of view are not so much wrong or incorrect as they are limited and partial. Their essence fits very nicely into a larger and inclusive structure. Of course integrating them into this larger and more inclusive structure certainly changes them in some ways, corrects them, points to certain mistakes, but yet includes their most essential, though partial, characteristics. There can be the enmity-amity complex among intellectuals, in which loyalty to Freud or to Clark Hull, or for that matter to Galileo or Einstein or Darwin, can be a kind of local excluding-others type of patriotism in which one forms a club or fraternity as much to keep other people out as to include some in. This is a special case of inclusiveness or hierarchical integration or holism, but it is useful to make a special point of it for psychologists, as well as for philosophers, scientists, and intellectual areas where there is a tendency to divide into so-called "schools of thought." This is to say that one can take either the dichotomous or the integrative attitude toward a school of thought.

A condensed statement. Transcendence refers to the very highest and most inclusive or holistic levels of human consciousness, behaving and relating, as ends rather than as means, to oneself, to significant others, to human beings in general, to other species, to nature, and to the cosmos. (Holism in the sense of hierarchical integration is assumed; so also is cognitive and value isomorphism.)

22
Theory Z

I have recently found it more and more useful to differentiate between two kinds (or better, degrees) of self-actualizing people, those who were clearly healthy, but with little or no experiences of transcendence, and those in whom transcendent experiencing was important and even central. As examples of the former kind of health, I may cite Mrs. Eleanor Roosevelt, and, probably, Truman and Eisenhower. As examples of the latter, I can use Aldous Huxley, and probably Schweitzer, Buber, and Einstein.

It is unfortunate that I can no longer be theoretically neat at this level. I find not only self-actualizing persons who transcend, but also *non*healthy people, non-self-actualizers who have important transcendent experiences. It seems to me that I have found some degree of transcendence in many people other than self-actualizing ones as I have defined this term. Perhaps it will be found even *more* widely as we develop better techniques and better conceptualizations. After all, I am reporting here my impressions from the most preliminary of explorations. In any case, it is my tentative impression that I am more likely to find cognizing of transcendence not only in self-actualizing but also in highly creative or talented people, in highly intelligent people, in very strong characters, in powerful and responsible leaders and managers, in exceptionally good (virtuous) people and in "heroic" people who have overcome adversity and who have been strengthened by it rather than weakened.

To some as yet unknown extent the latter are what I have referred to as "peakers" rather than "nonpeakers" (85), and Yea-sayers rather than Nay-sayers (159), life-positive rather than life-negative (in Reich's sense), eager for life rather than nauseated or irritated by it.

The former are more essentially practical, realistic, mundane, capable, and secular people, living more in the here-and-now world; i.e., what I have called the D-realm for short, the world of deficiency-needs and of deficiency-cognitions. In this *Weltanschauung*, people or things are taken essentially in a practical, concrete, here-now, pragmatic way, as deficiency-need suppliers or frustrators; i.e., as useful or useless, helpful or dangerous, personally important or unimportant.

"Useful" in this context means both "useful for survival" *and* "useful for growth toward self-actualization and freedom from basic deficiency-needs." More specifically, it means a way of life and a world view generated not only by the hierarchy of basic needs (for sheer physical survival, for safety and security, for belongingness, friendship, and love, for respect, esteem, and dignity, for self-esteem and feelings of worth), but also by the need for the actualization of one's personal, idiosyncratic potentialities (i.e., identity, Real Self, individuality, uniqueness, self-actualization). That is, it refers to the fulfillment not only of one's species-hood, but also of one's *own* idiosyncratic potentialities. Such people live in the world, coming to fulfillment in it. They master it, lead it, use it for good purposes, as (healthy) politicians or practical people do. That is, these people tend to be "doers" rather than meditators or contemplators, effective and pragmatic rather than aesthetic, reality-testing and cognitive rather than emotional and experiencing.

The other type (transcenders?) may be said to be much more often aware of the realm of Being (B-realm and B-cognition), to be living at the level of Being; i.e., of ends, of intrinsic values (85); to be more obviously metamotivated; to have unitive consciousness and "plateau experience" (Asrani) more or less often; and to have or to have had peak experiences (mystic, sacral, ecstatic) with illuminations or insights or cognitions which changed their view of the world and of themselves, perhaps occasionally, perhaps as a usual thing.

It may fairly be said of the "merely-healthy" self-actualizers that, in an overall way, they fulfill the expectations of McGregor's Theory Y (83). But of the individuals who have transcended self-actualization we must say that they have not only fulfilled but also transcended or surpassed Theory Y. They live at a level which I shall here call Theory Z for convenience and because it is on the same continuum as Theories X and Y and with them forms a hierarchy.

Obviously, we are dealing here with extraordinarily intricate matters, and as a matter of fact, with philosophies of life in general. Extended and discursive treatment would lead to volumes and sets of volumes.

It occurred to me, however, that a condensed beginning could be achieved with the aid of Table 1. Using Keith Davis' (27) very convenient summary table as a base, I have extended it in the ways indicated by italicizing. It can hardly be said to be light reading, but I do think that anyone who is really curious or interested can catch something of what I am trying to communicate. More extended treatment may be found in the various items listed in the bibliography.

One final caution: It should be noted that this hierarchical arrangement by levels leaves open the difficult and, as yet, unsolved problem of the degrees of overlap or correlation between the following progressions or hierarchies:

1. The hierarchy of needs (which can be taken either as coming to crises in a chronological progression à la Erikson *or* with age held constant).
2. A progression of basic-need gratifications from infancy through childhood, youth, adulthood, to old age, but at any time.
3. Biological, phyletic evolution.
4. From illness (diminution, stunting) to health and full humanness.
5. From living under bad environmental conditions to living under good conditions.
6. From being constitutionally or generally a "poor specimen" (in the biologist's sense) to being a "good specimen" in the zoo keeper's sense.

Of course all these complexities make the concept "psychological health" even more moot than it usually is and strengthen the case for using instead the concept of "full humanness," which applies well to all these variations without difficulty. Conversely, we can then use the one concept "stunting or diminution of humanness" instead of immature, unlucky, sick, born defective, underprivileged. "Diminution of humanness" covers them all.

Differences (in Degree) Between Transcenders and Merely Healthy People

Nontranscending and transcending self-actualizers (or Theory-Y and Theory-Z people) share in common all the characteristics described for self-actualizing (95) with the one exception of presence or absence or, more probably, greater or lesser number and importance of peak experiences and B-cognitions and what Asrani has called plateau experiences (serene and contemplative B-cognitions rather than climactic ones).

But it is my strong impression that the nontranscending self-actualizers do *not* have the following characteristics or have less of them than do the transcenders.

1. For the transcenders, peak experiences and plateau experiences become *the* most important things in their lives, the high spots, the validators of life, the most precious aspect of life.

2. They (the transcenders) speak easily, normally, naturally, and unconsciously the language of Being (B-language), the language of poets, of mystics, of seers, of profoundly religious men, of men who live at the Platonic-idea level or at the Spinozistic level, under the aspect of eternity. Therefore, they should better understand parables, figures of speech, paradoxes, music, art, nonverbal communications, etc. (This is an easily testable proposition.)

3. They perceive unitively or sacrally (i.e., the sacred within the secular), or they see the sacredness in all things *at the same time* that they also see them at the practical, everyday D-level. They can sacralize everything at will; i.e., perceive it under the aspect of eternity. This ability is in *addition* to—not mutually exclusive with—good

TABLE 11

Levels of Organization Related to Other Hierarchical Variables

	AUTOCRATIC	CUSTODIAL (MAINTENANCE)	SUPPORTIVE (MOTIVATIONAL)	COLLEGIAL Familial Colleagues	Theory-Z Organization; Organization-Transcending
Depends on:	Power	Economic resources	Leadership	Mutual contribution	Devotion to Being-itself and to B-Values.
Managerial orientation:	Authority	Material rewards	Support	Integration	Assumption that all are devoted. Signal giver. Fellow workers.
Employee orientation:	Obedience	Security	Performance	Responsibility	Admiration; Love; Acceptance of factual superiority.
Employee psychological result:	Personal dependency	Organizational dependency	Participation	Self-discipline	Oblation; Self-sacrifice.
Employee needs met:	Subsistence	Maintenance	Higher-order	Self-realization	Metaneeds; B-Values.
Morale measure:	Compliance	Satisfaction	Motivation	Commitment to task and team	Commitment to B-Values.
RELATION TO OTHER IDEAS:					
McGregor's theories:	Theory X		Theory Y		Theory Z
Maslow's need-priority model:	Physiological	Safety and security	Middle-order	Higher-order	Metaneeds; B-Values.
Herzberg's factors:	Maintenance	Maintenance	Motivational	Motivational	
W. H. Whyte's thesis:		Organization man			
Blake and Mouton's managerial grid:	9,1	3,5	6,6	8,8	
Motivational environment:	Extrinsic	Extrinsic	Intrinsic	Intrinsic	Fusion
Motivational style:	Negative	Mostly neutral on job	Positive	Positive	
Managerial power style:	Autocratic		Participative		Aggrident; Alpha; Excellence: Impersonal, transpersonal, including voluntary abdication of power.
Modal level of personal development:	*Owner*	*Boss; Father; Patriarch.*	*Equality of Immature*	*Healthy; Mature.*	*Transcendent; B-level beyond the ego; Transpersonal.*
Image of man:	*Thing to be used; Interchangeable; Without individuality. Owner.*	*Pet; Child; Doll; or Benevolent dictator.*	*Partnerships for mutual gain and mutual need-fulfillment. D-love.*	*Every man a general. Strong identities. Alliances between sovereign persons. Real Self. Self-actualizing.*	*Saint-Sage-Politician-Pragmatist. Mystic. Bodhisattva. Tsaddik. B-Person. Priestly oblation & impersonality. Heraclitean.*

	...identification; Possession-objectivity; Spectator-objectivity.			objectivity	...objectivity; Objectivity of non-interference. Objectivity of love.
Politics:	Slaves; Things.	Patriarch	Allies for mutual advantage	Senators; Every man a general; Full sovereignty.	B-politics: Anarchy; B-humility: Decentralization. Impersonality. Transpersonality.
Religion:	God of fear and wrath	Father God	Loving-kindness	Humanism	Transhumanism (centering in the cosmos rather than in the human species).
Male-female:	Ownership; Exploitation.	Responsible & affectionate ownership	Loving-kindness;	Mutual respect; Equality; B-love (?); Full sovereignty.	B-love: Fusion; The easy state.
Economics:	Keeping alive. Materialism. Lowest-need economics.	Benevolent ownership; Noblesse oblige.	Democratic; Partnership; Higher-need economics.	Ethical-economics; Moral-economics; Social indicators included in the accounting system.	Anarchy; Decentralization; B-Values as the most valuable pay. Spiritual economics. Metaneed economics. Transpersonal economics.
Level of science:	Thing-science	Infrahuman science	Humanistic science ————→		Transhuman science; Cosmo-centric science with transpersonal scientists.
Level of values:	Value-free	Infrahuman "value"	Humanistic values ————→		Transhuman values. B-Values. Cosmic values.
Method:	Atomistic-Dichotomizing-Reducing-Analyzing ——→ Hierarchical-integration. Synergic. Integrative. Structuring-with; Holism.				
Fear-courage:	Fear ←————→ Courage ————→ Transcendence of courage and fear; Beyond courage and fear.				
Degree of humanness:	Diminution of humanness; stunting ————→ Fully human				
Vector direction:	Regression ←————→ Becoming-Progression-Growth-Being ————→ Transhuman; Transpersonal.				
Excellence:	Increasing degrees of excellence ————→				
Psychological health:	Full humanness ←————→ Increasing degrees of health & humanness ————→				
Education:	Training	Dominating education	Mutual education	Intrinsic education. Training for improvisation. Confidence to face situation without preparation.	Transhuman education. Education personal, Taoistic. Heraclitean man. "Not my will but thine." Oblation. Embracing your fate. Duty. Responsibility.

————— Extrinsic education ————→

TABLE 1 (CONTINUED)

LEVELS OF ORGANIZATION RELATED TO OTHER HIERARCHICAL VARIABLES

	AUTOCRATIC	CUSTODIAL (MAINTENANCE)	SUPPORTIVE (MOTIVATIONAL)	COLLEGIAL Familial Colleagues	Theory-Z Organization; Organization-Transcending
Levels of therapist and therapy; Levels of help:	Machinist; Surgeon.	Veterinarian; Patriarch Authoritarian (feared and trusted); Gives orders.	Benevolent and all-powerful kind father (can be loved and is felt as loving; caring but inscrutable). Mirror.	Existential I-Thou Colleagues Older brother Identity—finding Fate—finding Value—finding	Taoistic guide. Consultant. Guru. Sage. Let-be. B-Values shared. Bodhisattva. Tsaddik. Sad—loving—compassion.
Sex:	Dirty; Evil; Unilateral; Transitive: Exploitative (done to another).	"Natural" desacralized.	Love-sex. Ecstasy. Joy.	Sacralized; Path to heaven; Tantric.	Heaven—state of being. The trans-sexual erotic.
Communication style or level:	Orders	Orders		Mutuality	B-language
Level of grumbles:	Lower	Middle		High	Metagrumbles
Pay; Wages; Rewards:	Material goods & possessions	Security now and in the future	Friendship. Affection. Group belongingness.	Dignity. Status. Glory. Praise. Honor. Freedom. Self-actualization.	B-Values. Justice. Beauty. Goodness; Excellence; Perfection; Truth, etc. Peak experiences. Plateau experiences.

reality testing within the D-realm. (This is well described by the Zen notion of "nothing special.")

4. They are much more consciously and deliberately metamotivated. That is, the values of Being, or Being itself seen both as fact and value, e.g., perfection, truth, beauty, goodness, unity, dichotomy-transcendence, B-amusement, etc. (85) are their main or most important motivations.

5. They seem somehow to recognize each other, and to come to almost instant intimacy and mutual understanding even upon first meeting. They can then communicate not only in all the verbal ways but also in the nonverbal ways as well.

6. They are *more* responsive to beauty. This may turn out to be rather a tendency to beautify all things, including all the B-Values, or to see the beautiful more easily than others do, or to have aesthetic responses more easily than other people do, or to consider beauty most important, or to see as beautiful what is not officially or conventionally beautiful. (This is confusing, but it is the best I can do at this time.)

7. They are *more* holistic about the world than are the "healthy" or practical self-actualizers (who are also holistic in this same sense). Mankind is one and the cosmos is one, and such concepts as the "national interest" or "the religion of my fathers" or "different grades of people or of IQ" either cease to exist or are easily transcended. If we accept as the ultimate political necessities (as well as today the most urgent ones), to think of all men as brothers, to think of national sovereignties (the right to make war) as a form of stupidity or immaturity, then transcenders think this way more *easily*, more reflexively, more naturally. Thinking in our "normal" stupid or immature way is for them an *effort*, even though they can do it.

8. Overlapping this statement of holistic perceiving is a strengthening of the self-actualizer's natural tendency to synergy—intrapsychic, interpersonal, intraculturally and internationally. This cannot be spelled out fully here because that would take too long. A brief—and perhaps not very meaningful—statement is that synergy transcends the dichotomy between selfishness and unselfishness and includes them both under a single superordinate concept. It is a transcendence of competitiveness, of zero-sum of win-lose games-

manship. The reader who is interested enough is referred to what has already been written on the subject (83).

9. Of course there is more and easier transcendence of the ego, the Self, the identity.

10. Not only are such people lovable as are all of the most self-actualizing people, but they are also more awe-inspiring, more "unearthly," more godlike, more "saintly" in the medieval sense, more easily revered, more "terrible" in the older sense. They have more often produced in me the thought, "This is a great man."

11. As one consequence of all these characteristics, the transcenders are far more apt to be innovators, discovers of the new, than are the healthy self-actualizers, who are rather apt to do a very good job of what has to be done "in the world." Transcendent experiences and illuminations bring clearer vision of the B-Values, of the ideal, of the perfect, of what *ought* to be, what actually *could* be, what exists *in potentia*—and therefore of what might be brought to pass.

12. I have a vague impression that the transcenders are less "happy" than the healthy ones. They can be more ecstatic, more rapturous, and experience greater heights of "happiness" (a too weak word) than the happy and healthy ones. But I sometimes get the impression that they are *as* prone and maybe more prone to a kind of cosmic-sadness or B-sadness over the stupidity of people, their self-defeat, their blindness, their cruelty to each other, their shortsightedness. Perhaps this comes from the contrast between what actually is and the ideal world that the transcenders can see so easily and so vividly, and which is in principle so easily attainable. Perhaps this is a price these people have to pay for their direct seeing of the beauty of the world, of the saintly possibilities in human nature, of the non-necessity of so much of human evil, of the seemingly obvious necessities for a good world; e.g., a world government, synergic social institutions, education for human goodness rather than for higher IQs or greater expertness at some atomistic job, etc. Any transcender could sit down and in five minutes write a recipe for peace, brotherhood, and happiness, a recipe absolutely within the bounds of practicality, absolutely attainable. And yet he sees all this *not* being done; or where it is being done, then so slowly that the holocausts may come first. No wonder he is sad or angry or impatient at the same time that he is also "optimistic" in the long run.

13. The deep conflicts over the "elitism" that is inherent in *any* doctrine of self-actualization—they are after all superior people whenever comparisons are made—is more easily solved—or at least managed—by the transcenders than by the merely healthy self-actualizers. This is made possible because they can more easily live in both the D- and B-realms simultaneously, they can sacralize everybody so much more easily. This means that they can reconcile more easily the absolute necessity for some form of reality-testing, comparing, elitism in the D-world (you *must* pick a good carpenter for the job, not a poor carpenter; you *must* make some distinction between the criminal and the policeman, the sick man and the physician, the honest man and the fake, the intelligent man and the stupid one) on the one hand, and on the other hand, the transfinite and equal, noncomparable sacredness of everybody. In a very empirical and necessary sense, Carl Rogers talks about the "unconditional positive regard" that is *a priori* necessary for effective psychotherapy. Our laws forbid "cruel and unusual" punishment; i.e., no matter *what* crime a man has committed, he must be treated with a dignity not reducible below a certain point. Seriously religious theists say that "each and every person is a child of God."

This sacredness of every person and even of every living thing, even of nonliving things that are beautiful, etc. is so easily and directly perceived in its reality by every transcender that he can hardly forget it for a moment. Fused with his highly superior reality-testing of the D-realm, he could be the godlike punisher, the comparer, noncontemptuous, *never* the exploiter of weakness, stupidity, or incapability even while he realistically recognized these gradable qualities in the D-world. The way of phrasing this paradox that I have found useful for myself is this: The factually-superior transcending self-actualizer acts always to the factually-inferior person as to a brother, a member of the family who must be loved and cared for no matter what he does because he is after all a member of the family. But he can still act as a stern father or older brother, and not only as an all-forgiving mother or motherly father. This punishment is quite compatible with godlike transfinite love. From a transcendent point of view, it is easy to see that even for the good of the transgressor himself it may be better to punish him, frustrate him, to say "No," rather than to gratify him or please him now.

14. My strong impression is that transcenders show more strongly a positive correlation—rather than the more usual inverse one—between increasing knowledge and increasing mystery and awe. Certainly by most people scientific knowledge is taken as a *lessener* of mystery and therefore of fear, since for most people mystery breeds fear. One then pursues knowledge as an anxiety-reducer (89).

But for peak-experiencers and transcenders in particular, as well as for self-actualizers in general, mystery is *attractive* and challenging rather than frightening. The self-actualizer is somewhat apt to be bored by what is well known, however useful this knowledge may be. But this is especially so for the peaker for whom the sense of mystery of reverence and of awe is a reward rather than a punishment.

In any case, I have found in the most creative scientists I have talked with that the more they know, the *more* apt they are to go into an ecstasy in which humility, a sense of ignorance, a feeling of smallness, awe before the tremendousness of the universe, or the stunningness of a hummingbird, or the mystery of a baby are all a part, and are all felt subjectively in a positive way, as a reward.

Hence the humility and self-confessed "ignorance" and yet also the happiness of the great transcender-scientist. I think it a possibility that we *all* have such experiences, especially as children, and yet it is the transcender who seems to have them more often, more profoundly, and values them most as high moments in life. This statement is meant to include both scientists and mystics as well as poets, artists, industrialists, politicians, mothers, and many other kinds of people. And in any case, I affirm as a theory of cognition and of science (for testing) that at the highest levels of developemnt of humanness, knowledge is positively rather than negatively correlated with a sense of mystery, awe, humility, ultimate ignorance, reverence, and a sense of oblation.

15. Transcenders, I think, should be less afraid of "nuts" and "kooks" than are other self-actualizers, and thus are more likely to be good selectors of creators (who sometimes look nutty or kooky). I would guess that self-actualizers would generally value creativeness more and therefore select it more efficiently (and therefore should make the best personnel managers or selectors or counselors) and yet to value a William Blake type takes, in principle, a greater experience with transcendence and therefore a greater valuation of it. Something like

this should be true at the opposite pole: A transcender should also be more able to screen out the nuts and kooks who are *not* creative, which I suppose includes most of them.

I have no experience to report here. This follows from theory and is presented as an easily testable hypothesis.

16. It follows from theory that transcenders should be more "reconciled with evil" in the sense of understanding its occasional inevitability and necessity in the larger holistic sense, i.e., "from above," in a godlike or Olympian sense. Since this implies a better understanding of it, it should generate *both* a greater compassion with it *and* a less ambivalent and a more unyielding fight against it. This sounds like a paradox, but with a little thought can be seen as not at all self-contradictory. To understand more deeply means, at this level, to have a stronger arm (not a weaker one), to be more decisive, to have less conflict, ambivalence, regret, and thus to act more swiftly, surely and effectively. One can *compassionately* strike down the evil man if this is necessary.

17. I would expect another paradox to be found in transcenders: namely, that they are more apt to regard themselves as *carriers* of talent, *instruments* of the transpersonal, temporary custodians so to speak of a greater intelligence or skill or leadership or efficiency. This means a certain peculiar kind of objectivity or detachment toward themselves that to nontranscenders might sound like arrogance, grandiosity, or even paranoia. The example I find most useful here is the attitude of the pregnant mother toward herself and her unborn child. What is self? What is not? How demanding, self-admiring, arrogant does she have a right to be?

I think we would be just as startled by the judgment, "I am the best one for his job and therefore I demand it," as by the equally probable judgment, "You are the best one for this job and therefore it is your duty to take it away from me." Transcendence brings with it the "transpersonal" loss of ego.

18. Transcenders are in principle (I have no data) more apt to be profoundly "religious" or "spiritual" in either the theistic or non-theistic sense. Peak experiences and other transcendent experiences are in effect also to be seen as "religious or spiritual" experiences if only we redefine these terms to exclude their historical, conventional, superstitious, institutional accretions of meaning. Such experiences

can indeed be seen as "antireligious" from the merely conventional point of view or as religion-surrogates, or religion-replacements or as a "new version of what *used* to be called religion or spirituality." The paradox that some atheists are far more "religious" than some priests can be easily enough tested and thus given operational meaning.

19. Perhaps another quantitative difference that may show up between these two kinds of self-actualizers—I am not at all sure of it —is that the transcenders, I suspect, find it easier to transcend the ego, the self, the identity, to go beyond self-actualization. To sharpen what I think I see: Perhaps we could say that the description of the healthy ones is more exhausted by describing them *primarily* as strong identities, people who know who they are, where they are going, what they want, what they are good for, in a word, as strong Selves, using themselves well and authentically and in accordance with their own true nature. And this of course does not sufficiently describe the transcenders. They are certainly this; but they are also more than this.

20. I would suppose—again as an impression and without specific data—that transcenders, because of their easier perception of the B-realm, would have more end experiences (of suchness) than their more practical brothers do, more of the fascinations that we see in children who get hypnotized by the colors in a puddle, or by raindrops dripping down a windowpane, or by the smoothness of skin, or the movements of a caterpillar.

21. In theory, transcenders should be somewhat more Taoistic, and the merely healthy somewhat more pragmatic. B-cognition makes everything look more miraculous, more perfect, just as it *should* be. It therefore breeds less impulse to *do* anything to the object that is fine just as it is, less needing improvement, or intruding upon. There should then be more impulse simply to stare at it and examine it than to do anything about it or with it.

22. A concept that adds nothing new but which ties all the foregoing in with the whole rich structure of Freudian Theory is the word "postambivalent" that I think tends to be more characteristic of all self-actualizers and *may* turn out to be a little more so in some transcenders. It means total wholehearted and unconflicted love, accept-

ance, expressiveness, rather than the more usual mixture of love and hate that passes for "love" or friendship or sexuality or authority or power, etc.

23. Finally I call attention to the question of "levels of pay" and "kinds of pay" even though I am not sure that my two groups differ much, if at all, in this regard. What is crucially important is the fact itself that there are many kinds of pay other than money pay, that money as such steadily recedes in importance with increasing affluence and with increasing maturity of character, while higher forms of pay and metapay steadily *increase* in importance. Furthermore, even where money pay continues to *seem* to be important, it is often so not in its own literal, concrete character, but rather as a symbol for status, success, self-esteem with which to win love, admiration, and respect.

This is an easily researched subject. I have been collecting ads for some time now which seek to attract professional, administrative, or executive employees, ads for Peace Corps and VISTA-type work, and sometimes even for less skilled, blue collar employees in which the attractions that are set forth to lure the applicant are not only money but also higher-need gratifications and metaneed gratifications, e.g., friendly co-workers, good surroundings, a secure future, challenge, growth, idealistic satisfactions, responsibility, freedom, an important product, compassion for others, helping mankind, helping the country, a chance to put one's own ideas into effect, a company of which one can be proud, a good school system, even good fishing, beautiful mountains to climb, etc. The Peace Corps goes so far as to *stress* as an attraction low money wages and great hardships, self-sacrifice, etc., all for the sake of helping others.

I assume that greater psychological health would make these kinds of pay more valuable especially with sufficient money and with money held constant as a variable. Of course, a large proportion of self-actualizing people have probably fused work and play anyway: i.e., they love their work. Of them, one could say, they get paid for what they would do as a hobby anyway, for doing work that is intrinsically satisfying.

The only difference I can think of, that further investigation may turn up between my two groups, is that the transcenders may actively seek out jobs that make peak experiences and B-cognition more likely.

One reason for mentioning this in this context is my conviction that it is a theoretical necessity in planning the Eupsychia, the good society, that leadership must be separated from privilege, exploitation, possessions, luxury, status, power-over-other-people, etc. The only way that I can see to protect the more capable, the leaders and managers from *ressentiment*, from the impotent envy of the weak, of the underprivileged, of the less capable, of those who need to be helped, i.e., from the Evil Eye, from overturn by the underdog, is to pay them, *not* with more money but with less, to pay them rather with "higher pay" and with "metapay." It follows from the principles so far set forth here and elsewhere (83) that this would please both the self-actualizers and the less psychologically developed, and would abort the development of the mutually exclusive and antagonistic classes or castes that we have seen throughout human history. All we need to do to make practical this post-Marxian, post-historical possibility is to learn not to pay too much for money, i.e., to value the higher rather than the lower. Also it would be necessary here to desymbolize money; i.e., it must *not* symbolize success, respectworthiness, or loveworthiness.

These changes should in principle be quite easily possible since they already accord with the preconscious or not-quite-conscious value-life of self-actualizing people. Whether or not this *Weltanschauung* is or is not more characteristic of transcenders remains to be discovered. I suspect so, mostly on the grounds that mystics and transcenders have throughout history seemed spontaneously to prefer simplicity and to avoid luxury, privilege, honors, and possessions. My impression is that the "common people" have therefore mostly tended to love and revere them rather than to fear and hate them. So perhaps this could be a help in designing a world in which the most capable, the most awakened, the most idealistic would be chosen and loved as leaders, as teachers, as obviously benevolent and unselfish authority.

24. I cannot resist expressing what is only a vague hunch; namely, the possibility that my transcenders seem to me somewhat more apt to be Sheldonian ectomorphs while my less-often-transcending self-actualizers seem more often to be mesomorphic. (I mention this only because it is in principle easily testable.)

Epilogue

Because it will be so difficult for so many to believe, I must state explicitly that I have found approximately as many transcenders among businessmen, industrialists, managers, educators, political people as I have among the professionally "religious," the poets, intellectuals, musicians, and others who are *supposed* to be transcenders and are officially labeled so. I must say that each of these "professions" has different folkways, different jargon, different personae, and different uniforms. Any minister will talk transcendence even if he hasn't got the slightest inkling of what it feels like. And most industrialists will carefully conceal their idealism, their metamotivations, and their transcendent experiences under a mask of "toughness," "realism," "selfishness," and all sorts of other words which would have to be marked off by quotes to indicate that they are only superficial and defensive. Their more real metamotivations are often not repressed but only suppressed, and I have sometimes found it quite easy to break through the protective surface by very direct confrontations and questions.

I must be careful also not to give any false impressions about numbers of subjects (only three or four dozen who have been more or less carefully talked with and observed, and perhaps another hundred or two talked with, read, and observed but not as carefully or in depth), or about the reliability of my information (this is all exploration or investigation or reconnaissance rather than careful final research, a first approximation rather than the normally verified science which will come later), or the representativeness of my sample (I used whomever I could get, but mostly concentrated on the *best* specimens of intellect, creativeness, character, strength, success, etc.).

At the same time, I must insist that it is an empirical exploration and reports what I have *perceived*, rather than anything I dreamed up. I have found that it helps to remove scientific uneasiness about my freewheeling explorations, affirmations, and hypotheses if I am willing to call them prescientific rather than scientific (a word which for so many means verification rather than discovery). In any case, every affirmation in this paper is in principle testable, provable or disprovable.

PART VIII

Metamotivation

23

A Theory of Metamotivation:
The Biological Rooting of the Value-Life

I

Self-actualizing individuals (more matured, more fully human), by definition, already suitably gratified in their basic needs, are now motivated in other higher ways, to be called "metamotivations."[1]

By definition, self-actualizing people are gratified in all their basic needs (of belongingness, affection, respect, and self-esteem). This is to say that they have a feeling of belongingness and rootedness, they are satisfied in their love needs, have friends and feel loved and loveworthy, they have status and place in life and respect from other people, and they have a reasonable feeling of worth and self-respect. If we phrase this negatively—in terms of the frustration of these basic needs and in terms of pathology—then this is to say that self-actualizing people do not (for any length of time) feel anxiety-ridden, insecure, unsafe, do not feel alone, ostracized, rootless, or isolated, do not feel unlovable, rejected, or unwanted, do not feel despised and looked down upon, and do not feel deeply unworthy, nor do they

[1] The twenty-eight italicized theses listed here are presented as testable propositions.

have crippling feelings of inferiority or worthlessness (95, Chap. 12).

Of course this can be phrased in other ways and this I have done. For instance, since the basic needs had been assumed to be the only motivations for human beings, it was possible, and in certain contexts also useful, to say of self-actualizing people that they were "unmotivated" (95, Chap. 15). This was to align these people with the Eastern philosophical view of health as the transcendence of striving or desiring or wanting. (And something of the sort was also true of the Roman Stoic view.)

It was also possible to describe self-actualizing people as expressing rather than coping, and to stress that they were spontaneous, and natural, that they were more easily themselves than other people. This phrasing had the additional usefulness of being compatible with the view of neurosis as an understandable coping mechanism and as a reasonable (though stupid and fearful) effort to satisfy the needs of a deeper-lying, more intrinsic, more biological self.

Each of these phrasings has its own operational usefulness in particular research contexts. But it is also true that for certain purposes it is best to ask the questions, "What motivates the self-actualizing person? What are the psychodynamics in self-actualization? What makes him move and act and struggle? What drives (or pulls) such a person on? What attracts him? For what does he hope? What makes him angry, or dedicated, or self-sacrificing? What does he feel loyal to? Devoted to? What does he value, aspire to, and yearn for? What would he die (or live) for?"

Clearly we must make an immediate distinction between the ordinary motives of people below the level of self-actualization—that is, people motivated by the basic needs—and the motivations of people who are sufficiently gratified in all their basic needs and therefore are no longer motivated by them primarily, but rather by "higher" motivations. It is therefore convenient to call these higher motives and needs of self-actualizing persons by the name "metaneeds" and also to differentiate the category of motivation from the category of "metamotivation."

(It is now more clear to me that gratification of the basic needs is not a sufficient condition for metamotivation, although it may be a necessary precondition. I have individual subjects in whom apparent basic-need-gratification is compatible with "existential neurosis," meaninglessness, valuelessness, or the like. Metamotivation now seems *not* to ensue automatically after basic-need-gratification. One must speak also of the additional variable of "defenses against metamotivation." This implies that, for the strategy of communication and of theory building, it may turn out to be useful to add to the definition of the self-actualizing person, not only [a] that he be sufficiently free of illness, [b] that he be sufficiently gratified in his basic needs, and [c] that he be positively using his capacities, but also [d] that he be motivated by some values which he strives for or gropes for and to which he is loyal.)

II

All such people are devoted to some task, call, vocation, beloved work ("outside themselves").

In examining self-actualizing people directly, I find that in all cases, at least in our culture, they are dedicated people, devoted to some task "outside themselves," some vocation, or duty, or beloved job. Generally the devotion and dedication is so marked that one can fairly use the old words vocation, calling, or mission to describe their passionate, selfless, and profound feeling for their "work." We could even use the words destiny or fate. I have sometimes gone so far as to speak of oblation in the religious sense, in the sense of offering oneself or dedicating oneself upon some altar for some particular task, some cause outside oneself and bigger than oneself, something not merely selfish, something impersonal.

I think it is possible to go pretty far with the notion of destiny or fate. This is a way of putting into inadequate words the feeling that one gets when one listens to self-actualizing people (and some others) talking about their work or task (83). One gets the feeling of a beloved job, and, furthermore, of something for which the person is a "natural," something that he is suited for, something that is right for him, even something that he was born for. It is easy to sense something like a pre-established harmony or, perhaps one could say, a good match like the perfect love affair or friendship, in which it seems that people belong to each other and were meant for each other. In the best instances, the person and his job fit together and belong together perfectly like a key and a lock, or perhaps resonate together like a sung note which sets into sympathetic resonance a particular string in the piano keyboard.

It should be said that the above seems to hold true for my female subjects even though in a different sense. I have at least one woman subject who devoted herself entirely to the task of being the mother, the wife, the housewife, and the clan matriarch. Her vocation, one could very reasonably call it, was to bring up her children, to make her husband happy, and to hold together a large number of relatives in a network of personal relations. This she did very well and, as nearly as I could make out, this she enjoyed. She loved her lot completely and totally, never yearning for anything else so far as I could tell, and using all her capacities well in the process. Other women subjects have had various combinations of home life and professional work outside the home which could produce this same sense of dedication to something perceived simultaneously, both as beloved and also as important and worthwhile doing. In some women, I have also been tempted to think of "having a baby" as fullest self-actualization all by itself, at least for a time. However, I should say that I feel less confident in speaking of self-actualization in women.

III

In the ideal instance, inner requiredness coincides with external requiredness, "I want to" with "I must."

I often get the feeling in this kind of situation that I can tease apart two kinds of determinants of this transaction (or alloying, fusion, or chemical reaction) which has created a unity out of a duality, and that these two sets of determinants can and sometimes do vary independently. One can be spoken of as the responses within the person, e.g., "I love babies (or painting, or research, or political power) more than anything in the world. I am fascinated with it. . . . I am inexorably drawn to . . . I need to . . ." This we may call "inner requiredness" and it is felt as a kind of self-indulgence rather than as a duty. It is different from and separable from "external requiredness," which is rather felt as a response to what the environment, the situation, the problem, the external world calls for or requires of the person, as a fire "calls for" putting out, or as a helpless baby demands that one take care of it, or as some obvious injustice calls for righting. Here one feels more the element of duty, or obligation, or responsibility, of being compelled helplessly to respond no matter what one was planning to do, or wished to do. It is more "I must, I have to, I am compelled" than "I want to."

In the ideal instance, which fortunately also happens in fact in many of my instances, "I want to" coincides with "I must." There is a good matching of inner with outer requiredness. And the observer is then overawed by the degree of compellingness, of inexorability, of pre-ordained destiny, necessity, and harmony that he perceives. Further-more, the observer (as well as the person involved) feels not only that "it has to be" but also that "it ought to be, it is right, it is suitable, appropriate, fitting, and proper." I have often felt a Gestaltlike quality about this kind of belonging together, the formation of a "one" out of "two."

I hesitate to call this simply "purposefulness" because that may imply that it happens only out of will, purpose, decision, or calculation, and doesn't give enough weight to the subjective feeling of being swept along, of willing and eager surrender, or yielding to fate and happily embracing it at the same time. Ideally, one also *discovers* one's fate; it is not only made or constructed or decided upon. It is recognized as if one had been unwittingly waiting for it. Perhaps the better phrase would be "Spinozistic" or "Taoistic" choice or decision or purpose—or even will.

The best way to communicate these feelings to someone who doesn't intuitively, directly understand them is to use as a model "falling in love." This is clearly different from doing one's duty, or doing what is sensible or logical. And clearly also "will," if mentioned at all, is used in a very special sense. And when two people love each other fully, then each one knows what it feels like to be magnet and what it feels like to be iron filings, and what it feels like to be both simul-taneously.

IV

This ideal situation generates feelings of good fortune and also of ambivalence and unworthiness.

This model also helps to convey what is difficult to communicate in words, that is, their sense of good fortune, of luck, of gratuitous grace, of awe that this miracle should have occurred, of wonder that they should have been chosen, and of the peculiar mixture of pride fused with humility, of arrogance shot through with the pity-for-the-less-fortunate that one finds in lovers.

Of course the possibility of good fortune and success also can set into motion all sorts of neurotic fears, feelings of unworthiness, counter-values, Jonah-syndrome dynamics, etc. These defenses against our highest possibilities must be overcome before the highest values can be wholeheartedly embraced.

V

At this level the dichotomizing of work and play is transcended; wages, hobbies, vacations, etc., must be defined at a higher level.

And then, of course, it can be said of such a person with real meaningfulness that he is being his own kind of person, or being himself, or actualizing his real self. An abstract statement, an extrapolation out from this kind of observation toward the ultimate and perfect ideal would run something like this: This person is the best one in the whole world for this particular job, and this particular job is the best job in the whole world for this particular person and his talents, capacities, and tastes. He was meant for it, and it was meant for him.

Of course, as soon as we accept this and get the feel of it, then we move over into another realm of discourse, i.e., the realm of being (89), of transcendence. Now we can speak meaningfully only in the language of being ("The B-language," communication at the mystical level, etc.). For instance, it is quite obvious with such people that the ordinary or conventional dichotomy between work and play is transcended totally (80, 83). That is, there is certainly no distinction between work and play in such a person in such a situation. His work is his play and his play is his work. If a person loves his work and enjoys it more than any other activity in the whole world and is eager to get to it, to get back to it after any interruption, then how can we speak about "labor" in the sense of something one is forced to do against one's wishes?

What sense, for instance, is left to the concept "vacation"? For such individuals it is often observed that during their vacations, that is, during the periods in which they are totally free to choose whatever they wish to do and in which they have no external obligations to anyone else, that it is precisely in such periods that they devote themselves happily and totally to their "work." Or, what does it mean "to have some fun," to seek amusement? What is now the meaning of the word "entertainment"? How does such a person "rest"? What are his "duties," responsibilities, obligations? What is his "hobby"?

What meaning does money or pay or salary have in such a situation? Obviously the most beautiful fate, the most wonderful good fortune that can happen to any human being, is to be paid for doing that which he passionately loves to do. This is exactly the situation, or almost the situation, with many (most?) of my subjects. Of course money is welcome, and in certain amounts is needed. But it is certainly not the finality, the end, the ultimate goal (that is, in the affluent society, and for the fortunate man). The salary check such a man gets is only a small part of his "pay." Self-actualizing work or B-work (work at the level of being), being its own intrinsic reward, transforms the money or paycheck into a byproduct, an epiphenomenon. This is, of course, very different from the situation of the large majority of human beings who do something they do not want to do in order to get money, which they then use to get what they really want. The role of money in the realm of being is certainly different from the role of money in the realm of deficiencies and of basic needs.

It will help to make my point that these are scientific questions, and can be investigated in scientific ways, if I point out that they already have been investigated in monkeys and apes to a degree. The most obvious example, of course, is the rich research literature on monkey curiosity and other precursors of the human yearning for and satisfaction with the truth (89). But it will be just as easy in principle to explore the aesthetic choices of these and other animals under conditions of fear, and of lack of fear, by healthy specimens or by unhealthy ones, under good-choice conditions or bad ones, etc. So also for such other B-Values as order, unity, justice, lawfulness, completion; it should be possible to explore these in animals, children, etc.

Of course, "highest" means also weakest, most expendable, least urgent, least conscious, most easily repressed (95, Chap. 8). The basic needs, being prepotent, push to the head of the line, so to speak, being more necessary for life itself, and for sheer physical health and survival. And yet metamotivation *does* exist in the natural world and in ordinary human beings. Supernatural intervention is not needed in this theory, nor is it necessary to invent the B-Values arbitrarily, or *a priori*, nor are they merely logical products or the products by fiat of an act of will. They can be uncovered or discovered by anyone who is willing and able to repeat these operations. That is, these propositions are verifiable or falsifiable, and they are repeatable. They can be operationally stated. Many of them can be made public or demonstrable, that is, perceived simultaneously by two or more investigators.

If, then, the higher life of values is open to scientific investigation and clearly lies within the jurisdiction of (humanistically defined) science (82, 126), we may reasonably affirm the likelihood of progress in this realm. The advancement of knowledge of the higher life of values should make possible not only greater understanding, but also should open up new possibilities of self-improvement, of improvement of the human species and of all its social institutions (83). Of course, it goes without saying that we need not shiver at the thought of "the strategy of compassion" or of "spiritual technologies": obviously, they would have to be extremely different in kind from the "lower" strategies and technologies we now know.

VI

Such vocation-loving individuals tend to identify (introject, incorporate) with their "work" and to make it into a defining-characteristic of the self. It becomes part of the self.

If one asks such a person, i.e., self-actualizing, work-loving, "Who are you?" or "What are you?" he often tends to answer in terms of his "call," e.g., "I am a lawyer." "I am a mother." "I am a psychiatrist." "I am an artist," etc. That is, he tells you that he identifies his call with his identity, his self. It tends to be a label for the whole of him, i.e., it becomes a defining characteristic of the person.

Or, if one asks him, "Supposing you were not a scientist (or a teacher, or a pilot), then what would you be?" Or, "Supposing you were not a psychologist, then what?" It is my impression that his response is apt to be one of puzzlement, thoughtfulness, being taken aback, i.e., not having a ready answer. Or the response can be one of amusement, i.e., it is funny. In effect, the answer is, "If I were not a mother (anthropologist, industrialist), then I wouldn't be *me*. I would be someone else. And I can't imagine being someone else."

This kind of response parallels the confused response to the question, "Supposing you were a woman rather than a man?"

A tentative conclusion is then that in self-actualizing subjects, their beloved calling tends to be perceived as a defining characteristic of the self, to be identified with, incorporated, introjected. It becomes an inextricable aspect of one's being.

(I do not have experience with deliberately asking this same question of less-fulfilled people. My impression is that the above generalization is less true for some people [for whom it is an extrinsic job] and that in other individuals the job or profession can become functionally autonomous, i.e., the person is *only* a lawyer and not a person apart from this.)

VII

The tasks to which they are dedicated seem to be interpretable as embodiments or incarnations of intrinsic values (rather than as a means to ends outside the work itself, and rather than as functionally autonomous). The tasks are loved (and introjected) BECAUSE they embody these values. That is, ultimately it is the values that are loved rather than the job as such.

If one asks these people why they love their work (or, more specifically, which are the moments of higher satisfaction in their work, which moments of reward make all the necessary chores worthwhile and acceptable, which are the peak moments or peak experiences), one gets many specific and *ad hoc* answers of the type listed and summarized in Table 1.

In addition, of course, one gets many "end answers" of the type— "I just love my baby, that's all. Why do I love him? I just do"; or "I just get a big kick out of improving the efficiency of my plant. Why? I just get a big bang out of it." Peak experiences, intrinsic pleasures, worthwhile achievements, whatever their degree, need no further justification or validation. They are intrinsic reinforcers.

It is possible to classify these moments of reward, and to boil them

TABLE 1

Motivations and Gratifications of Self-Actualizing People, obtained through their work as well as in other ways. (These are in addition to basic-need gratifications.)

Delight in bringing about justice.

Delight in stopping cruelty and exploitation.

Fighting lies and untruths.

They love virtue to be rewarded.

They seem to like happy endings, good completions.

They hate sin and evil to be rewarded, and they hate people to get away with it.

They are good punishers of evil.

They try to set things right, to clean up bad situations.

They enjoy doing good.

They like to reward and praise promise, talent, virtue, etc.

They avoid publicity, fame, glory, honors, popularity, celebrity, or at least do not seek it. It seems to be not awfully important one way or another.

They do not *need* to be loved by everyone.

They generally pick out their own causes, which are apt to be few in number, rather than responding to advertising or to campaigns or to other people's exhortations.

They tend to enjoy peace, calm, quiet, pleasantness, etc., and they tend *not* to like turmoil, fighting, war, etc. (they are *not* general-fighters on every front), and they can enjoy themselves in the middle of a "war."

They also seem practical and shrewd and realistic about it, more often than impractical. They like to be effective and dislike being ineffectual.

Their fighting is not an excuse for hostility, paranoia, grandiosity, authority, rebellion, etc., but is for the sake of setting things right. It is problem-centered.

They manage somehow simultaneously to love the world as it is and to try to improve it.

In all cases there was some hope that people and nature and society could be improved.

In all cases it was as if they could see both good and evil realistically.

They respond to the challenge in a job.

A chance to improve the situation or the operation is a big reward. They enjoy improving things.

Observations generally indicate great pleasure in their children and in helping them grow into good adults.

They do not need or seek for or even enjoy very much flattery, applause, popularity, status, prestige, money, honors, etc.

Expressions of gratitude, or at least of awareness of their good fortune, are common.

They have a sense of *noblesse oblige*. It is the duty of the superior, of the one who sees and knows, to be patient and tolerant, as with children.

They tend to be attracted by mystery, unsolved problems, by the unknown and the challenging, rather than to be frightened by them.

They enjoy bringing about law and order in the chaotic situation, or in the messy or confused situation, or in the dirty and unclean situation.

They hate (and fight) corruption, cruelty, malice, dishonesty, pompousness, phoniness, and faking.

They try to free themselves from illusions, to look at the facts courageously, to take away the blindfold.

They feel it is a pity for talent to be wasted.

They do not do mean things, and they respond with anger when other people do mean things.

They tend to feel that every person should have an opportunity to develop to his highest potential, to have a fair chance, to have equal opportunity.

They like doing things well, "doing a good job," "to do well what needs doing." Many such phrases add up to "bringing about good workmanship."

One advantage of being a boss is the right to give away the corporation's money, to choose which good causes to help. They enjoy giving their own money away to causes they consider important, good, worthwhile, etc. Pleasure in philanthropy.

They enjoy watching and helping the self-actualizing of others, especially of the young.

They enjoy watching happiness and helping to bring it about.

They get great pleasure from knowing admirable people (courageous, honest, effective, "straight," "big," creative, saintly, etc.). "My work brings me in contact with many fine people."

They enjoy taking on responsibilities (that they can handle well), and certainly don't fear or evade their responsibilities. They respond to responsibility.

They uniformly consider their work to be worthwhile, important, even essential.

They enjoy greater efficiency, making an operation more neat, compact, simpler, faster, less expensive, turning out a better product, doing with less parts, a smaller number of operations, less clumsiness, less effort, more foolproof, safer, more "elegant," less laborious.

down into a smaller number of categories. As I tried to do this, it quickly became apparent that the best and most "natural" categories of classification were mostly or entirely abstract "values" of an ultimate and irreducible kind, such values as truth, beauty, newness, uniqueness, justice, compactness, simplicity, goodness, neatness, efficiency, love, honesty, innocence, improvement, orderliness, elegance, growth, cleanliness, authenticity, serenity, peacefulness, and the like.

For these people the profession seems to be *not* functionally autonomous, but rather to be a carrier of, an instrument of, or an incarnation of ultimate values. For them the profession of law, for example, is a means to the end of justice, and not an end in itself. Perhaps I can communicate my feeling for the subtle difference in this way: For one man the law *is* loved because it *is* justice, while another man, the pure value-free technologist, might love the law simply as an intrinsically lovable set of rules, precedents, procedures without regard to the ends or products of their use. He may be said to love the vehicle itself without reference to its ends, as one loves a game which has no end other than to be a game, e.g., chess.

I have had to learn to differentiate several kinds of identification with a "cause" or a profession or a calling. A profession can be a means to covert and repressed ends as easily as it can be an end in itself. Or, better said, it can be motivated by deficiency-needs or even neurotic needs as well as by metaneeds. It can be multiply-determined or overdetermined by all or any of those needs and metaneeds in any patterning. From the simple statement, "I am a lawyer and I love my work," one cannot assume very much.

It is my strong impression that the closer to self-actualizing, to full-humanness, etc., the person is, the more likely I am to find that his "work" is metamotivated rather than basic-need-motivated. For more highly evolved persons, "the law" is apt to be more a way of seeking justice, truth, goodness, etc., rather than financial security, admiration, status, prestige, dominance, masculinity, etc. When I ask the questions: Which aspects of your work do you enjoy most? What gives you your greatest pleasures? When do you get a kick out of your work? etc., such people are more apt to answer in terms of intrinsic values, of transpersonal, beyond-the-selfish, altruistic satisfactions, e.g., seeing justice done, doing a more perfect job, advancing the truth, rewarding virtue and punishing evil, etc.

VIII

These intrinsic values overlap greatly with the B-Values, and perhaps are identical with them.

While my "data," if I may call them that, are certainly not firm enough to permit me any exactness here, I have been proceeding on the assumption that my classification of B-Values already published (85) is close enough to the above list of found final or intrinsic values to be useful here. Clearly, there is considerable overlap between the two lists, and they may yet approach identity. I feel it desirable to use my description of the B-Values, not only because it would be theoretically pretty if I could, but also because they are operationally definable in so many different ways (85, Appendix G). That is to say, they are found at the end of so many different investigative roads that the suspicion arises that there is something in common between these different paths, e.g., education, art, religion, psychotherapy, peak experiences, science, mathematics, etc. If this turns out to be so, we may perhaps add as another road to final values, the "cause," the mission, the vocation, that is to say, the "work" of self-actualizing people. (It is also theoretically advantageous to speak of the B-Values here because of my strong impression that self-actualizing, or more fully human people show, *outside* their calling, as well as in it and through it, a love for and satisfaction in these same values.)

Or, to say it in another way, people who are reasonably gratified in all their basic needs now become "metamotivated" by the B-Values, or at least by "final" ultimate values in greater or lesser degree, and in one or another combination of these ultimate values.

In another phrasing: Self-actualizing people are not primarily motivated (i.e., by basic needs); they are primarily metamotivated (i.e., by metaneeds = B-Values).

IX

This introjection means that the self has enlarged to include aspects of the world and that therefore the distinction between self and not-self (outside, other) has been transcended.

These B-Values or metamotives are, therefore, no longer *only* intrapsychic or organismic. They are equally inner and outer. The meta-needs, insofar as they are inner, and the requiredness of all that is outside the person are each both stimulus and response to each other. And they move toward becoming indistinguishable, that is, toward fusion.

This means that the distinction between self and not-self has broken down (or has been transcended). There is now less differentiation between the world and the person because he has incorporated into himself part of the world and defines himself thereby. He becomes an enlarged self, we could say. If justice or truth or lawfulness have now become so important to him that he identifies his self with them, then where are they? Inside his skin or outside his skin? This distinction comes close to being meaningless at this point because his self no longer has his skin as its boundary. The inner light now seems to be no different than the outer light.

Certainly simple selfishness is transcended here and has to be defined at higher levels. For instance, we know that it is possible for a person to get more pleasure (selfish? unselfish?) out of food through having his child eat it than through eating it with his own mouth. His self has enlarged enough to include his child. Hurt his child and you hurt him. Clearly the self can no longer be identified with the biological entity which is supplied with blood from his heart along his blood vessels. The psychological self can obviously be bigger than its own body.

Just as beloved people can be incorporated into the self, become defining characteristics of it, so also can beloved causes and values be similarly incorporated into a person's self. Many people, for instance, are so passionately identified with trying to prevent war, or racial injustice, or slums, or poverty, that they are quite willing to make great sacrifices, even to the point of risking death. And very clearly, they don't mean justice for their own biological bodies alone. Something personal has now become bigger than the body. They mean justice as a general value, justice for everyone; justice as a principle. Attack upon the B-Values is then also an attack upon any person who has incorporated these values into his self. Such an attack becomes a *personal* insult.

To identify one's highest self with the highest values of the world out there means, to some extent at least, a fusion with the non-self. But this is true not only for the world of nature. It is also true for other human beings. That is to say that the most highly valued part of such a person's self, then, is the same as the most highly valued part of the self of other self-actualizing people. Such selves overlap.

There are other important consequences of this incorporation of values into the self. For instance, you can love justice and truth in the world or in a person out there. You can be made happier as your friends move toward truth and justice, and sadder as they move away from it. This is easy to understand. But suppose you see yourself moving successfully toward truth, justice, beauty, and virtue? Then of course you may find that, in a peculiar kind of detachment and objectivity toward oneself, for which our culture has no place, you will be loving and admiring yourself, in the kind of healthy self-love that Fromm (36) has described. You can respect yourself, admire yourself, take tender care of yourself, reward yourself, feel virtuous, loveworthy, respectworthy. So also may a person with a great talent protect it and himself as if he were a carrier of something which is simultaneously himself and not himself. He may become his own guardian, so to speak.

X

Less evolved persons seem to use their work more often for achieving gratification of lower basic needs, of neurotic needs, as a means to an end, out of habit, or as a response to cultural expectations, etc. However, it is probable that these are differences of degree. Perhaps all human beings are (potentially) metamotivated to a degree.

These people, though concretely working for, motivated by, and loyal to the law, or to family, or to science, or to psychiatry, or to teaching, or the arts, that is, to some conventional category of work, seem then to be motivated by the intrinsic or ultimate values (or ultimate facts, or aspects of reality) for which the profession is only a vehicle (85, 89). This is my impression from observing them, and interviewing them, e.g., asking them why they like doctoring, or just which are the most rewarding moments in running a home, or chairing a committee, or having a baby, or writing. They may meaningfully be said to be working for truth, for beauty, for goodness, for law and for order, for justice, for perfection, if I boil down to a dozen or so intrinsic values (or values of Being) all the hundreds of concrete or specific reports of what is yearned for, what gratifies, what is valued, what they work for from day to day, and why they work. (This is, of course, in addition to lower values.)

I have not deliberately worked with an *ad hoc* control group, i.e., non-self-actualizing people. *I could say that most of humanity is a control group, which is certainly true.* I *do* have a considerable fund of experience with the attitudes toward work of average people, immature people, neurotic and borderline people, psychopaths, etc., and there is no question whatsoever that their attitudes cluster around money, basic-need gratifications (rather than B-Values), sheer habit, stimulus-binding, neurotic needs, convention, and inertia (the unexamined and nonquestioned life), and from doing what other people expect or demand. However, this intuitive common sense or naturalistic conclusion is certainly easily susceptible to more careful, more controlled, and predesigned examination which could confirm or disconfirm.

It is my strong impression that there is not a sharp line between my subjects chosen as self-actualizing and other people. I believe that each self-actualizing subject with whom I have worked more or less fits the description I have given; but it seems also true that some percentage of other, less healthy people also are metamotivated to some degree by the B-Values, especially individuals with special talents and people placed in especially fortunate circumstances. Perhaps all people are metamotivated to some degree.[2]

The conventional categories of career, profession, or work may serve as channels of many other kinds of motivations, not to mention sheer habit or convention or functional autonomy. They may satisfy or seek vainly to satisfy any or all of the basic needs as well as various neurotic needs. They may be a channel for "acting out" or for "defensive" activities as well as for real gratifications.

My guess, supported both by my "empirical" impressions and by general psychodynamic theory, is that we will find it ultimately most true and most useful to say that all these various habits, determinants, motives, and metamotives are acting simultaneously in a very complex pattern which is centered more toward one kind of motivation or

---

[2] I feel confident enough about this to suggest the founding of companies for metamotivational research. These should be as lucrative as those that specialize in so-called motivation research.

determinedness than the others. This is to say that the most highly developed persons we know are metamotivated to a much higher degree, and are basic-need-motivated to a lesser degree than average or diminished people are.

Another guess is that the dimension of "confusion" will also be relevant. I have already reported (95, Chap. 12) my impression that my self-actualizing subjects seemed quite easily and decisively to "know right from wrong" for themselves. This contrasts sharply with the current and widely prevalent value-confusion. Not only is there confusion, but also a queer kind of turning black into white, and an active hatred of the good (or trying-to-become-good) person, or of superiority, excellence, beauty, talent, etc.

> "Politicians and intellectuals bore me. They seem to be unreal; the people I see a lot of these days are the ones who seem real to me: whores, thieves, junkies, etc." (From an interview with Nelson Algren.)

This hatred I have called "counter-valuing." I could as easily have called it Nietzschean *ressentiment*.

XI

The full definition of the person or of human nature must then include intrinsic values, as part of human nature.

If we then try to define the deepest, most authentic, most constitutionally based aspects of the real self, of the identity, or of the authentic person, we find that in order to be comprehensive we must include not only the person's constitution and temperament, not only anatomy, physiology, neurology, and endocrinology, not only his capacities, his biological style, not only his basic instinctoid needs, but also the B-Values, which are also *his* B-Values. (This should be understood as a flat rejection of the Sartre type of arbitrary existentialism in which a self is created by fiat.) They are equally part of his "nature," or definition, or essence, along with his "lower" needs, at least in my self-actualizing subjects. They must be included in any ultimate definition of "the human being," or of full humanness, or of "a person." It is true that they are not fully evident or actualized (made real and functionally existing) in most people. And yet, so far as I can see at this time, they are not excluded as potentials in any human being born into the world. (Of course, it is conceivable that we may discover new data in the future to contradict this assumption. Also strictly semantic and theory-building considerations will ultimately be involved, e.g., what meaning shall we assign to the concept "self-actualization" in a feebleminded person?) And in any case, I maintain that this is true for some people at least.

A fully inclusive definition of a fully developed self or person includes this kind of value system, by which he is metamotivated.

XII

These intrinsic values are instinctoid in nature, i.e., they are needed (a) to avoid illness and (b) to achieve fullest humanness or growth. The "illnesses" resulting from deprivation of intrinsic values (metaneeds) we may call metapathologies. The "highest" values; the spiritual life, the highest aspirations of mankind are therefore proper subjects for scientific study and research. They are in the world of nature.

I wish now to advance another thesis, which comes also from (unsystematized and unplanned) observations on the contrasts between my subjects and the population in general. It is this: I have called the basic needs instinctoid or biologically necessary for many reasons (95, Chap. 7) but primarily because the person *needs* the basic gratifications in order to avoid illness, to avoid diminution of humanness, and, positively stated, in order to move forward and upward toward self-actualization or full humanness. It is my strong impression that something very similar holds true for the metamotivations of self-actualizing people. They seem to me to be also biological necessities in order (a) negatively, to avoid "illness" and (b) positively, to achieve full humanness. Since these metamotivations are the intrinsic values of being, singly or in combination, then this amounts to contending that the B-Values are instinctoid in nature.

These "illnesses" (which come from deprivation of the B-Values or metaneeds or B-facts) are new and have not yet been described as such, i.e., as pathologies, except unwittingly, or by implication, or, as by Frankl (34), in a very general and inclusive way, not yet teased apart into researchable form. In general, they have been discussed through the centuries by religionists, historians, and philosophers under the rubric of spiritual or religious shortcomings, rather than by physicians, scientists, or psychologists under the rubric of psychiatric or psychological or biological "illnesses" or stuntings or diminutions. To some extent also there is some overlap with sociological and political disturbances, "social pathologies," and the like (Table 2).

I will call these "illnesses" (or, better, diminutions of humanness) "metapathologies" and define them as the consequences of deprivation of the B-Values either in general or of specific B-Values (see Tables

TABLE 2

General Metapathologies

Alienation.
Anomie.
Anhedonia.
Loss of zest in life.
Meaninglessness.
Inability to enjoy. Indifference.
Boredom; ennui.
Life ceases to be intrinsically worthwhile and self-validating.
Existential vacuum.
Noogenic neurosis.
Philosophical crisis.
Apathy, resignation, fatalism.
Valuelessness.
Desacralization of life.
Spiritual illnesses and crises. "Dryness," "aridity," staleness.
Axiological depression.
Death wishes; letting go of life. One's death doesn't matter.
Sense of being useless, unneeded, of not mattering. Ineffectuality.
Hopelessness, apathy, defeat, cessation of coping, succumbing.
Feeling totally determined. Helplessness. No feeling of free will.
Ultimate doubt. Is *anything* worthwhile? Does anything matter?
Despair, anguish.
Joylessness.
Futility.
Cynicism; disbelief in, loss of faith in, or reductive explanation of all high values.
Metagrumbles.
"Aimless" destructiveness, resentment, vandalism.
Alienation from all elders, parents, authority, from *any* society.

TABLE 3
B-Values and Specific Metapathologies

B-Values	Pathogenic Deprivation	Specific Metapathologies
1. Truth	Dishonesty	Disbelief; mistrust; cynicism; skepticism; suspicion.
2. Goodness	Evil	Utter selfishness. Hatred; repulsion; disgust. Reliance only upon self and for self. Nihilism. Cynicism.
3. Beauty	Ugliness	Vulgarity. Specific unhappiness, restlessness, loss of taste, tension, fatigue. Philistinism. Bleakness.
4. Unity; Wholeness	Chaos. Atomism, loss of connectedness.	Disintegration; "the world is falling apart." Arbitrariness.
4A. Dichotomy-Transcendence	Black and white dichotomies. Loss of gradations, of degree. Forced polarization. Forced choices.	Black-white thinking, either/or thinking. Seeing everything as a duel or a war, or a conflict. Low synergy. Simplistic view of life.
5. Aliveness; Process	Deadness. Mechanizing of life.	Deadness. Robotizing. Feeling oneself to be totally determined. Loss of emotion. Boredom (?); loss of zest in life. Experiential emptiness.
6. Uniqueness	Sameness; uniformity; interchangeability.	Loss of feeling of self and of individuality. Feeling oneself to be interchangeable, anonymous, not really needed.
7. Perfection	Imperfection; sloppiness; poor workmanship, shoddiness.	Discouragement (?); hopelessness; nothing to work for.
7A. Necessity	Accident; occasionalism; inconsistency.	Chaos; unpredictability. Loss of safety. Vigilance.
8. Completion; Finality	Incompleteness	Feelings of incompleteness with perseveration. Hopelessness. Cessation of striving and coping. No use trying.
9. Justice	Injustice	Insecurity; anger; cynicism; mistrust; lawlessness; jungle world-view; total selfishness.
9A. Order	Lawlessness. Choas Breakdown of authority.	Insecurity. Wariness. Loss of safety, of predictability. Necessity for vigilance, alertness, tension, being on guard.
10. Simplicity	Confusing complexity. Disconnectedness. Disintegration.	Overcomplexity; confusion; bewilderment, conflict, loss of orientation.

11.	Richness; Totality; Comprehensiveness	Poverty. Coarctation.	Depression; uneasiness; loss of interest in world.
12.	Effortlessness	Effortfulness	Fatigue, strain, striving, clumsiness, awkwardness, gracelessness, stiffness.
13.	Playfulness	Humorlessness	Grimness; depression; paranoid humorlessness; loss of zest in life. Cheerlessness. Loss of ability to enjoy.
14.	Self-sufficiency	Contingency; accident; occasionalism.	Dependence upon (?) the perceiver (?). It becomes his responsibility.
15.	Meaningfulness	Meaninglessness	Meaninglessness. Despair. Senselessness of life.

2 and 3). Extrapolating out from my previous descriptions and cataloguing of the various B-Values, arrived at by various operations, it is possible to form a kind of periodic table (Table 3) in which illnesses not yet discovered may be listed, to be looked for in the future. To the extent that they will be discovered and described, to that extent will my impressions and hypotheses be confirmed. (I have used the world of television and especially of television advertising as a rich source of metapathologies of all types, i.e., of the vulgarization or destruction of all intrinsic values, although, of course, many other sources of data are readily available.)

The third column in Table 3 is a very tentative effort and should not be taken too seriously except as a pointing toward future tasks. These specific metapathologies seem to be as figure against the ground of general metapathology. The only specific metapathology with which I have dealt at length is the first one (89, Chap. 5), and perhaps this publication could serve as a stimulus to other efforts, quite feasible, I think, to describe other metapathologies. I suspect that reading in the literature of religious pathology, especially in the mystical tradition, would be suggestive. I would guess that leads would also be found in the realm of "chic" art, of social pathology, of homosexual subcultures, in the literature of Nay-saying existentialism (159). The case histories of existential psychotherapy, spiritual illness, existential vacuum, the "dryness" and "aridity" of the mystics, the dichotomizing, verbalizing, and overabstracting dissected by the general semanticists, the philistinism against which artists struggle, the mechanization, robotizing, and depersonalizing that social psychiatrists talk about, alienation, loss of identity, extrapunitiveness, whining, complaining and the feeling of helplessness, suicidal tendencies, the religious pathologies that Jung talked about, Frankl's noogenic disorders, the psychoanalyst's character disorders—these and many other value disturbances are undoubtedly relevant sources of information.

To summarize: If we agree that such disturbances, illnesses, pathologies, or diminutions (coming from deprivation of metaneed gratifications) are indeed a diminishing of full humanness or of the human potential, and if we agree that the gratification, or fulfilling, of the B-Values enhances or fulfills the human potential, then clearly these intrinsic and ultimate values may be taken as instinctoid needs (83, pp. 33–47) in the same realm of discourse with basic needs and on the same hierarchy. These metaneeds, though having certain special characteristics which differentiate them from basic needs, are yet in the same realm of discourse and of research as, for instance, the need for vitamin C or for calcium. They fall within the realm of science, broadly conceived, and are certainly *not* the exclusive property of theologians, philosophers, or artists. The spiritual or value-life then falls well *within* the realm of nature, rather than being a different and opposed realm. It is susceptible to investigation at once by psychologists and social scientists, and in theory will eventually become also a problem for neurology, endocrinology, genetics, and biochemistry as these sciences develop suitable methods.

XIII

The metapathologies of the affluent and indulged young come partly from deprivation of intrinsic values, frustrated "idealism," from disillusionment with a society they see (mistakenly) motivated only by lower or animal or material needs.

This theory of metapathology generates the following easily testable proposition: I believe that much of the social pathology of the affluent (already lower-need-gratified) is a consequence of intrinsic-value-starvation. To say it in another way: Much of the bad behavior of affluent, privileged, and basic-need-gratified high school and college students is due to frustration of the "idealism" so often found in young people. My hypothesis is that this behavior can be a fusion of continued search for something to believe in, combined with anger at being disappointed. (I sometimes see in a particular young man total despair or hopelessness about even the *existence* of such values.)

Of course, this frustrated idealism and occasional hopelessness is partially due to the influence and ubiquity of stupidly limited theories of motivation all over the world. Leaving aside behavioristic and positivistic theories—or rather non-theories—as simple refusals even to see the problem, i.e., a kind of psychoanalytic denial, then what is available to the idealistic young man and woman?

Not only does the whole of official nineteenth-century science and orthodox academic psychology offer him nothing, but also the major motivation theories by which most men live can lead him only to depression or cynicism. The Freudians, at least in their official writings (though not in good therapeutic practice), are still reductionistic about all higher human values. The deepest and most real motivations are seen to be dangerous and nasty, while the highest human values and virtues are essentially fake, being not what they seem to be, but camouflaged versions of the "deep, dark, and dirty." Our social scientists are just as disappointing in the main. A total cultural determinism is still the official, orthodox doctrine of many or most of the sociologists and anthropologists. This doctrine not only denies intrinsic higher motivations, but comes perilously close sometimes to denying "human nature" itself. The economists, not only in the West but also in the East, are essentially materialistic. We must say harshly of the "science" of economics that it is generally the skilled, exact, technological application of a totally false theory of human needs and values, a theory which recognizes only the existence of lower needs or material needs (133, 154, 163).

How could young people not be disappointed and disillusioned? What else could be the result of *getting* all the material and animal gratifications and then *not being happy*, as they were led to expect, not only by the theorists, but also by the conventional wisdom of parents and teachers, and the insistent gray lies of the advertisers?

What happens then to the "eternal verities"? to the ultimate truths? Most sections of the society agree in handing them over to the churches and to dogmatic, institutionalized, conventionalized religious organizations. But this is also a denial of high human nature! It says in effect that the youngster who is looking for something will definitely *not* find it in human nature itself. He must look for ultimates to a non-human, non-natural source, a source which is definitely mistrusted or rejected altogether by many intelligent young people today.

> The end product of such surfeit conditions is that material values have come more and more to dominate the scene. In the result, man's thirst for values of the spirit has remained unquenched. Thus the civilization has reached a stage which virtually verges on disaster. [E. F. Schumacher]

I have focused on the "frustrated idealism" of the young here because I consider it to be a hot research topic today. But, of course, I consider all metapathologies in anybody to be also "frustrated idealism."

XIV

This value-starvation and value-hunger come both from external deprivation and from our inner ambivalence and counter-values.

Not only are we passively value-deprived into metapathology by the environment; we also fear the highest values, both within ourselves and outside ourselves. Not only are we attracted; we are also awed, stunned, chilled, frightened. That is to say, we tend to be ambivalent and conflicted. We defend ourselves against the B-Values. Repression, denial, reaction-formation, and probably all the Freudian defense-mechanisms are available and are used against the highest within ourselves just as they are mobilized against the lowest within ourselves. Humility and a sense of unworthiness can lead to evasion of the highest values. So also can the fear of being overwhelmed by the tremendousness of these values.

It is reasonable to postulate that metapathologies will result from self-deprivation as from externally imposed deprivation.

XV

The hierarchy of basic needs is prepotent to the metaneeds.

Basic needs and metaneeds are in the same hierarchical-integration, i.e., in the same continuum, in the same realm of discourse. They have the same basic characteristic of being "needed" (necessary, good for the person) in the sense that their deprivation produces "illness" and diminution, and that their "ingestion" fosters growth toward full humanness, toward greater happiness and joy, toward psychological "success," toward more peak experiences, and in general toward living more often at the level of being. That is, they are *all* biologically desirable, and *all* foster biological success. And yet, they are also different in definable ways. Biological value or success has been seen only negatively, i.e., as simple endurance in life, viability, avoidance of illness, survival of the individual and of his offspring. But we here imply also positive criteria of biological or evolutionary success, i.e., not only survival values, but also fulfillment values. Basic-need and metaneed gratification help to make "better specimens," biological superiors, high in the dominance-hierarchy. Not only does the stronger, more dominant, more successful animal have more satisfactions, a better territory, more offspring, etc.—not only is the weaker animal lower in the dominance-hierarchy, more expendable, more likely to get eaten and less likely to reproduce, more likely to go hungry, etc., but the better specimen also lives a fuller life with more gratification and less frustration, pain, and fear. Without getting involved in trying to describe pleasure in animals—which, however, I think could be done —we can yet legitimately ask, "Is there no difference in the biological life as well as the psychological life of an Indian peasant and an American farmer, even though they both reproduce?"

First of all, it is clear that the whole hierarchy of the basic needs is prepotent to the metaneeds, or, to say it in another way, the metaneeds are postpotent (less urgent or demanding, weaker) to the basic needs. I intend this as a generalized statistical statement because I find some single individuals in whom a special talent or a unique sensitivity makes truth or beauty or goodness, for that single person, more important and more pressing than some basic need.

Secondly, the basic needs can be called deficiency-needs, having the various characteristics already described for deficiency-needs, while the metaneeds seem rather to have the special characteristics described for "growth motivations" (89, Chap. 3).

XVI

The metaneeds are equally potent among themselves, on the average—i.e., I cannot detect a generalized hierarchy of prepotency. But in any given individual, they may be and often are hierarchically arranged according to idiosyncratic talents and constitutional differences.

The metaneeds (or B-Values, or B-facts) so far as I can make out are not arranged in a hierarchy of prepotency, but seem, all of them, to be equally potent *on the average*. Another way of saying this, a phrasing that is useful for other purposes, is that each individual seems to have his own priorities or hierarchy or prepotency, in accordance with his own talents, temperament, skills, capacities, etc. Beauty is more important than truth to one person, but for his brother it may be the other way about with equal statistical likelihood.

XVII

It looks as if any intrinsic or B-Value is fully defined by most or all of the other B-Values. Perhaps they form a unity of some sort, with each specific B-Value being simply the whole seen from another angle.

It is my (uncertain) impression that any B-Value is fully and adequately defined by the total of the other B-Values. That is, truth, to be fully and completely defined, must be beautiful, good, perfect, just, simple, orderly, lawful, alive, comprehensive, unitary, dichotomy-transcending, effortless, and amusing. (The formula, "The truth, the whole truth, and nothing but the truth," is certainly quite inadequate.) Beauty, fully defined, must be true, good, perfect, alive, simple, etc. It is as if all the B-Values have some kind of unity, with each single value being something like a facet of this whole.

XVIII

The value-life (spiritual, religious, philosophical, axiological, etc.) is an aspect of human biology and is on the same continuum with the "lower" animal life (rather than being in separated, dichotomized, or mutually exclusive realms). It is probably therefore species-wide, supracultural even though it must be actualized by culture in order to exist.

What all of this means is that the so-called spiritual or value-life, or "higher" life, is on the same continuum (is the same *kind* or *quality* of thing) with the life of the flesh, or of the body, i.e., the animal life, the material life, the "lower" life. That is, the spiritual life is part of our biological life. It is the "highest" part of it, but yet part of it.

The spiritual life is then part of the human essence. It is a defining-characteristic of human nature, without which human nature is not full human nature. It is part of the Real Self, of one's identity, of one's inner core, of one's specieshood, of full humanness. To the extent that pure expressing of oneself, or pure spontaneity, is possible, to that extent will the metaneeds also be expressed. "Uncovering" or Taoistic or existential therapeutic or logotherapeutic (34) or "on-togogic" techniques (20), should uncover and strengthen the meta-needs as well as the basic needs.

Depth-diagnostic and therapeutic techniques should ultimately also uncover these same metaneeds because, paradoxically, our "highest nature" is also our "deepest nature." The value life and the animal life are not in two separate realms as most religions and philosophies have assumed, and as classical, impersonal science has also assumed. The spiritual life (the contemplative, "religious," philosophical, or value-life) is within the jurisdiction of human thought and is attainable in principle by man's own efforts. Even though it has been cast out of the realm of reality by the classical, value-free science which models itself upon physics, it can be reclaimed as an object of study and technology by humanistic science. That is, such an expanded science must consider the eternal verities, the ultimate truths, the final values, and so on, to be "real" and natural, fact-based rather than wish-based, human rather than superhuman, legitimate scientific problems calling for research.

In practice, of course, such problems are more difficult to study. The lower life is prepotent over the higher life, which means that the higher is just less likely to occur. The preconditions of the metamoti-vated life are far more numerous, not only in terms of prior gratifica-tion of the whole hierarchy of basic needs, but also in terms of the greater number of "good conditions" (85) which are needed to make the higher life possible, i.e., a far better environment is required, economic scarcity must have been conquered, a wide variety of choices must be freely available along with conditions that make real and efficient choosing possible, synergic social institutions are almost a requirement (83), etc. In a word, we must be very careful to imply only that the higher life is in principle *possible*, and never that it is probable, or likely, or easy to attain.

Let me also make quite explicit the implication that metamotivation is species-wide, and is, therefore, supracultural, common-human, not created arbitrarily by culture. Since this is a point at which misunderstandings are fated to occur, let me say it so: The metaneeds seem to me to be instinctoid, that is, to have an appreciable hereditary, species-wide determination. But they are potentialities, rather than actualities. Culture is definitely and absolutely needed for their actualization; but also culture can fail to actualize them, and indeed this is just what most known cultures actually seem to do and to have done throughout history. Therefore, there is implied here a supracultural factor which can criticize any culture from outside and above that culture, namely, in terms of the degree to which it fosters or suppresses self-actualization, full humanness, and metamotivation (85). A culture can be synergic with human biological essence or it can be antagonistic to it, i.e., culture and biology are not in principle opposed to each other.

Can we, therefore, say that everyone yearns for the higher life, the spiritual, the B-Values, etc.? Here we run full-tilt into inadequacies in our langauge. Certainly we can say in principle that such a yearning must be considered to be a potential in every newborn baby until proven otherwise. That is to say, our best guess is that this potentiality, if it is lost, is lost after birth. It is also socially realistic today to bet that most newborn babies will never actualize this potentiality, and will never rise to the highest levels of motivation because of poverty, exploitation, prejudice, etc. There is, in fact, inequality of opportunity in the world today. It is also wise to say of adults that prognosis varies for each of them, depending on how and where they live, their social-economic-political circumstances, degree and amount of psychopathology, etc. And yet is also unwise (as a matter of social strategy, if nothing else) to give up the possibility of the metalife completely and in principle for any living person. "Incurables" have, after all, been "cured" in both the psychiatric sense and in the sense of self-actualization, for example by Synanon. And most certainly, we would be stupid to give up this possibility for future generations.

The so-called spiritual (or transcendent, or axiological) life is clearly rooted in the biological nature of the species. It is a kind of "higher" animality whose precondition is a healthy "lower" animality, i.e., they are hierarchically integrated (rather than mutually exclusive). But this higher, spiritual "animality" is so timid and weak, and so easily lost, is so easily crushed by stronger cultural forces, that it can become widely actualized *only* in a culture which approves of human nature, and therefore actively fosters its fullest growth.

It is this consideration that offers a possible resolution of many unnecessary conflicts or dichotomies. For instance, if "spirit" à la Hegel and "nature" à la Marx are in fact hierarchically integrated on the same continuum, which means also the usual versions of "idealism" and "materialism," then various solutions are given by the nature of this hierarchical continuum. For instance, lower needs (animal, nature, material) are prepotent in quite specific, empirical, operational, limited senses to so-called higher basic needs, which in turn are prepotent to metaneeds (spirit, ideals, values). This is to say that the "material" conditions of life are meaningfully prior to (have precedence over, are stronger than) high ideals and are even prepotent to ideology, philosophy, religion, culture, etc., also in definitely definable and limited ways. Yet these higher ideals and values are far from being mere epiphenomena of the lower values. They seem rather to have the same quality of biological and psychological reality even though differing in strength, urgency, or priority. In any hierarchy of prepotency, as in the nervous system, or as in a pecking order, the higher and the lower are equally "real" and equally human. One can certainly see history, if one wishes, from the point of view of struggle toward full humanness, or as the unfolding of an immanent, German-professor-type Idea, i.e., from above downward. Or one can equally find first or basic or ultimate causes in material circumstances, i.e., from below upward. (One can then accept as true the statement that "self-interest is the basis of all human nature," in the sense that it is prepotent. But it is not true in the sense of being a sufficient description of *all* human motives.) They are both useful theories for different intellectual purposes, and both have assignable psychological meanings. We need not argue over "the primacy of spirit to matter," or the other way about. If the Russians today get worried over the emergence of idealism, and of spiritual philosophies, they needn't. From what we know of developments within individuals and within societies, a certain amount of spirituality is the extremely probable consequence of a satisfied materialism. (It is a great mystery to me why affluence releases some people for growth while permitting other people to stay fixated at a strictly "materialistic" level.) But it is just as probable that the religionist, fostering spiritual values, had better start with food, shelter, roads, etc., which are more basic than sermons.

Placing our lower-animal inheritance on the same scale as our "highest," most spiritual, axiological, valuable, "religious" (thereby saying that spirituality is *also* animal, i.e., higher-animal) helps us to transcend many other dichotomies as well. For instance, the voice of the devil, depravity, the flesh, evil, the selfish, the egocentric, self-seeking, etc., have all been dichotomized from, and opposed to, the divine, the ideal, the good, the eternal verities, our highest aspirations, etc. Sometimes the divine or the best has been conceived to be within human nature. But far more often, in the history of mankind, the good has been conceived of as external to human nature, above it, supernatural.

My vague impression is that most religions, philosophies, or ideologies have been somewhat more likely to accept the evil or the worst as intrinsic to human nature. But even our "worst" impulses have sometimes been exteriorized as, e.g., the voice of Satan, or the like.

Frequently, also, our "lowest" animal nature has automatically been maligned as "bad" (95) although in principle it could just as easily have been thought of as "good"—and in some cultures, has been, and is. Perhaps this maligning of our lower-animal nature is due in part to the dichotomizing itself (dichotomizing pathologizes, and pathology encourages dichotomizing, which, in a holistic world, is usually incorrect). If so, then the concept of metamotivation should supply a theoretical basis for solving all these (mostly) false dichotomies.

XIX

Pleasures and gratifications can be arranged in hierarchy of levels from lower to higher. So also can hedonistic theories be seen as ranging from lower to higher, i.e., metahedonism.

The B-Values, seen as gratifications of metaneeds, are then also the highest pleasures or happinesses that we know of.

I have suggested elsewhere (81) the need for and usefulness of being conscious that there is a hierarchy of pleasures, ranging from, e.g., relief from pain, through the contentment of a hot tub, the happiness of being with good friends, the joy of great music, the bliss of having a child, the ecstasy of the highest love-experiences, on up to the fusion with the B-Values.

Such a hierarchy suggests a solution of the problem of hedonism, selfishness, duty, etc. If one includes the highest pleasures among the pleasures in general, then it becomes true in a very real sense that fully human people also seek only for pleasure, i.e., metapleasure. Perhaps we can call this "metahedonism" and then point out that at this level there is then no contradiction between pleasure and duty since the highest obligations of human beings are certainly to truth, justice, beauty, etc., which however are also the highest pleasures that the species can experience. And of course at this level of discourse the mutual exclusiveness between selfishness and unselfishness has also disappeared. What is good for us is good for everyone else, what is gratifying is praiseworthy, our appetites are now trustworthy, rational and wise, what we enjoy is good for us, seeking our own (highest) good is also seeking the general good, etc.

If one speaks of lower-need hedonism, of higher-need hedonism, and of metaneed hedonism, then this is an order from lower to higher (95), implying operational and testable meanings of various sorts. For instance, the higher we go, the less the frequency found in the population, the greater the number of preconditions, the better must the social environment be, the higher the quality of education must be, etc.

XX

Since the spiritual life is instinctoid, all the techniques of "subjective biology" apply to its education.

Since the spiritual life (B-Values, B-facts, metaneeds, etc.) is part of the Real Self, which is instinctoid, it can in principle be introspected. It has "impulse voices" or "inner signals" which, though weaker than basic needs, can yet be "heard," and which therefore come under the rubric of the "subjective biology."

In principle, therefore, all the principles and exercises which help to develop (or teach) our sensory awarenesses, our body awarenesses, our sensitivities to the inner signals (given off by our needs, capacities, constitution, temperament, body, etc.)—all these apply also, though less strongly, to our inner metaneeds, i.e., to the education of our yearnings for beauty, law, truth, perfection, etc. Perhaps we can also invent some such term as "experientially rich" to describe those who are so sensitive to the inner voices of the self that even the metaneeds can be consciously introspected and enjoyed.

It is this experiential richness which in principle should be "teachable" or recoverable at least in degree, perhaps with the proper use of psychedelic chemicals, with Esalen-type, nonverbal methods[3] with meditation and contemplation techniques, with further study of the peak experiences, or of B-cognition, etc.

I do not wish to be understood as deifying the inner signals (the voices from within, the "still, small voice of conscience," etc.). It seems to me that experiential knowledge is certainly the beginning of all knowledge, but it is definitely not the end of all knowledge. It is necessary, but not sufficient. The voice from within can occasionally be wrong even in the wisest individual. In any case, such wise individuals generally test their inner commands against external reality whenever they can. Empirical testing and verifying of experiential knowledge is thus always in order, for sometimes the inner certainty, even of a veritable mystic, turns out to be the voice of the devil (53). It is not yet wise to permit the private conscience of one person to outweigh all other sources of knowledge and wisdom, however much we respect inner experiencing.

XXI

But B-Values seem to be the same as B-facts. Reality then is ultimately fact-values or value-facts.

[3] The Esalen Institute at Big Sur, California, specializes in such methods. The tacit assumption underlying this new kind of education is that both the body and the "spirit" can be loved, and that they are synergic and hierarchically integrated rather than mutually exclusive, i.e., one can have both.

The B-Values can equally be called B-facts (or ultimate reality) at the highest levels of perspicuity (of illumination, awakening, insight, B-cognition, mystical perception, etc.) (89, Chap. 6). When the highest levels of personality development, of cultural development, of perspicuity, of emotional freeing (from fears, inhibitions, defenses), and of noninterference all coincide, then there are now some good reasons for affirming that human-independent reality is seen most clearly in its own (human-independent) nature, least distorted by observer-intrusions (82). Then reality is *described* as true, good, perfect, integrated, alive, lawful, beautiful, etc. That is, the reality-describing words that are most accurate and suitable to report what is perceived are the very same words which have been traditionally called value-words. The traditional dichotomizing of *is* and *ought* turns out to be characteristic of lower levels of living, and is transcended at the highest level of living, where fact and value fuse. For obvious reasons, those words which are simultaneously descriptive and normative can be called "fusion-words."

At this fusion level "love for the intrinsic values" is the same as "love of ultimate reality." Devotion *to* the facts here implies love *for* the facts. The sternest effort at objectivity or perception, i.e., to reduce as much as possible the contaminating effect of the observer, and of his fears and wishes and selfish calculations, yields an emotional, aesthetic, and axiological result, a result pointed toward and approximated by our greatest and most perspicuous philosophers, scientists, artists, and spiritual inventors and leaders.

Contemplation of ultimate values becomes the same as contemplation of the nature of the world. Seeking the truth (fully defined) may be the same as seeking beauty, order, oneness, perfection, rightness (fully defined) and truth may then be sought *via* any other B-Value. Does science then become indistinguishable from art? love? religion? philosophy? Is a basic scientific discovery about the nature of reality also a spiritual or axiological affirmation?

If all this is so, then our attitude toward the real, or at least the reality we get glimpses of when we are at our best and when *it* is at *its* best, can no longer be only "cool," purely cognitive, rational, logical, detached, uninvolved assent. This reality calls forth also a warm and emotional response, a response of love, of devotion, of loyalty, even peak experiences. At its best, reality is not only true, lawful, orderly, integrated, etc.; it is also good and beautiful and lovable as well.

Seen from another angle, we could be said to be offering here implied answers to the great religious and philosophical questions about, e.g., the philosophical quest, the religious quest, the meaning of life, etc.

The theoretical structure proposed here is offered tentatively as a set of hypotheses for testing and verification, or possibly nonverification. It is a network of "facts" at various levels of scientific reliability, of clinical and personological reports, and also of sheer intuitions and hunches. Or to say it in another way, I believe it in advance of the verifications which I confidently predict or gamble will come. But *you* (the reader) shouldn't. You should be more tentative even if it feels right, and even if it sits well. It is after all a set of guesses which *may* be true and which had better be checked.

If the B-Values are identified with and become defining characteristics of one's self, does this mean that reality, the world, the cosmos are therefore identified with and become defining characteristics of the self? What can such a statement mean? Certainly this sounds like the classical mystic's fusion with the world or with his god. Also it reminds us of various Eastern versions of this meaning, e.g., that the individual self melts into the whole world and is lost.

Can we be said to be raising into meaningfulness the possibility of absolute values, at least in the same sense that reality itself may be said to be absolute? If something of the sort turned out to be meaningful, would it be merely humanistic, or might it be transhuman?

By this time, we have reached the limits of meaning-power that these words can convey. I mention them only because I wish to leave doors open, questions unanswered, problems unsolved. Clearly this is not a closed system.

XXII

Not only is man PART *of nature, and it part of him, but also he must be at least minimally isomorphic with nature (similar to it) in order to be viable in it. It has evolved him. His communion with what transcends him therefore need not be defined as non-natural or supernatural. It may be seen as a "biological" experience.*

Heschel (47, p. 87) claims that "Man's true fulfillment depends upon communion with that which transcends him." And of course this is obviously true in one sense. But this sense needs spelling out.

We have seen that there is not an absolute chasm between man and the reality which is beyond him. He can identify with this reality, incorporate it into his own definition of his self, be loyal to it as to his self. He then becomes part of it and it becomes part of him. He and it overlap.

Phrasing it in this way builds a bridge to another realm of discourse, i.e., to the theory of biological evolution of man. Not only is man *part* of nature, but he must also be isomorphic with it to some extent. That is, he cannot be in utter contradiction to nonhuman nature. He cannot be utterly different from it or else he would not now exist.

The very fact of his viability proves that he is at least compatible with, acceptable to nature. He agrees with its demands and, as a species, has yielded to them at least to the extent of remaining viable. Nature has not executed him. He is politic enough, biologically speaking, to accept the laws of nature which, were he to defy them, would mean death. He gets along with it.

This is to say that in some sense he must be similar to nature. When we speak of his fusion with nature, perhaps this is part of what we mean. Perhaps his thrilling to nature (perceiving it as true, good, beautiful, etc.) will one day be understood as a kind of self-recognition or self-experience, a way of being oneself and fully functional, a way of being at home, a kind of biological authenticity, of "biological mysticism," etc. Perhaps we can see mystical or peak-fusion not only as communion with that which is most worthy of love, but also as fusion with that which *is*, because he belongs there, being truly part of what is, and being, so to speak, a member of the family:

> . . . one direction in which we find increasing confidence is the conception that we are basically one with the cosmos instead of strangers to it. [Gardner Murphy]

This *biological* or evolutionary version of the mystic experience or the peak experience—here perhaps no different from the spiritual or religious experience—reminds us again that we must ultimately outgrow the obsolescent usage of "highest" as the opposite of "lowest" or "deepest." Here the "highest" experience ever described, the joyful fusion with the ultimate that man can conceive, can be seen simultanously as the deepest experience of our ultimate personal animality and specieshood, as the acceptance of our profound biological nature as isomorphic with nature in general.

This kind of empirical, or at least naturalistic, phrasing seems to me also to make it less necessary or less tempting to define "that which transcends him" as nonhuman and non-natural or supernatural as Heschel does. Communion by the person with that which transcends him can be seen as a biological experience. And although the universe cannot be said to *love* the human being, it can be said at least to accept him in a nonhostile way, to permit him to endure, and to grow and, occasionally, to permit him great joy.

XXIII

The B-Values are not the same as our personal attitudes toward these values, nor our emotional reactions to them. The B-Values induce in us a kind of "requiredness feeling" and also a feeling of unworthiness.

The B-Values had better be differentiated from our human attitudes toward these B-Values, at least to the extent that is possible for so difficult a task. A listing of such attitudes toward ultimate values (or reality) included: love, awe, adoration, humility, reverence, unworthiness, wonder, amazement, marveling, exaltation, gratitude, fear, joy, etc. (85, p. 94). These are clearly emotional-cognitive reactions within a person witnessing something not the same as himself, or at least verbally separable. Of course, the more the person fuses with the world in great peak or mystic experiences, the less of these intraself reactions there would be and the more the self would be lost as a separable entity.

I suppose the main reason for keeping this separability—that is, beyond the obvious advantages for theorizing and researching—is that great peak experiences, illuminations, desolations, ecstasies, mystical fusions do not occur very often. A rather small percentage of clock time is spent in such exceptional moments even in the most reactive individuals. Far more time is spent in relatively serene contemplation and enjoyment *of* the ultimate (rather than climactic fusion *with* them) which have been revealed in the great illuminations. It is thus quite useful to speak of Royce-type "loyalty" (131) to the ultimates, and of duty, responsibility, and devotion as well.

In addition, the theoretical structure being herein set forth makes it impossible to think of these reactions to the B-Values as being in any way arbitrary or accidental. From what has gone before, it is much more natural to think of these reactions as in some degree required, commanded, called-for, suitable, fitting and proper, appropriate, i.e., in some sense or other the B-Values are felt to be worthy of, and even to require or command love, awe, devotion. The fully-human person presumably can't help having such reactions.

Nor should we forget that witnessing these ultimate facts (or values) often makes the person acutely conscious of his own unworthiness, of his inadequacies and shortcomings, of his ultimate existential smallness, finiteness, and powerlessness simply as a human being and as a member of the human species.

XXIV

The vocabulary to describe motivations must be hierarchical, especially since metamotivations (growth motivations) must be characterized differently from basic needs (deficiency-needs).

This difference between intrinsic values and our attitudes toward these values also generates a hierarchical vocabulary for motives (using this word most generally and inclusively). In another place I have called attention to the levels of gratification, pleasures, or happiness corresponding to the hierarchy of needs to metaneeds (82). In addition to this, we must keep in mind that the concept of "gratification" itself is transcended at the level of metamotives or growth-motives, where satisfactions can be endless. So also for the concept of happiness which can also be altogether transcended at the highest levels. It may then easily become a kind of cosmic sadness or soberness or nonemotional contemplation. At the lowest basic-need levels we can certainly talk of being driven and of desperately craving, striving, or needing, when, e.g., cut off from oxygen or experiencing great pain. As we go on up the hierarchy of basic needs, words like desiring, wishing, or preferring, choosing, wanting, become more appropriate. But at the highest levels, i.e., of metamotivation, all these words become subjectively inadequate, and such words as yearning for, devoted to, aspiring to, loving, adoring, admiring, worshiping, being drawn to or fascinated by, describe the metamotivated feelings more accurately.

In addition to these feelings, we shall certainly have to face the difficult task of finding words which are capable of conveying the meaning of the *felt appropriateness*, the duty, the suitability, the sheer justice, of loving that which is intrinsically loveworthy, which deserves to be loved, which requires and even commands love, which calls for love, which one ought to love.

But all these words still assume a separation between the wanter and what he wants. How shall we describe what happens when this separation is transcended and there is some degree of identity or fusion between the person who wants and that which he wants? or between the person who wants and that which, in a sense, wants him?

This can also be phrased as a kind of Spinozistic transcendence of the free will vs. determinism dichotomy. At the level of metamotivation, one freely, happily, and wholeheartedly embraces one's determinants. One chooses and wills one's fate, not reluctantly, not "ego-dystonically," but lovingly and enthusiastically. And the greater the insight, the more "ego-syntonic" is this fusion of free will and determinism.

XXV

The B-Values call for behavioral expression or "celebration" as well as inducing subjective states.

We must agree with Heschel's (47, p. 117) stress on "celebration" which he describes as "an act of expressing respect or reverence for that which one needs or honors. . . . Its essence is to call attention to the sublime or solemn aspects of living. . . . To celebrate is to share in a greater joy, to participate in an eternal drama."

It is well to notice that the highest values are not only receptively enjoyed and contemplated, but that they often also lead to expressive and behavioral responses, which of course would be easier to investigate than subjective states.

Here we find still another phenomenological meaning of the

"ought feeling." It feels suitable, fitting and proper, a pleasantly pressing duty, to celebrate the B-Values, as if it were due them that we should, as if we owed them at least this, as if it were only fair, just, and natural that we should protect them, foster, enhance, share, and celebrate them.

XXVI

There are certain educational and therapeutic advantages in differentiating the realm (or level) of being from the realm (or level) of deficiencies, and in recognizing language differences at these levels.

I have found it most useful for myself to differentiate between the realm of being (B-realm) and the realm of deficiencies (D-realm), that is, between the eternal and the "practical." Simply as a matter of the strategy and tactics of living well and fully and of choosing one's life instead of having it determined for us, this is a help. It is so easy to forget ultimates in the rush and hurry of daily life, especially for young people. So often we are merely responders, so to speak, simply reacting to stimuli, to rewards and punishments, to emergencies, to pains and fears, to demands of other people, to superficialities. It takes a specific, conscious, *ad hoc* effort, at least at first, to turn one's attention to intrinsic things and values, e.g., perhaps seeking actual physical aloneness, perhaps exposing oneself to great music, to good people, to natural beauty, etc. Only after practice do these strategies become easy and automatic so that one can be living in the B-realm even without wishing or trying, i.e., the "unitive life," the "metalife," the "life of being," etc.

I have found this vocabulary useful also in teaching people to be more aware of values of being, of a language of being, of the ultimate facts of being, of the life of being, of unitive consciousness, etc. The vocabulary is certainly clumsy and sometimes grates on the sensibilities, but it does serve the purpose (85, Appendix I: An example of B-analysis). In any case, it has already proven to be operationally useful in the planning of research.

A subhypothesis emerges here from my occasional observation that highly developed or matured individuals ("metapersons"?), even when meeting for the first time, can make extraordinarily quick communication with each other at the highest level of living with what I have called the B-language. At this point I will say of it only that it speaks as if B-Values existed, were true and real, and were easily perceived by some but not by others, and that communication with these others can be also true and real, but must occur at a lower and less mature level of significance or of meaning.

At this moment I do not know how to put this hypothesis to the test because I have found that some people can use the vocabulary without really understanding it, as some people can talk glibly about music or love without really experiencing either.

Other impressions, even more vague, are that along with this easy communication with the B-language also may go a great intimacy, a feeling of sharing common loyalties, of working at the same tasks, of being "simpatico," of feeling kinship, perhaps of being fellow servants.

XXVII

"Intrinsic conscience" and "intrinsic guilt" are ultimately biologically rooted.

Stimulated by Fromm's discussion of "humanistic conscience" (37) and Horney's (50) reconsideration of Freud's "superego," other humanistic writers have agreed that there is an "intrinsic conscience" beyond the superego, as well as "intrinsic guilt" which is a deserved self-punishment for betrayal of the intrinsic self.

I believe that the biological rooting of metamotivation theory can clarify and solidify these concepts further.

Horney and Fromm, revolting against the specific content of Freud's instinct theory, and probably also because of a too ready acceptance of social determinism, rejected any version of biological theory and "instinct theory." That this a serious mistake is more readily discerned against the background of this chapter.

One's personal biology is beyond question a *sine qua non* component of the "Real Self." Being oneself, being natural or spontaneous, being authentic, expressing one's identity, all these are also biological statements since they imply the acceptance of one's constitutional, temperamental, anatomical, neurological, hormonal, and instinctoid-motivational nature. Such a statement is in both the Freudian line and in the Neo-Freudian line (not to mention Rogerian, Jungian,

Sheldonian, Goldsteinian, *et al.*). It is a cleansing and a correction of what Freud was groping toward and of necessity glimpsed only vaguely. I therefore consider it to be in the *echt*-Freudian or "*epi*-Freudian" tradition. I think Freud was trying to say something like this with his various instinct theories. I believe also that this statement is an acceptance of, plus an improvement upon, what Horney was trying to say with her concept of a Real Self.

If my more biological interpretation of an intrinsic self is corroborated, then it would also support the differentiation of neurotic guilt from the intrinsic guilt which comes from defying one's own nature and from trying to be what one is not.

But in view of what has gone before, we should have to include the intrinsic values or values of being in this intrinsic self. In theory, then, a betrayal of truth or justice or beauty or any other B-Value should be expected to generate intrinsic guilt (metaguilt?), a guilt that would be deserved and biologically sound. This is in about the same sense that pain is ultimately a blessing because it tells us that we are doing something that is bad for us. When we betray the B-Values, we hurt, and in a certain sense, we should hurt. Furthermore, this implies a reinterpretation of the "need for punishment," which can also be positively phrased as a wish, via expiation, to feel "clean" again (118).

XXVIII

Many of the ultimate religious functions are fulfilled by this theoretical structure.

From the point of view of the eternal and absolute that mankind has always sought, it may be that the B-Values could also, to some extent, serve this purpose. They are *per se*, in their own right, not dependent upon human vagaries for their existence. They are perceived, not invented. They are transhuman and transindividual. They exist beyond the life of the individual. They can be conceived to be a kind of perfection. They could conceivably satisfy the human longing for certainty.

And yet they are also human in a specifiable sense. They are not only his, but him as well. They command adoration, reverence, celebration, sacrifice. They are worth living for and dying for. Contemplating them or fusing with them gives the greatest joy that a human being is capable of.

Immortality also has a quite definite and empirical meaning in this context, for the values incorporated into the person as defining characteristics of his self live on after his death, i.e., in a certain real sense, his self transcends death.

And so for other functions that the organized religions have tried to fulfill. Apparently all, or almost all, the characteristically religious experiences that have ever been described in any of the traditional religions, in their own local phrasings, whether theist or nontheist, Eastern or Western, can be assimilated to this theoretical structure and can be expressed in an empirically meaningful way, i.e., phrased in a testable way.

Appendices

Comments on "Religions, Values, and Peak-Experiences"

Since *Religions, Values, and Peak-Experiences* was first written, there has been much turmoil in the world and, therefore, much to learn. Several of the lessons I have learned are relevant here, certainly in the sense that they are helpful supplements to the main thesis of the book. Or perhaps I should call them warnings about overextreme, dangerous, and one-sided *uses* of this thesis. Of course this is a standard hazard for thinkers who try to be holistic, integrative, and inclusive. They learn inevitably that most people think atomistically, in terms of either-or, black-white, all in or all out, of mutual exclusiveness and separativeness. A good example of what I mean is the mother who gave her son two ties for his birthday. As he put on one of them to please her, she asked sadly, "And why do you hate the other tie?"

I think I can best state my warning against polarization and dichotomizing by a historical approach. I see in the history of many organized religions a tendency to develop two extreme wings: the "mystical" and individual on the one hand, and the legalistic and organizational on the other. The profoundly and authentically religious person integrates these trends easily and automatically. The forms, rituals, ceremonials, and verbal formulae in which he was reared remain for him experientially rooted, symbolically meaningful, archetypal, unitive. Such a person may go through the same motions and behaviors as his more numerous coreligionists, but he is never *reduced* to the behavioral, as most of them are. Most people lose or forget the subjectively religious experience, and redefine Religion as a set of habits, behaviors, dogmas, forms, which at the extreme becomes entirely legalistic and bureaucratic, conventional, empty, and in the truest meaning of the word, antireligious. The mystic experience, the illumination, the great awakening, along with the charismatic seer who started the whole thing, are forgotten, lost, or transformed into their opposites. Organized Religion, the churches, finally may become the major enemies of the religious experience and the religious experiencer.

But on the other wing, the mystical (or experiential) also has its traps which I have not stressed sufficiently. As the more Apollonian type can veer toward the extreme of being reduced to the merely behavioral, so does the mystical type run the risk of being reduced to the merely experiential. Out of the joy and wonder of his ecstasies and peak experiences he may be tempted to *seek* them, *ad hoc*, and to value them exclusively, as the only, or at least the highest goods of life, giving up other criteria of right and wrong. Focused on these wonderful subjective experiences, he may run the danger of turning away from the world and from other people in his search for triggers to peak experiences, *any* triggers. In a word, instead of being temporarily self-absorbed and inwardly searching, he may become simply a selfish person, seeking his own personal salvation; trying to get into "heaven" even if other people can't, and finally even perhaps *using* other people as triggers, as means to his sole end of higher states of consciousness. In a word, he may become not only selfish but also evil. My impression, from the history of mysticism, is that this trend can sometimes wind up in meanness, nastiness, loss of compassion, or even in the extreme of sadism.

Another possible booby trap for the (polarizing) mystics throughout history has been the danger of needing to escalate the triggers, so to speak. That is, stronger and stronger stimuli are needed to produce the same response. If the *sole* good in life becomes the peak experience, and if all means to this end become good, and if more peak experiences are better than fewer, then one can *force* the issue, push actively, strive, and hunt, and fight for them. So they have often moved over into magic, into the secret and esoteric, into the exotic, the occult, the dramatic and effortful, the dangerous, the cultish. Healthy openness to the mysterious, the realistically humble recognition that we don't know much, the modest and grateful acceptance of gratuitous grace and of just plain good luck—all these can shade over into the antirational, the antiempirical, the antiscientific, the antiverbal, the anticonceptual. The peak experience may then be exalted as the best or even the *only* path to knowledge, and thereby all the tests and verifications of the *validity* of the illumination may be tossed aside.

The possibility that the inner voices, the "revelations," may be mistaken, a lesson from history that should come through loud and clear, is denied, and there is then no way of finding out whether the voices within are the voices of good or of evil. (George Bernard Shaw's *Saint Joan* confronts this problem.) Spontaneity (the impulses from our best self) gets confused with impulsivity and acting out (the impulses from our sick self) and there is then no way to tell the difference.

Impatience (especially the built-in impatience of youth) dictates shortcuts of all kinds. Drugs, which can be helpful when wisely used, become dangerous when foolishly used. The sudden insight becomes "all" and the patient and disciplined "working through" is postponed or devalued. Instead of being "surprised by joy," "turning on" is scheduled, promised, advertised, sold, hustled into being, and can get to be regarded as a commodity. Sex-love, certainly one possible path to the experience of the sacred, can become mere "screwing," i.e., desacralized. More and more exotic, artificial, striving "techniques" may escalate further and further until they become *necessary* and until jadedness and impotence ensue.

The search for the exotic, the strange, the unusual, the uncommon, has often taken the form of pilgrimages, of turning away from the world, the "Journey to the East," to another country or to a different Religion. The great lesson from the true mystics, from the Zen monks, and now also from the Humanistic and Transpersonal psychologists—that the sacred is *in* the ordinary, that it is to be found in one's daily life, in one's neighbors, friends, and family, in one's back yard, and that travel may be a *flight* from confronting the sacred—this lesson can be easily lost. To be looking elsewhere for miracles is to me a sure sign of ignorance that *everything* is miraculous.

The rejection of a priestly caste that claimed to be exclusive custodians of a private hotline to the sacred was, in my opinion, a great step forward in the emancipation of mankind, and we have the mystics among others—to thank for this achievement. But this valid insight can also be used badly when dichotomized and exaggerated by foolish people. They can distort it into a rejection of the guide, the teacher, the sage, the therapist, the counselor, the elder, the helper along the path to self-actualization and the realm of Being. This is often a great danger and always an unnecessary handicap.

To summarize, the healthily Apollonian (which means integrated with the healthily Dionysian) can become pathologized into an extreme, exaggerated, and dichotomized compulsive-obsessional sickness. But also the healthily Dionysian (which means integrated with the healthily Apollonian) can become pathologized at its extreme into hysteria, with all *its* symptoms.[1]

Obviously, what I am suggesting here is a pervasively holistic attitude and way of thinking. The experiential must be not only stressed and brought back into psychology and philosophy as an opponent of the merely abstract and abstruse, of the *a priori*, of what I have called "helium-filled words." It must then also be *integrated* with the abstract, and the verbal, i.e., we must make a place for "experientially based concepts," and for "experientially filled words," that is, for an experience-based rationality in contrast to the *a priori* rationality that we have come almost to identify with rationality itself.

The same sort of thing is true for the relations between experientialism and social reform. Shortsighted people make them opposites, mutually exclusive. Of course, historically this has often happened and does today still happen in many. But it need not happen. It is a mistake, an atomistic error, an example of the dichotomizing and pathologizing that goes along with immaturity. The empirical fact is that self-actualizing people, our best experiencers, are also our most compassionate, our great improvers and reformers of society, our most *effective* fighters against injustice, inequality, slavery, cruelty, exploitation (and also our best fighters *for* excellence, effectiveness, competence). And it also becomes clearer and clearer that the best "helpers" are the most fully human persons. What I may call the Bodhisattvic path is an *integration* of self-improvement and social

[1] Colin Wilson's "Outsider" series will furnish all the examples necessary.

zeal, i.e., the best way to become a better "helper" is to become a better person. But one necessary aspect of becoming a better person is *via* helping other people. So one must and can do both simultaneously. (The question "Which comes first?" is an atomistic question.)

In this context I would like to refer to my demonstration in the Preface to the revised edition of my *Motivation and Personality* (95) that normative zeal is *not* incompatible with scientific objectivity, but can be integrated with it, eventuating in a higher form of objectivity, i.e., the Taoistic.

What this all adds up to is this: small "r" religion is quite compatible, at the higher levels of personal development, with rationality, with science, with social passion. Not only this, but it can, in principle, quite easily integrate the healthily animal, material, and selfish with the naturalistically transcendent, spiritual, and axiological.

For other reasons also, I now consider that my book *Religions, Values, and Peak-Experiences* (85) was too imbalanced toward the individualistic and too hard on groups, organizations, and communities. Even within the last six or seven years we have learned not to think of organizations as *necessarily* bureaucratic, as we have learned more about humanistic, need-fulfilling kinds of groups, from, e.g., the research in Organization Development and Theory-Y management, the rapidly accumulating experience with T-groups, encounter groups, and personal-growth groups, the successes of the Synanon community, of the Israeli kibbutzim, etc. (See my listing of the Eupsychian Network, an appendix in the revised edition [89] of my *Toward a Psychology of Being.*)

As a matter of fact, I can say much more firmly than I ever did, for many empirical reasons, that basic human needs can be fulfilled *only* by and through other human beings, i.e., society. The need for community (belongingness, contact, groupiness) is itself a basic need. Loneliness, isolation, ostracism, rejection by the group—these are not only painful but also pathogenic as well. And of course it has also been known for decades that humanness and specieshood in the infant is only a potentiality and must be actualized by the society.

My study of the failure of most Utopian efforts has taught me to ask the basic questions themselves in a more practicable and research-able way. "How good a society does human nature permit?" and, "How good a human nature does society permit?"

Finally, I would now add to the peak-experience material a greater consideration, not only of nadir experiences, the psycholytic therapy of Grof (40), confrontations with and reprieves from death, post-surgical visions, etc., but also of the plateau experience.[2] This is serene and calm, rather than poignantly emotional, climactic, auto-nomic response to the miraculous, the awesome, the sacralized, the Unitive, the B-Values. So far as I can now tell, the high-plateau ex-perience always has a noetic and cognitive element, which is not always true for peak experiences, which can be purely and exclusively emotional. It is far more voluntary than peak experiences are. One can learn to see in this Unitive way almost at will. It then becomes a witnessing, an appreciating, what one might call a serene, cogni-tive blissfulness which can, however, have a quality of casualness and lounging about it.

There is more an element of surprise, and of disbelief, and of aesthetic shock in the peak experience, more the quality of having such an experience for the *first time*. I have pointed out elsewhere that the aging body and nervous system is less capable of tolerating a really shaking peak-experience. I would add here that maturing and aging means also some loss of first-time-ness, of novelty, of sheer unpreparedness and surprise.

Peak and plateau experiences differ also in their relations to death. The peak experience can often meaningfully itself be called a "little death," a rebirth in various senses. The less intense plateau-experi-ence is more often experienced as pure enjoyment and happiness, as let's say, a mother sitting quietly looking, by the hour, at her baby playing and marveling, wondering, philosophizing, not quite believ-ing. She can experience this as a very pleasant, continuing, contem-plative experience rather than as something akin to a climactic explosion, which then ends.

Older people, making their peace with death, are more apt to be profoundly touched, with (sweet) sadness and tears at the contrast between their own mortality and the eternal quality of what sets off the experience. This contrast can make far more poignant and pre-cious what is being witnessed, e.g., "The surf will be here forever

[2] This is a very brief anticipation of a more detailed study of "plateau experi-ences" (R. Johnson, Asrani), and the "Easy State" (Asrani), which I hope to write soon.

and you will soon be gone. So hang on to it; appreciate it; be fully conscious of it. Be grateful for it. You are lucky."

Very important today in a topical sense is the realization that plateau experiencing can be achieved, learned, earned by long hard work. It can be meaningfully aspired to. But I don't know of any way of bypassing the necessary maturing, experiencing, living, learning. All of this takes time. A transient glimpse is certainly possible in the peak experiences which may, after all, come sometimes to anyone. But, so to speak, to take up residence on the high plateau of Unitive consciousness, that is another matter altogether. That tends to be a lifelong effort. It should not be confused with the Thursday evening turn-on that many youngsters think of as *the* path to transcendence. For that matter, it should not be confused with *any* single experience. The "spiritual disciplines," both the classical ones and the new ones that keep on being discovered these days, all take time, work, discipline, study, commitment.

There is much more to say about these states which are clearly relevant to the life of transcendence and the transpersonal, and to experiencing life at the level of Being. All I wish to do here with this brief mention is to correct the tendency of some to identify experiences of transcendence as only dramatic, orgasmic, transient, "peaky," like a moment on the top of Mt. Everest. There is also the high plateau where one can *stay* "turned-on."

To summarize in a few words, I would say it this way: Man has a higher and transcendent nature, and this is part of his essence, i.e., his biological nature as a member of a species which has evolved. This means to me something which I had better spell out clearly, namely, that this is a flat rejection of the Sartre-type of Existentialism, i.e., its denial of specieshood, and of a biological human nature, and its refusal to face the existence of the biological sciences. It is true that the word "Existentialism" is by now used in so many different ways by different people, even in contradictory ways, that this indictment does not apply to all who use the label. But just *because* of this diversity of usage, the word is now almost useless, in my opinion, and had better be dropped. The trouble is that I have no good alternative label to offer. If only there were some way to say simultaneously: "Yes, man is in a way his own project and he does make himself.

But also there are limits upon what he can make himself into. The 'project' is predetermined biologically for all men; it is to become a man. He cannot adopt as his project for himself to become a chimpanzee. Or even a female. Or even a baby." The right label would have to combine the humanistic, the transpersonal, and the transhuman. Besides, it would have to be experiential (phenomenological), at least in its basing. It would have to be holistic rather than dissecting. And it would have to be empirical rather than *a priori*, etc.

The reader who is especially interested in continuing developments along the lines of this book may be referred to the recently established (1969) *Journal of Transpersonal Psychology* (P. O. Box 4437, Stanford, California 94305) and to the older weekly *Manas* (P. O. Box 32112, El Sereno Station, Los Angeles, California 90032).

Some Parallels Between Sexual and Dominance Behavior of Infrahuman Primates[1] and the Fantasies of Patients in Psychotherapy

A. H. Maslow, Ph.D.; H. Rand, M.D.; and S. Newman, M.A.

It is our purpose in this paper to present some parallels between human and infrahuman primates in respect to dominance-subordination, and to male and female sexuality and character, that have arisen in our own work.

What appears openly in the behavior of these animals often shows an astonishing resemblance to the content of secret human wishes and fantasies, dreams, myths, characterological adaptations, neurotic and psychotic acts and symptoms, as well as overt and covert social and psychological interactions especially between parent and child, male and female, therapist and patient, and in general, between the strong and the weak, the rulers and the ruled. Thus, this resemblance offers a perspective on aspects of human psychology not easily accessible to behavioral observation.

We wish to stress as strongly as we can that we are dealing with

[1] No effort has been made to survey the entire literature on this subject: This paper is based almost entirely on the investigations of the senior author listed in the Bibliography (94, 95, 97–109).

interesting and suggestive *parallels*, not with proofs of anything. Monkeys and apes prove nothing whatsoever about human beings; but they *suggest* a great deal, as we can testify. These parallels have certainly enriched *our* perceptions, giving another dimension to many human psychological problems, enabling us to see much that we had not noticed before. They have also raised many questions, specula- tions, and hypotheses which were new for us, and which, of course, await validation by other techniques.

This is quite definitely an intellectual game we are playing and is quite appropriate, even perhaps necessary, at the idea-producing level of scientific work, at the level of scientific work, at the level of "pri- mary process creativity" (95). It is certainly necessary to be cau- tious in science and we wish to be, too (especially by our stress on *parallels*). But it is not well to be *only* cautious. A certain boldness in the forward elements of science, in speculation and theories, is also needed.

The Dominance-Subordination Syndrome in Infrahuman Primates

This syndrome may be generalized to all infrahuman primates and indeed, in its basic schema, to most other animals. It has been de- scribed for all vertebrate classes from the teleost fishes to the human being (except for amphibians). For our purposes, however, it is most useful, to begin with, to concentrate on the *Old* World monkeys and baboons in whom the syndrome is seen most nakedly in its sado- masochistic form. Apes and New World monkeys vary in certain respects described in a previous communication (101) and discussion of them may be postponed for later consideration.

In brief, it is observed that when a pair of monkeys are introduced to each other for the first time, they will, without exception, form at once into a dominance-subordination hierarchy, i.e., one will assume the status of boss or overlord and the other will become the subor- dinate one. Under experimental conditions this status is independent of gender. Either male or female can become either the dominant or the subordinate individual. When there is a real discrepancy in size, the larger one will usually be the dominant. Sexual dimorphism therefore almost always guarantees male dominance in the wild. In the laboratory, however, one can select as one pleases. If a female is selected who is larger than the male, she becomes dominant and he becomes subordinate. So also when two males or two females are paired, the larger one ordinarily becomes dominant. Since prior to these experiments only observations in the wild or in herds or flocks were available, we can understand why it should have been believed that dominance was an exclusively male prerogative. When the factor of size is ruled out by pairing equally large monkeys, more subtle determinants emerge into view. Sureness, lack of hesitation, a confident posture, cockiness—in short, what the observer is irresistibly impelled to call self-confidence, determines the issue. It is as if the animals somehow knew at first glance which was dominant and which subordinate. Since there are two animals involved, sometimes it looks as if this occurs by one animal conceding dominance, sometimes by one animal assuming or taking dominance, but more often these two attitudes are assumed simultaneously. Characteristically one maintains a level stare and the other drops his eyes or looks off to a corner. The postures become different, the subordinate one assumes a craven and appeasing attitude, his tail drooping, his belly closer to the floor. He looks hesitant and uncertain. He may chatter in fear or back into a corner or get out of the way.

Often, however, the difference in status shows itself very soon by a pseudosexual act. The subordinate animal, whether male or female, presents (assumes the female sexual position); the dominant one, whether male or female, mounts. This must be called pseudosexual because most often it is a token act. Sexual excitement may not be seen. Erection may be absent in the mounting male. There may be no pelvic thrusts or they may be weak and nominal. The head may be mounted instead of the pelvis, etc. There may be no penetration. The only desideratum at times seems to be getting above the subordinate, regardless of its posture or position. Sometimes the subordinate animal goes eagerly or willingly into this situation; sometimes reluctantly. In a few cases, reluctant subordination shows itself by an assumption of a face-to-face sexual position rather than the presenting for dorso-ventral mounting. This kind of dominance mounting and subordinate presenting probably occurs more often at the beginning of a relationship rather than after status has been stabilized.

In addition, the dominant animal pre-empts the food supply without opposition. It can and does bully the subordinate animal in various ways. But this, too, occurs much less often in a stable relationship. The dominant animal pre-empts *anything* that is desirable—the best place to sit, a new object in the cage, the front of the cage, etc.

Within the limits of observation of pairs in zoo or laboratory this relative status is normally permanent. It has been observed to change when females come into heat and readjustments take place (105), or when alliances of several subordinates occur to dethrone an overlord (106). There have also been reports of changes under certain experimental conditions; e.g., hormone injections, traumatizing, drugs.

Dominance-Subordination in Humans

In subprimate species, dominance may involve actual use of physical strength as it does, for example, in the gang or group of preadolescent or adolescent boys. Punching or formal boxing may establish a boy in the dominance hierarchy: Often the combat takes the form of wrestling, which is won when the winner lies on top of the loser for specified amounts of time, frequently defined by counting, or by admission of defeat ("say 'uncle' ").

But the very *threat* of use of force, or an obvious external evidence —bigger size, obvious self-confidence, strong muscles, swagger, strutting or cockiness—may be enough, as it is in monkeys. This again we may observe among boys; also in preadolescents of both sexes, when some girls may try to measure up their strength against boys, but eventually acknowledge that boys are stronger. This is also accepted tacitly by most children in regard to their parents and other adults.

In later life also the struggle for dominance manifests itself in all areas of interpersonal relationships: both in overt behavior, in dreams, fantasies, neurotic and psychotic symptoms. However, in the sexual realm especially we can see parallels between our data from primates and human behavior patterns and fantasies.

If maturation does not result in a healthy integration under the hegemony of (Freudian) genitality, masculine sexual activity may be identified with dominance, control, manipulation, aggression, and even sadistic behavior. This may extend over a wide range of phenomena. At the extreme, the partner may be bound and actual pain inflicted. Or he may be immobilized, frightened, made passive, manipulated, dominated, used. Here, as in the dominance struggle of the primates, the power, dominance, and aggression aspects overshadow the genital drives and use them to channel through. The pattern of the struggle is basically nonsexual, regardless of the gender of the participants. Thus in the dominance struggle there are several possible combinations:

1. Male-male relationship.
2. Female-female relationship.
3. Male-female relationship in which the man is dominant.
4. Male-female relationship in which the woman is dominant.

Cases 3 and 4 are often deceptive and masquerade frequently as the "normal" genital adjustment.

Yet even here, in the behaviorally "normal" sexual act, dominance and subordination fantasies are often found.

1. A case of a homosexual woman, whose strong masculine aspirations appeared in the course of treatment, spontaneously found herself in her first heterosexual experience, on top of her male partner, feeling herself as the thrusting dominant one.

2. A male patient with an anesthetic penis seeks out sexual intercourse to feel powerful; he has repetitive fantasies of wielding a whip over a harem of women.

3. A patient reports fantasies of sucking the breast during "normal" intercourse. Even though his behavior is dominant, his fantasy is submissive.

4. An active homosexual woman feels that the climax of her seductive campaign has been reached when an innocent girl succumbs sexually, *not* when she herself has sexual pleasure. Indeed, it is almost irrelevant for her.

In the behaviorally "normal" (to the eye of the camera) sexual intercourse, the fantasies may express a dominant-subordinate impulse, rather than a love, a sex, or reproductive impulse. One way in which this is commonly reflected is in the use of the words screwing, fucking, to express overpowering aggression, contempt, conquest, assumption of the dominant status or even cruelty. These words are used in many nonsexual situations. "Did I get screwed!" a man may exclaim to say that he was taken advantage of. "I got 'raped'" (or "shafted"), a man or woman may say in situations in which he or she was taken advantage of, fooled, swindled, or exploited; or of an irritatingly superior or hoity-toity woman, males are apt to say "She ought to be raped" as if this would humble her properly.

Human adults—consciously, preconsciously, and unconsciously—frequently perceive and describe the sexual act in terms of the infantile perception of it as the male ("overpowering, cruel, bad") doing something harmful to the female ("helpless, unwilling, weak"). The child may perceive his father as killing the mother or hurting her in the act. So also when he sees animals copulating.

The perception of the sexual act may be sadomasochistic and manipulative in its essence and express itself correspondingly in language.

This is the (masturbation) fantasy of a dominant woman: She is an Oriental queen, all powerful. She is surrounded by huge male slaves, almost naked. She selects one for a sexual partner and commands him to serve her. He does this in the way that she prefers, she on her back and he above her. She likes the feeling of being crushed by his weight. He is very potent and with a huge penis performs to her complete satisfaction. She lets herself go entirely in an orgiastic way. But after it is over, because he has committed *lèse-majesté*, she commands that he be decapitated, which is done. He does not protest but recognizes that this is inevitable, proper, and suitable. She then commands another slave to do the same.

This woman is frigid in actual sexual intercourse. She has the common rape and prostitution fantasies. Apparently these enable her to surrender enough to enjoy sexuality. Several of these high-dominance women who were sexually neurotic, and who "dominatized" the sexual act, managed some compromise pleasure in sexuality by such fantasies as the following:

1. By being in the above position, and insisting that the man remain immobile, these women could imagine that *they* were the males and that *they* had the penis ("as if it were part of *my* body and I were entering him").

2. The fantasy that the penis was attached to her body and that she was "screwing" him has been reported by some females even though they assumed the below position.

3. That the man was really "serving" her, was her slave, working hard, sweating and grunting at his job of pleasing her rather than himself, while she saw herself as taking her ease, not working, making no effort and secretly using him.

4. By stretching and pulling the clitoris to resemble a penis in masturbation.

5. By decontaminating the "surrender," i.e., refusing to submit (even though sexually submitting) by refusing to enjoy it, by hiding the enjoyment, by contemptuous gestures, e.g., smoking casually during the act, yawning, laughing contemptuously at his excitement.

Modes of Adjustment of the Subordinated Ones

In Animals. "Presentation" to the dominant animal may range from a kind of symbolic gesture of recognition of the other's superiority to actual "*giving up*" of the male role in an acute situation and thus trying to escape injury and punishment by the other animal.

The completely subordinate animal flees to a far corner of the cage when food is thrown in, and thus makes it clear that he is not competing for it. To obtain food it may often engage in what Kempf (59) called "prostitution behavior," i.e., it may present itself sexually to the dominant one. This it does also to avoid attack or to obtain protection. These presentations are frequently merely nominal, vestigial, one is tempted to say "symbolic." They are different from real sexual behavior in heat. The following responses have been observed in the subordinate animal in a dominance mounting: fear, apprehension, disinterest, mere complaisance, annoyance, impatience, passivity, cringing, waxy flexibility, or attempts at flight. In many cases (but not in all) the response pattern indicates that being dominance-mounted is unpleasant.

Sexual presentation and subordination may serve as a *means* for achieving several aims that can be summarized under the headings of self-preservation and handling fear in threatening situations. This includes warding off attacks, avoiding punishment, obtaining access to food, and other benefits and privileges.

In Man. Man learns subordinate patterns of behavior from early childhood on. While he is factually helpless, he learns to submit to his parents, and to other adults. He has to do this, for his (or her) very survival depends on parental care. Also, threatening situations and fears can be handled by the child only with the help of parents (or their substitutes). The child can assert its will only if the parents let him do so and are not threatened by his asserting his will. By and large, he can strive for security, when he is young, only by being and becoming the *object* of parental love and care. He cannot really be the *subject* of masculine assertive behavior toward the parents, unless they let him; or when they do not realize that he is asserting himself by various covert compromise formations, e.g., apparent inability to get the good grades in school that his parents demand.

This helpless situation, as long as the child is young, leaves deep impressions both upon the human individual and upon the cultural, artistic, and social aspects of mankind. Leonardo Da Vinci, in his notebooks, mentions the (unsubstantiated) legend of the beaver[2] that pursued by enemies castrates itself, to save its life: not being a male it might be spared. So also the boy or the adult man tries sometimes to escape the danger of competition or attack, or the threat of punishment by denial or renunciation of his masculinity.[3]

The adult, too, may use the subordinate pattern as a means of handling threats, escaping punishment, and obtaining favors and approval. In other words, such an adult will not assert his will, will not fight, compete or challenge, but rather will try to escape dangers by "degrading" himself, by surrendering or ingratiation, by voluntary subordination and appeasement. This is not an all-or-none situation—there are many intermediate grades. A monkey that has to submit unwillingly may, for instance, retain some degree of dominance by facing his sexual partner rather than presenting his rear. Such compromise formations are common also in humans. Complete subor-

[2] See the discussion of the problem of masochism at the Midwinter Meeting, 1955, of the American Psychoanalytic Association, reported in the *Journal of the American Psychoanalytic Association*, July 1956, by Dr. Martin H. Stein, especially Rudolph M. Loewenstein's presentation in which a distinction is made between the various forms of masochism. He maintains that masochism does play a role in survival. It is "the weapon of the weak . . . of every child . . . faced with the danger of human aggression" (*ibid.*, p. 537). Giving up dominance or masculinity can be seen as preferable to giving up life itself.

[3] This is probably a human projection only, for we do not know of animals castrating other animals: They either kill, fight, run, or present. Only the human being castrates literally.

dination is rare. An effort is made to preserve as much self-assertion, will, freedom, as is possible under the circumstances.

Ingratiation, continued smilings, being unable to win, some forms of kindness—all these can be seen as attempts at avoiding danger by voluntarily accepting dominance and making clear that one is no threat to the dominant one. Other techniques are appeasement, submissiveness, fawning, humility, propitiation, meekness, lack of demandingness or challenge, whimpering, cringing, showing fear, whining, compliance, wheedling, reducing, appealing via incapacity, helplessness or fearfulness or illness, dependence, the call to pity, the giving of constant admiration, being "good," looking up to, adoration, worship, passivity, the "you are always right" technique. These are all accommodations whereby the subordinate child, the weaker one, can adapt himself to living with the sadomasochistic parent, the strong one. Observe that these are also customary techniques whereby a weak minority group can accommodate to a stronger group.

That these subordinance techniques ("presenting techniques") can all be seen as sexualized is obvious, for most of these techniques may also be called "feminine" even in our culture and *are* in *fact* feminine in more traditional sadomasochistic cultures where women are valued less than men. Weakness can appease strength and avert its dangers by sexualizing itself and by offering in a symbolic way a sexual service to the strong. Also strength and would-be strength may assert itself and prove itself via sexual channels.

Why does presenting and its variations work so well in appeasing and forestalling the wrath of the strong? We do not really know. We know that it does work and that we have infrahuman parallels which force us to think of at least the possibility of instinctoid sources. For instance, the ethologists have described for us the "chivalry reflex" in the wolf and the dog. Two animals may be fighting hard, even to the death. However, if one *concedes* defeat by rolling over and exposing its throat and belly, not fighting any longer, the conqueror will no longer attack but will turn away. In one or another isomorphic form, something of the sort can be seen in many other species. In the infrahuman primates, it is sexual presenting which apparently has the same meaning, or at least the same appeasing and lifesaving effect.

In some lower species, this is the mechanism that differentiates male from female objects for the attacking male. If it fights back, it's a male and fighting ensues; if it doesn't fight back but instead assumes another kind of posture, varying with the species, it is a female and sexual activity ensues. In some birds, the females indicate subordinance not only by assuming a sexually inviting position, but also by soliciting food from the male in the way that a half-grown fledgling does. No instance is known in which a male does this in the wild. Here also human parallels strongly suggest themselves. The appeal to many males of admitted fear, helplessness, passivity, receptiveness, etc. in the female or in the child suggests a parallel to the "chivalry reflex." Most males, especially immature males, in our culture are not sexually drawn to the female who is strong, assertive, self-confident, self-sufficient, and if he *is*, we may suspect that his feminine component is attracted to her masculine component; that is, at the unconscious and fantasy level, this may simply be a reversal of roles, for the strong woman can also be drawn to the dependent male as a man is to a woman or perhaps as a mother is to a son. Even this reminds us of the chivalry reflex. (Of course, we must not forget that in the human beings we find, in our own culture at least, that psychologically mature and strong males can be drawn to psychologically mature females who may look too "strong" for the average, more delicate male.)

Dominance, Subordination, Masculinity, Femininity

The young or neurotic human being in many cultures has a tendency to identify or confuse subordinate status with feminine status and the dominant status with masculine status. The man in subordinate status, whether willingly or unwillingly arrived at, in relation to a boss, superior officer, or anybody who gives him orders, may react as if he had been made female, as if even justifiable orders were like being mounted or raped. He may respond to a realistic situation as if he had been ordered to become feminine; i.e., to present. This, as in the monkeys, is without relationship to gender, i.e., it may happen in response to either male or female boss. Some respond to this subordination by submitting willingly or even eagerly but these are often despised.

Army lingo examples: Such a person or act is called "brownnose," "being cornholed," "asskisser," "asslicker," "being browned." The phrase "he is prostituting himself" also applies. Other men may fight against this as if against an assault upon their masculinity, even when the demands or orders are perfectly natural or justifiable. That is, such dominance relations are sexualized just as sexual relations are seen as dominance-subordination metaphors.

Furthermore, in those cultures which value masculinity more than femininity, being pushed into subordinate status means being degraded or demoted. In such cultures this attitude is shared by both men and women. Women who feel that their femininity is synonymous with inferior status or subordination may repudiate their femininity in various unconscious ways or unconsciously emulate the male, or they may in their striving for esteem or status or self-respect fantasy being male. This is as if they thought that the only way to be strong or capable or intelligent or successful were to be male. So also, following the same assumption, the woman in order to be a good female may feel it necessary to give up her strength, intelligence, or talent, fearing them as somehow masculine and defeminizing.

This has been observed overtly in female children who will openly demand some phallic equivalent, e.g., will urinate in the standing position. In adults, this is not seen overtly very often (exceptions are in psychotics or in some female homosexuals) but is rather seen in fantasy or desexualizing and castrating of the male, or of various forms of resistance to being pushed into the female position, either literally or figuratively.

Homosexuality

We have learned from Evelyn Hooker to speak of the many kinds of homosexualities and to give up monistic explanations and theories. However, the homosexual behavior that is so easily and parsimoniously explained in monkeys, that is, as a function of dominance and subordination status, can also be paralleled in *some* forms of human homosexuality, overt as well as covert. The dominating Lesbian certainly exists and she so strongly identifies the female sexual role with total domination by the male, with obliteration of her personality, her selfhood, that she could not possibly accept the role of "weakness."

Feeling herself to be so strong she identifies with the conquering male. So also for the pansy type of male homosexual who feels himself to be so weak that he cannot possibly fit into *his* distorted image of the dominant male, the raper, the exploiter, the selfish, arrogant taker of what he wants. But also his sexual presenting can be a way of protecting himself or winning favors, as in men's prisons. The same mechanism may be seen in the "normal" man.

> An unconsciously passive, fearful man, ingratiating and appeasing his therapist, had the following dream: "I was following a narrow snowy path some place in the wilds of Alaska. Suddenly there is a huge frightening bear standing on his hind legs in front of me, blocking the path. In terror I turn around and put my rear up to him, eagerly and quickly fitting his penis into my anus in the hope that he won't attack me. It works and I can go on." He was disturbed by this dream, seeing it as homosexual.

Let us say that at least *one* factor in the complex web of human homosexuality is the dominance-subordination determinant in its sado-masochistic version, in the version that so many children report and adults covertly fantasy, that "Daddy is killing Mommy" or, upon watching animals copulate, "He is hurting her." Some males cannot stand to identify with the hurter and/or prefer to identify with the hurtee. Some females cannot or will not identify with the hurtee and/or prefer to identify with the hurter. Presumably in such cases differentiating sex from dominance instead of confounding them should cure *this* aspect of the illness.

Sexualizing of the Transference

The actual subordination of the therapeutic patient, his factual weakness, his necessary humility, the lowering of self-esteem implied in asking someone for help and in exposing oneself in all one's shame and embarrassment, leads not only to the customary hostility fantasies and verbalizations, but also encourages a sexualization of the relationship. Whatever character style or defenses the patient has lived by will reveal themselves here in a sexual translation, most often in a dominatized form. That is, it will be either raping or castrating, or otherwise dominating the analyst or, more frequently, of winning his love by offering oneself to him as a sexual object (although of course there are also many other fantasied ways of winning his love). All this can be independent of the gender of either the analyst or the patient, just as in monkeys. "Presenting to the analyst" this may be called, and must very frequently be isomorphic with the ways in which long ago as a child, the patient "presented" to his parents, especially to the one seen as more powerful (regardless of gender). It may be hypothesized that any therapeutic atmosphere or technique which minimized the factual status of subordination would reduce sexualization of the relationship.

The patient, a twenty-three-year-old single man, had been for most of his life fearful of older men, especially those in the authoritative position. He was never conscious of any hostile feelings, wishes, or fantasies toward these men; toward the original man, his father, he had the same attitude. In fact, if someone criticized his father he would passionately defend him. In analytic treatment the patient developed the same attitudes toward the analyst. He came in one day with the following dream:

> He is in some kind of prison atmosphere where he is to be forced to submit to penile intercourse by some big man. The man approaches him ready to penetrate him, and the dream ends.

In association to the dream the patient suddenly remembered something that had occurred the day before and represented for the first time a conscious, hostile fantasy toward an older man. When he left the analyst's office and got into his car, he saw the analyst's car nearby. His fantasy was that he wanted to crash his car into the rear of the analyst's car. This fantasy had apparently been transient and had gone into repression. The dream apparently was a projected retaliative gesture.

Religious Oblation

We may speak not only of the "feminine aspects of Christianity" in the Nietzschean sense (and of other religions as well), but also we can get a richer understanding of the oblative and homonomous aspects of all religious experience, and especially of the conversion experience, by separating the fusion of sexuality and dominance-subordination (pride-humility). The conversion experience as depicted by James, Begbie, and many others is often described in a clearly sexual way, but also as a giving up of pride and autonomy in favor of surrender and oblation, with ensuing peace of mind in the "successful" cases. The necessary giving up of will and of self-sufficiency, as presented in these accounts, can be understood better if we are clearly aware of the simultaneous and ambitendent urges to rule and be ruled, to dominate and to submit, and if we are also aware of the delights of surrender. In the Western male, these are felt especially as dangerous to the (unevolved) conception of masculinity, are felt even as a castration, as a becoming feminine, as a homosexual reaction, i.e., they are sexualized.

> A patient in homosexual panic ran away and hid in a hotel room in another city. He couldn't sleep and felt frightened much of the time. Suddenly during the night, as he lay in bed on his back, he felt the weight of a presence on top of him. He submitted to it lovingly and felt, This is God. He felt peaceful and slept deeply for the first time in months. Next morning, he awoke refreshed and relaxed and determined to serve God by good works, which he now does. He returned to his wife and is heterosexual with her.

We may hypothesize that man's bisexual or ambitendent urges (to be masculine and feminine simultaneously *or*, what amounts to the same thing, to master and to submit) are generally dangerous to him because he interprets femininity as submission, and submission as feminine, feels himself thereby castrated, lower in self-esteem, emasculated. He generally has few outlets for, or legitimate expressions of, his feminine-submitting, or oblative impulses. *But*, it seems to be somewhat more possible for him to satisfy these tendencies without threat to his picture of himself as masculine if he can surrender to a God, to some omnipotent, omniscient figure, where rivalry is out of the question. Kneeling before a God is less an unmanly act than kneeling before a rival or competitor or peer. It is "suitable" in the Gestalt psychological sense, appropriate, "fittin' and proper," called for; it is not a defeat.

And of course this satisfying oblation is also possible before a human if that person is seen as Godlike enough, "great" enough, e.g., Napoleon, Hitler on the one hand, Lincoln, Schweitzer on the other.

It is also interesting to observe that most women in most cultures that we know are apt to be more religious (in this sense) than their men are. They seem to be less threatened by oblation, and to be more able to enjoy it in an uncomplicated way. So also are women apt to be less destroyed and less rebellious, made less "neurotic," by conquest of their society from without. Their admiration for the conqueror is less threatening to their integrity as persons than it is in men who must fight against their oblative tendencies or else lose self-respect. Or to put it in another way, being raped (in whatever sense) is less psychologically damaging to women than to men. Women are more able to permit themselves to "relax and enjoy it" than men are.

Healthy Differentiation of Dominance from Sexuality: Desexualization

One hoped-for effect of depth therapy is to separate and unconfound these two areas of life, and to keep them differentiated, to learn that the penis is in fact not a club or a sword or a rending instrument, that the vagina is not a garbage pail or a biting mouth or an engulfing well; that the above or below position in the sexual act is meaningful only for sexual convenience and pleasure; that taking orders from a superior is not equivalent to being raped; that stronger people need not be made a sexual oblation to in order to avert their anger. It is hoped for the woman that her sexual surrender becomes *not* a giving up of her ego or self-respect; it is *not* a conquest in which by surrendering she concedes her slavish status thereafter. The male must learn that by penetrating his wife, he has neither conquered nor asserted mastery nor committed a sadistic act. Nor has she thereby conceded submission in other areas of life. Nor need he feel guilty or fearful after the sexual act if he can feel that he is welcomed rather than resented, if he has not conquered but collaborated. And so on.

What all this amounts to is the differentiation of sex from dominance and subordination. It seems likely that this is really, *fully* possible only for the human being, although there seem to be some approaches to this separation in the chimpanzee.

A paper (101) whose theoretical implications have been overlooked, called attention to the qualitative differences in what was called "dominance-quality" in the three large families of infrahuman primates. Briefly, all the New World monkeys show a laissez-faire quality of dominance. All the Old World monkeys and baboons show the kind of sadomasochistic or dominating, tyrannical quality of dominance we have mostly talked about in this paper. The anthropoid apes (of whom we really know only the chimpanzees) show a more friendly, altruistic, cooperative quality of dominance. We do not have enough data, even on the chimpanzee, to be very confident of this. But what we *do* have indicates that there is absolutely less pseudosexual behavior, less dominance-sexual equivalence, less dominance mounting, and the like. Certainly there is less bullying, cringing, and cowering.

This suggests (nothing more, of course) that the dominance-sexual fusion is a lower evolutionary development than the differentiation of sex from dominance and parallels our suspicion that such a differentiation in the human being may be a correlate or epiphenomenon of greater psychological maturity or development. Considering the importance of such a speculation, it certainly calls for more investigation than it has received.

The obverse implication is that the confounding of sex and dominance in the human being may be an evidence of immaturity or of neurosis, of the loss of a distinctively human capacity, of mild psychopathology, of human diminution.

Healthy Femininity and Masculinity

Of course, there are many theoretical possibilities, and all fascinating. We mention one only because we have data that bear on this puzzle. It *may* turn out that healthy growth or psychotherapy in the human being has as its hoped-for consequence *not the abolition* of the dominance-subordination relationships as between male or female at their deepest levels, or between parents and children. What may rather be the case is a change in what has been called "dominance-quality" from the baboon quality to the chimpanzee quality. In chimpanzees, the dominance-subordination syndrome can also be seen but it has taken on an entirely different flavor, one of kind and fostering and responsible strength which is at the service of the weak; older-brotherly dominance it was called. By this time the words "dominance" and "subordination" become misnomers and can be very misleading. Substitutes might be, for instance, "kind and loving strength" and "trusting dependence."

In any case in the human being, the healthward shift is away from devaluation of the subordinate status, with mutual hostility, toward an accepting and loving attitude. Concomitant with this is a desexualizing of the statuses of strength and weakness, and of leadership so that either man or woman can be, without anxiety and without degradation, either weak or strong, as the situation demands. Either must be capable of both leadership or surrender, e.g., a therapist has to be motherly, unfortunate widows must be ready also to "father" their children.

We have in essence been concerned with the old problem of bisexuality, of the conflict between "maleness" and "femaleness" in either male or female, penis envy, castration anxieties, masculine protest, and phallic masculinity.

Without trying at this point to spell out consequences in detail, we may point to the following pregnant fact. There is evidence available to indicate that the sexual hormones produce not only sexual but also dominance desires. That is to say, the same hormones may produce both the sexual syndrome and the dominance-subordination syndrome. No wonder they are so intimately interconnected. Indeed, the problem then is transformed into understanding how they become separated, independent, e.g., how position in the sexual act becomes detached from dominance-subordination meaning, how the penis can become *only* a sexual tool and not a power weapon, how the anus can become only a defecating organ and no more a sexual receptacle, how an employee can come to take necessary orders without feeling feminized-subordinated.

Postscript

In sum, for those of you who enjoy the game of theoretical speculation and manipulation, there is much here to play with. For instance, with respect to Freudian theory, we have opened up the possibility of combining Oedipal theory and castration theory in a single and unified system. They can both be pushed into the more general phrasing of "the mutual accommodations of the strong and the weak to each other and the pathological sexualization of these accommodations." We have opened up another possibility with respect to Freudian and Adlerian theory, namely, that they may be, in the respects we have dealt with, isomorphic parallel languages, at an archaic level saying the same thing, one from the sexual side of the fusion, the other from the dominance side of the same fusion. The so-far mysterious problem of the definition of healthy masculinity and femininity have been touched on, and this is clearly *one* way of playing with this mystery. We have only barely mentioned the strong thread of sexualization that can be plucked out of the web of interclass and caste relationships. We have bypassed altogether the intricate questions of the relationships of culture to our primate inheritance even though we are quite convinced that the study of infrahuman primates has much to teach the sociologist. We imply another approach to the psychoanalytic theory of instincts and still another toward the understanding of sadism-masochism, of authoritarianism, of hypnosis, of the need for achievement, of the definition of the various types of love, of religious oblation, even of the servant problem. And so on, and so on.

Adolescence and Juvenile Delinquency in Two Different Cultures

A. H. Maslow and R. Díaz-Guerrero

The visitor to Mexico very soon notices that Mexican children behave differently from American children. The general impression is that the Mexican children are "better behaved," more polite, more helpful. They seem to get along well with adults, enjoying their company, trusting them, obeying them, respecting them, and showing no overt signs of hostility. At the same time they are quite able to play with other children (not clinging to adults), giving the impression that they can enjoy both adults and children more than American children can. Another common observation, also reported from, e.g., Italy, is that to the naked eye, there seems to be no sibling rivalry. Life in Mexico is so arranged that children are confined to sibling playmates more than are children in the United States. Older Mexican children, both boys and girls, not only have to take care of their younger siblings, but also seem to want to. At any rate, to the parent who has brought up children in the United States the contrast is startling and unmistakable, or to put it another way, Mexican parents seem to have less trouble with their children than do U.S. parents. Their children seem to resent authority less, to demand less, to be less whining and complaining, to be less of a nuisance and to cry less often. Also they laugh more and seem to enjoy themselves more.

They are seldom, if ever, disrespectful to their parents, or openly defiant or rebellious. There are more often expressions of affection for adults, i.e., kissing fathers, arms around mothers and grandmothers, etc. Following up this impression one finds that though statistics are inadequate, all agree who know both cultures,[1] that there is far less juvenile delinquency in Mexico, far less juvenile vandalism and destruction, and practically never does there occur a juvenile gang attack upon adults.[2] Traditionally, adolescent gangs fight gangs, but not adults, perhaps also police who are not respected by either young men or adults.

Assuming that these impressions are confirmed, where do these differences come from? Some of the usual explanations of American sociologists and criminologists don't seem to work. Mexican children are more deprived, even to the point of hunger (and yet they seem to feel more secure than do U.S. children). The Mexican family, especially the lower-class family, is far more often broken than its American counterpart. (Estimates of abandonment by the father run as high as 32 per cent.)[3]

In any Mexican family the likelihood is much greater, than in the United States, that the father isn't home very often after work (he usually prefers the company of men friends, except, perhaps, on Sunday) (24, 12). The Mexican father is far more apt to have

[1] Drs. Rosenquist and Solís Quiroga, sociologists of the University of Texas and the National University of Mexico respectively, start from this agreement in their comparative study of juvenile delinquency in Mexico and the United States.

[2] Several editorial statements have appeared recently in Mexican newspapers complaining of the recent appearance of "juvenile delinquency" in the large cities. *Excelsior*, May 14, 1959, says: "Youth has become fond . . . of the belief that the adolescent has to be daring, vile, irresponsible, and a gypsy." The preoccupation refers to adolescents that in groups get inside movie houses and break furniture, adolescents that molest women and especially adolescents —sons of well-to-do families—that organize thefts and brutally attack other adolescents. Very rarely is there an attack upon adults, so far. The break-in, previously quoted from *Excelsior*, was in a movie house showing a picture in which Elvis Presley was the star. This has happened no more than three or four times in the history of Mexico.

[3] Cited by Ramírez (127). His sampling of families was taken from the population of a public hospital. The 1950 census for Mexico shows that the head of the family is a female 17 per cent of the time in Mexico City, 15 per cent of the time in the state of Jalisco to the West, and 10 per cent of the time in Nuevo León to the North. Male heads of the family made up the remaining per cents.

mistresses, more or less openly,[4,5] and is far less likely to make a "pal" or partner of his wife, or to participate in the day-to-day bringing up of his children. The Mexican father, though physically absent is however always psychologically present (77, 158, 28, 12)—the American father is much more physically present but is more apt to be a psychological nonentity. Even where the American father wants to impose discipline, he is usually regarded as a sadist by his children, because most other fathers in the neighborhood set a more indulgent standard. Parents in Mexico will consider weak a parent who permits his child to throw a temper tantrum. "Niño malcriado." His parents are blamed for this.

We wish to suggest that part of the answer probably lies in another direction, easily observed and easily checked on.

1. First of all, the Mexican culture, in spite of rapid industrialization, remains far more a traditional culture than the United States. We mean here far more than the influence of the Catholic Church, for there are very strong anticlerical forces at work in Mexico also and extremely strong traditional sociocultural beliefs. What we do mean is that with respect to bringing up children there is a shared and agreed-upon value system which is still quite homogeneous, unified and widespread. All fathers (and mothers and children too) know how a father "should" behave toward his children, and in fact, the degree of sameness in father's behavior to his children is far greater than in the United States, caste and clan differences and urban and rural differences notwithstanding (24, 12, 28, 158, 77). Or to put it another way, the Mexican father (or mother) "knows" far more definitely what the "right" way is to bring up children (unconsciously and preconsciously rather than with full rationality). By comparison, the American parent is confused, uncertain, guilty, and conflicted. His traditions have gone and no new ones are yet available to him (habitual, unquestioned, automatic reflexlike certainties). He must try to figure things out rationally, to study the subject, to read books

---

[4] To the question: "Do you think most married men have lovers?" 51 per cent of the male population, and 63 per cent of the female population, from a sample of the City of Mexico, answered yes (29).
[5] Thirty-six per cent of the males and 42 per cent of the females, in a sample of Puerto Rican college students, agreed with the statement: "Most married men have lovers" on a declarative-sentence approach (33).

by "authorities" (he is no authority, but every Mexican parent is an "authority" in a sense). Each American parent must solve the problem by himself anew, as if it were a brand-new problem for him. Hardly any American father today could act with the sureness, the decisiveness, the certainty, the feeling of virtue, the lack of conflict or guilt shown, for example, by the father in Alan Wheeler's *Quest for Identity*.

The Mexican children can therefore more surely "count" on what the father will do. This, in spite of the fact that, frequently, presence, absence, and degree of punishment depend upon his mood. The limits set by the Mexican parent, especially by the father, are far more definite, unchanging, consistent than those of the American parent, if, indeed the latter sets any limits at all (within these definite limits, the Mexican child is certainly loved and indulged and permitted freedom, especially by the mother). The parent, especially the father, will punish, surely and quickly, any serious transgression of these limits, without the lingering doubts and fears and guilts characteristic of the American parent. However far apart mother and father may be, in Mexico they will agree absolutely on the necessity of respect to either of them (*a su madre se la respeta*).

More difference is found in these between fathers of the two cultures than between mothers. We postulate that the major task of the mother, qua mother, is to love unconditionally, to gratify, to heal and comfort and smooth over; and that the major task of the father, qua father, is to support and protect, to mediate between the family and reality (the world), and to prepare his children to live in the extra-familial world by discipline, toughening, instruction, reward and punishment, judging, differential valuing, reason and logic (rather than by unconditioned love), and by being able to say "NO" when necessary. The Mexican father seems to be able to do this job more easily than does the American father. For instance, it is our observation that in the United States, far more than in Mexico, the father is not only afraid of his wife, but of his children as well (and is therefore often afraid to punish, to refuse, to frustrate).[6]

6 Fernández-Marina *et al.* (33) say that 63 per cent of the male and 67 per cent of the female Puerto Rican students selected, among others, the statement: "Many boys are afraid of their fathers." Sixty-nine per cent of the males and 76 per cent of the females selected: "Many girls are afraid of their fathers." A significantly smaller percentage selected the same statement about the mother.

Patriarchy, long dead in the United States, is still very much alive in the Mexican family. Not only is it maintained by the men, but also by the women. Even the wife who is neglected by the husband and who is hurt by his running around with other women is not apt to complain openly when he does show up, but will rather suffer in silence, meanwhile serving him, making much of him, treating him like visiting royalty, especially being careful to help maintain his authority with the children.[7]

We shall not speak here of the deeper family dynamics that are covered over by the foregoing picture, at any rate insofar as the child is concerned, e.g., the greater "strength," responsibility, reliability of the Mexican woman, the deeper passivity, irresponsibility, and inferiority feeling of the Mexican male, etc. The surface "behavioral" patriarchial front, at any rate, postpones the inevitable disillusion of the child with the father, the loss of paternal godliness, omniscience, omnipotence, etc., which certainly comes earlier in life for the American child than for the Mexican child. We shall advance below the various effects of the clear dichotomizing of masculinity and femininity, so much more distinct still in Mexico than in the United States, where the gender roles are much more apt to be blurred for the child. In addition, we wish to stress that we are not concerned with the effects of these regimes on the adult, only upon children and adolescents.[8]

We wish to stress as relevant to the problem in hand that the Mexican child is confronted by a more stable, widely agreed-upon set of adult values with respect to child rearing. The child's life is run by adult values which are clear, unmistakable, and leave him no room for doubt about what is "right" and "wrong" for him to do.

2. But there is another striking and interesting difference between the Mexican and the American adolescent; traditionally in Mexico the masculine and feminine roles have been kept apart. The most intense cultural forces have maintained this differentiation. Implicit and with the force of an axiom (28) there is the goal to keep them apart. The

[7] Convers-Vergara (24) considers one of her most striking findings, in her study of twenty-five low-income workers' families, the incredible importance that the mother gives the father in his family role and her almost infinite self-sacrificial submission. This contrasts with the average wife's behavior in the United States when she fails to respect him or is angry at him, or tears him down in public, or makes fun of him to their own children.

[8] Díaz-Guerrero has discussed some of these effects for the adult (28).

Minister of Public Education of Mexico (1943), Lic. Véjar Vázquez, said the following in defense of a change in the Laws of Public Education:

> The ideal of education is to make women more feminine and men more masculine, or in different words, education should enable the boy and the girl to refine or emphasize the characteristics of their sex instead of obscuring, nullifying or substituting them.[9]

and in his message to the Mexican nation:

> An education in search of a spiritual renaissance that will precise and deepen masculinity and femininity.[10]

Fernández-Marina *et al.* (33) conclude from the available evidence a clear and persistent sex role definition in several Latin American countries and go on to demonstrate its intense existence in Puerto Rico. Whatever the interpretation of this separation of the masculine and feminine roles, writers, psychologists, anthropologists, etc., in Mexico, agree on its existence. Thus, for example, Santiago Ramírez (127), a Mexican psychoanalyst, wants to see this extreme separation of masculine and feminine roles as explainable through the facts of the conquest of Mexico. He is historically correct when he says that originally the man, the father, was the Spaniard; and the woman, the mother, was the Indian. That the male was the powerful, dominant conqueror and the female the overpowered, humiliated, and submitted. One may disagree with Ramírez about the cause for the sex-role differentiation, but accept that present-day sex roles are nicely illustrated by the four-centuries-old historical state of affairs.

One does not need to cite evidence. Anyone visiting Mexico will observe the differential behavior exhibited by the males and the females. It is easily realized that the female dresses, walks, and generally behaves constantly as if her main goal in life was to further her femininity and femaleness. The behavior of the male is more complex but two aspects are interesting. On one hand he will show an extreme exaggeration of the male pattern (if we understand for the male pattern a sexually forward attitude, sex bragging, domi-

[9] *Novedades*, Dec. 12, 1943.
[10] *Ley Orgánica de la Educación Pública*, Secretaría de Educación Pública, México, 1942.

nance, and dominance bragging, and the final word on abstract and intellectual matters as well as in the home). On the other hand he will show no anxiety, better yet, he will show enthusiasm in regard to his spontaneous expressions of affect, hand shakes, embraces, and many other types of bodily contact with other males. One of us remembers an amusing incident: A young Mexican psychiatrist, in training with American psychoanalysts, related with great distress, that he just could not understand them, that whenever he wanted to throw one of his arms around them (a perfectly natural gesture among Mexicans), they would withdraw, as he put it, "frightened to death." He later found out that they were not at all sure of his intentions!

From the cradle to the tomb, in every stage of development, there are clearly stipulated chores, ways of behaving and anticipations for the male and the female. This is true in the urban (28) as well as in most rural areas (158, 77).

3. The Mexican child is much more apt to be brought up exclusively in the bosom of the family than is the American child. The Spanish tradition of closing off the family within walls and gates that shut out most of the outside world (except relatives) is still active. Siblings are more apt to play with each other exclusively, rather than with street gangs, or peer groups of the same age, and they are more apt to play within the walls or within the home, under the eye of adults, than are American children. Especially in the urban environment, the eight-year-old American boy is likely to play with other eight-year-old boys rather than with his four-year-old brother, and certainly rather than with any of his sisters.

We see this as giving additional support to the foregoing picture of children living by adult values.[11] Furthermore, we see the pos-

[11] Evidence that Mexican children and adolescents live by adult values in Mexico comes from many sources. Dr. Aaron Shore studied the children of a Mexican village with a Mexican T.A.T. (136). His *a priori* intentions were to study authority and aggression. The study was carried out in forty children of both sexes ranging in age from six to fifteen years, but with the bulk between six and twelve. He found himself with the fact that 34 per cent of the statements of his children did not meet any of his criteria of authority or aggression. These expressions referred to thoughts and activities of the following nature: to pacify, to be industrious, to get along with others, to enjoy working, to obey, to be good children, to be good pupils, to say that one is happy, to ask for excuses, to ask for forgiveness, to forgive, to praise, to caress, to embrace a child, to carry a child in one's arms, to put a child to sleep, to give water and to feed other people, to show "buena educación" (good manners), to give thanks, to respect, to express love and affection, to follow orders,

sibility of interpreting the American picture by contrast as throwing the American child back upon child values rather than adult values. American adults, especially fathers, can be seen as having abdicated their ideal roles of structuring the world for the child, of providing him with a clear set of values, or "rights" and "wrongs," and thus of leaving him with the task of deciding right and wrong long before he is willing and able to do so. This, we conceive, breeds in him, not only insecurity and anxiety, but also a deeply "justified" hostility, contempt, and resentment against the parents (especially the father), who have failed him and set him a task too great for his powers by not giving the answers, and who in effect are frustrating his deep need for a system of values, *Weltanschauung*, and for the limits and controls that these involve. Left to themselves then, we see the children, needing values and feeling the dangers of a state of valuelessness, as turning to the only other external source of values, i.e., other children, especially older ones.

What this involves we think we can communicate best by asking, "What would happen to children's security and values if all people

---

to pay attention, to listen, etc. He had to invent a new category to classify this assortment. He needed help to define it and finally called it A-4 and indicated that it implicated at least two factors: internalization of the social culture (values?) and spontaneous expressions of affect.

But the omnipresence of adult or humanistic evaluations is evident by the following example. The national commission for primary textbooks just published the announcement of a contest to select the reading books for the first and second grades. Philosophers, writers, educators, etc., form part of this commission, named by the Minister of Education, Torres Bodet. Besides the technical details of the books, it is forcefully stated that they must teach the child, through clear exemplification (especially in the paired workbook)— within the natural-science study for instance—that "I am happy when I do physical exercise, when I help my mother and my father in their chores, when I am friendly to all and have no enemies, when I am an enemy of filth and lack of order, when I help in what I can to improve my house, my school and the place where I live, when I help my neighbor or any other person that needs help" (Revista *Tiempo*, May 25, 1959). Among the goals stated about arithmetic and geometry: "To develop habits of preciseness, certainty, exactitude, self-criticism and respect to truth. . . ." Among the history and civic studies: "To become aware that understanding, tolerance, justice, respect and mutual help are the only bases of good human relations," and later, as an important goal: "respect, obedience and love among the members of the family" (*ibid.*).

J. Giraldo Angel cites (3) an unpublished study on Mexican adolescent values of Profesora Margarita Zendejas. She found that in an almost stereotyped fashion, the adolescents (men as well as women) keep completing the incomplete sentence, "The persons that I most respect are characterized . . . by being older than I am."

died at the age of twenty or so?" It seems to us clear that what must happen in such a science-fiction world would be almost exactly what now does actually happen in the juvenile-gang cultures (in the middle and upper classes as well as the lower classes) in the United States today, and what we can actually see projected before our eyes for study in the eastern cowboy movies, beautiful examples, in a classic form, of adolescent value systems (or it can be said in the Freudian language, of phallic-stage value systems).

We postulate that juvenile violence, vandalism, cruelty, defiance of authority, and war against adults is not only a matter of growth dynamics of the standard Freudian variety (trying to be grown-up, fighting one's dependency needs, counterphobic mechanisms against weakness, childishness, cowardice, etc.), but also implies a hostile and contemptuous lashing-out in understandable retaliation against the weak adults who have failed them. We feel this to be more directed toward the father than the mother, and more vehemently by boys than by girls, and would expect that the most common interpersonal attack would be attacks upon males (and everything that they represent), by boys.

To make our postulations explicit:

1. It is implied here that all human beings, including children, "need a value system," (93) "a system of understanding," (95) "a frame of orientation and devotion," (35) "the ordered demand for a conceptual grip on the universe and its meaning for us" (120).

2. The lack of such a system, or the breaking up of such a system, breeds certain psychopathologies.

3. It also releases a craving for such a system and search for values will ensue.

4. Any value system, good or bad, is preferred to the lack of system, i.e., to chaos.

5. If there is no adult value system, then a child or adolescent value system will be embraced.

6. Juvenile delinquency (so called) is an example of such an adolescent value system.

7. It is distinguished from other adolescent value systems, e.g., the cowboy world, or the college fraternity world, by the addition of hostility and contempt to the adults who have failed them.

8. We postulate that the value system, insofar as it involves principles

of law, order, justice, judgments of right and wrong, are communicated primarily by the father.

9. To the extent that he, the father, has no value system, or is uncertain or weak about it, to that extent, will his children be thrown back upon their own inadequate resources.

10. A psychologically weak (no values, no clear masculine role) father figure interferes even with the kind of primary identification (the ideal self) of which Freudians speak. As a result, the child is confused further regarding "how he should be." He grabs the ideals of the cowboy and of his equally confused peers.

11. These resources are inadequate.

Criteria for Judging
Needs to Be Instinctoid

I have approached the problem of discovering the deepest wishes, urges, and needs of the human being as Freud did rather than as the animal behaviorists have been doing (95). I have searched via the route of psychopathogenesis, reasoning backward from adult sickness to its earlier origins. My question was, What made people neurotic? Where does neurosis come from? More recently, I have asked also where do character disturbances and value distortions come from? And it has also turned out to be useful and instructive to ask where do fully human, psychologically sound people come from? Or even, what is the fullest height to which the human being can attain? And what prevents him from attaining it?

My conclusion was, speaking very generally, that neuroses, as well as other psychic illnesses, were due primarily to absence of certain gratifications (of objectively and subjectively perceivable demands or wishes). These I called basic needs and called them instinctoid because they had to be gratified or else illness (or diminution of humanness, i.e., loss of some of the characteristics that define humanness) would result. It was implied that neuroses were closer to being deficiency diseases than had been thought.[1] And it was further hypothesized that health is impossible unless these needs are gratified, i.e., basic-need gratification is a necessary, even though not a sufficient, condition.

[1] But basic-need frustrations are not the only determinants of psychopathology.

This reconstructive biological technique has a very respectable history in the biological and medical sciences. For instance, it has been used for ferreting out hidden biological needs, e.g., by the nutritionists who discovered our "instinctoid" needs for vitamins, minerals, etc. Here too the searching back started from confrontation by an illness like rickets or scurvy, whose origins were traced back to a deficiency, which was then called a "need." A "need for vitamin C" meant that this was a *sine qua non* for achieving health and avoiding sickness. This could then be checked further and the hypothesis supported by other control experiments, e.g., the prophylactic control, the replacement control, etc., tests which can also be applied to the basic psychological needs.

This appendix is an extension and improvement of my 1954 presentation, "The Instinctoid Nature of Basic Needs" (Chapter 7 in my *Motivation and Personality* [95]). In summary, the main points that I made there were:

1. The human organism has a nature of its own and is more trustworthy and more self-governing than it has been given credit for;

2. There are good reasons for postulating an intrinsic or innate tendency to growth toward self-actualization;

3. Most psychotherapists are forced to some version of instinct-like needs whose frustration results in psychopathology;

4. These needs supply him with a ready-made foundation framework of biological ends, goals, or values.

In that chapter the mistakes of older instinct theory were listed and carefully considered to see if they could be avoided. Consequent conclusions were than drawn.

1. The effort to define human instinct in behavioral terms ("actones") was foredoomed to failure. Behavior (in humans) can be, and often is, a defense *against* impulse, and expresses not impulse alone, but rather is the resultant of the impulses to action and the controls upon such impulses, and their expression. It is rather the conative element, the urge or need, which seems to give promise of being innate, in some sense, and in some degree;

2. The full animal instinct is not found in the human being. There seem to be only parts of remnants of old animal instincts, e.g., *only* urges, or *only* capacities;

3. There is no reason why human beings should not have species-

specific needs or capacities, and, in fact, there is some clinical evidence that they *do* in fact have motivations (possibly innate) which are uniquely human;

4. Instinctlike urges in the human are generally weak and not strong, as they are in animals. They are easily overcome and repressed by culture, by learning, by defensive processes. Psychoanalysis can be seen as the lengthy, laborious process of uncovering these instinctoid needs, and of permitting them to grow strong enough to resist suppression by fears and habits! That is, they need help to appear;

5. There is imbedded in most discussions of human instinctoid needs the belief that the animal in us is a bad animal, and that our most primitive impulses are only greedy, evil, selfish, destructive. This is inaccurate;

6. Instinctoid impulses in the human being can disappear altogether with disuse;

7. Instinct should not be dichotomized from learning and rationality. Reason itself is also conative. And in any case, in the good human specimen impulse and reason tend to be synergic rather than antagonistic. Furthermore, instinctoid urges are very quickly canalized to instrumental behaviors and to goals, i.e., they become "sentiments";

8. I believe much of the confusion over instinct and heredity comes from the unconscious and erroneous assumption that the hereditarian must be politically conservative or reactionary, and that the environmentalist must be liberal or progressive. While this *has* been the case it *need* not be the case. It is a mistake;

9. It was assumed that the deeper urges in man could be seen most clearly in the insane, the neurotic, the alcoholic, the animal, the feebleminded, the child. This is a mistake. They may perhaps be seen best in the *healthiest*, most evolved and matured individuals; and in such people, it can be seen that these deepest urges and needs can be "high" as well as "low," e.g., a need for truth, a need for beauty, etc.

Various criteria were then offered by which to judge the probability that a need was likely to be instinctoid in nature. It is these criteria that I wish to discuss now, along with some improvements that can be added. Also I wish to compare the applicability of each of these criteria; first, to the need for vitamins; second, to the need for love; third, to the curiosity need, and finally to neurotic needs.

You will see how close the fit is between the need for vitamins and the need for love. Deny the one, and you pretty well have to deny the other. Curiosity, or the need to know, is what I have called a growth-need (or metaneed or B-Value) in contradistinction to the deficiency-need (87, 89) because, though instinctoid in nature, it yet shows important differences from the basic needs. As for the neurotic need, it will be quite apparent that it does *not* conform to these criteria and cannot therefore be called instinctoid. Something similar could be shown for addiction-needs and for habitual or learned needs.

A need is instinctoid if:

1. The chronic lack of the satisfier produces pathology, especially if this lack occurs early in life. (But it must not be overlooked that the *transient* lack of the satisfier can also produce desirable effects, e.g., appetite, frustration-tolerance, healthy ability to delay, self-control, etc.)

Vitamins: + (+ means "true," or "it fulfills the criterion")

Love: +

Curiosity: +

Neurotic Needs: Lack of satisfier produces anxiety and other symptoms but does not produce character pathology; on the contrary, deprivation of the satisfier of a neurotic need may produce increased psychological health.

1a. Deprivation at a critical period can cause the total and permanent loss of the desire and/or of the need, possibly never to be relearned or reinstated; the person is thereby permanently diminished and has lost a defining characteristic of the human species; he is no longer fully human.

Vitamins: We do not know enough to be able to say whether this is true or not. Deprivation of the various vitamins produces differential consequences which we do not know well enough.

Love: + (as exemplified by psychopathic personalities)

Curiosity: Again we do not have enough data to be quite sure of ourselves here, but cultural data and clinical data indicate pretty clearly that curiosity itself can be lost and is often enough permanently lost in institutionalized children, for instance, who are given no satisfaction of early curiosity, e.g., dulling, contented ignorance, permanent stupidity, obscurantism, stultification, superstition, etc.

Neurotic Needs: The criterion does not apply.

1b. Direct-deprivation effects, e.g., as described by Rosenzweig (130).

Vitamins: the avitaminoses, etc.

Love: yearnings for love and love figures; the "kissing bug" reaction of D. M. Levy (70,72).

Curiosity: increased curiosity, compulsive curiosity, perseveration of curiosity, scoptophilia, etc.

Neurotic Needs: The lack of the neurotic satisfier can produce anxiety, conflict, hostility, etc., but it can also produce *relief* from conflict, *relief* from anxiety, etc.

1c. Neuroticizing of the basic need, e.g., it becomes uncontrollable, insatiable, ego-alien, rigid, inflexible, compulsive, indiscriminating, choosing wrong objects, accompanied by anxiety, etc. The attitudes toward the need become conflicted, fearful, ambivalent, rejecting. The need becomes dangerous.

Vitamins: doesn't apply (?)

Love: +

Curiosity: ? (scoptophilia?)

Neurotic Needs: −

1d. Deformations of character, of value system, and of *Weltanschauung;* warping and pathologizing of the means to the goal (93). The organism develops a coping system to deal with this lack.

Vitamins: ?

Love: +

Curiosity: + (cynicism, nihilism, boredom, mistrust, anomie, etc.)

Neurotic Needs: −

1e. Diminution of humanness; loss of defining characteristics of humanness; loss of essence; regression; blocking of growth toward self-actualization.

Vitamins: + (There tends to be a regression down the hierarchy of basic needs toward any prepotent need which is being frustrated.)

Love: +

Curiosity: +
Neurotic Needs: −

1f. Emotional reactions of various kinds, both acute and chronic, e.g., anxiety, threat, anger, depression, etc.
Vitamins: +
Love: +
Curiosity: +
Neurotic Needs: ± mixed, ambivalent, and conflicting emotions.

2. Restoration of the missing satisfier, if it is not too late, restores health (more or less) and cures illness (more or less) to the extent that the pathology is not irreversible, i.e., the replacement control, anaclitic therapy.
Vitamins: +
Love: +
Curiosity: +
Neurotic Needs: −

3. The need has intrinsic (real) satisfiers; which in fact *do* satisfy, and *only* which satisfy; canalization rather than associative or arbitrary learning. No fully satisfying sublimation or substitution is possible.
Vitamins: +
Love: +
Curiosity: +
Neurotic Needs: −

4. Suitable availablity of a "real" satisfier throughout the life span avoids pathologies, i.e., the prophylactic control.
Vitamins: +
Love: +
Curiosity: +
Neurotic Needs: −

4a. Suitable availability of a "real" satisfier throughout the life span positively helps healthy growth toward self-actualization, toward contemporary health, and goodness of personality. Gratification has good effects on organism in general and personality in particular. (See my *Motivation and Personality*, Chapter 6, "The Role of Basic-Need Gratification in Psychological Theory.")

Vitamins: +
Love: +
Curiosity: +
Neurotic Needs: −

5. The chronically need-satisfied person (the healthy person) shows no craving; his need is at optimal level; he is able to control or postpone satisfaction or to do without for a period of time; he is better able to do without for a *long* period of time than are other people; the need is accepted and enjoyed openly; there are no defenses against the need. The need is satisfiable, as a neurotic need is not.

Vitamins: +

Love: +

Curiosity: − The satisfaction of curiosity often breeds increased rather than decreased curiosity.

Neurotic Needs: − (Satisfaction of the neurotic need by a neurotic satisfier has no effect on craving except transiently.)

6. The "real" satisfier is preferred and chosen behaviorally by a healthy organism in a real free-choice situation; the healthier the individual the stronger the preferences and the more likely he is to be a "good chooser." Referred to in another way, there is a strong clinical correlation between the psychological health of the individual and the likelihood that he will prefer and choose the real satisfier of his needs rather than a false satisfier.

Vitamins: − (But there are some synthetic substances like saccharin [165] which can fool the organism.)

Love: +

Curiosity: +

Neurotic Needs: −

7. The "real" satisfier tastes good, or tastes better than false satisfiers in particular, phenomenologically describable ways, e.g., the real satisfier leaves a satisfied, contented, or happy feeling, perhaps even peak experiences or mystic experiences (even when there was no felt need, as with some underprivileged people before the real satisfier came to him for the first time, to tell him how much he had wanted it, or to tell him that this was what he had been missing all his life, etc.).

This is one source of difficulty in a final definition of the words "need" or "desire," i.e., that there is an occasional instance in which a person does not know what he is missing, and has no object for his restlessness, but knows very well *after* he has experienced the satisfaction that this was what he had wanted, desired, or needed.

Vitamins: + (But again the saccharin, certain sweet lead salts, etc., are exceptions which can fool the organism.)

Love: +

Curiosity: +

Neurotic Needs: − or? Neurotic-need gratifications may taste good, but this seems to be less frequent, not to last as long, to be mixed with other feelings, is more likely to be regretted, and to be judged differently in retrospect, etc.

8. There tends to be an open expression of the need in the early (precultural) life of the individual. Any expression of the need or of a desire before the culture could have had its say, or before learning could have taken place, generally increases the presumption that the need is instinctoid.

Vitamins: +

Love: +

Curiosity: +

Neurotic Needs: −

9. It is uncovered, accepted, approved of, and strengthened by insight therapy, uncovering therapy (or by increase in health in general), (or by "good conditions" in society), i.e., by the lifting of defenses, controls, fears.

Vitamins: + (probably)

Love: +

Curiosity: +

Neurotic Needs: −

9a. The preference for the real satisfier is increased by any improvement in physical, psychological, or social health.

Vitamins: + (probably)

Love: +

Curiosity: +

Neurotic Needs: −

10. It is crosscultural, crossclass, crosscaste. The closer it comes toward universality throughout the species, the greater the likelihood that it is instinctoid. (This is not an absolute proof because all human cultures present certain experiences to every infant. Or it must be demonstrated that the needs have been killed permanently or repressed temporarily.)

Vitamins: +
Love: +
Curiosity: +
Neurotic Needs: −

11. All those cultures or subcultures or work situations called secure, healthy, or synergic satisfy the basic needs more sufficiently and threaten them less. All insecure, sick, or low-synergy cultures, subcultures, or work situations *fail* to gratify some basic needs, threaten them, exert too heavy a price for their satisfaction, throw them into inevitable conflict with other basic-need satisfactions, etc.

Vitamins: +
Love: +
Curiosity: +
Neurotic Needs: −

12. Cross-species occurrence of needs certainly increases the probability that the need is instinctoid, but it is not a necessary criterion or a sufficient one because there are also species-specific "instincts" in *all* species including the human.

Vitamins: +
Love: +
Curiosity: +
Neurotic Needs: −

13. The need shows dynamic persistence throughout life in the manner that Freud has described (unless killed off early in life).

Vitamins: +
Love: +
Curiosity: ?
Neurotic Needs: −

14. Neuroses are discovered to be covert, fearful, compromise, timid, roundabout ways of seeking these need-gratifications.

Vitamins: ?
Love: +
Curiosity: +
Neurotic Needs: −

15. There is easier learning of appropriate instrumental behavior, and easier canalization of appropriate goal objects and goal states, etc. (121). The need itself in its beginnings must be considered to be potential rather than actual because it must be used, rehearsed, exercised, "drawn out" by a cultural representative before it is actualized. This *might* be considered a kind of learning, but I think that such a usage would be confusing. The word "learning" already carries too many meanings.

Vitamins: +
Love: +
Curiosity: +
Neurotic Needs: −

16. The need is ultimately ego-syntonic (meaning that if it is not so, it can be made so as a result of uncovering therapy).

Vitamins: +
Love: +
Curiosity: +
Neurotic Needs: − (Here the opposite is true, the need is most often felt to be ego-alien or dystonic.)

17. If everybody enjoys the need and its gratification, it is more apt to be basic and instinctoid. Neurotic, addictive, and habitual needs are enjoyed only by *some* individuals.

Vitamins: +
Love: +
Curiosity: +
Neurotic Needs: −

18. Finally, I can offer as a very tentative future possibility to think about various findings from the use of the psychedelic drugs, and perhaps other disinhibiting drugs as well, e.g., alcohol. It may be that inhibiting the highest control centers, as alcohol does, may release the more intrinsically biological and noncultural aspects of the

personality, i.e., the deeper core-self. I detect some such possibilities from the work with LSD. (This is *not* the Freudian superego which is rather a set of arbitrary social controls imposed *upon* the biological or intrinsic organism, and which inhibit its functioning.)

I have not referred to two criteria which have been used by others because they do not seem to me to differentiate successfully biological needs, from neurotic needs, learned needs, or addictive needs; a) the willingness to face pain or discomfort for the gratification in question; b) arousal of pugnacity or anxiety upon frustration.

I have confined myself to species-wide instinctoid characteristics, and have said nothing of the innate idiosyncratic individuality which is so crucial for the psychotherapist and the personality theorist. Though the immediate goal of psychotherapy may be the recovery of specieshood, of healthy animality, it is still true that a basic *far* goal of psychotherapy is the recovery of identity (of the individual person), of real-self, of authenticity, individuation, self-realization, etc. That is, it is the effort to discover the natural bent of the person, his innate individuality, the answers to life problems which are subtly suggested to him (*not* dictated forcefully) by his constitution, his temperament, his nervous system, his endocrine system, in a word, his body and its preferred ways of functioning, his "biological destiny," the direction in which his greatest and easiest happiness is to be sought. Here we concern ourselves with the special talents and capacities not only of the Mozarts, but also of more ordinary people. Vocational guidance, for instance, ultimately involves, in theory if not in practice, the innate capacities which are unique to this particular person.

Perhaps one day the clinical intuitions upon which we must rely so heavily in the absence of better data may be tested and systematized in a more reliable way. As therapists, we try to discover what is easier for the person to do, what fits his nature best and suits him most comfortably (as a shoe fits well or badly), what feels "right" for him, what strains and presses him least, what he is best suited *for*, what is most in conformity with his particular personality. (These are what Goldstein [39] has called "preferred behaviors.") We can ask the same questions as experimenters. We have already learned how to ask such questions fruitfully of different breeds of dogs, as at the Jackson Laboratories. Perhaps one day, we shall be able to do as well for human beings.

Furthermore, in order to concentrate on the main point I wish to make, I have omitted from consideration all the more direct biological techniques of the human geneticist (twin studies, direct micro-study of genes, etc.), of the experimental embryologist, and of the neurophysiologist (electrode-implantation studies, etc.), as well as the rich literatures of animal behavior, of child and developmental psychology.

Such an integration is urgently needed to tie together the two great sets of data which today have so little contact with each other, i.e., the biological-behavioral-ethological on the one hand, and the psychodynamic on the other hand. That this task can be achieved, I have no doubt. (We already have at least one such effort that I know about, namely, Kortlandt's brilliant monograph [63].)

Most of what I have presented here is based on clinical evidence and experience, and is therefore not nearly as reliable as evidence from controlled experimentation. However, it is mostly cast in such a form as to be susceptible of experimental confirming or disconfirming.

Abraham H. Maslow: A Bibliography

1932

Delayed reaction tests on primates from the lemur to the orangoutan. (With Harry Harlow and Harold Uehling.) *Journal of Comparative Psychology*, 13: 313-343.

Delayed reaction tests on primates at Bronx Park Zoo. (With Harry Harlow.) *Journal of Comparative Psychology*, 14: 97-101.

The "emotion of disgust in dogs." *Journal of Comparative Psychology*, 14: 401-407.

1933

Food preferences of primates. *Journal of Comparative Psychology*, 16: 187-197.

1934

Influence of differential motivation on delayed reactions in monkeys. (With Elizabeth Groshong.) *Journal of Comparative Psychology*, 18: 75-83.

The effect of varying external conditions on learning, retention and reproduction. *Journal of Experimental Psychology*, 17: 36-47.

The effect of varying time intervals between acts of learning with a note on proactive inhibition. *Journal of Experimental Psychology*, 17: 141-144.

1935

Appetites and hungers in animal motivation. *Journal of Comparative Psychology*, 20: 75-83.

Individual psychology and the social behavior of monkeys and apes. *International Journal of Individual Psychology*, 1: 47-59. Reprinted in German translation in *Internationale Zeitschrift für Individual Psychologie*, 1936, 1: 14-25.

1936

The role of dominance in the social and sexual behavior of infrahuman primates. I: Observations at Vilas Park Zoo. *Journal of Genetic Psychology*, 48: 261-277.

Part II: An experimental determination of the dominance-behavior syndrome. (With Sydney Flanzbaum.) *Journal of Genetic Psychology*, 48: 278-309. Reprinted in W. Dennis (Ed.), *Readings in general psychology*. New York: Prentice-Hall, 1949.

III: A Theory of sexual behavior of infrahuman primates. *Journal of Genetic Psychology*, 48: 310-338.

IV: The determination of hierarchy in pairs and in groups. *Journal of Genetic Psychology*, 49: 161-198.

1937

The comparative approach to social behavior. *Social Forces*, 15: 487-490.

The influence of familiarization on preferences. *Journal of Experimental Psychology*, 21: 162-180.

Dominance feeling, behavior and status. *Psychological Review*, 44: 404-420.

Personality and patterns of culture. In R. Stagner, *Psychology of personality*. New York: McGraw-Hill. Reprinted in S. Britt (Ed.), *Selected readings in social psychology*. New York: Rinehart, 1950.

An experimental study of insight in monkeys. (With Walter Grether.) *Journal of Comparative Psychology*, 24: 127-134.

1939

Dominance-feeling, personality and social behavior in women. *Journal of Social Psychology*, 10: 3-39.

1940

Dominance-quality and social behavior in infrahuman primates. *Journal of Social Psychology*, 11: 313-324.

A test for dominance-feeling (self-esteem) in college women. *Journal of Social Psychology*, 12: 255-270.

1941

Principles of abnormal psychology: The dynamics of psychic illness. (With Bela Mittelmann.) New York: Harper & Bros. Recorded as Talking Book for the Blind.

Deprivation, threat and frustration. *Psychological Review*, 48: 364-366. Reprinted in T. Newcomb and E. Hartley (Eds.), *Readings in social psychology*. New York: Holt, 1947. Reprinted in M. Marx (Ed.), *Psychological theory: contemporary readings*. New York: Macmillan, 1951. Reprinted in C. Stacy and M. DeMartino (Eds.), *Understanding human motivation*. Cleveland: Howard Allen Publishers, 1958.

1942

Liberal leadership and personality. *Freedom*, 2: 27-30.

The social personality inventory for college women. Palo Alto, Calif.: Consulting Psychologists Press.

The dynamics of psychological security-insecurity. *Character and Personality*, 10: 331-344.

A comparative approach to the problem of destructiveness. *Psychiatry*, 5: 517-522.

Self-esteem (dominance-feeling) and sexuality in women. *Journal of Social Psychology*, 16: 259-294. Reprinted in M. DeMartino (Ed.), *Sexual behavior and personality characteristics*. New York: Citadel Press, 1963. Reprinted in H. M. Ruitenbeek (Ed.), *Psychoanalysis and female sexuality*. New Haven: College and University Press, 1966.

1943

A preface to motivation theory. *Psychosomatic Medicine*, 5: 85-92.

A theory of human motivation. *Psychological Review*, 50: 370-396.

Reprinted in P. Harriman (Ed.), *Twentieth century psychology.* New York: Philosophical Library, 1946. Reprinted in H. Remmers, *et al.* (Eds.), *Growth, teaching and learning.* New York: Harper & Bros., 1957. Reprinted in C. Stacy and M. DeMartino (Eds.), *Understanding human motivation.* Cleveland: Howard Allen Publishers, 1958. Reprinted in W. Lazer and E. Kelly (Eds.), *Managerial marketing.* Homewood, Ill.: Richard Irwin, 1958. Reprinted in W. Baller (Ed.), *Readings in psychology of human growth and development.* New York: Holt, Rinehart & Winston, 1962. Reprinted in J. Seidman (Ed.), *The child.* New York: Rinehart, 1958. Reprinted in L. Gorlow and W. Katkowsky (Eds.), *Readings in the psychology of adjustment.* New York: McGraw-Hill, 1959. Reprinted in I. Heckman and S. Hunryager (Eds.), *Human relations in management.* Cincinnati: South-Western Publishing Co., 1960. Reprinted in P. Hountras (Ed.), *Mental hygiene: A text of readings.* Columbus, Ohio: Merrill, 1961. Reprinted in J. A. Dyal (Ed.), *Readings in psychology: Understanding human behavior.* New York: McGraw-Hill, 1962. Reprinted in T. Costello and S. Zalkind (Eds.), *Psychology in administration: A research orientation.* Englewood Cliffs, N.J.: Prentice-Hall, 1963. Reprinted in R. Sutermeister (Ed.), *People and productivity.* New York: McGraw-Hill, 1963. Reprinted in H. J. Leavitt and L. R. Pondy (Eds.), *Readings in managerial psychology.* University of Chicago Press, 1964. Reprinted in J. Reykowski (Ed.), *Problemy Osobowosci I Motywacji W Psychologii Amerykanskiej.* Warsaw: Panstwowe Wydawnictwo Naokowe, 1964. Reprinted in D. E. Hamachek (Ed.), *The self in growth, teaching and learning.* Englewood Cliffs, N.J.: Prentice-Hall, 1965. Reprinted in Bobbs-Merrill Reprint Series, 1966. Reprinted in Y. Ferreira Balcao and L. Leite Cordeiro (Eds.), *O Comportamento Humano Na Empresa, Fundação Getulio Vargas.* Rio de Janeiro, 1967. Reprinted in M. S. Wadia (Ed.), *Management and the behavioral sciences.* Boston: Allyn & Bacon, 1968. Reprinted in H. Kassarjian and T. Robertson (Eds.), *Perspectives in consumer behavior.* Glenview, Ill.: Scott, Foresman, 1968. Reprinted in D. Hampton, C. Summer, R. Weber (Eds.), *Organizational behavior and the practice of management.* Glenview, Ill.: Scott, Foresman, 1968. Reprinted in R. G. Brown, R. Newell, and H. G. Vonk

(Eds.), *Behavioral implications for curriculum and teaching.* Dubuque, Iowa: W. C. Brown Book Co., 1969. Reprinted in S. Frey and E. Haugen (Eds.), *Readings in learning.* New York: American Book Co., 1969. Reprinted in L. D. Grebstein (Ed.), *Toward self-understanding: Studies in personality and adjustment.* Glenview, Ill.: Scott, Foresman, 1969.

Conflict, frustration and the theory of threat. *Journal of Abnormal and Social Psychology*, 38: 81-86. Reprinted in S. Tomkins (Ed.), *Contemporary psychopathology: A sourcebook.* Cambridge, Mass.: Harvard University Press, 1943.

The dynamics of personality organization: I & II. *Psychological Review*, 50: 514-539; 541-558.

The authoritarian character structure. *Journal of Social Psychology*, 18: 401-411. Reprinted in P. Harriman (Ed.), *Twentieth century psychology: Recent developments in psychology.* New York: Philosophical Library, 1946. Reprinted in R. S. Ross (Ed.), *Speech-communication.* Englewood Cliffs, N.J.: Prentice-Hall.

1944

What intelligence tests mean. *Journal of General Psychology*, 31: 85-93.

1945

A clinically derived test for measuring psychological security-insecurity. *Journal of General Psychology*, 33: 21-41. (With E. Birsh, M. Stein, and I. Honigman.)

A suggested improvement in semantic usage. *Psychological Review*, 52: 239-240. Reprinted in *Etc., A Journal of General Semantics*, 1947, 4: 219-220.

Experimentalizing the clinical method. *Journal of Clinical Psychology*, 1: 241-243.

1946

Security and breast feeding. *Journal of Abnormal and Social Psychology*, 41: 83-85. (With I. Szilagyi-Kessler.)

Problem-centering vs. means-centering in science. *Philosophy of Science*, 13, 326-331.

1947

A symbol for holistic thinking. *Persona*, 1: 24-25.

1948

"Higher" and "lower" needs. *Journal of Psychology*, 25: 433-436. Reprinted in C. Stacy and M. DeMartino (Eds.), *Understanding human motivation*. Cleveland: Howard Allen Publishers, 1958. Reprinted in K. Schultz (Ed.), *Applied dynamic psychology*. Berkeley: University of California Press, 1958.

Cognition of the particular and the generic. *Psychological Review*, 55: 22-40.

Some theoretical consequences of basic-need gratification. *Journal of Personality*, 16: 402-416.

1949

Our maligned animal nature. *Journal of Psychology*, 28: 273-278. Reprinted in S. Koenig *et al.* (Eds.), *Sociology: A book of readings*. New York: Prentice-Hall, 1953.

The expressive component of behavior. *Psychology Review*, 56: 261-272. Condensed in *Digest of neurology and psychiatry*, Jan., 1950. Reprinted in Howard Brand (Ed.), *The study of personality: A book of readings*. New York: John Wiley, 1954.

1950

Self-actualizing people: a study of psychological health. *Personality Symposia:* Symposium #1 on Values. New York: Grune & Stratton, pp. 11-34. Reprinted in C. Moustakas (Ed.), *The self*. New York: Harper & Bros., 1956. Reprinted in G. B. Levitas (Ed.), *The world of psychology*. New York: George Braziller, 1963. Reprinted in C. G. Kemp (Ed.), *Perspectives on the group process*. Boston: Houghton Mifflin, 1964.

1951

Social theory of motivation. In M. Shore (Ed.), *Twentieth century mental hygiene*. New York: Social Science Publishers. Reprinted in K. Zerfoss (Ed.), *Readings in counseling*. New York: Association Press, 1952.

Personality. In H. Helson (Ed.), *Theoretical foundations of psychology*. New York: Van Nostrand. (With D. MacKinnon.)

Higher needs and personality. *Dialectica* (University of Liege), 5: 257-265.

Resistance to acculturation. *Journal of Social Issues*, 7: 26-29.

Principles of abnormal psychology (Rev. Ed.). New York: Harper & Bros. (With B. Mittelmann.) Recorded as Talking Book for the Blind. Chapter 16 reprinted in C. Thompson *et al.* (Eds.), *An outline of psychoanalysis*. New York: Modern Library, 1955.

1952

Volunteer-error in the Kinsey study. (With J. Sakoda.) *Journal of Abnormal and Social Psychology*, 47: 259-262. Reprinted in J. Himelhock and S. Fava (Eds.), *Sexual behavior in American society*. New York: W. W. Norton, 1955.

The S-I Test (A measure of psychological security-insecurity). Palo Alto, Calif.: Consulting Psychologists Press. Spanish translation, 1961, Instituto de Pedagogia, Universidad de Madrid. Polish translation, 1963.

1953

Love in healthy people. In A. Montagu (Ed.), *The meaning of love*. New York: Julian Press, pp. 57-93. Reprinted in M. DeMartino (Ed.), *Sexual behavior and personality characteristics*. New York: Citadel Press, 1963.

College teaching ability, scholarly activity and personality. *Journal of Educational Psychology*, 47: 185-189. Reprinted in *Case book: Education beyond the high school*. (With W. Zimmerman.) Vol. 1. Washington, D.C.: U.S. Department of Health, Education, and Welfare, 1958.

1954

The instinctoid nature of basic needs. *Journal of Personality*, 22: 326-347.

Motivation and personality. New York: Harper & Bros. Spanish translation, Barcelona: Sagitario, 1963. Selections reprinted in W. Sahakian (Ed.), *Psychology of personality: Readings in theory.* Chicago: Rand McNally, 1965. Japanese translation, Tanki Daigaku, Sangyo Noritsu, 1967.

Abnormal psychology. *National encyclopedia.*

Normality, health and values. *Main Currents,* 10: 75-81.

1955

Deficiency motivation and growth motivation. In M. R. Jones (Ed.), *Nebraska symposium on motivation: 1955.* Lincoln, Nebr.: University of Nebraska Press. Reprinted in *General Semantics Bulletin,* 1956, 18 and 19: 33-42. Reprinted in J. Coleman, *Personality dynamics and effective behavior.* Glenview, Ill.: Scott, Foresman, 1960. Reprinted in J. A. Dyal (Ed.), *Readings in psychology: understanding human behavior.* New York: McGraw-Hill, 1962. Reprinted in R. C. Teevan and R. C. Birney (Eds.), *Theories of motivation in personal and social psychology.* Princeton, N.J.: Van Nostrand, 1964.

Comments on Professor McClelland's paper. In M. R. Jones (Ed.), *Nebraska symposium on motivation, 1955.* Lincoln, Nebr.: University of Nebraska Press, pp. 65-69.

Comments on Professor Old's paper. In M. R. Jones (Ed.), *Nebraska symposium on motivation, 1955.* Lincoln, Nebr.: University of Nebraska Press. pp. 143-147.

1956

Effects of esthetic surroundings: I. Initial effects of three esthetic conditions upon perceiving "energy" and "well-being" in faces. (With N. Mintz.) *Journal of Psychology,* 41: 247-254. Reprinted in D. C. Barnlund (Ed.), *Interpersonal communication.* Boston: Houghton Mifflin, 1968.

Personality problems and personality growth. In C. Moustakas (Ed.), *The self.* New York: Harper & Bros. Reprinted in J. Coleman, F. Libaw and W. Martinson, *Success in college.* Glenview, Ill.: Scott, Foresman, 1961. Reprinted in F. Matson (Ed.), *Being, becoming and behavior.* New York: George Braziller, 1967.

Reprinted in D. Hamachek (Ed.), *Human dynamics in psychology and education*. Boston: Allyn & Bacon, 1968.

Defense and growth. *Merrill-Palmer Quarterly*, 3: 36-47. Reprinted in T. Millon (Ed.), *Theories of psychopathology*. Philadelphia: W. B. Saunders, 1967.

A philosophy of psychology. *Main Currents*, 13: 27-32. Reprinted in *Etc.*, 1957, 14: 10-22. Reprinted in J. Fairchild (Ed.), *Personal problems and psychological frontiers*. New York: Sheridan House, 1957. Reprinted in *Manas*, 1958, 11, Nos. 17 & 18. Reprinted in S. I. Hayakawa (Ed.), *Our language and our world*. New York: Harper & Bros., 1959. Reprinted in L. Hamalian and E. Volpe (Eds.), *Essays of our times*. New York: McGraw-Hill, 1963. Reprinted in *Human Growth Institute Buzz Sheet*, 1964. Reprinted in F. T. Severin (Ed.), *Humanistic viewpoints in psychology*. New York: McGraw-Hill, 1965. Reprinted in *Forum for Correspondence and Contact*, 1968, 1: 12-23. Translated into Urdu in *Fikr-O-Nazar*. India: Muslim University of Alibarh, 1968.

1957

Power relationships and patterns of personal development. In A. Kornhauser (Ed.), *Problems of power in American democracy*. Detroit: Wayne University Press.

Security of judges as a factor in impressions of warmth in others. (With J. Bossom.) *Journal of Abnormal and Social Psychology*, 55: 147-148.

Two kinds of cognition and their integration. *General Semantics Bulletin*, 20 & 21: 17-22. Reprinted in *New Era in Home and School*, 1958, 39: 202-205.

1958

Emotional blocks to creativity. *Journal of Individual Psychology*, 14: 51-56. Reprinted in *Electro-Mechanical Design*, 2, 66-72. Reprinted in *The Humanist*, 1958, 18: 325-332. Reprinted in *Best articles and stories*, 1959, 3: 23-35. Reprinted in S. Parnes and H. Harding (Eds.), *A source book for creative thinking*. New York: Charles Scribner's Sons, 1962. Reprinted in *Humanitas*, 1966, 3: 289-294.

1959

Psychological data and human values. In A. H. Maslow (Ed.), *New knowledge in human values*. New York: Harper & Bros. Reprinted in B. J. Ard, Jr. (Ed.), *Counseling and psychotherapy: Classics on theories and issues*. Palo Alto, Calif.: Science and Behavior Books, 1966.

Editor, *New knowledge in human values*. New York: Harper & Bros. Hebrew translation, Tel Aviv, Israel: Daga Books, 1968. Paperback edition, Chicago: Regnery, 1970.

Creativity in self-actualizing people. In H. H. Anderson (Ed.), *Creativity and its cultivation*. New York: Harper & Bros. Reprinted in *Electro-Mechanical Design*, 1959 (January and August). Reprinted in *General Semantics Bulletin*, 1959, 24 & 25: 45-50. Reprinted in L. Nelson and B. Psaltis (Eds.), *Fostering creativity*, S.A.R., 1967.

Cognition of being in the peak experiences. *Journal of Genetic Psychology*, 94: 43-66. Reprinted in *International Journal of Parapsychology*, 1960, 2: 23-54. Reprinted in B. Stoodley (Ed.), *Society and self: A reader in social psychology*. New York: Free Press, 1962. Reprinted in W. Fullager, H. Lewis and C. Cumbee (Eds.), *Readings in educational psychology*. (2nd Ed.) New York: Crowell, 1964. Reprinted in D. E. Hamachek (Ed.), *The self in growth, teaching and learning*. Englewood Cliffs, N.J.: Prentice-Hall, 1965.

Mental health and religion. In *Religion, science and mental health*. Academy of Religion and Mental Health, New York University Press.

Critique of self-actualization; I: Some dangers of Being-cognition, *Journal of Individual Psychology*, 15: 24-32.

1960

Juvenile delinquency as a value disturbance. (With R. Díaz-Guerrero.) In J. Peatman and E. Hartley (Eds.), *Festschrift for Gardner Murphy*. New York: Harper & Bros.

Remarks on existentialism and psychology. *Existentialist Inquiries*, 1: 1-5. Reprinted in *Religious Inquiry*, No. 28: 4-7. Reprinted in R. May (Ed.), *Existential Psychology*. New York: Random House,

1961 (Japanese translation, 1965). Reprinted in D. E. Hamachek (Ed.), *The self in growth, teaching and learning.* Englewood Cliffs, N.J.: Prentice-Hall, 1965.

Resistance to being rubricized. In B. Kaplan and S. Wapner (Eds.), *Perspectives in psychological theory, essays in honor of Heinz Werner.* New York: International Universities Press.

Some parallels between the dominance and sexual behavior of monkeys and the fantasies of patients in psychotherapy. (With H. Rand and S. Newman). *Journal of Nervous and Mental Disease,* 131: 202-12. Reprinted in M. DeMartino (Ed.), *Sexual behavior and personality characteristics.* New York: Citadel Press, 1963. Reprinted in W. Bennis, *et al., Interpersonal dynamics* (2nd Ed.) Homewood, Ill.: Dorsey, 1968.

1961

Health as transcendence of the environment. *Journal of Humanistic Psychology,* No.1: 1-7. Reprinted in *Pastoral Psychology,* 1968, 19: 45-49.

Peak experience as acute identity experiences. *American Journal of Psychoanalysis,* 21: 254-260. Reprinted in A. Combs (Ed.), *Personality theory and counseling practice.* Gainesville: University of Florida Press, 1961. Digested in *Digest of neurology and psychiatry,* 1961, p. 439. Reprinted in C. Gordon and K. Gergen (Eds.), *The self in social interaction,* Vol. I. New York: John Wiley, 1968.

Eupsychia—The good society. *Journal of Humanistic Psychology,* 1, No. 2: 1-11.

Are our publications and conventions suitable for the Personal Sciences? *American Psychologist,* 16: 318-319. Reprinted in *WBSI Report,* No. 8, 1962. Reprinted in *General Semantics Bulletin,* 1962, 28 & 29, 92-93. Reprinted in A. A. Hitchcock (Ed.), *Guidance and the utilization of new educational media: Report of 1962 conference.* Washington, D.C.: American Personnel and Guidance Association, 1967.

Comments on Skinner's attitude to science. *Daedalus,* 90: 572-573.

Some frontier problems in mental health. In A. Combs (Ed.), *Personality theory and counseling practice.* Gainesville: University of Florida Press.

Summary Comments: Symposium on Human Values. In L. Solomon (Ed.), *WBSI Report*, No. 17, 1961, 41-44. Reprinted in *Journal of Humanistic Psychology*, 2, No. 2: 110-111.

1962

Some basic propositions of a growth and self-actualization psychology. In A. Combs (Ed.), *Perceiving, behaving, becoming: A new focus for education. 1962 Yearbook of Association for Supervision and Curriculum Development*, Washington, D.C. Reprinted in C. Stacy and M. DeMartino (Eds.), *Understanding human motivation*. (Rev. Ed.) Cleveland: Howard Allen, 1963. Reprinted in G. Lindzey and L. Hall (Eds.), *Theories of personality: Primary sources and research*. New York: John Wiley, 1965. Reprinted in B. J. Ard, Jr. (Ed.), *Counseling and psychotherapy: Classics on theories and issues*. Palo Alto, Calif.: Science and Behavior Books, 1966. Reprinted in W. Sahakian (Ed.), *History of psychology: A source book*. Itasca, Ill.: F. E. Peacock, 1968.

Toward a psychology of being. Princeton, N.J.: Van Nostrand. Preface reprinted in *General Semantics Bulletin*, 1962, 28 & 29: 117-118. Japanese translation, Tokyo: Charles E. Tuttle Co., 1964 (Y. Ueda, translator).

Book review: John Schaar, Escape from Authority. *Humanist*, 22: 34-35.

Lessons from the peak experiences. *Journal of Humanistic Psychology*, 2, No. 1: 9-18. Reprinted as *WBSI Report*, No. 6, 1962. Digested in *Digest of Neurology and psychiatry*, 1962, p. 340. Reprinted in *Turning On*, 1963, No. 2. Reprinted in R. Farson (Ed.), *Science and human affairs*. Palo Alto, Calif.: Science and Behavior Books, Inc., 1965.

Notes on Being-Psychology. *Journal of Humanistic Psychology*, 2: 47-71. Reprinted in *WBSI Report*, No. 7, 1962. Reprinted in H. Ruitenbeek (Ed.), *Varieties of personality theory*. New York: E. P. Dutton, 1964. Reprinted in A. Sutich and M. Vich (Eds.), *Readings in humanistic psychology*. New York: Free Press, 1969.

Was Adler a disciple of Freud? A note. *Journal of Individual Psychology*, 18: 125.

Summer notes on social psychology of industry and management.

Delmar, Calif.: Non-Linear Systems, Inc., 1962. Edited and improved revision published as *Eupsychian management: A journal.* Homewood, Ill.: Irwin-Dorsey, 1965.

1963

The need to know and the fear of knowing. *Journal of General Psychology*, 68: 111-124. Reprinted in H. J. Peters and M. J. Bathroy (Eds.), *School counseling: Perspectives and procedures.* Itasca, Ill.: F. E. Peacock, 1968. Reprinted in D. Lester (Ed.), *Explorations in exploration.* New York: Van Nostrand–Reinhold, 1969.

The creative attitude. *The Structurist*, No. 3: 4-10. Reprinted as a separate by *Psychosynthesis Foundation*, 1963. Reprinted in the *Ethical Forum*, 1966, No. 5. Reprinted in R. Mooney and T. Razik (Eds.), *Explorations in creativity.* New York: Harper & Row, 1967.

Fusions of facts and values. *American Journal of Psychoanalysis*, 23: 117-131. Reprinted in *The Ethical Forum*, 1966, No. 5.

Criteria for judging needs to be instinctoid. *Proceedings of 1963 International Congress of Psychology.* Amsterdam: North-Holland Publishers, 1964, pp. 86-87.

Further notes on the Psychology of Being. *Journal of Humanistic Psychology*, 3, No. 1: 120-135.

Notes on innocent cognition. In L. Schenk-Danzinger and H. Thomas (Eds.), *Gegenwartsprobleme der Entwicklungspsychologie: Festschrift für Charlotte-Bühler.* Gottingen: Verlag für Psychologie, 1963. Reprinted in *Explorations*, 1964, 1: 2-8.

The scientific study of values. *Proceedings 7th Congress of Interamerican Society of Psychology.* Mexico, D.F., 1963.

Notes on unstructured groups. *Human Relations Training News*, 7: 1-4.

1964

The superior person. *Trans-action*, 1: 10-13.

Religions, values, and peak-experiences. Columbus, Ohio: Ohio State University Press. Chap. 3 reprinted in *The Buzz Sheet*, Dec. 1964. Paperback edition, New York: The Viking Press, 1970.

Synergy in the society and in the individual. (With L. Gross.) *Journal of Individual Psychology*, 20, 153-164. Reprinted in *Humanitas*, 1964, 1: 161-172. Reprinted in M. C. Katz, *Sciences of man and social ethics*. Boston: Branden Press, 1969.

Further notes on the Psychology of Being. *Journal of Humanistic Psychology*, 4, No. 1: 45-58.

Preface to Japanese translation of *Toward a psychology of being*. Tokyo: Seishin-Shobo.

1965

Observing and reporting education experiments. *Humanist*, 25: 13.

Foreword to Andras Angyal, *Neurosis and treatment: A holistic theory*. New York: John Wiley, pp. v-vii.

The need for creative people. *Personnel Administration*, 28: 3-5; 21-22.

Critique and discussion. In J. Money (Ed.), *Sex research: New Developments*. New York: Holt, Rinehart & Winston, pp. 135-143; 144-146.

Humanistic science and transcendent experiences. *Journal of Humanistic Psychology*, 5, No. 2: 219-227. Reprinted in *Manas*, July 28, 1965, 18, 1-8. Reprinted in *Challenge*, 1965, 21 & 22. Reprinted in *American Journal of Psychoanalysis*, 1966, 26: 149-155. Reprinted in E. P. Torrance and W. F. White (Eds.), *Issues and advances in educational psychology*. Itasca, Ill.: F. E. Peacock, 1969.

Criteria for judging needs to be instinctoid. In M. R. Jones (Ed.), *Human motivation: A symposium*. Lincoln, Nebr.: University of Nebraska Press, pp. 33-47.

Eupsychian management: A journal. Homewood, Ill.: Irwin-Dorsey. Japanese translation, Tokyo: Charles E. Tuttle Co., 1967.

Art judgment and the judgment of others. A preliminary study. (With R. Morant.) *Journal of Clinical Psychology*, 21: 389-391.

1966

Isomorphic interrelationships between knower and known. In G. Kepes (Ed.), *Sign, image, symbol*. New York: George Braziller. Reprinted in F. W. Matson and A. Montagu (Eds.), *The human dialogue: Perspectives on communication.* New York: Free Press, 1966.

The psychology of science: A reconnaissance. New York: Harper & Row. Paperback edition, Chicago: Regnery, 1969.

Toward a psychology of religious awareness. *Explorations*, 9: 23-41.

Comments on Dr. Frankl's paper. *Journal of Humanistic Psychology*, 6, No. 2: 107-112. Reprinted in A. Sutich and M. Vich (Eds.), *Readings in humanistic psychology.* New York: Free Press, 1969.

1967

Neurosis as a failure of personal growth. *Humanitas*, 3: 153-169. Reprinted in *Religious Humanism*, 1968, 2: 61-64. Reprinted in W. Bennis, *et al.* (Eds.), *Interpersonal Dynamics.* (2nd Ed.) Homewood, Ill.: Dorsey, 1968.

Synanon and Eupsychia. *Journal of Humanistic Psychology*, 7, No. 1: 28-35. Reprinted in H. Ruitenbeek (Ed.), *Group Therapy Today.* New York: Atherton, 1969.

Preface to Japanese translation of *Eupsychian management.*

A theory of metamotivation: The biological rooting of the value-life. *Journal of Humanistic Psychology*, 7, No. 2: 93-127. Reprinted in *The Humanist*, 1967, 27: 83-84; 127-129. Condensed in *Psychology Today*, 1968, 2: 38-39; 58-61. Reprinted in P. Kurtz (Ed.), *Moral problems in contemporary society: Essays in humanistic ethics.* Englewood Cliffs, N.J.: Prentice-Hall, 1969. Reprinted in A. Sutich and M. Vich (Eds.), *Readings in humanistic psychology.* New York: Free Press, 1969. Reprinted in *Humanitas*, 1969, 4: 301-343. Reprinted in H. M. Chiang and A. H. Maslow (Eds.), *The healthy personality: Readings.* New York: Van Nostrand–Reinhold, 1969. Reprinted in Bobbs-Merrill Reprint Series in Psychology, 1970.

Dialogue on communication. (With E. M. Drews.) In A. Hitchcock (Ed.), *Guidance and the utilization of New Educational media: Report of the 1962 Conference.* Washington, D.C.: American Personnel and Guidance Association, pp. 1-47; 63-68.

Foreword to Japanese translation of *Motivation and personality.*

Self-actualizing and beyond. In J. F. Bugental (Ed.), *Challenges of humanistic psychology.* New York: McGraw-Hill. Reprinted in D. Hamachek (Ed.), *Human dynamics in psychology and education.* Boston: Allyn and Bacon, 1968.

1968

Music education and peak experiences. *Music Educators Journal,* 54: 72-75; 163-171. Reprinted in *The arts and education: A new beginning in higher education.* New York: Twentieth Century Fund, 1969.

Human potentialities and the healthy society. In H. Otto (Ed.), *Human potentialities.* St. Louis, Mo.: Warren H. Green, Inc.

The new science of man. In papers on *"The human potential."* New York: Twentieth Century Fund.

Toward a psychology of being. (2nd Ed.) Princeton, N.J.: Van Nostrand. Italian translation. Rome: Ubaldini Editore, 1970.

Conversation with Abraham H. Maslow. *Psychology Today,* 2: 35-37; 54-57.

Toward the study of violence. In L. Ng (Ed.), *Alternatives to violence.* New York: Time-Life Books.

Some educational implications of the humanistic psychologies. *Harvard Educational Review,* 38: 685-696. Reprinted in *Forum for Correspondence and Contact,* 1969, 2: 43-52. Reprinted in *California Elementary Administrator,* 1969, 32: 23-29. Reprinted in *Reflections,* 1969, 4: 1-13.

Goals of humanistic education. *Esalen Papers.* Big Sur, Calif.: Esalen Institute, pp. 1-24.

Maslow and Self-actualization. (Film.) Santa Ana, Calif.: Psychological Films.

Some fundamental questions that face the normative social psychologist. *Journal of Humanistic Psychology,* 8, No. 2: 143-154.

Eupsychian network. Mimeographed.

1969

The farther reaches of human nature. *Journal of Transpersonal Psychology,* 1, No. 1: 1-9. Reprinted in *Psychological Scene* (South Africa), 1968, 2: 14-16. Reprinted in *Philosophical Research and Analysis,* 1970, 3: 2-5.

Theory Z. *Journal of Transpersonal Psychology*, 1, No. 2: 31-47.

Various meanings of transcendence. *Journal of Transpersonal Psychology*, 1, No. 1: 56-66. Reprinted in *Pastoral Psychology*, 1968, 19, No. 188: 45-49.

A holistic approach to creativity. In C. W. Taylor (Ed.), *A climate for creativity: Reports of the Seventh National Research Conference on Creativity, University of Utah, Dec., 1968*. Salt Lake City, Utah.

The healthy personality: Readings. (With Hung-Min Chiang.) New York: Van Nostrand–Reinhold.

Notice biographique et bibliographique. *Revue de Psychologie Appliquée*, 18: 167-173.

Toward a humanistic biology. *American Psychologist*, 24: 724-735.

Humanistic education vs. professional education. *New Directions in Teaching*, No. 2: 6-8.

1970

Motivation and personality. (Rev. Ed.) New York: Harper & Row.

Humanistic education vs. professional education. *New Directions in Teaching*, No. 2: 3-10.

Bibliography

1. ABRAMSON, H. (ed.). *The Use of LSD in Psychotherapy.* New York: Josiah Macy Foundation, 1961.
2. ALLPORT, G. *The Individual and His Religion.* New York: Macmillan, 1950.
3. ANGEL, J. G. *La Adolescencia, del Vivir al Existir.* Unpublished doctoral dissertation. Universidad Nacional de México, Mexico, D.F., 1957.
4. ANGYAL, A. *Neurosis and Treatment: A Holistic Theory.* New York: John Wiley, 1965.
5. ———. *Foundations for a Science of Personality*, Cambridge, Mass.: Commonwealth Fund, 1941.
6. ARDREY, R. *The Territorial Imperative.* New York: Atheneum Press, 1966.
7. ASCH, S. *Social Psychology.* New York: Prentice-Hall, 1952.
8. ASSAGIOLI, R. *Psychosynthesis: A Manual of Principles and Techniques.* New York: Hobbs, Dorman, 1965; paperback ed., New York: The Viking Press, 1971.
9. BENEDICT, R. Synergy: Patterns of the good culture. *American Anthropologist*, 1970, 72: 320-333.
10. ———. *Patterns of Culture*, Boston: Houghton Mifflin, 1934.
11. BENNETT, E., DIAMOND, M., KRECH, D., and ROSENZWEIG, M. Chemical and anatomical plasticity of brain. *Science*, 1964, 146: 610-619.
12. BERMUDEZ, E. *La Vida Familiar del Mexicano.* Mexico, D.F.: Ed. Antiqua Libreria Robredo, 1955.
13. BOSSOM, J., and MASLOW, A. H. Security of judges as a factor in impressions of warmth in others. *Journal of Abnormal and Social Psychology*, 1957, 55: 147-148.
14. BOWLBY, J. *Maternal Care and Mental Health.* Geneva: World Health Organization, 1952.

15. BRADEN, W. *The Private Sea: LSD and the Search for God*. Chicago: Quadrangle, 1967.
16. BRONOWSKI, J. The values of science. In A. H. Maslow (ed.), *New Knowledge in Human Values*. New York: Harper & Row, 1959.
17. BUBER, M. *I and Thou*. New York: Charles Scribner's Sons, 1958.
18. BUCKE, R. *Cosmic Consciousness*. New York: E. P. Dutton, 1923.
19. BUGENTAL, J. F. (ed.). *Challenges of Humanistic Psychology*. New York: McGraw-Hill, 1967.
20. ———. *The Search for Authenticity*. New York: Holt, Rinehart and Winston, 1965.
21. BUHLER, C. *Values in Psychotherapy*. Glencoe, Ill.: Free Press, 1962.
22. CHILD, I. The experts and the bridge of judgment that crosses every cultural gap. *Psychology Today*, 1968, 2: 24-29.
23. CLUTTON-BROCK, A. *The Ultimate Belief*. New York: E. P. Dutton, 1916.
24. CONVERS-VERGARA, J. *Dinámica Familiar Frente a la Enfermedad en un Grupo de la Clase Humilde Laborante del Distrito Federal*. Unpublished doctoral dissertation. Universidad Nacional de México, Mexico, D. F., 1958.
25. CORTES, J. Religious aspects of mental illness. *Journal of Religion and Health*, 1965, 4: 315-321.
26. CRAIG, R. Trait lists and creativity. *Psychologia*, 1966, 9: 107–110.
27. DAVIS, K. *Human Relations at Work* (3rd ed.). New York: McGraw-Hill, 1967.
28. DÍAZ-GUERRERO, R. Neurosis and the Mexican family structure. *American Journal of Psychiatry*, 1955, 6: 411-417.
29. ———. Teoría y Resultados Preliminares de un Ensayo de Determinación de Grado de Salud Mental, Personal y Social de Mexicano de la Ciudad. *Psiquis*, 1952, 2: 31.
30. DUNBAR, H. F. *Psychosomatic Diagnosis*. New York: Hoeber, 1943.
31. ELIADE, M. *The Sacred and the Profane*. New York: Harper & Row, 1961.
32. ESALEN INSTITUTE. *Residential Program Brochure*. Big Sur, Calif.: Esalen Institute, 1965–1969.
33. FERNÁNDEZ-MARINA, M. R., MALDONADO-SIERRA, S., and TRENT, D. R. Three basic themes in Mexican and Puerto Rican family values. *Journal of Social Psychology*, 1958, 48: 167-181.
34. FRANKL, V. Self-transcendence as a human phenomenon. *Journal of Humanistic Psychology*, 1966, 6: 97-106.
35. FROMM, E. *The Sane Society*. New York: Rinehart, 1955.

36. ———. *Man for Himself.* New York: Rinehart, 1947.
37. ———. *Escape from Freedom.* New York: Farrar and Rinehart, 1941.
38. GLOCK, C. Y., and STARK, R. *Religion and Society in Tension.* Chicago: Rand McNally, 1965.
39. GOLDSTEIN, K. *The Organism.* New York: American Book Co., 1939.
40. GROF, S. *Theory and Practice of LSD Psychotherapy*, Palo Alto, Calif.: Science and Behavior Books, in press.
41. HARRIS, T. G. About Ruth Benedict and her lost manuscript. *Psychology Today*, 1970, 4: 51-52.
42. HARTMAN, R. S. *The Structure of Value: Foundations of Scientific Axiology.* Carbondale, Ill.: Southern Illinois University Press, 1967.
43. ———. The science of value. In A. H. Maslow (ed.), *New Knowledge in Human Values.* New York: Harper & Row, 1959.
44. HEIDER, F. *The Psychology of Interpersonal Relations.* New York: John Wiley, 1958.
45. HENLE, M. (ed.). *Documents of Gestalt Psychology.* Berkeley: University of California Press, 1961.
46. HERZBERG, F. *Work and the Nature of Man.* New York: World, 1966.
47. HESCHEL, A. *Who Is Man?* Stanford, Calif.: Stanford University Press, 1965.
48. HOLT, J. *How Children Fail.* New York: Pitman, 1964.
49. HORNEY, K. *Neurosis and Human Growth.* New York: W. W. Norton, 1950.
50. ———. *New Ways in Psychoanalysis.* New York: W. W. Norton, 1939.
51. HULL, C. L. *Principles of Behavior.* New York: Appleton-Century-Crofts, 1943.
52. HUXLEY, A. *Island.* New York: Harper & Row, 1962.
53. ———. *Grey Eminence.* New York: Meridian Books, 1959.
54. HUXLEY, L. *You Are Not the Target.* New York: Farrar, Straus & Giroux, 1963.
55. ISHERWOOD, M. *Faith without Dogma.* London: G. Allen and Unwin, 1964.
56. *Journal of Applied Behavioral Sciences.* (Periodical.)
57. *Journal of Humanistic Psychology.* (Periodical.) Association for Humanistic Psychology, San Francisco, Calif.
58. KAMIYA, J. Conscious control of brain waves. *Psychology Today*, 1968, 1: 56-61.

59. KEMPF, E. J. The social and sexual behavior of infrahuman primates. *Psychoanalytic Review*, 1917, 4: 127-154.

60. KING, C. D. The meaning of normal. *Yale Journal of Biology and Medicine*, 1945, 17: 493-501.

61. KIRKENDALL, L. *Premarital Intercourse and Interpersonal Relationships*. New York: Julian Press, 1961.

62. KÖHLER, W. *The Place of Values in a World of Facts*. New York: Liveright, 1938.

63. KORTLANDT, A. *Aspects and Prospects of the Concept of Instinct (Vicissitudes of the Hierarchy Theory)*. Leiden: E. J. Brill, 1955.

64. KUBIE, L. The forgotten man in education. *Harvard Alumni Bulletin*, 1953–1954, 56: 349-353.

65. LAING, R. D. *The Divided Self: A Study of Sanity and Madness*. London: Tavistock Publishers. 1960.

66. LASKI, M. *Ecstasy*. London: Cresset Press, 1961.

67. LEONARD, G. *Education and Ecstasy*. New York: Delacorte Press, 1968.

68. LEVY, D. M. The deprived and indulged form of psychopathic personality. *American Journal of Orthopsychiatry*, 1951, 21: 250–254.

69. ———. On the problem of movement-restraint. *American Journal of Orthopsychiatry*, 1944, 14: 644-671.

70. ———. *Maternal Overprotection*. New York: Columbia University Press, 1943.

71. ———. On instinct-satiation: an experiment on the pecking-behavior of chickens. *Journal of General Psychology*, 1938, 18: 327-348.

72. ———. Primary affect hunger. *American Journal of Psychiatry*, 1937, 94: 643-652.

73. ———. A note on pecking in chickens. *Psychoanalytic Quarterly*, 1935, 4: 612-613.

74. ———. Experiments on the suckling reflex and social behavior of dogs. *American Journal of Orthopsychiatry*, 1934, 4: 203-224.

75. LEWIN, K. *The Conceptual Representation and Measurement of Psychological Forces*. Durham, N.C.: Duke University Press, 1938.

76. ———. *Principles of Topological Psychology*. New York: McGraw-Hill, 1936.

77. LEWIS, O. *Life in a Mexican Village*. Urbana: University of Illinois Press, 1951.

78. LIKERT, B. *New Patterns of Management*. New York: McGraw-Hill, 1961.

79. *Manas.* (Periodical.) P.O. Box 32112, El Sereno Station, Los Angeles, Calif. 90032.

80. MARCUSE, H. *Eros and Civilization.* Boston: Beacon Press, 1955.

81. MASLOW, A. H. *The Psychology of Science: A Reconnaissance.* New York: Harper & Row, 1966.

82. ———. Comments on Dr. Frankl's paper. *Journal of Humanistic Psychology*, 1966, 6: 107-112.

83. ———. *Eupsychian Management: A Journal.* Homewood, Ill.: Irwin-Dorsey, 1965.

84. ———. Further notes on the Psychology of Being. *Journal of Humanistic Psychology*, 1964, 4: 45-58.

85. ———. *Religions, Values, and Peak-Experiences.* Columbus, Ohio: Ohio State University Press, 1964; Paperback ed., New York: The Viking Press, 1970.

86. ———. Further notes on the Psychology of Being. *Journal of Humanistic Psychology*, 1963, 3: 120-135.

87. ———. The need to know and the fear of knowing. *Journal of General Psychology*, 1963, 68: 111-124.

88. ———. Lessons from the peak experiences. *Journal of Humanistic Psychology*, 1962, 2: 9-18.

89. ———. *Toward a Psychology of Being.* Princeton, N.J.: Van Nostrand, 1962. (Rev. ed., 1968.)

90. ———. Some frontier problems in mental health. In A. Combs (ed.), *Personality Theory and Counseling Practice.* Gainesville: University of Florida Press, 1961.

91. ———. Eupsychia—the good society. *Journal of Humanistic Psychology*, 1961, 1: 1-11.

92. ———. Comments on Skinner's attitude to science. *Daedalus*, 1961, 90: 572-573.

93. ——— (ed.). *New Knowledge in Human Values*, New York: Harper & Row, 1959.

94. ———. Power relationships and patterns of personal development. In A. Kornhauser (ed.), *Problems of Power in American Democracy.* Detroit, Mich.: Wayne University Press, 1957.

95. ———. *Motivation and Personality.* New York: Harper & Bros., 1954. (Rev. ed., 1970.)

96. ———. Resistance to acculturation. *Journal of Social Issues*, 1951, 7: 26-29.

97. ———. The authoritarian character structure. *Journal of Social Psychology*, 1943, 18: 401-411.

98. ———. Self-esteem (dominance-feeling) and sexuality in women. *Journal of Social Psychology*, 1942, 16: 259-294.

99. ———. *The Social Personality Inventory for College Women.* Palo Alto, Calif.: Consulting Psychologists Press, 1942.

100. ———. A test for dominance-feeling (self-esteem) in college women. *Journal of Social Psychology*, 1940, 12: 255-270.

101. ———. Dominance-quality and social behavior in infrahuman primates. *Journal of Social Psychology*, 1940, 11: 313-324.

102. ———. Dominance-feeling, personality and social behavior in women. *Journal of Social Psychology*, 1939, 10: 3-39.

103. ———. Dominance-feeling, behavior and status. *Psychological Review*, 1937, 44: 404-420.

104. ———. The comparative approach to social behavior. *Social Forces*, 1937, 15: 487-490.

105. ———. A theory of sexual behavior of infrahuman primates. *Journal of Genetic Psychology*, 1936, 48: 310-338.

106. ———. The determination of hierarchy in pairs and in groups. *Journal of Genetic Psychology*, 1936, 49: 161-198.

107. ———. The role of dominance in the social and sexual behavior of infrahuman primates. I: Observations at Vilas Park Zoo. *Journal of Genetic Psychology*, 1936, 48: 261-277.

108. ———. Individual psychology and the social behavior of monkeys and apes. *International Journal of Individual Psychology*, 1935, 1: 47-59.

109. ———, and FLANZBAUM, S. An experimental determination of the dominance-behavior syndrome. *Journal of Genetic Psychology*, 1936, 48: 278-309.

110. ———, and MITTELMANN, B. *Principles of Abnormal Psychology.* New York: Harper & Bros., 1941.

111. MATSON, F. *The Broken Image.* New York: George Braziller, 1964.

112. MAY, R. *Psychology and the Human Dilemma.* Princeton, N.J.: Van Nostrand, 1967.

113. ———. *Existential Psychology.* New York: Random House, 1961.

114. MCGREGOR, D. *The Human Side of Enterprise.* New York: McGraw-Hill, 1960.

115. MEAD, M., and METRAUX, R. Image of the scientist among high-school students. *Science*, 1957, 126: 384-390.

116. MOGAR, R. E. Psychedelic (LSD) research: a critical review of methods and results. In J. F. Bugental (ed.), *Challenges of Humanistic Psychology.* New York: McGraw-Hill, 1967.

117. MOUSTAKAS, C. *The Authentic Teacher*. Cambridge, Mass.: Howard A. Doyle Publishing Co., 1966.

118. MOWRER, O. H. *The New Group Therapy*. Princeton, N.J.: Van Nostrand, 1964.

119. MUMFORD, L. *The Conduct of Life*. New York: Harcourt, Brace, 1951.

120. MURPHY, G. *Human Potentialities*. New York: Basic Books, 1958.

121. ———. *Personality*. New York: Harper & Bros., 1947.

122. OLDS, J. Physiological mechanisms of reward. *Nebraska Symposium on Motivation*, 1955, 3: 73-138.

123. OPPENHEIMER, O. Toward a new instinct theory. *Journal of Social Psychology*, 1958, 47: 21-31.

124. OTTO, H. The Minerva Experience: an initial report. In J. F. Bugental (ed.), *Challenges of Humanistic Psychology*. New York: McGraw-Hill, 1967.

125. OTTO, R. *The Idea of the Holy*. New York: Oxford University Press, 1958.

126. POLANYI, M. *Personal Knowledge*. Chicago: University of Chicago Press, 1958.

127. RAMÍREZ, S. *El Mexicano, Psicología de sus Motivaciones*. Mexico, S.A.: Editorial Pax, 1959.

128. ROGERS, C. R. *On Becoming a Person*. Boston: Houghton Mifflin, 1961.

129. ———. A therapist's view of personal goals. *Pendle Hill Pamphlet*, 1960.

130. ROSENZWEIG, S. Need-persistive and ego-defensive reactions to frustration. *Psychological Review*, 1941, 48: 347-349.

131. ROYCE, J. *The Philosophy of Loyalty*. New York: Macmillan, 1908.

132. SCHELER, M. *Ressentiment*. Glencoe, Ill.: Free Press, 1961.

133. SCHUMACHER, E. F. Economic development and poverty. *Manas*, Feb. 15, 1967, 1-8.

134. SEVERIN, F. (ed.). *Humanistic Viewpoints in Psychology*. New York: McGraw-Hill, 1965.

135. SHELDON, W. H. *Psychology and the Promethean Will*. New York: Harper & Bros., 1936.

136. SHORE, A. *Autoritarismo y Agresión en una Aldea Mexicana*. Unpublished doctoral dissertation. Universidad Nacional de México, Mexico, D.F., 1954.

137. SHOSTROM, E. *Personal Orientation Inventory (POI)*. Educational and Industrial Testing Service, 1963.

138. SIMPSON, G. G. Naturalistic ethics and the social sciences. *American Psychologist*, 1966, 21: 27-36.

139. SINNOTT, E. W. *The Bridge of Life*, New York: Simon and Schuster, 1966.

140. SKINNER, B. F. *Walden Two*. New York: Macmillan, 1948.

141. SOHL, J. *The Lemon Eaters*. New York: Dell, 1967.

142. SPINLEY, B. *The deprived and the privileged*. London: Routledge and K. Paul, 1953.

143. SUTICH, A. J. The growth-experience and the growth-centered attitude. *Journal of Psychology*, 1949, 28: 293-301.

144. SUZUKI, D. *Mysticism: Christian and Buddhist*. New York: Harper & Bros., 1957.

145. TANZER, D. W. *The Psychology of Pregnancy and Childbirth: An Investigation of Natural Childbirth*. Unpublished doctoral dissertation. Brandeis University, 1967.

146. TILLICH, P. *The Courage to Be*. New Haven: Yale University Press, 1952.

147. TORRANCE, E. P. *Guiding Creative Talent*. New York: Prentice Hall, 1962.

148. VAN KAAM, A. *Existential Foundations of Psychology*. Pittsburgh: Duquesne University Press, 1966.

149. WATSON, J. B. *Behaviorism*. New York: W. W. Norton, 1924. (Rev. ed., 1930.)

150. ———. *Psychology from the Standpoint of a Behaviorist*. Philadelphia: Lippincott, 1924.

151. WATTS, A. W. *Psychotherapy East and West*. New York: Pantheon Books, 1961.

152. WEINBERG, A. *Reflections on Big Science*. Cambridge, Mass.: M.I.T. Press, 1967.

153. WEISS, F. A. Emphasis on health in psychoanalysis. *American Journal of Psychoanalysis*, 1966, 26: 194-198.

154. WEISSKOPF, W. Economic growth and human well-being. *Manas*, Aug. 21, 1963.

155. WERTHEIMER, M. Some problems in the theory of ethics. In M. Henle (ed.), *Documents of Gestalt Psychology*. Berkeley: University of California Press, 1961.

156. ———. *Productive Thinking*. New York: Harper & Bros., 1959.

157. WHEELIS, A. *The Seeker*. New York: Random House, 1960.

158. WHETTEN, N. L. *Rural Mexico*. Chicago: University of Chicago Press, 1948.

159. WILSON, C. *Introduction to the New Existentialism.* Boston: Houghton Mifflin, 1967.

160. ———. *Beyond the Outsider.* London: Arthur Barker, 1965.

161. ———. *Origins of the Sexual Impulse.* London: Arthur Barker, 1963.

162. ———. *The Stature of Man.* Boston: Houghton Mifflin, 1959.

163. WOOTON, G. *Workers, Unions and the State.* New York: Schocken, 1967.

164. YABLONSKY, L. *The Tunnel Back: Synanon.* New York: Macmillan, 1965.

165. YOUNG, P. T. *Motivation and Emotion.* New York: John Wiley, 1961.

Index